# The Lost Colony of Roanoke
## New Perspectives

BRANDON FULLAM

McFarland & Company, Inc., Publishers
*Jefferson, North Carolina*

Library of Congress Cataloguing-in-Publication Data

Names: Fullam, Brandon, 1944– author.
Title: The lost colony of Roanoke : new perspectives / Brandon
  Fullam.
Description: Jefferson, North Carolina : McFarland & Company, Inc.,
  Publishers, 2017. | Includes bibliographical references and index.
Identifiers: LCCN 2017009138 | ISBN 9781476667867 (softcover :
  acid free paper) ∞
Subjects: LCSH: Roanoke Colony. | Roanoke Island (N.C.)—History—
  16th century.
Classification: LCC F229 .F85 2017 | DDC 975.6/17501—dc23
LC record available at https://lccn.loc.gov/2017009138

British Library cataloguing data are available

ISBN (print) 978-1-4766-6786-7
ISBN (ebook) 978-1-4766-2849-3

On the cover: *White's party find traces of the colonists, 1590* (New
York Public Library, Digital Collections); *background*: map of early
America 1585, John White, Theodor de Bry, Thomas Harriot (Library
of Congress); old paper banner (© 2017 cranach/iStock)

Printed in the United States of America

*McFarland & Company, Inc., Publishers*
  *Box 611, Jefferson, North Carolina 28640*
  *www.mcfarlandpub.com*

For Ann, Alexis, and Evelyn

# Table of Contents

## Part II: The Jamestown Intelligence

## Part III: Lost Colony Survivors and Descendants

# Introduction

The focus of the present work is the 1587 Lost Colony, but its approach is a significant departure from the traditional method of dealing with the subject matter. On the one hand the book promises to provide the reader with *fresh* perspectives—supported by documentary evidence and previously unexamined sources—about the activities, decisions, challenges, disappointments, and disappearance of the 1587 colony and the many subsequent attempts to locate it. The chapters are presented in specific, continuous, chronological segments so that the events that make up the story of the Lost Colony can more readily be seen in their proper sequence of cause and effect. The strict chronology also allows for the Lost Colony story to be understood in its larger context, with the historical record serving as a permanent backdrop to the narrative.

But this book intends to do more than offer new evidence and solutions to the Lost Colony mystery. It also promises to identify and challenge the difficulties and shortcomings of the theories and assumptions contained in virtually all past and present nonfiction books and published material on the Lost Colony. That endeavor is also facilitated by the aforementioned chronology, because it allows for a focused examination of those past and current assumptions at every key step in the Lost Colony narrative. A few of those key steps include the decision to alter the original settlement destination at the Chesapeake Bay, the condition and circumstances surrounding the colony at Roanoke, the selection of a mainland settlement site, the departure from Roanoke, and—most importantly—the ultimate fate of the colony. In a few crucial places the book also ventures into the field known as historical criticism, where it becomes necessary to challenge traditional misconceptions about the precise meaning of certain words and phrases penned by one particular Jamestown chronicler when he referenced the Lost Colony. This dual, comprehensive approach is unique among previously published books dealing with the Lost Colony.

The motivation for writing this book was a long-standing dissatisfaction and fundamental disagreement with the theories and explanations about the

1

Lost Colony that have appeared in print over the years. For well over four centuries, in fact, there has been little or no progress made in solving the mystery of the disappearance of the 1587 colonists, despite the many attempts by authors and historians to persuade us that the Lost Colonists went here or there upon leaving Roanoke, and that eventually they were victims of a slaughter that occurred in one of several supposed locations. Unfortunately, these explanations are contradicted by a close examination of the contemporary references and details contained in the late 16th and early 17th century documents and accounts. Virtually all of the published material attempting to explain what happened to the Lost Colony has only provided slight variations of earlier theories and assumptions, which—as will be proposed in the pages that follow—were flawed from the very beginning.

Historian David Beers Quinn once wrote that all Lost Colony authors are faced with three options concerning their approach to the subject matter. The first is to adhere consistently and faithfully to the facts and details as presented in the late 16th and early 17th century documents and accounts relating to the topic. While this may seem like a reasonable goal of every serious historical writer, it is surprising how many basic factual errors one will encounter in the nonfiction books about the Lost Colony to be found on the library shelf today. Quinn himself was occasionally wrong in a broader sense—his Chesapeake theory is one notable example—but he probably was on target when he chided his contemporaries for their "inadequate knowledge" of the writings of Jamestown chroniclers John Smith and William Strachey on the subject of the Lost Colony. Yet even if we concede someone's adequate knowledge of the source material, his or her strict adherence to the information *as presented* in those sources will tend to result in yet another repetition of the recycled versions mentioned above.

The second approach is the opposite of the first and relies more on imagination than facts in order to produce a fanciful tale about the Lost Colony. There are a number of such books on the library shelves too, but these are arranged alphabetically by the author's last name and need not be mentioned further in the context of nonfiction.

The third approach is the most challenging and potentially the most rewarding. Its prerequisite is an exceptional familiarity with the documents and relevant source materials that pertain to the Lost Colony, an attribute not shared equally by everyone, as Quinn noted. Then there must be the commitment to adhere as closely as possible to the details in those accounts, but *not indiscriminately* as in the first approach. The early chroniclers must first be identified as primary, secondary, or even tertiary sources in order to properly assess their historical reliability, a factor that will be of particular importance in the examination of the Lost Colony references contained in the Jamestown documents. The documents themselves must be carefully analyzed for textual contradictions and ambiguities, conflicts with the larger contemporary historical record, and other more subtle textual clues, all of which may then be used to verify, clarify, expand—and in some cases *challenge and correct*—the traditional narrative. As suggested above, books produced by authors who consistently and resolutely attach universal credibility to the traditional assumptions about the information contained in the early sources, particularly non-primary sources, are bound to repeat the same Lost Colony narrative over and over again.

As with all mysteries, resolution must start with a careful and impartial examination of all the available evidence, in this case the clues contained in those pertinent 16th and 17th century sources, and *not* with a preconceived hypothesis. To do otherwise would be to fall victim to what Thomas Jefferson once observed: "The moment a person forms a theory, his imagination sees in every object only the traits which favor that theory." Unfortunately, Jefferson's warning aptly describes the general state of Lost Colony theory today. Authors who promote theories that are rooted in long-standing preconceptions and assumptions will necessarily produce books with predisposed outcomes. Consequently, as Jefferson noted, they tend to see "only the traits which favor" their preconceived assumptions, and are blind to other potentially important clues and outcomes. In one remarkable case, to be cited below, a critical clue was misinterpreted in order to fit a preexisting assumption about the fate of the Lost Colony.

Although it is hoped that this book will rest entirely on its own merits, a few autobiographical notes are inserted here. My background, like my approach to this topic, is somewhat unusual in that my interest in the Lost Colony developed relatively late. I received a B.A. degree from Providence College in 1966 and immediately embarked on a thirty-four year career of teaching English and a few years of Latin in South Huntington on Long Island. I received an M.A. from the State University of New York at Stony Brook in 1973. That same year I was invited to join the doctoral program at Stony Brook for my research on American authors Emerson and Melville and English poet Lord Byron. This work had nothing at all to do with the subject of the Lost Colony, but I mention it here because my research involved close textual analysis, an aptitude which would prove instrumental in my later examination of the documents and accounts related to the Lost Colony. The Byron research, in particular, provided fresh evidence and a new hypothesis concerning his unfinished *Don Juan*, a work which has been debated in literary circles since Byron's untimely death in 1824. The doctoral program at Stony Brook required a full-time commitment, however, and the stipend I was offered was insufficient either to cover the mortgage on our house or to persuade me to leave my established teaching career. I did, however, complete a number of postgraduate courses in English and history.

I had always taken an interest in the history of the early European-Native American contact period, and my wife and I spent many summer months exploring the ancient Puebloan cliff dwellings in the Southwest and examining the accounts of the early Spanish expeditions there. After my retirement from teaching in 2000 we visited the 1607 "James Town" settlement site, where the Jamestown Rediscovery project had been at work for nearly a decade. At that time the archaeological excavations were concentrated near the west wall of the original palisade of what was called James Fort, and the team had discovered several building foundations, gravesites, and many early 17th century artifacts. That experience inspired me to explore the writings of the early Jamestown chroniclers: George Percy, Edward Maria Wingfield, Henry Spelman, and Ralph Hamor, to name a few, and of course John Smith and William Strachey, where the references to the Lost Colony are found. Those problematic references led inevitably to research into the earlier accounts of the Roanoke voyages contained in Richard Hakluyt's *The Principal Navigations, Voyages, Traffiques and Discoveries of the English Nation*, as well as other late 16th and early 17th century sources and histories. It was during that period of research that a number of deficiencies in the traditional Lost Colony narrative became evident.

In 2012 I became associated with the Lost Colony Research Group, an alliance co-founded by Roberta Estes and Ann Poole in 2007. The LCRG consists of dedicated and knowledgeable individuals pursuing multi-faceted disciplines related to the Lost Colony in the fields of archaeology, genealogy, genetics, and historical research. The LCRG has sponsored and funded a number of archaeological digs since 2009 and enjoys an ongoing collaboration with the Phelps Archaeology Laboratory at East Carolina University, as well as the North Carolina Office of State Archaeology. The LCRG also remains in the forefront of genetic research with endeavors such as the Lost Colony Y DNA and the Lost Colony Family Projects, both of which are overseen by co-founder Estes, who has won a number of awards for her work in this field, including two Paul Jehu Barringer Awards of Excellence and two Paul Green Multimedia Awards. In addition to its work in archaeology, genealogy, and genetics, the group has also published, reviewed, and collaborated with other authors on many articles of historical interest related to the Lost Colony and has won several awards from the North Carolina Historical Society, including the Malcolm Fowler Society Award and three Joe M. McLaurin Awards.

I have written a number papers and reports on the Lost Colony, some of which have appeared in publications of the aforementioned Lost Colony Research Group. Many of my earlier papers are also archived at the Office of State Archaeology in Raleigh, NC, as well as the Sampson-Clinton Public Library in Clinton, NC. Some of my work has appeared in the newsletter of the Sampson County Historical Society. I am also a member of the Virginia Historical Society.

What follows in this volume is the product of years of research which challenges the foundation of current and past Lost Colony theory in a number of key areas. It is proposed here that virtually all past and current Lost Colony theories have been based upon one or more of the following four fallacies, which have become, through reiteration over time, what are hereafter referred to as "institutionalized assumptions."

1. The first and oldest of the institutionalized assumptions is that master pilot Simon Fernandez was a scurrilous individual who, through incompetence or villainy, was directly responsible for the failure of the 1587 colony.

2. The second erroneous assumption is that John Smith's references to the "men cloathed" at Ocanahonan and Pakrakanick were Lost Colonists.

3. The third assumption is that Wahunsunacock, known to the English as Chief Powhatan, slaughtered the 1587 colony.

4. The fourth and final institutionalized assumption is that William Strachey's reference to the "slaughter at Roanoke" does not refer specifically to Roanoke Island, but rather *anywhere* in the vast area separating Albemarle Sound and Jamestown.

Three of these fallacies have been with us for more than 400 years. The first is based entirely on John White's inconsistent account of the 1587 voyage and his blatant mischaracterization of the flagship *Lyon*'s master pilot, Simon Fernandez. The second fallacy originated more than two decades later, when John Smith and the composer of the so-called Zúñiga Map—probably fellow Jamestown Council member John Martin—mistakenly concluded that the "men cloathed" at the distant locations of Ocanahonan and Pakrakanick were surviving members of the 1587 Lost Colony. The third fallacy was also born at Jamestown, about a year later, when John Smith reported the disturbing— but erroneous—news that Chief Powhatan had slaughtered the 1587 Lost Colony. The combination of these three assumptions is responsible for all the current variations of the flawed narrative which claims that the Lost Colonists were intentionally abandoned by the villainous Simon Fernandez at Roanoke; that they hastily relocated from Roanoke to the Chesapeake Bay, the Chowan River, Weapemeoc, or elsewhere to the north or west; that they were eventually massacred by Chief Powhatan's warriors or another tribe; and that a few escaped to distant locations where they remained alive in 1607–8.

The fourth fallacy is a somewhat more recent and remarkable misinterpretation of a single phrase written by William Strachey, Secretary of the Jamestown Colony from June 13 of 1610 to the summer of 1611. Strachey's troublesome claim that the slaughter of the English colonists occurred "at Roanoke," was not widely known until his *Historie of Travaile Into Virginia*

*Britannia* was eventually published by the Hakluyt Society in 1857, and it has baffled historians ever since. The inability to explain Strachey's phrase satisfactorily has resulted in attempts either to circumvent or re-interpret his meaning in order to suit existing theories about the colony's fate. The distortion of Strachey's "slaughter at Roanoke" phrase is directly responsible for many of the theories promoted today which place the imagined massacre of the Lost Colony anywhere south of Jamestown from the Atlantic coast to the far reaches west of Albemarle Sound.

These four long-standing institutionalized assumptions have become cornerstones of mainstream Lost Colony doctrine, and they have attained an uncontested, authoritative status of their own. Consequently, they have had a major impact on the direction of Lost Colony theory. As proposed in the pages that follow, these assumptions have stifled any real progress in unraveling the Lost Colony mystery, and have resulted in many of the established— but misguided–theories that still persist today.

These flawed assumptions, particularly the first three, have endured for so long and have been repeated so often that they have attained a level of unchallenged, but undeserved, credibility. They are typical examples of "proof by repeated assertion," the logical fallacy whereby something is accepted as being true or false simply because it has been asserted as such over and over again. As stated, it has been consistently alleged that Simon Fernandez was a villain, that Wahunsunacock slaughtered the 1587 colony, and that the "men cloathed" at Ocanahonan and Pakrakanick were surviving Lost Colonists. A closer look at the evidence, however, will challenge those assumptions. The fourth and more recently asserted (and repeated) assumption, regarding William Strachey's references to the "slaughter at Roanoke," has also been aided by an "appeal to authority," another logical fallacy that holds something to be true or false because some authority had declared it so.

Carl Sagan focused on this particular problem when he wrote, "One of the great commandments of science is, 'Mistrust arguments from authority.... Too many such arguments have proved too painfully wrong. Authorities must prove their contentions like everybody else."[1] Historians are no different than scientists in that regard. When they make historical assertions that seem controversial or questionable, they are obliged to provide convincing facts and evidence to support their contentions if we are to take their assertions seriously. In the case of the Lost Colony some (failing to heed either Jefferson or Sagan) have asserted that we should interpret Strachey's seemingly straightforward phrase, "the slaughter at Roanoke," in a way that conforms to their own theories about what happened to the Lost Colony. Their assertions, however, stand almost entirely upon the authority of the asserters, and are contradicted by the evidence from Strachey himself as well as his contemporaries.

A few words should be inserted here about an unappreciated investigative tool (also expounded upon by Sagan), which can be useful in reconstructing a credible Lost Colony narrative: proving that something did *not* happen. The oft-repeated notion that "you can't prove a negative" is generally misunderstood and has no real foundation in the real world and certainly not in Lost Colony analysis. It would be very helpful, for example, to know where the colonists did *not* go when they left Roanoke, where they could *not* have been when the Jamestown settlers arrived, and what did *not* ultimately happen to them. "Reasonably conclude" is a more accurate expression to use in this line of inductive reasoning than the mathematically oriented "prove," as Carl Sagan demonstrated by "reasonably concluding" that there was no fire-breathing dragon in his garage.[2] Like Sagan, we can *reasonably conclude*, for example, that aliens did not abduct the Lost Colonists (a theory that can actually be found on the Internet), yet we cannot actually "prove" it.

The Internet has been both a blessing and a curse for historical research. On the one hand it has brought a virtually limitless volume of information within reach of a few keystrokes, and along with it, accessibility to previously unavailable documents and records, all of which have been a boon for historical investigators, Lost Colony researchers included. On the other hand so much of the information found on the Internet is inaccurate and unreliable, and this is perhaps even more prevalent when it comes to material related to the Lost Colony. In fact not only is the Internet rife with misinformation pertaining to the Lost Colony, much of the erroneous material is repeated—often verbatim—on one site after another, further exemplifying the dangers presented by the two logical fallacies referenced above.

The chapters that follow not only challenge the foundations and specific elements of current and past Lost Colony theory, but offer new research into the alteration of the original plan to settle at the Chesapeake, the colonists' selection of a new mainland settlement location, the options available after Governor John White failed to return in 1588, and the events that resulted in the disappearance of the colony. Also analyzed are the several attempts by the Spanish and the English to locate the colonists between 1588 and 1608, including John White's dubious assertions that his colony was safe at Croatoan when he finally returned to Roanoke in 1590. An entire section is devoted to the misunderstood information acquired from the Powhatan Indians during the Jamestown years, particularly by John Smith and William Strachey, which led directly to three of the four flawed institutionalized assumptions mentioned above. The troublesome Zúñiga Map is also included in that analysis. The final section examines the claims and possibilities of survivors and the existence of Lost Colonist descendants down through the centuries. All the information presented here is derived from a close examination of the contemporary 16th and 17th century accounts, the historical record, previously unknown or unexamined documentary sources, native oral tradition, and even a North Carolina legend or two.

Sir Walter preferred to spell his own surname "Ralegh," but there are at least a dozen other known spellings of that surname employed by his contemporaries. Today's more familiar "Raleigh" is used throughout the body of this text, unless of course it appears in excerpts from late 16th or early 17th century documents in which case the original spelling is retained. Conversely, the traditional "Croatoan" is used, though one is more apt to see it spelled "Croatan" today, and especially in contexts not specific to the Lost Colony. The use of "Powhatan" in the following pages is intended to mean the individual "king" or chief called Powhatan, otherwise known as Wahunsunacock. Exceptions to this would be its use as a proper adjective as in "Powhatan" Indians, or a plural proper noun as in "Powhatans." The term "Lost Colony" itself did not come into use until the 19th century, but, since it is the glue that holds these pages together, it is utilized throughout the chapters as a proper noun regardless of its historical context or timeframe. The same is true of "Lost Colonists." Another term used throughout the book is the original "tun," a measure of volume applied to 16th and 17th century ships, as opposed to the later "ton" or "tonnage" which can have several different meanings.

Finally, the evidence and conclusions in the following pages do not pretend to represent the absolute final word on the Lost Colony. There are certainly clues yet to be found through archaeological endeavors, or perhaps in still undiscovered documents in England, or among the 75,000,000 manuscript pages in the Archivo General de Indias in Seville, or maybe from some clue in the existing documents that this analysis may have overlooked. The following pages do, however, offer a coherent, comprehensive, chronological narrative based on careful, independent research, undertaken without the slightest allegiance to a preconceived theory. They also suggest that current Lost Colony theory needs to be re-evaluated, and it is hoped that these pages represent a positive step in that direction.

# 1

# *Setting the Stage*
## 1496–1586

Raleigh's involvement in New World colonization is all the more remarkable because of what had preceded it. Prior to the reign of Elizabeth I, the English considered the land mass across the Atlantic to the west as little more than an obstacle which needed to be piloted through in order to discover the fabled Northwest Passage and an all-water access to the valuable spice trade in the Orient. The Venetians had already established control of the trade routes through the Mediterranean, and the Portuguese and Spanish were exploring routes around Africa and South America respectively. For the English the only remaining potential sea route to the Orient was across the north Atlantic and through the frozen Arctic. Up until about a decade before Raleigh sent out the first of the Roanoke voyages, England's focus had remained on the Northwest Passage, not colonization.

In 1496 the Italian Giovanni Caboto, or John Cabot, sailing for England, obtained a patent from King Henry VII to search for a northern route to China, which was thought to lie not far beyond the Atlantic. Cabot returned from his first voyage on August 6, 1497, mistakenly claiming to have discovered the "new founde land" of Asia. Cabot's mysterious second voyage of discovery departed from Bristol in May of 1498, and was believed to have been lost at sea, until evidence was discovered in the 1960s suggesting that Cabot may have reached Newfoundland and then sailed south along the coast as far as South America before returning to England in 1500.[1]

The next significant attempt by the English to find the Northwest Passage, by Sir Martin Frobisher, was not undertaken until 1576. Frobisher had been convinced since as early as 1561 that a Northwest Passage not only existed, but that he was capable of finding it. However, it took Frobisher many years to gain sufficient support, financial backing, and of course the license for the venture. In the summer of 1576 Frobisher finally set sail with a small fleet of three vessels, the *Gabriell*, the *Michaell*, and a small pinnace. The pinnace sank during a storm, and the *Michaell*, having been separated from the *Gabriell*, returned to England. Frobisher continued on with the *Gabriell* and sailed as far as Baffin Bay before returning to England in October with a captured native Inuit and some iron pyrite mineral samples, which were mistaken for gold.

Encouraged by the prospects of a great gold ore source, investors formed the Company of Cathay, backed by a royal charter. The new company seems to have been less interested in Cathay, a 16th century term for part of China, than it was in gold. In May of 1577 Frobisher was sent on a second voyage specifically to search for more gold, and he returned in September with 200 tons of ore. Joining the expedition was artist John White, who painted Eskimo scenes, and would become an instrumental figure years later during the Roanoke voyages. A third expedition was sent in May of 1578 with the dual purpose of finding even more of what was thought to be gold, and also of establishing a mining settlement near the source of the ore. Frobisher brought back a huge quantity of ore, but the planned settlement was not established. After several years of failed attempts to extract gold from Frobisher's tons of ore, the Cathay Company was dissolved.

In the meantime Sir Humphrey Gilbert, Walter Raleigh's older half-brother, had petitioned Queen Elizabeth for a patent to search for the Northwest Passage to "Cathaia," and by 1574 he had revised his treatise titled *A discourse of a discouerie for a new passage to Cataia*. Gilbert's *Discourse* is remarkable, not for its arguments in support of the discovery of the Northwest Passage, but for its early proposal to colonize the New World. Gilbert wrote,

> Also we might inhabite some parte of those Countreys, and settle there suche needie people of our Countrie, which now trouble the common welth, and through want here at home, are inforced to commit outragious offences, whereby they are dayly consumed with the Gallowes. Moreouer, we might from all the aforesaid places, haue a yerely retourne, inhabiting for our staple some conuenient place of *America*, about *Sierra Neuada* [reference to Coronado's 1540–2 expedition through the Southwest], or some other part, wheras it shal seeme best for the shortening of the voyage.[2]

On June 11, 1578, the queen granted Letters Patent to Gilbert authorizing him to discover and colonize a location on the coast of North America, but there was no mention of the Northwest Passage. By September 1578, Gilbert had assembled a large ten-vessel fleet for the colonization venture, one of the ships being the *Falcon*, with Walter Raleigh as captain and Simon Fernandez as master and pilot. However, bad weather, inadequate provisions, poor timing, and leaking ships thwarted his several attempts to cross the Atlantic in late 1578 and early 1579. Gilbert probably regretted his recommendation in the *Discourse* about the type of "needie people" to be used for colonization, because quarrels and dissention aboard the ships were also constant problems.

In late 1579 Gilbert sent the small 8 tun *Squirrel* and a crew of ten commanded by Simon Fernandez on a reconnaissance across the Atlantic. It is not known what part of the coastline Fernandez scouted, but the voyage was accomplished in a remarkable three months. By 1581 Gilbert was once again making preparation for a voyage to America and by June of 1583 he had assembled five ships at Plymouth: the flagship *Delight*, the *Bark Raleigh* owned and commanded by Walter Raleigh, the *Golden Hind*, the *Swallow*, and the *Squirrel*, which had made the reconnaissance voyage a few years earlier.

The fleet sailed on June 11, but the voyage was once again marked by dissention and poor planning. In addition sickness had spread among the crews, forcing the *Bark Raleigh* to return to England. Nevertheless, the remaining ships managed to cross the north Atlantic and on the morning of August 5 Gilbert and his men went ashore at St. John's, where in a formal ceremony he read his royal patent and took possession of Newfoundland in the name of the queen. His intention was to establish the first English colony in America, but the coastal area at St. John's was not deemed to be a suitable location for a settlement, and so he headed southward in search of a better site. After the *Delight* ran aground and broke up, taking with her most of the expedition's supplies and the crew, Gilbert was forced to return to England with the intention of completing the colonization effort the following year, before his charter expired. Despite advice to the contrary, Gilbert chose to sail aboard the *Squirrel* on the return voyage. On September 9 the small vessel sank in stormy weather near the Azores and all aboard perished.

Since Raleigh was clearly involved with his half-brother Gilbert in England's first colonization effort, one wonders what role he would have played if Gilbert had lived. Given Gilbert's possession of Newfoundland and his intention to establish a colony there in 1584, it can reasonably be concluded that Raleigh would have played a part in that enterprise, although very likely a less prominent one than he would eventually play farther south. Upon Humphrey Gilbert's death the Newfoundland patent was given to his brother Adrian, who continued to search Newfoundland for precious metals and an all-water route to Asia. Newfoundland would not be permanently settled by Englishmen until John Guy arrived at Cuper's Cove with thirty-nine colonists more than a quarter-century later.

On March 25, 1584, Queen Elizabeth conferred new Letters Patent to Sir Walter Raleigh "to discouer, search, finde out, and view such remote, heathen and barbarous lands, countreis, and territories ... within the space of two hundreth leagues ... not actually possessed of any Christian Prince, nor inhabited by Christian People...."[3] The royal charter provided Raleigh with the legal entitlement for colonizing the New World, but—like Gilbert's charter—it was contingent upon actually establishing a permanent colony, and would otherwise expire after "six yeeres and no more." Raleigh's rights extended 200 leagues—600 miles—to the north and south of his settlement. Since Humphrey Gilbert had already claimed Newfoundland for the crown and Adrian Gilbert would soon be actively exploring there, Raleigh chose to look farther south along the Atlantic coast for settlement opportunities. It is very likely that thirty-five degrees north latitude or thereabouts was *pre-selected* at this time as a target location for a new settlement. Both Gilbert's and Raleigh's patents included the 200 league restriction, and 35 degrees north latitude was approximately 1,200 miles or 400 leagues from Newfoundland, thus fulfilling the 200 league separation requirement for both patents. Raleigh employed his former *Falcon* pilot, Simon Fernandez, for the new venture at this time, since Fernandez had more knowledge of that part of the coast than any other pilot in England.

Raleigh wasted little time. On April 27, 1584, he sent Philip Amadas and Arthur Barlowe "with two barkes well furnished with men and victuals" on a reconnaissance voyage to America in search of a suitable settlement location. Unlike Gilbert's North Atlantic course to Newfoundland, Amadas and Barlowe sailed the known route south to the Canary Islands and then across the Atlantic, finally arriving at the islands in the West Indies on June 10, where, "hauing refreshed our selues with sweet water, and fresh victuall," they continued up the Atlantic coast. On July 13 they landed along the Outer Banks and took "possession of the same, in the right of the Queenes most excellent Maiestie," at Wokokon according to Hakluyt, which was very close to thirty-five degrees north latitude (35.0861°). Three days later at Roanoke the Englishmen made first contact with a native Algonquian, "And after he had spoken of many things not vnderstood by vs, we brought him with his owne good liking, aboord the ships, and gaue him a shirt, a hat and some other things, and made him taste of our wine, and our meat, which he liked very wel...."[4] Shortly thereafter the Algonquian returned to his own small boat and "fell to fishing," catching more than enough to share with all the English in both ships, a tradition author Seth Mallios defines as a strict "gift-exchange system" common in many Indian cultures.[5] The following day the king's brother Granganimeo arrived with forty or fifty men and more gifts were exchanged, which, according to historian David Beers Quinn, "meant, from the Indian side, that relations had now been formally established and the parties could treat each other as equals."[6]

The English were able to learn that the king, Wingina, was recovering at a village six days away from wounds he had received in "mortall warre" with tribes farther south. The English also learned that "the king is called Wingina, the countrey Wingandacoa, and now by her Maiestie Virginia." According to Barlowe, the soil at Wingandacoa "is the most plentifull, sweete, fruitfull and wholsome of all the worlde." As for the trees, "there were aboue fourteene seuerall sweete smelling timber trees, and the most part of their vnderwoods are Bayes and such like: they haue those Okes that we haue, but farre greater and better."[7]

Although the published account of the Amadas-Barlowe reconnaissance was most likely edited to present a favorable picture to potential colonists and investors in England, relations seem to have remained cordial between the English and the natives at Wingandacoa. Some of the men visited the village at the north end of the island called Roanoke where, Barlowe wrote, "We were entertained with all loue and kindnesse, and with as much bountie (after their maner) as they could possibly deuise."[8] Many more gifts were exchanged during their approximately one month stay, and the English learned much concerning the local customs and beliefs and about the neighboring territories and tribes. In mid–August Amadas and Barlowe departed for England, taking with them "two of the Sauages being lustie men, whose names were Wanchese and Manteo,"[9] each of whom would take different paths in the years to come.

At about the same time that Amadas and Barlowe set sail for the New World, Raleigh turned to his friend Richard Hakluyt, writer and geographer, to further advance his colonization endeavors with the queen. Hakluyt immediately went to work on a treatise known by its abbreviated title, *A Discourse of Western Planting.* The *Discourse,* written "at the requeste and direction of the righte worshipfull Mr. Walter Raghly, nowe Knight," and "before the comynge home of his twoo barkes," was a twenty-chapter promotional piece advocating the numerous benefits likely to result from the initial Amadas-Barlowe reconnaissance voyage and future colonization enterprises. The *Discourse* concluded with "A note of some thinges to be prepared for the voyadge," quite an understatement since the "note" consisted of a remarkably exhaustive listing of every imaginable item to be brought as well as the numerous skills and occupations required for such a venture.

The *Discourse* was written primarily to obtain Queen Elizabeth's financial support for Raleigh's colonization efforts, to assure the queen regarding England's legitimate right to colonize the New World, and to outline the many rewards England would reap from colonization. The topic of finding the Northwest Passage was brought up again, but was far outweighed in importance by the benefits of colonization. Hakluyt spent most of his twenty chapters claiming that Raleigh's efforts would "yelde unto us all the commodities of Europe, Affrica and Asia; limit ... the kinge of Spaines domynions ... [and] ... bringe Kinge Phillippe from his highe throne"; and "be greately for thinlargemente of the gospell of Christe." The Northwest Passage was not mentioned until Chapter 17: "by these colonies the north west passage to Cathaio and China may easely, quickly, and perfectly be searched oute."[10] By 1584 it was clear that England's focus had changed from the Northwest Passage to colonization. Inspired by Hakluyt's *Discourse* as well as the reports from the

Amadas-Barlowe reconnaissance that returned in September, Queen Elizabeth and her Principal Secretary of State, Francis Walsingham, supplied two ships for Raleigh's 1585 colonization venture.[11]

On April 9, 1585, a seven-vessel fleet departed to establish Raleigh's first permanent colony in what the English now called "Virginia" in honor of their monarch, the "Virgin Queen" Elizabeth.

> … we departed from Plymmouth, our Fleete consisting of the number of seuen sailes, to wit, the Tyger, of the burden of seuen score tunnes, a Flie-boat called the Roebucke, of the like burden, the Lyon of a hundred tunnes or thereabouts, the Elizabeth, of fiftie tunnes, and the Dorothie, a small barke: whereunto were also adioyned for speedy seruices, two small pinnesses.[12]

The all-male colony was essentially intended to be fortified base from which exploratory ventures could be launched into the areas surrounding Roanoke. It was most likely hoped that the base could eventually be used as a stopover for English privateers. The expedition was led by Sir Richard Grenville, who commanded the flagship *Tyger*, with Simon Fernandez as master pilot. Fernandez had piloted the Amadas-Barlowe reconnaissance the previous year and would also serve as master pilot on the 1587 voyage which transported what would come to be known as the Lost Colony. Other notables on the 1585 voyage included Ralph Lane, "Generall" of the soldiers; Thomas Harriot, the brilliant mathematician, astronomer, and translator, who—with the help of Manteo—constructed a phonetic alphabet for the Algonquian language; and John White, artist and cartographer, who would become governor of the ill-fated Lost Colony the following year. Wanchese and Manteo, the two native Algonquians who had traveled to England with Amadas and Barlowe, also returned to their homeland.

The exploratory nature of the new colony was immediately evident when, on June 26, they anchored for three weeks at Wokokon before proceeding to Roanoke. During that time Grenville, Lane, and a contingent of men in three vessels explored Pamlico Sound and visited a number of native Indian villages, including Pomeiok, Aquascogoc, and Secota, and "were well entertained there of the Sauages."[13] Unfortunately, an incident occurred at Aquascogoc which would begin to unravel whatever amicable relations had been established during the Amadas-Barlowe reconnaissance. On July 16 the English discovered that a silver cup was missing and apparently had last been seen three days earlier at Aquascogoc. The English returned, demanded the cup, and when it was not produced, "wee burnt, and spoyled their corne, and Towne, all the people being fled."[14]

The activities conducted by the English during this three week period are revealing in several respects. First of all the fact that Grenville delayed his arrival at Roanoke that long and spent a full week exploring mainland locations across Pamlico Sound suggests that he may have been instructed to investigate alternative settlement locations. Grenville knew that he would be returning the following spring with more colonists, and Raleigh may have already realized, from the post-voyage reports of Amadas and Barlowe, that a better—or maybe an additional—settlement location was needed. Roanoke was an inadequate location for a growing, permanent colony or military base which would require a better harbor. This consideration would be of particular relevance in 1587.

The episode at Aquascogoc speaks volumes about the English attitude toward the native tribes. Hakluyt had explained in his 1584 *Discourse* that the English would win over the natives "with discretion and myldenes," and he devoted an entire chapter condemning the terrible cruelties afflicted upon the native people by the Spanish in the West Indies. As he wrote, "So many and so monstrous have bene the Spanishe cruelties, suche straunge slaughters and murders of those peaceable, lowly, milde, and gentle people, together with the spoiles of townes...."[15] The harsh treatment of the Indians at Aquascogoc would indicate that "discretion and myldenes" were in short supply among the English. On the other side, the Indians witnessed, probably for the first time, what the English were capable of. Burning the village, an act specifically denounced by Hakluyt as one of the Spanish atrocities, was a severe penalty to pay for the alleged theft of a cup. An additional consequence, one which the English may not have recognized, was the fact that the last planting for the native Indians had already occurred in June, so when the English "spoyled their corne" they may have unwittingly ruined the remaining year's harvest. News of this incident was undoubtedly relayed to Wingina and probably contributed to the growing suspicions about these newcomers who were about to establish a settlement and construct a fort at Roanoke. To add insult to injury, after having ruined the corn supply at Aquascogoc, the English then turned to Wingina's tribe to provide corn for the colony, a demand which further strained Anglo-native relations.

It is also interesting that Philip Amadas, who was recorded as "Admirall of the countrey" in 1585, was the man who was responsible for the retribution at Aquascogoc. As recorded in one account, Grenville sent "one of our boates with the Admirall ... to Aquascogoc, to demaund a siluer cup which one of the Sauages had stollen from vs." The treatment of the Indians at Aquascogoc seems at odds with Barlowe's description of a native "people most gentle, louing, and faithfull, voide of all guile and treason, and such as liue after the maner of the golden age." It also makes one wonder if the English-Indian relations described in Barlowe's account of the 1584 reconnaissance were actually as uniformly amicable as it would have its readers believe.

On August 25 Grenville left Lane and more than 100 men at Roanoke and sailed for England, promising to return by the following Easter with fresh supplies, equipment, and additional colonists. Lane's account is difficult to follow chronologically, but he must have quickly undertaken the construction of the fort and begun to explore the area for the precious metals, copper, and pearls which the English hoped to find. "Our discouerie," Lane wrote, "hath beene extended from the Island of Roanoak, (the same hauing bene the place of our settlement or habitation) into the South, into the North, into the Northwest, and into the West."[16] They explored as far as Secota to the south, but decided to postpone any further discovery in that area until Grenville's return in the spring. To the northwest they ventured as far as "Chawanook distant from Roanoak about 130. Miles" and "it selfe is the greatest Prouince and Seigniorie lying vpon that Riuer." Lane's most favorable assessment was reserved for the exploration to the north:

> ... the Territorie and soyle of the Chesepians (being distant fifteene miles from the shore) was for pleasantnes of seat, for temperature of Climate, for fertilitie of soyle and for the commoditie of the Sea, besides multitude of Beares (being an excellent good victuall) with great woods of Sassafras, and Wallnut trees, is not to be excelled by any other whatsoeuer.[17]

Lane was immediately intrigued, however, by what the Chowanoke king, Menatonon, told him about the Moratico (Roanoke) River to the west. Far up the Moratico there was said to be a place called Chaunis Temoatan, where "a marueilous and most strange Minerall" called "Wassador" could be found. This mineral was most likely copper, but Lane was told, "is very soft, and pale: they say that they take the saide mettall out of a riuer that falleth very swift from the rockes and hils," and he may have thought it could be gold. Lane hoped that the Moratico would lead to "the discouery of a good Mine, by the goodnesse of God, or a passage to the South-sea, or some way to it," an indication that finding an all-water passage to the Orient, albeit much farther south than Newfoundland, was still considered feasible. It was during his unsuccessful quest up the Moratico River in 1586 that, according to Lane, he and his party were attacked and then nearly starved to death as the result of a plot arranged by Wingina. On the return trip down the Moratico Lane and his men were forced to cook and eat their two mastiffs, after which "wee had nothing in the world to eate but pottage of Sassafras leaues."[18]

Lane's relations with the natives, uneasy at best and marked by growing suspicions and distrust, would have repercussions for the 1587 colony. Aside from Manteo, who proved to be an enduring and trustworthy friend to the English, only Ensenore, Wingina's aged father, and Granganimeo, Wingina's brother who had welcomed Amadas and Barlowe the previous year, recommended cooperation with Lane's Englishmen. Ensenore's deference, however, was derived from his belief that the English were servants of God and had come back from the dead with the capability of killing their enemies with sickness and other means "being 100 miles from any of vs." As Harriot explained it:

There could at no time happen any strange sicknesse, losses, hurts, or any other crosse vnto them, but that they would impute to vs the cause or meanes thereof, for offending or not pleasing vs…. There was no towne where wee had any subtle deuise practised against vs, wee leauing it vnpunished or not reuenged … but that within a few dayes after our departure from euery such Towne, the people began to die very fast, and many in short space, in some Townes about twentie, in some fourtie, and in one sixe score, which in trueth was very many in respect of their numbers. This happened in no place that we could learne, but where we had bin, where they vsed some practise against vs, and after such time. The disease also was so strange, that they neither knewe what it was, nor how to cure it, the like by report of the oldest men in the Countrey neuer happened before, time out of minde.[19]

Some authors have referred to the friendly relations that Lane had established with Menatonon, the king of the Chowanokes, and his son, Skiko, but that is somewhat misleading. The cooperation Lane received from the Chowanokes was only accomplished through coercion and threats. Lane had seized both Menatonon and Skiko, and, "hauing dismissed Menatonon vpon a ransome agreed for," he sent "his best beloued sonne prisoner" to Roanoke where he "kept me companie in an handlocke." At one point Skiko attempted to escape and Lane "laid him in the bylboes [leg shackles], threatening to cut off his head."[20]

Relations took a dramatic turn for the worse in April of 1586, by which time both Granganimeo and Ensenore had died. Wingina changed his name to Pemisapan, a significant event, and was openly hostile to the English. Wingina's name change, as historian Karen Kupperman noted, announced his intention to form an alliance against the English, just as Opechancanough would do before the assault by the Powhatans on the Virginia settlers in 1622.[21] Wanchese, too, who had quickly abandoned the English upon his return to Roanoke with Manteo, was specifically named by Lane as one of "our great enemies about Pemisapan" who "were in hand againe to put their old practises in vse against vs."

According to Lane, Pemisapan had organized a great conspiracy involving a number of tribes to destroy the English at Roanoke. Among the conspiring tribes Lane mentioned "the Mandoaks, who were a great people, with the Chesepians and their friends to the number of 700," a probable gross exaggeration. Nevertheless, the conspiracy seems to have been widespread and is an indication of the extent and depth of the hostility that existed toward the English by the spring of 1586. The plan was apparently to surprise Lane first, "the instant whereof they would haue knocked out my braines," followed by "certaine of his fellowes, for M. Heriots: so for all the rest of our better sort."[22] However Lane struck first, at Dasamonguepeuk, before the conspiracy could be executed by Pemisapan. Shouting the signal "Christ our victory," Lane's force attacked the village, and during the course of battle one of his men, Edward Nugent, chased down and beheaded Pemisapan.

About a week later, in early June of 1586, Sir Francis Drake arrived at Roanoke with a large fleet after his successful raids of the Spanish possessions at Santo Domingo, Cartagena de Indias, and San Augustín. By this time Lane had become disillusioned about colonization at Roanoke in particular, and Virginia in general. This was illustrated by the stark contrast between his letter to Hakluyt and "another gentleman," written "from the New Fort in Virginia, this third of September, 1585," and his comments in early April following his exploration of the Moratico River. In the former, Lane wrote effusively about the many wonders of Virginia:

> The goodliest soyle vnder the cope of heauen … sweete trees … sortes of Apothecarie drugs … flaxe … one kind like silke…. Maiz … and the climate so wholsome, that wee had not one sicke since we touched the land here…. If Virginia had but horses and kine … being inhabited with English, no realme in Christendome were comparable to it…. And sundry other rich commodities, that no parts of the world, be they West or East Indies, haue, here wee finde great abundance of…. The people naturally are most curteous.[23]

Contrast this with his offhand comment in April that the "healthfullest climate, and … most fertile soyle … and Sassafras, and many other rootes and gummes" do not in themselves justify colonization in Virginia. Unless "either of the two aboue" was discovered—a passage to the South Sea or the mine at Chaunis Temoatan—all those commodities "otherwise of themselues will not be worth fetching."[24]

It is little wonder, then, that Lane did not insist on preserving the colony at Roanoke when Drake arrived in June. Drake had offered to provide two or three ships for Lane's use while he awaited Grenville's return with supplies and colonists, but in the end it was clear that everyone wanted to return to England. As Lane put it, "considering the case that we stood in, the weaknesse of our company, the small number of the same," he accepted Drake's offer to transport the entire colony back to England. On June 19 the fleet set sail, and Manteo, who had proven to be a loyal friend to the English, returned once again to England.

Drake's account of this evacuation generally corroborates Lane's, but adds a detail not mentioned by Lane about two of his men who were left behind. (Note—parentheticals contain insertions by the editor due to torn margins in the original document):

> Then we sailed along the coast of the land until we came to the place where those men did live that Sir Walter Raleigh had sent thither to inhabit the year before. (Mr. Lane) and others, as soon as they saw us, (thin)king we had been a new supply (came from the) shore, and tarried certain days, and (afterwards we carried) thence all those men with us except two (who had gone furt)her into the country and the wind gre(w so that) we could not stay for them.[25]

Not long after Lane abandoned Roanoke, Grenville arrived belatedly with three ships, supplies, and additional colonists. Finding the fort deserted, he searched the area but found no trace of the colony. In order to retain possession of "Virginia" for Raleigh, Grenville "landed fifteene men in the Isle of Roanoak, furnished plentifully with all maner of prouisions for two yeeres, and so departed for England."[26] It is interesting to note that the published account of the Grenville supply voyage was obviously written sometime after Grenville's and Drake's return to England, since it spoke disparagingly of Lane's dealings with the Indians. Regarding the evacuation by Drake it stated, "for feare they [Lane's colonists] should be left behinde they left all things confusedly, as if they had bene chased from thence by a mighty army: and no doubt so they were; for the hand of God came vpon them for the cruelty and outrages committed by some of them against the natiue inhabitants of that countrey."[27]

There is another account of Grenville's attempt to resupply Lane's colony, and that was provided by Pedro Diaz, a Spaniard who had been captured by Grenville the previous year and was pressed into service aboard the *Tyger*. Although Diaz was not permitted to go ashore, he reported in a deposition taken a few years later in Havana that Grenville left eighteen men, as opposed to the fifteen mentioned in Hakluyt.[28]

In the end, the Grenville-Lane colonization attempt accomplished none of its immediate goals. No permanent base of any significance was established, and no precious metals or valuable commodities were found. Furthermore, the English had alienated virtually all of the native Algonquians except for Manteo and his small coastal tribe at Croatoan. On the positive side, John White and Thomas Harriot did produce important maps and charts of the area, and White provided Elizabethan England with the first views of America through his many sketches and watercolors.

Perhaps the most useful outcome of the Grenville-Lane colonization effort was the realization that the inlets near Roanoke were inadequate for a permanent, thriving settlement. The inlets there were too shallow or narrow to allow access to the sounds by vessels any larger than a pinnace, making it difficult and time-consuming to transport supplies and material to and from larger ships which had to remain anchored offshore. Lane made several complaints about "our bad harborow" and the need for "a better harborough then yet there is." He also concluded that the better harbor "must be to the Northward."[29]

Based on the reports of the 1585–86 Grenville/Lane expedition, therefore, future colonization plans shifted northward to the Chesapeake Bay. Once again Raleigh sought the advice of his friend, Richard Hakluyt, who replied, "If yow proceed, which I longe much to knowe, in yor enterprise of Virginia, yor best planting wilbe about the bay of Chesepians."[30]

The stage was now set for Raleigh's 1587 colonization venture.

# 2

## Planning the Cittie of Ralegh
### July 27, 1586–July 22, 1587

For all the expense and effort Raleigh had committed to colonization over the previous two years, the results were rather disappointing. Roanoke proved to be an inadequate location for either a thriving colony or a base for exploration, which had turned up neither any precious metals nor a passage to the Orient. The Indians were now openly hostile to the English, and the first colony, established with great expectations, had been unexpectedly abandoned. Grenville's resupply ships, with additional settlers intended to expand the colony, had gotten a late start and arrived at Roanoke only to find that the entire colony had already left, and so they returned to England. All that remained of Raleigh's grand plan at Roanoke was the small contingent Grenville had left to preserve Raleigh's claim. To make matters worse, on July 27 Ralph Lane and the first colonists arrived back in England, and they brought with them troubling stories about their difficult experiences in Virginia. The spread of these pessimistic accounts, particularly by those who had actually been to Virginia, could only dissuade prospective investors and dampen future colonist enlistment.

Harriot had apparently already started work on "a discourse by it selfe in maner of a Chronicle" concerning "the naturall inhabitants, their natures and maners." This work, he wrote, "when time shall be thought conuenient, shall be also published,"[1] but no copies of this earlier "Chronicle" are known to exist. Instead Harriot turned his attention to the publication of his *A briefe and true report of the new found land of Virginia*, probably written in large part to dispel the negative stories being circulated at the time. Although *A brief and true report* is considered today to be the first and most influential work about North America, it still can easily be read, at least in part, as damage control for Raleigh.

Harriot tells his readers that the report was undertaken at the request of "some [of] my particular friends," Raleigh no doubt the most prominent

20

and eager among them. After addressing his report "To the Aduenturers, Fauourers, and Welwillers of the enterprise for the inhabiting and planting in Virginia," he moved quickly to deflect the rumors and "diuers and variable reports with some slanderous and shameful speeches bruted abroad by many that returned from thence: especially of that discouery which was made by the Colony transported by Sir Richard Grinuile in the yere 1585." Those reports, he continued, "haue not done a little wrong to many that otherwise would haue also fauoured and aduentured in the action."[2]

Harriot's *brief and true report,* however, was neither very brief—some 13,000 words—nor completely true, particularly in his portrayal of "the nature and maners of the people," especially considering the state of affairs that existed by the summer of 1586. Harriot assured prospective colonists that if they were worried about the natives resisting "our inhabiting and planting, [they] are not to be feared, but that they shall haue cause both to feare and loue vs, that shall inhabite with them." Besides, he wrote,

> neither haue they any thing to defend themselues but targets made of barkes, and some armours made of sticks wickered together with thread.... If there fall out any warres betweene vs and them..., the turning vp of their heeles against vs in running away was their best defence ... it is probable that they should desire our friendship and loue, and haue the greater respect for pleasing and obeying vs.[3]

Harriot mentioned Wingina twice, but in sharp contrast with Lane's assessment of him. To Lane, Wingina/Pemisapan was a scheming savage who continually plotted to destroy the English, but for Harriot, Wingina was submissive to the English and was in awe of their god-like powers. He wrote, "Twise this Wiroans [Wingina] was so grieuously sicke ... and thinking hee was in such danger for offending vs and thereby our God, sent for some of vs to pray and bee a meanes to our God that it would please him either that he might liue, or after death dwell with him in blisse." And then again, "some of the inhabitants which were our friends, and especially the Wiroans Wingina," believed, as previously mentioned, that the sickness which struck several villages "was the worke of our God through our meanes, and that we by him might kill and slay whom we would without weapons, and not come neere them."[4]

Harriot neglected to mention the fact that Wingina/Pemisapan had been beheaded by one of Lane's men, or the events that led up to it, but he did admit that "some of our company ... shewed themselues too fierce in slaying some of the people in some Townes, vpon causes that on our part might easily ynough haue bene borne withall." However, he wrote, the killing was "iustly deserued.... And whatsoever els they [the Indians] may be, by carefulnesse of our selues neede nothing at all to be feared."

Harriot concluded his report with more encouragement to prospective colonists and Raleigh's generous promise of vast acreage for every man who enlisted in the venture:

> Seeing therefore the aire there is so temperate and holsome, the soyle so fertile, and yeelding such commodities, as I haue before mentioned, the also thither to and fro being sufficiently experimented to be performed twise a yeere with ease, and at any season thereof: And the dealing of Sir Walter Ralegh so liberall in large giuing and granting land there, as is already knowen, with many helpes and furtherances else: (The least that he hath granted hath bene fiue hundreth acres to a man onely for the aduenture of his person) I hope there remaines no cause whereby the action should be misliked.[5]

Whether or not Harriot's *brief and true report* had an immediate effect or any at all is not known, but plans were certainly under way towards the end of 1586 to send out another colony the following year. Recruitments for the new colony seem to have come mostly from densely populated London,[6] where the prospect of 500 acres would have been particularly enticing. The promised acreage also affirms Raleigh's intent that the main industry of the new colony would be agriculture. Harriot had listed the wide variety of "merchantable commodities" which could be grown in abundance in Virginia. Unlike the earlier 1585–86 colony, made up mostly of military men who became dependent upon the native Indians for sustenance, which in turn added to the friction between them, the new colony would have a completely different composition and purpose. The 1587 colony was designed and planned for agricultural self-sufficiency, and for the first time included women and children, essential elements for a permanent colony.

As mentioned previously, by 1586 it was clear that Roanoke itself was not only ill-suited for a large, permanent colony, but that the inlets at the Outer Banks at Roanoke did not provide adequate access by anything larger than a pinnace. Lane's colony did not accomplish much, but it had at least determined that a far "better harborough" was to be found "to the Northward." The new 1587 colony, therefore, was intended to be situated on the mainland somewhere beyond the broad and deep-channel entrance to the Chesapeake Bay. Lane had also indicated, however, that lacking the availability of precious metals or access to the Orient, there was no justification for establishing a colony anywhere. A healthy climate and fertile soil were not enough. A viable colony, according to Lane and certainly investors, required monetary justification and the likelihood of profit. An agricultural-based colony would provide self-sufficiency, but not enough profit potential.

It is probable, then, that Raleigh saw the 1587 colony as just the first step in an expanding enterprise which would eventually include a base for the most profitable of all enterprises: privateering. As Quinn noted, Sir George Carey's unexplained association with the 1587 colony may have originated from his hope to use the Chesapeake as a future safe harbor for his privateering ventures. Cary, a well-known promoter of privateering ventures, sent out a small three-vessel fleet in early 1587 and, as Quinn suggested, may have intended to stop at the new settlement at the Chesapeake and test its viability as a base for privateering.[7]

As unsuitable as Roanoke was, however, it does not seem to have been eliminated from Raleigh's future plans. His directions for the 1587 voyage included a stop at Roanoke, "to finde those fifteene Englishmen, which Sir Richard Grinuile had left there the yeere before, with whom he meant to haue conference, concerning the state of the Countrey, and Sauages." Furthermore, a ceremony was to occur at Roanoke whereby the loyal Croatoan, Manteo, "by the commandement of Sir Walter Ralegh, was [to be] christened in Roanoak, and called Lord thereof, and of Dasamonguepeuk, in reward of his faithfull seruices."[8] There would be no need to consult with the fifteen Englishmen "about the state of the Countrey, and Sauages" if Roanoke had no place in Raleigh's future plans. Manteo's christening and title conferral are also significant. Manteo would become the first native Indian to have an official English title, and would oversee both Roanoke and Dasamonguepeuk, the previous realm of Wingina/Pemisapan. Manteo, therefore, would hold the status of Raleigh's assignee, as sanctioned by the 1583 royal charter. It is clear that the primary colony was to be located at the Chesapeake, and it seems that Roanoke was intended to be a unique satellite entity of sorts, perhaps a protectorate of the Chesapeake colony, which, if all went according to plan, would eventually have the military presence of privateers. The Roanoke-Dasamonguepeuk "colony" was to be ruled by a thoroughly anglicized Indian, who, it was hoped, could consolidate the neighboring tribes in Raleigh's name and thereby tighten Raleigh's grip on the New World.

The primary colony at the Chesapeake was to be named the "Cittie of Ralegh" and would be governed by John White, the artist and cartographer, a seemingly odd choice, and whose leadership qualities would not be particularly evident in the months ahead. White, though, had at least explored the Chesapeake with Harriot the previous year and was enthusiastic enough about the new venture to include his pregnant daughter Elyoner and son-in-law Ananias Dare. A group of twelve "Assistants" would help White in the organization and governance of the colony, although several of them would remain in England presumably to represent the colony's interests. Very little is known about these assistants. One of them was White's son-in law, Ananias Dare, and another was Dyonis Harvie, who was probably the husband of the pregnant Margery Harvie, who would give birth to a child the day after White's daughter. It seems that the Assistants had invested more heavily, at least on a personal level, in the 1587 venture. Simon Fernandez, the well-known master pilot who had guided the previous Roanoke voyages, was also one of the Assistants.

Hakluyt wrote that Raleigh "prepared a newe Colonie of one hundred and fiftie men to be sent thither," but his list of "The names of all the men, women and children, which safely arriued in Virginia, and remained to inhabite there" totals just 117, made up of ninety-one men, seventeen women, and nine children. Hakluyt's list, however, contains a few names like Simon Fernandez and John White, both of whom certainly did not remain "to inhabite there." It is possible that the rest of the 150 either changed their minds or would have been among the additional colonists who were scheduled to join the original settlers once the colony had been established.

The 1587 fleet consisted of three ships. The flagship was the 120 tun *Lyon* commanded by John White, with Simon Fernandez as master pilot. The two other vessels were an unnamed "flyboat" under the command of Edward Spicer, and an unnamed pinnace with Edward Stafford in command. Flyboats were generally used to transport cargo and could have a capacity of up to 150 tuns.[9] The unnamed pinnace was a smaller vessel, probably about 30 tuns, as will be seen in a later chapter, with a shallow draft barely capable of navigating the main inlet at Roanoke. The fleet departed from England most likely with 118[10] settlers, and the native Croatoan, Manteo, on May 8, 1587, with high hopes of establishing the Cittie of Ralegh on Chesapeake Bay.

By June 19 the *Lyon* arrived at the island of Dominica, the first landfall in the Caribbean after crossing the Atlantic and a traditional rendezvous location. On July 22 they arrived at the Hatorask inlet off Roanoke, where they anchored and sent the pinnace on to the island in order to confer with the contingent of men Grenville had left the year before, after which—according to White—they meant "to returne againe to the fleete, and passe along the coast, to the Bay of Chesepiok where we intended to make our seate and forte, according to the charge giuen us among other directions in writing, vnder the hande of Sir Walter Ralegh."[11]

That last short leg of the voyage from Roanoke to the Chesapeake would never happen.

# 3

# Simon Fernandez and the Aborted Chesapeake Plan
## July 22–August 27, 1587

## The First Institutionalized Assumption

The only version we have of what happened on July 22, or for that matter the two months preceding the arrival of the *Lyon* and the pinnace at Roanoke, is John White's problematic account of the voyage. What is certain is that at some point during the voyage ship's master Simon Fernandez[1] aborted the original plan and decided to deposit the colony at Roanoke instead of proceeding to the originally intended destination at the Chesapeake Bay. Because of this decision, Fernandez has emerged as the most reviled of all the principal characters who participated in the Roanoke voyages. It is generally held today that Simon Fernandez was at best a thoroughly incompetent master pilot and at worst a villainous character who either plotted to sabotage the voyage or simply abandoned the colony at Roanoke in order to pursue his own selfish interests. Such critical views of Fernandez have been readily adopted by authors and historians, more recently by Lee Miller, who proposed that Fernandez was the key player in a grand scheme designed by Sir Francis Walsingham, the queen's Principal Secretary of State, to sabotage Raleigh's 1587 colonization effort.[2]

The long-standing view of Fernandez as villain is based entirely on the aforementioned account of John White, who displayed a deep, personal dislike for the man. White's account—composed and edited after his return to England and clearly biased—rarely missed an opportunity to complain about Fernandez's activities during the voyage, accusing him of incompetence, deceit, negligence, and even blasphemy when "he suddenly began to sweare, and teare God in pieces."[3]

Simon Fernandez was certainly not without his faults. He was apparently arrogant and headstrong, but so were most of the leading adventurers of his day. Fernandez had also been a pirate, but so were virtually all the English sea captains who engaged—as Fernandez did—in piracy under the guise of privateering. His rough language and manner may have alienated some with more refined sensibilities, like the artist John White, but rough language and factionalism aboard ships on extended voyages were commonplace. Furthermore, such divided loyalties were not just confined to the coarser sort. It was very evident during the 1585 voyage, during which Grenville and Lane were often at odds and each had his own followers and supporters. As mentioned, between 1578 and 1579 dissention aboard Gilbert's ships had constantly plagued his efforts to reach Newfoundland.

White's derogatory depiction of Fernandez has not only persisted to this day, but has also inadvertently contributed to many of the misinformed theories which have been promoted concerning the relocation and fate of the 1587 "lost" colony. It is proposed here that the view of master pilot Simon Fernandez as a villain, who, through intention or neglect, was directly responsible for the failure of the 1587 colony is a myth. And because that negative view of Fernandez has been taken for granted for so long, it represents the first of the four flawed institutionalized assumptions identified in the Introduction. The body of evidence presented below will suggest that the universal condemnation of Simon Fernandez has been fundamentally mistaken, and that he had, in fact, good reason to alter the colony's destination. If that is the case, all the traditional assumptions about the condition, activities, and location of the 1587 colonists—based on the false narrative about Fernandez—must be reevaluated.

First, then, who was this supposedly villainous character, Simon Fernandez, and what was his involvement in the English colonization effort?

Fernandez, a Portuguese by birth, was first recorded in English service in 1574 as pilot of the *Elephant,* a ship owned in part by Queen Elizabeth's cousin, Henry Knollys, and commanded by the well-known pirate, John Challice. The following year Fernandez purchased a small vessel and joined Challice in attacking both Spanish and Portuguese shipping in the Atlantic. Although Queen Elizabeth unofficially approved of these privateering activities, Fernandez was arrested for piracy as a result of strenuous protests by the Portuguese ambassador and brought to London for trial. Possibly due to political influence exerted on his behalf, Fernandez was acquitted and released in 1577.[4]

Fernandez soon entered the service of Sir Francis Walsingham, the queen's Principal Secretary of State and an ardent proponent of English colonization in America. Walsingham knew that Fernandez would be an extremely valuable asset to the English colonization effort. Prior to severing relations with Spain, Fernandez had piloted Spanish ships to America between 1561 and 1573, and probably discovered the inlet near Roanoke Island originally called Port Fernando, which bore his name. He may also have been the pilot on the unsuccessful 1566 expedition, when Florida Governor Pedro Menéndez de Aviles first attempted to send the captive Indian Paquiquineo and two Dominican friars to the Bahia de Santa Maria (Chesapeake Bay).[5] The pilot and master of the ship *La Trinidad* on that voyage was a Domingo Fernandez, who "was considered one of the two most knowledgeable pilots for the east coast of North America."[6] It is possible that, when Fernandez later cut his ties with Spain, he may have left his given name behind as well. During this time Fernandez would have had detailed information about the *Padrón Real*, a confidential map used by Spanish pilots on ocean-going ships. Walsingham understood that Fernandez not only had first-hand knowledge of Spanish charts and shipping routes, but was also more familiar with the North American Atlantic coast than any other pilot in England at that time. His only known surviving map is one dated 1580 that he lent to mathematician-astrologer John Dee, an advisor to Queen Elizabeth and proponent of England's colonization of the New World.[7]

Fernandez sailed with Sir Francis Drake to the West Indies in 1577, and it was undoubtedly because of his recognized skill and experience, as well as his possession of valuable charts and maps, that he was chosen as pilot and master of the *Falcon*, part of Sir Humphrey Gilbert's seven-vessel fleet in the 1578 expedition which failed in its attempt to establish a colony at Newfoundland. As mentioned earlier, Gilbert's younger half-brother, Walter Raleigh, was captain of the *Falcon*, and it was during this voyage that Raleigh and Fernandez became well acquainted. The expedition encountered a fierce storm, however, during which the ships were scattered and forced to return to England. In 1579 Gilbert sent Fernandez on the previously mentioned reconnaissance voyage to North America aboard the small *Squirrel*, and Fernandez accomplished the mission in a remarkable three months. In 1582–83 Fernandez was pilot of the *Leicester*, the flagship of a large venture under Sir Edward Fenton that was intended to find a route to the East Indies by way of the South Atlantic. The expedition only made it as far as Brazil, but did capture several Spanish ships along the way.

After Sir Humphrey Gilbert's death at sea in 1583, Queen Elizabeth issued the Letters Patent to Raleigh, giving him the rights of exploration, trade, and colonization in the New World. As mentioned, Raleigh employed Fernandez as master and pilot of the Amadas-Barlowe reconnaissance in 1584, and again in 1585 as master pilot of the *Tiger*, Grenville's flagship. In 1587 Raleigh once again employed Fernandez as master pilot of the flagship *Lyon* on the voyage for which Fernandez has been vilified.

Authors invariably close the book on Simon Fernandez at this point, claiming that Raleigh severed relations with him because of the 1587 debacle, and implying that Fernandez was held responsible for the failure and disappearance of what came to be called the Lost Colony. This is simply an extension of the Fernandez-as-villain assumption and ignores the facts. When Fernandez returned from Roanoke in late 1587, England was gearing up for the imminent clash with the Spanish Armada. While it is probably true that Fernandez was not employed again by Raleigh, that outcome had nothing to do with any blame directed at Fernandez. Even though Fernandez would have been about fifty years old by then, both he and Raleigh were involved with the mobilization against the Spanish invaders. Fernandez, in fact, fought against the Armada as a deck officer aboard the *Triumph*, the largest ship in the English fleet, commanded by Martin Frobisher.[8] Such a position of importance and distinction argues convincingly against any notion that Fernandez was considered culpable for sabotaging the 1587 venture.

As alluded to briefly above, an assortment of unpersuasive reasons, all of which are based on the presumption of Fernandez' duplicity, have been offered to explain his decision to alter the original plans. White, whose references to Fernandez were almost always tainted by personal animosity, claimed that as soon as they arrived at Roanoke on July 22, Fernandez gave the order "to leaue them in the Island … saying that the Summer was farre spent, wherefore hee would land all the planters in no other place."[9]

Most authors account for this turn of events by suggesting that Fernandez's selfish and urgent thirst for privateering was what made him abort the original plan. These explanations, however, along with White's above-cited claim, are based on the assumption that *time* was a pressing factor, and that Fernandez—whatever his intention was—did not wish to waste time transporting the colony to the Chesapeake. Yet Fernandez did not hurry off after depositing the colony at Roanoke. On the contrary, we know from White's own account that Fernandez remained anchored off Roanoke for nearly five weeks until August 27, far more than enough time to convey the colony to the Chesapeake and be on his way.

As mentioned, author Lee Miller proposed that Fernandez left the colony at Roanoke because he was part of a plot orchestrated by Walsingham to sabotage Raleigh's colonization plans. The motives, Miller suggested, were Walsingham's jealousy of Raleigh's growing influence, Walsingham's mounting debts and expenses, and his view of Raleigh as an obstacle to his own political ends. Raleigh was "a loose cannon," Miller wrote, and needed to be restrained by Walsingham.[10]

This theory is unconvincing. In the first place Walsingham had always been an ardent supporter of England's colonial expansion. His backing for the exploration in the New World had long been evident and is illustrated in his 1582 letter to Hakluyt:

… you haue endeuoured, and giuen much light for the discouery of the Westerne partes yet vnknowen: as your studie in those things is very commendable, so I thanke you much for the same; wishing you do continue, your trauell in these and like matters, which are like to turne not only to your owne good in priuate, but to the publike benefice of this Realme.[11]

Walsingham's support for Gilbert's discoveries in Newfoundland is also clear in his letter to Thomas Aldworth, mayor of Bristol. As mentioned previously, Gilbert's voyage, probably the one referenced here, was an attempt to establish the first English colony in the New World.

Your good inclination to the Westerne discouerie I cannot but much commend. And for that sir Humfrey Gilbert, as you haue heard long since, hath bene preparing into those parts being readie to imbarke within these 10. dayes, who needeth some further supply of shipping then yet he hath, I am of opinion that you shall do well if the ship or 2. barkes you write of, be put in a readinesse to goe alongst with with him, or so soone after as you may.[12]

As already noted, Queen Elizabeth *and* Walsingham provided ships for Raleigh's 1585 colonization attempt, and Walsingham invested capital in the enterprise.[13] Historian David Beers Quinn wrote that "Walsingham … had so much to do with getting backing for the voyages in 1584 and 1585…."[14] These actions seem completely at odds with the notion that Walsingham plotted to destroy Raleigh's colonization effort.

Part of Walsingham's support for colonization was rooted in his deep antipathy for Spain and its dominance in the New World. An English settlement at the Chesapeake, with its deep harbor, would make an ideal base for refitting ships on their way to or from raids against Spanish treasure ships or settlements to the south, as Drake had done in 1586. It would make little sense for Walsingham to sabotage a voyage intended for the Chesapeake which could establish a foothold for just such a base.

Miller contends that Fernandez owed Walsingham a debt of gratitude for arranging his acquittal in his piracy trial in 1577 and was thereby induced into a conspiracy to sabotage Raleigh's expedition. Walsingham may have played a role in Fernandez' acquittal, but he would have done so because, as mentioned earlier, Fernandez was a valuable asset. He was the most experienced pilot in England at that time and would be extremely useful in future English colonization. The previously mentioned Martin Frobisher had also been arrested for piracy a number of times, but also managed to avoid prosecution, possibly with help from the crown. Even if one assumes for a moment that Fernandez felt indebted to Walsingham, it would seem an impossible leap to conclude that he would intentionally turn on his own patron, Raleigh, in 1587 and sabotage a major English colonization venture. There is no indication whatsoever that Fernandez and Raleigh had anything but a trustworthy relationship. Fernandez had been associated with Raleigh for almost a decade, since they sailed together on the *Falcon* in 1578, and he was Raleigh's choice to guide all three of the Roanoke voyages.

Furthermore, Fernandez was one of the twelve Assistants appointed by Raleigh to be, along with Governor White, the overseeing administration of the new Cittie of Ralegh. These Assistants were elevated to the status of gentlemen by virtue of the coats of arms which Raleigh had arranged to be conferred on them. As members of the governing body the twelve Assistants would have enjoyed certain advantages unavailable to the rest of the colonists. The Assistants would make up the "ruling class" of the colony and would likely have been entitled to larger shares of land plus whatever other benefits their successful enterprise might produce. They may also have put up "a minimum investment in money and goods"[15] to be part of that elite group, and as mentioned earlier probably had a greater personal interest in the venture. The Assistants who had either remained behind in England or returned to England—Fernandez being among these latter—probably also had the rights to sell subscriptions to investors or participants in the new enterprise. Fernandez, then, may have had a personal and perhaps a financial interest in the colony's success.

Finally, Fernandez had a golden opportunity to abandon the colony on August 21, when a storm rolled in forcing him to cut the *Lyon's* cables and put to sea. If his intention was to sabotage the venture, the storm would have been a perfect excuse to do so. Instead, he rode out the storm and then anchored once again at Roanoke to complete the final arrangements. One of those arrangements was to bring on board his harshest critic, John White, for the voyage to England. If he were part of a conspiracy to intentionally ruin Raleigh's enterprise, a criminal act, it seems inconceivable that he would risk transporting his most potentially incriminating witness, John White, safely back to England. Such actions do not seem compatible with Miller's conspiracy theory.

There are further details in White's version of their arrival at Roanoke which raise questions about his credibility as a narrator. White claimed that he first learned about the decision to leave the colony at Roanoke on July 22 when "...a Gentleman who was appointed to returne for England, called to the sailers in the pinnesse, charging them not to bring any of the planters backe again, but to leaue them in the Island."[16] The identity of the "Gentleman" is not stated, but it is unlikely that any gentlemen would have been aboard the *Lion* other than White's Assistants. This particular "Gentleman" had been "appointed to returne for England," which raises the possibility that he could have been William Fullwood or James Plat, two of the known Assistants who do not appear on Hakluyt's passenger list of those who "remained to inhabite there." In that case White seems to be saying that he first heard about the change of plans from one of his own Assistants, an implausible occurrence.

Moreover, when White heard from that "Gentleman" what should have been very shocking and unexpected news—that his settlement location was inexplicably changed—he seemed strangely impassive. As he put it, "it booted not the Gouernour to contend with them,"[17] an extremely odd and passive reaction. White was not only the governor of the colony, but also the principal authority on the *Lyon* during the entire voyage. His inexplicable lack of any response to this crucial turn of events demonstrates much more than poor leadership; it strongly suggests that his version of what happened on July 22 is not plausible. White claimed he heard the news when he was in the pinnace with "fortie of his best men,"[18] and yet not a single one of those forty men apparently voiced an objection either. If this was indeed the first time that White and his men had heard of the change, it is difficult to understand why neither he nor anyone in the pinnace raised a single word of protest.

This reaction becomes all the more perplexing when the promises and expectations of this 1587 venture are recalled. As already noted, the colonists departed from England intending to establish the "Cittie of Ralegh" at the Chesapeake Bay in "Virginia" and expecting to acquire 500 acres of land as reward for participation in the 1587 colonization effort.[19] Many of the would-be colonists sold everything they had in England for the opportunity to be part of this exciting new venture and become large landowners in what was purported to be a New World paradise. It is impossible to believe that no one, including the governor of the colony, raised a single word of complaint at the supposedly sudden and shocking news that the plans had been inexplicably changed. White went on to say that "Vnto this [the decision to leave the colony at Roanoke] were all the saylers, both in the pinnesse, and shippe, perswaded by the Master [Fernandez]."[20] It begins to sound like White was the last to learn of the decision to abort the original plan. It is equally strange that White never brought up the issue of the settlement relocation again. After his improbable comments about the change of plans on July 22, he made no further mention of it at all.

White's version of events is not credible. A far more plausible explanation is that the decision to change the colony's settlement location, as disappointing as it must have been at the time, had been made long before the arrival at Roanoke on July 22. This conclusion is supported by White's own statement that on July 25 "our Flyboate and the rest of our planters arriued all safe at Hatoraske [the inlet near Roanoke]."[21] The wording here seems to indicate that Roanoke was their intended destination. If the decision to deposit the colony at Roanoke was *not prearranged*, how did the flyboat's captain, Edward Spicer, know to set a course *to Roanoke*, instead of sailing with his cargo and the remaining settlers directly to the Chesapeake, the original settlement destination? The decision must have been made earlier in the voyage and surely White and the principal colonists must not only have been aware of it, but probably agreed—perhaps reluctantly—with it as well. As mentioned, it seems that at least one of White's own Assistants, the "Gentleman" who called from the ship, had undoubtedly known of and had apparently supported the decision. The dubious claims in White's account, then, very likely served another purpose. They may have been intended to place the burden of the decision entirely on Fernandez, and at the same time to shield White from any personal liability which might later arise from the decision to change the settlement location.

It is obvious that Fernandez must have had *some* reason for his decision to change the location from the Chesapeake to Roanoke. Sabotage, it has been demonstrated, is not a plausible explanation, and White's claim that Fernandez was in a rush to get on his way because "the Summer was farre spent" is manifestly false. Since Fernandez was not motivated out of nefarious intentions or incompetency, the obvious question remains: Why did Simon Fernandez alter the destination of the 1587 colony from the Chesapeake Bay to Roanoke Island?

The Spanish had suspected as early as 1584 that the English were planning a settlement somewhere up the Atlantic coast. The precise location of the settlement, however, was unknown at that time other than it was to be "up toward the cod fisheries,"[22] probably a reference to Gilbert's colonization attempt in 1583. In early 1586 Sir Francis Drake's "Great Expedition" raided the Spanish cities of Santo Domingo and Cartagena and by May had looted and destroyed the settlement and fort at St. Augustine. Drake's intention after the raid was to proceed northward to assist Lane's colony at Roanoke. As it turned out, of course, Drake transported the entire colony back to England. The Spanish, however, still did not know the exact location of the colony and were unaware of its evacuation by Drake. They believed that the English settlement existed and would be used as a base from which further attacks could be launched on Spanish interests to the south. A concerted effort was begun to locate the English settlement.

In a letter to King Phillip II dated June 27, 1586, Alonso Suarez de Toledo claimed (mistakenly) that the 1585 Grenville/Lane expedition had established a colony at Bahia de Santa Maria, the Spanish name for the Chesapeake Bay. Suarez had been to that area more than a decade earlier and knew it to be a suitable location.[23] On November 26, 1586, the king sent orders to Pedro Menéndez Marques, Governor of La Florida, to find the English colony. By the time Menéndez Marques received the king's orders, the Spanish were certain that the English settlement would be near Ajacán, the location of the failed 1570 Jesuit settlement believed to be on the present-day James River near the Chesapeake Bay.[24] On May 7, 1587, *the day before White and his colonists set sail from England*, Menéndez Marques sailed north from Havana to find it.[25] Menéndez Marques stopped at the Spanish settlement of Santa

Elena, present-day Parris Island in South Carolina, where he was told by local Indians that they had no knowledge of an English settlement to the north. Menéndez Marques continued onward, but a storm drove him from the entrance to the Chesapeake Bay. He returned to Havana with plans to sail again in search of the English the following May.

At the same time, a letter was written by the military secretary in Madrid to the Junta de Puerto Rico indicating that the Spanish knew about Raleigh's latest venture to the Chesapeake Bay.[26] Two things are clear from the documentary evidence: first, that the Spanish were well aware of the English intention to establish a colony specifically at the Chesapeake Bay, and second, that the Spanish were actively searching for the colony in 1587, at the same time White and his colony were en route to the Chesapeake.

As noted, Fernandez was a well-known and highly experienced master pilot, and by 1587 he had been sailing the waters of the Caribbean for a quarter century. He was well acquainted with all the ports of call in the islands, and he undoubtedly had an established network of useful contacts from whom he would acquire supplies and important intelligence about Spanish activities. It is known, for example, that one of these contacts was a friend named Alanson in Hispaniola, present-day Dominican Republic and Haiti,[27] and surely there were many others. Such contacts would provide Fernandez with valuable information about Spanish port activities and ship movements as well as ongoing operations. The major news awaiting Fernandez in the Caribbean during the summer of 1587 would have been that the Spanish knew about and were attempting to locate the English colony at Bahia de Santa Maria to the north. Fernandez would have learned of this troubling development shortly after his arrival at Dominica on July 19.

The Spanish threat was very real and could not be taken lightly by the colonists at Roanoke. The English were well aware of the stories of Spanish cruelties. Pedro Menéndez Marques, in fact, was the nephew of Pedro Menéndez de Avilés, who had demonstrated the kind of treatment non–Catholic heretics could expect at the hands of the Spanish: In 1564 René de Laudonnière sailed up the St. Johns River with three ships loaded with French Huguenots—Protestants—and started construction of Fort Caroline. The French fort was a potential threat to the Spanish treasure fleet, which sailed along La Florida's coast en route to Spain. More importantly these settlers were Huguenots, heretics whose poisonous beliefs could not be allowed to spread among the natives in the new world.

On September 20, 1565, Pedro Menéndez de Avilés and a force of 500 soldiers from the garrison at St. Augustine assaulted the lightly defended Fort Caroline in the early morning hours during a fierce storm. About 140 of the French Huguenots were killed and their bodies piled in a heap on the bank of the St. Johns River. A number of prisoners were hanged from trees, but

Menéndez spared the remaining women and infants. In the meantime Jean Ribault had just crossed the Atlantic with new settlers for Ft. Caroline, but was caught in a hurricane and his fleet was scattered and wrecked along Florida's coast. Two groups of survivors headed north along the beach. Pedro Menéndez de Avilés met the first group of about 125 Frenchmen, who, expecting to be spared, surrendered to Pedro Menéndez de Avilés at an inlet south of St. Augustine on September 29. The Spaniards took the prisoners across the inlet in groups of ten and marched each group behind a dune out of sight of the others, and they were put to the sword. Twelve days later the second group of Frenchmen arrived at the inlet, where about 130, including Ribault, met the same fate. The inlet is still known today as Matanzas Inlet, the Spanish word for "slaughter."

Although the massacres of the French Protestants happened much farther south and a decade earlier, the English settlement to the north represented the identical threats to the Spanish in 1587. The English settlement could be used as a base from which Spanish treasure ships were attacked, which was indeed a large part of the English motivation for colonization. The Spanish were even more worried about that possibility after Drake had successfully raided their colonial settlements, including St. Augustine, in 1586. And of course England's break with the Catholic Church—the root cause of hostilities between England and Spain—would threaten to spread its heresy among the natives in the New World if an English settlement were to be established. In fact, "thinlargemente of the gospell of Christe," as Hakluyt had written in his 1584 *Discourse of Western Planting*, was the first motivation he listed for colonization.

Moreover, Hakluyt's claim that the English had the right to colonize the "parte of AMERICA from 30. degrees in Florida northewarde unto 63. degrees (which ys yet in no Christian princes actuall possession)" was little more than an exercise in wishful thinking. Spain's original claim to "La Florida" extended to virtually all of North America, and the Spanish had been exploring the present-day Carolina and Virginia latitudes long before the English. Santa Elena had been established in 1566, and the Spanish were cognizant of the strategic importance of the Chesapeake Bay. In a 1565 letter to King Philip II, Pedro Menéndez de Avilés wrote that the Bahia de Santa Maria was, "the key to the defense of these lands."[28]

In any event territorial boundaries had become irrelevant by 1587. After the beginning of the Anglo-Spanish War in 1585, England began raiding Spanish holdings in both America and Europe, and Spain was preparing to invade England. Fernandez and the colonists at Roanoke certainly knew this history, just as they would have been acutely aware that their settlement location must be kept hidden from the Spanish. The new and disturbing intelligence Fernandez learned in the Caribbean would have eliminated the possibility of landing the colony at the original destination, and it required a reassessment of potential locations. This was very likely the reason Fernandez made the decision to change the destination to Roanoke instead of the Chesapeake, and his decision may have saved the 1587 colony from certain discovery and possibly a similar fate as the one suffered by the French Huguenots. There was no other logical option. Roanoke, at least, was familiar territory for both White and Fernandez. The old settlement site and Lane's fort were located there, and they expected to find Grenville's small contingent waiting there as well. Most importantly, Roanoke was situated inside the barrier island chain and was shielded from Spanish ships patrolling the coast.

The evidence presented here has broader implications beyond the rehabilitation of Simon Fernandez. Much of the current theory regarding the relocation and ultimate fate of the Lost Colony hinges upon what was believed to be the negligent or villainous actions of Simon Fernandez during the summer of 1587. It has generally been assumed, for example, that White's colony would have relocated to their original destination at the Chesapeake, using the pinnace and smaller boats that are known to have been in their possession. Since it is clear, however, that the Spanish knew of their intentions to settle at the Chesapeake and were actively searching for them there, the Chesapeake location would have become—and would have remained—a toxic choice for White's colonists.

The activities of the colonists between July 22, the day they arrived at Roanoke, and August 27, when White departed for England, are fairly well documented: Toward evening on July 22 White and some of the colonists searched for the fifteen men whom Grenville had left the previous year, "but we found none of them, nor any signe that they had bene there, sauing onely wee found the bones of one of those fifteene, which the Sauages had slaine long before."[29] There is no way of knowing, of course, but the bones may not have been the remains of one of Grenville's contingent, but rather one of the two unfortunate members of Lane's colony who had been left behind during Drake's evacuation. On the morning of the 23rd White and some of his colonists walked to the north end of Roanoke Island where Lane had built his fort in 1585. They found the settlement "ouergrowen with Melons of diuers sortes," but most of the dwellings were still standing. White ordered that "euery man should be employed for the repayring of those houses ... and also to make other new Cottages, for such as should neede."[30]

As already mentioned, the flyboat commanded by Edward Spicer arrived with the rest of the colonists and supplies on July 25. Three days later George Howe, one of White's twelve appointed Assistants, wandered some distance from the settlement to catch crabs where some Indians from the mainland "shot at him in the water, where they gaue him sixteen wounds with their arrowes: and after they had slaine him with their woodden swords, they beat his head in pieces, and fled ouer the water to the maine."[31] George Howe left behind a young son, George Howe, Jr.

On July 30 Captain Stafford and a party of twenty men along with the faithful Manteo went to Croatoan, home of Manteo and the friendly Croatoan tribe. They learned from the Croatoans that the contingent left by Grenville in 1586 had been attacked by a combined force of tribesmen from Aquascogoc, Secota, and Dasamonguepeuk and were driven from the island. At White's behest the Croatoans agreed to invite the hostile tribal leaders to a conference to be held within seven days in an attempt at restoring peaceful relations. When none of the native leaders had arrived by August 8, White—perhaps urged on by one of his more aggressive Assistants—decided to destroy the village at Dasamonguepeuk, in revenge for the killing of George Howe ten days earlier.

In the very early morning hours of August 9 White, Stafford, Manteo, and twenty-four others attacked the village. As the assault began, the attackers learned to their dismay that the natives there were friendly Croatoans who had occupied Dasamonguepeuk after the hostile Indians had abandoned it shortly after the killing of George Howe. It took some explaining by White and Manteo, but the Croatoans were eventually convinced that the blame lay with the failure of the hostile native leaders to meet with White by the appointed time.

The next several days were occupied with happier occasions. On August 13 Manteo was baptized into the Church of England and installed as Lord of Roanoke and Dasamonguepeuk in reward for his faithful service. On August 18 White's daughter Elyoner Dare, wife of Ananias Dare, gave birth to a daughter, the first English child born in America. The following Sunday she was christened "Virginia."

By this time the supplies and stores for the colony had been unloaded and brought ashore, the old dwellings repaired and new ones built, and the colonists prepared letters to send back to England. On about August 21 a controversy arose over which of the Assistants should return to England as agent for the colony's interests. Christopher Cooper, one of White's Assistants, initially agreed to go, but he was dissuaded by his friends and changed his mind the next day, perhaps an indication that Cooper was considered a more useful asset to the colony than White. The Assistants and some of the other colonists, "the whole company" according to White, came to him with the plea that White himself be the one to return to England, another indication that his leadership abilities may have been in doubt.

White at first refused, citing the criticism he would receive back in England for abandoning his colony after persuading so many to take part in the venture. He also worried that in his absence the belongings he left behind would be spoiled or "pilfered away," another indication that he may not have had the level of respect normally attributed to a governor. It was only after White was actually provided with a written bond on August 25, properly signed and sealed, certifying that he was entreated to leave against his will and guaranteeing his personal belongings, that he agreed to go.

At some time prior to White's departure it was determined that the colonists would eventually seek a permanent settlement location somewhere on the mainland and that they would leave carved messages for White at Roanoke indicating where they had gone. As explained above, Chesapeake Bay would *no longer* have been a viable settlement option. Furthermore, since White clearly did not know where they planned to go, it seems likely that the Chesapeake had been eliminated from consideration.

On August 27, 1587, John White boarded the *Lyon* and departed from Roanoke Island, leaving behind 119[32] men, women, and children, including his daughter Elyoner Dare and his nine-day-old granddaughter, Virginia Dare. He fully intended to acquire supplies and additional colonists for his expected return in the early summer of the following year.

# 4

## *Decisions at Roanoke*
### August 28–September 30, 1587

After John White sailed for England, deliberations would have proceeded in earnest among the principal Assistants regarding the colony's settlement options. It is known that the colonists planned to relocate from Roanoke to the mainland, but, as mentioned, it is also clear that the location of the new settlement had not been resolved by August 27, when White departed. It was for this reason that, prior to his departure, the arrangement was made for the colonists to leave carved messages at Roanoke which would tell White where to look for them upon his expected return in the early summer of 1588.

Those carved messages left at Roanoke—"CRO" and "CROATOAN"—are the only indisputable primary source evidence we have from the Lost Colonists after August 27, 1587. They were clearly intended to direct John White to Croatoan, present-day Hatteras, upon his return the following year. As it turned out, of course, White did not return as planned, and the colonists' carved messages would not be discovered until 1590, by which time the colony had disappeared.

The question of the resettlement location has long been debated, but it can at least be said with a fair amount of assurance that the 1587 colonists did not relocate to Croatoan, at least not initially. First and foremost we have the colonists' known intention to settle somewhere on the mainland. Croatoan, as part of the barrier island chain, must therefore be eliminated as a settlement option. Furthermore, Croatoan's location as part of the Outer Banks would have been far more vulnerable to Spanish discovery and attack. As already seen, the Spanish were actively searching for the English colony at this time, and the colonists were well aware of the threat they posed. Also, the mainland would provide much better agricultural opportunities than Croatoan for what was expected to be a growing, self-sustaining colony. We know, for example, that when "On the thirtieth of Iuly Master Stafford and twenty of our men passed by water to the Island of Croatoan, ... some of them came vnto vs, embracing and entertaining vs friendly, desiring vs not to gather or spill any of their corne, for that they had but little."[1] By the end of July the corn crop would normally be plentiful, another indication that Croatoan would not have been a viable option for a large agriculture-based colony.

Finally, archaeological excavations at Croatoan to date support the conclusion that the colony did not relocate there. Because of the inscriptions left at Roanoke by the Lost Colonists, an extensive amount of archaeological attention has been directed at Hatteras Island, some of which was conducted and funded by the Lost Colony Research Group. Although a number of early European artifacts such as iron spikes, copper farthings, brass fragments, a snaphaunce (gunlock), gun flints, and pottery shards have been recovered, the origin and age of these findings remain uncertain. Shipwrecks alone could account for some. The artifacts *do* demonstrate that Hatteras Island was a contact site, but it was already known from the Roanoke accounts that Croatoan was visited by the English on a number of occasions between 1585 and 1587, sometimes for a period of weeks. There was also an English presence at Croatoan/Hatteras in the 17th century. The fact remains that no evidence has been discovered which link these artifacts directly to the Lost Colony.[2]

Perhaps the most dramatic discovery at Hatteras was a gold signet ring found by David Phelps, archaeologist at East Carolina University. The ring was alleged to bear the Kendall family crest and therefore thought to have belonged to "Master Kendall." The Kendall connection itself is disputed, but— even if accurate—"Master Kendall" was listed among "The names of those as well Gentlemen as others, that remained one whole yeere in Virginia, vnder the Gouernement of Master Ralph Lane." He was *not* a member of White's 1587 colony. In the final analysis no archaeological evidence of a large and permanent 16th century English settlement has been found at Hatteras/Croatoan.

Croatoan could not have been the colonists' choice for a permanent settlement location, but it *would* have been a logical place to position a small outpost to wait for White's expected return the following summer. The chosen settlement location on the mainland may not have had an established name or one recognized by the English, but Croatoan was very well known to White and the colonists and was home to Manteo's friendly tribe. From a strategic standpoint Croatoan's position on the Outer Banks may have been *en route* from Roanoke *to* the permanent settlement location on the mainland, which might reasonably place it across Pamlico Sound to the west or southwest of Croatoan. The messages left by the colony would have sent White to Croatoan, about fifty miles south of Roanoke, where he—along with the supplies and new colonists—could then have been guided to the nearby mainland settlement site.

Three of the prominent theories of the past several decades place the mainland settlement location either at the Chesapeake Bay to the north, at Weapemeoc bordering Albemarle Sound to the north and northwest, or somewhere near the Chowan River across Albemarle Sound far to the west of Roanoke. These theories also generally hold that the colonists left Roanoke almost immediately after White's departure on August 27. All of these hypotheses, however, have their roots in the problematic Fernandez-as-villain scenario, the first of the four institutionalized assumptions, which has been addressed in the preceding chapter.

The most eminent proponent of the Chesapeake theory was the previously mentioned historian David Beers Quinn, who was convinced that most if not all of the 1587 colonists, having been stranded at Roanoke by the villainous Simon Fernandez, would have logically relocated to their originally intended destination, the Chesapeake Bay, at the earliest opportunity. Quinn proposed that the colonists would have accomplished that relocation in September.[3] As already demonstrated, however, Fernandez had very likely aborted the Chesapeake settlement location because the Spanish not only knew of the English plans to settle there, but were actively searching for them. Consequently, the Chesapeake would have become an unlikely settlement option.

Furthermore, if White and his colonists had thought a move to the original location at the Chesapeake was a foregone conclusion, as Quinn suggested, the plan to relocate there would have been settled long before White departed for England on August 27. On the contrary, however, the new settlement location was *not* known, making it necessary to leave carved messages for White telling him where to look for them upon his return. As mentioned, such an arrangement would suggest that the colonists had already eliminated the Chesapeake as a viable settlement option.

The "Weapemeoc theory," promoted by Quinn's contemporary Thomas C. Parramore, claimed that "the colonists were already prepared, when John White left them, to move from Roanoke Island across Albemarle Sound to Weapemeoc."[4] The colonists chose the territory of the Weapemeoc tribe, he asserted, because "they were the only friendly mainland Indians within fifty miles of Roanoke Island." Furthermore, he continued, the colonists moved to Weapemeoc "within days or, at most, scant weeks after White left...."[5] There are several problems with this theory. As with the Chesapeake theory, if the decision had already been made and the colonists were "already prepared" to move to Weapemeoc by the time White left, the carved message system would have been unnecessary. Once again, the message system was required precisely because the mainland location had *not* been selected by the time White left.

In addition, the territory occupied by the Weapemeoc tribe was largely swampland and would have been a poor choice for a settlement, particularly one that was intended to be agricultural in nature. The Weapemeoc were also a small tribe that seemed more interested in keeping clear of the English than aiding them. While it is true that Okisco, chief of the Weapemeoc tribe, pledged his allegiance to Queen Elizabeth during the previous Grenville-Lane colonization attempt, he did that only because he was so ordered by his more powerful neighbor, Menatonon. When hostilities between Lane's colony and Wingina/Pemisapan's followers were intensifying in 1586, the Weapemeoc did not offer aid to the English, but rather retreated farther inland away from them. Another problem, to be addressed below, is Parramore's possible misinterpretation of White's fifty mile designation, which would have eliminated Weapemeoc as a settlement possibility.

The "Chesapeake," "Chowanoke," "Weapemeoc," and other similar theories claim that when John White departed Roanoke on August 27, 1587, his colony was left in a desperate state. It is asserted that the colonists were hopelessly ill-provisioned and that they had failed to obtain essential provisions in the West Indies. As historian James Horn wrote, "the failure to obtain cattle, salt, and supplies in the West Indies would necessitate short rations through much of the winter and spring."[6] Given such a bleak scenario, these theories continue, the colonists could not have survived the winter at Roanoke and therefore were forced to seek refuge and sustenance among the Indians at one of the aforementioned locations. These included the Chowanoke tribe about sixty miles or so across Albemarle Sound to the west of Roanoke along the Chowan River, where Ralph Lane had experienced some degree of cooperation during the previous 1585–6 expedition. Horn, Miller, Parramore, and Quinn all suggested that the main body of White's colonists abandoned Roanoke shortly after White's departure on August 27, 1587.[7]

The key premise of the these theories—that the colony was in desperate need of provisions in August of 1587—is once again based *entirely* on the dubious credibility of John White's account, and in particular his biased allegations against Simon Fernandez. White did accuse Fernandez of failing to obtain salt and other provisions during the voyage, but it is curious that he did not cite any problem whatsoever about a shortage of provisions *once they arrived* at Roanoke on July 22. White certainly would not have missed the opportunity to add a desperate food shortage at Roanoke to the list of complaints against Fernandez, if one had actually existed. White's silence on this point after their arrival at Roanoke is at odds with his previous accusations made during the voyage. In fact White did not even mention any need for "supplies"—and at that, not food stores or provisions in particular—until a month later on August 22, when the controversy arose about who "should goe backe as factors for the company into England."[8]

The most blatantly fictitious of White's allegations concerned the flyboat, the vessel used primarily for the purpose of transporting cargo and supplies, the very items White claimed Fernandez failed to obtain. On May 18 White made the preposterous claim that Fernandez "lewdly forsook our Fly-boate, leauing her distressed in the Bay of Portugal."[9] White not only would have his readers believe that the flyboat was intentionally abandoned in the Bay of Portugal only eight days after leaving Plymouth on May 8, but also that its whereabouts were unknown until July 25, when it arrived at Roanoke three days after the *Lyon*. Note White's remarkable entry for July 25:

> The 25 our Flyboate and the rest of our planters arriued all safe at Hatoraske [the inlet at Roanoke], to the great ioy and comfort of the whole company: but the Master of our Admirall Ferdinando grieued greatly at their safe comming: for hee purposely left them in the Bay of Portugal, and stole away from them in the night, hoping that the Master thereof, whose name was Edward Spicer, for that he neuer had bene in Virginia, would hardly finde the place, or els being left in so dangerous a place as that was, by meanes of so many men of warre, as at that time were abroad, they should surely be taken, or slaine: but God disappointed his wicked pretenses.[10]

In this passage White unequivocally charged Fernandez with intentionally abandoning the flyboat in the Bay of Portugal on May 16 in the hopes that the passengers and crew would be captured or killed. It was a virtual miracle, according to White, that the flyboat appeared once again at Roanoke on July 25.

This allegation is patently false. White's entire claim, in fact, is refuted by a detail he apparently overlooked in his own entry for June 19–21 when he wrote, "we fell with Dominica, and the same euening we sayled betweene it, and Guadalupe: the 21 the Fly-boat also fell with Dominica."[11] The flyboat was clearly in contact with the *Lyon* on June 21, which obviously contradicts White's allegation of its abandonment on May 16 and its seemingly miraculous appearance at Roanoke more than two months later on July 25. This inconsistency is persuasive evidence of White's intention to fabricate a false narrative about Fernandez.

It is probable that White kept an abbreviated journal during the 1587 voyage, logging the dates and location of the *Lyon* and perhaps a few brief notes during and after crossing the Atlantic. His expanded account of the voyage, containing the multiple allegations against Fernandez, must have been completed not long after his return to England on November 5, since he dated the account with "An. Dom. 1587." It would appear that in the rewriting and preparation of his manuscript, during which White gave vent to his personal animosity toward Fernandez and attempted to blame him for the colony's dilemma, he failed to delete the original June 21 detail from his original daily journal concerning the flyboat's arrival at Dominica. The final manuscript he delivered to Hakluyt contained the telltale contradiction, and it was eventually published by Richard Hakluyt in 1589,[12] along with the self-incriminating discrepancy.

Dominica is an island in the Lesser Antilles, the first island chain voyagers encountered in the West Indies after an Atlantic crossing. The *Lyon* arrived at Dominica on June 19 after the 3,000 mile trans–Atlantic voyage from the Canary Islands to the Caribbean, and remained in the area for several days. Two days later, on June 21, the flyboat arrived at Dominica. If Fernandez had intentionally stranded the flyboat in the Bay of Portugal, hoping that "they should surely be taken, or slaine," or to sabotage the expedition as Miller proposed, his delay at Dominica until the flyboat arrived would be inexplicable. Unless this meeting at Dominica had been charted and planned prior to the ocean crossing, the chances of Edward Spicer showing up in the flyboat at this particular island in the Caribbean more than a month later, while the *Lyon* just happened to be waiting there, would be infinitesimal. White's allegation about the flyboat was an intentional deception, the most serious in a succession of allegations motivated in part by his obvious hostility toward Fernandez and also by his intention to place the consequences for the colony's predicament at Roanoke squarely on Fernandez's shoulders.

A far more plausible scenario is that Edward Spicer and the flyboat were never abandoned at all. The recorded contact between the *Lyon* and the flyboat at the island of Dominica on June 21 was a pre-arranged and pre-charted rendezvous, common practice involving multiple vessels on voyages to the New World. As mentioned earlier, Dominica—the first landfall after crossing the Atlantic—was the traditional rendezvous point."[13] The Grenville/Lane colonization expedition had stopped there in 1585 and, in fact, the three-vessel fleet—which included White aboard the *Hopeful*—would also rendezvous at Dominica en route to Roanoke three years later in 1590.

Having rendezvoused safely with the *Lyon* at Dominica, the flyboat—whose essential function, as mentioned, was the transportation of the very cargo and supplies White claimed Fernandez neglected—would then have acquired the salt and whatever additional cargo was deemed necessary for the colony. The time it took to acquire this cargo would also explain the flyboat's arrival at Roanoke on July 25, three days after the *Lyon*. As explained previously, because the Spanish knew of the English plans to settle at the Chesapeake, the decision to abort the final leg of the voyage and leave the colony at Roanoke must have been made at this time. During the rendezvous, furthermore, the change of plans had to have been discussed with Edward Spicer, who otherwise would not have known to proceed to Roanoke rather than the Chesapeake with the flyboat loaded with supplies and the rest of the colonists.

White's accusations against Fernandez do not survive a close examination of the text, and therefore conclusions drawn from those accusations—such as the assumption that the colony was in a perilous state because of Fernandez' failure to obtain provisions in the West Indies—must be considered questionable as well.

It should also be remembered that the two previous Roanoke voyages started off well-provisioned with stores intended for the colony or expedition upon arrival at Roanoke. The three ships of the 1587 voyage were fitted out in Portsmouth and Plymouth where the food stores and supplies for the colony were stowed on board. Although White's account of the voyage says nothing about these preparations, some instruction can be taken from the previous expedition. The Grenville-Lane expedition of 1585, properly fitted out in England, had been crippled upon its arrival at the Carolinas when the *Tyger* ran aground at Wokokon and a major portion of the food supplies was ruined by seawater. This accident consequently forced the colony to rely more heavily on the native Indians for food.

White's 1587 voyage suffered no such misfortune. The crew, in fact, took weeks to unload supplies for the colony and it was not until mid to late August that "our ships had vnladen the goods and victuals of the planters."[14] It appears that there was a sizable supply of "goods and victuals" and that everything was unloaded without any difficulty or loss whatsoever. White would certainly have mentioned it and blamed Fernandez had such a problem occurred.

In addition, contemporary accounts cited an abundance of natural food sources to be had at Roanoke and its environs. The Amadas-Barlowe expedition of 1584 reported that Roanoke and the nearby islands were "replenished with Deere, Conies, Hares, and diuers beasts, and about them the goodliest and best fish in the world, and in greatest abundance."[15] White's 1587 colony found Lane's old fort and settlement "ouergrowen with Melons of diuers sortes, and Deere within them."[16] White also noted that Indians sometimes came from the mainland to Roanoke "to hunt Deere, whereof were many in the Island."[17] And then, of course, the colony had the assistance of the steadfastly loyal Manteo and his Croatoans, who would certainly have helped the colonists build weirs for a continual supply of fish.

It is noteworthy, too, that the colony's provisions were amply supplemented on August 9 after White's ill-advised attack at Dasamonguepeuk. The hostile natives "had fled immediately after they had slaine George Howe, and for haste had left all their corne. Tobacco, and Pompions…" and "…we gathered al the corne, Pease, Pompions, and Tobacco that we found ripe…."[18] The confiscation of Dasamonguepeuk's ripened harvest would have represented a major enhancement to what apparently was an already adequate food supply.

It appears that White's colony was not desperately short of food by any means, and therefore they would not have been forced to abandon Roanoke soon after White's departure and seek sustenance with the Chowanoke or any other tribe. On the contrary, if they had a sufficient food supply, there would have been no reason to winter any place other than Roanoke, where they already had the availability of "all the houses standing vnhurt" from the previous Grenville-Lane expedition. And furthermore, all the men were "... employed for the repayring of those houses, which wee found standing, and also to make other new Cottages, for such as should neede."[19] These activities seem more attuned to a colony preparing for an extended stay rather than a colony supposedly compelled to make a hasty departure in order to seek refuge among the Chowanoke tribe or elsewhere. Moreover, when White finally returned three years later, he discovered that the settlement had been "very strongly enclosed with a high palisado of great trees, with cortynes and flankers very Fortlike."[20] Apparently the colonists took the time and effort to fortify the Roanoke settlement after White departed in August 1587, and therefore must have spent the winter there.

Furthermore, finding refuge and sustenance with the Chowanoke tribe would not have been as promising a prospect as some suggest. The Indians had to depend upon their own food stores for sustenance through the winter. Even under the best of circumstances, mid to late winter through early spring was always the leanest time of year for the Indians, when the previous fall's stores of corn were gone and the spring berry crop had not yet ripened.[21] It seems very doubtful that the Chowanokes could have been persuaded to provide the colony with food through the winter, because an additional hundred-plus mouths would have placed an impossible strain on the tribe's own winter food stores. Moreover, as mentioned previously, the fragile "cooperation" Lane had received from the Chowanoke king, Menatonon, was hardly offered out of friendship towards the English. Lane had captured both Menatonon and his son Skiko, and after obtaining a ransom for the release of Menatonon, he guaranteed the king's cooperation because, as Lane noted, "I had his best beloued sonne prisoner with me."[22] It is unlikely that the Chowanokes would have been either willing or able to feed the 1587 colony.

Another relocation theory generated considerable excitement and press coverage in May of 2012 when a fort symbol was discovered beneath a patch on John White's 1585 "Virginea Pars map." The discovery was made after First Colony Foundation member Brent Lane initiated an inquiry which resulted in the employment of a light table to discover a painted symbol under the patch. In a joint announcement by the First Colony Foundation and the British Museum, the proposal was made that the fort symbol could represent a location where the English intended to establish a settlement.[23] Press reports at the time included announcements that the fort symbol "provides conclusive proof that they [the Lost Colonists] moved westward up the Albemarle Sound to the confluence of the Chowan and Roanoke Rivers."[24]

There were a few perceptible problems, though, with these conclusions. As mentioned previously, it had become obvious during the 1585–86 Grenville-Lane expedition that the inlet at Roanoke was not adequate and that future colonization efforts would focus on the Chesapeake, not Albemarle

Sound. There are a number of references in the contemporary documents supporting this conclusion. Since John White was a member of the party that explored the Chesapeake and drew his Virginea Pars map during the same 1585–86 expedition, he would have known firsthand about the likely prospects of a Chesapeake settlement. It is doubtful, then, that he would have drawn a fort symbol on his map at the western end of Albemarle Sound to designate a location for a future colony.

Moreover, Ralph Lane identified that specific location in his account and provided definitive information about what that location was intended to be used for, and it was *not* as a site for a future colony. Lane described the location as "very neere whereunto directly from the West runneth a most notable Riuer ... called the Riuer of Moratoc. This Riuer openeth into the broad Sound of Weapomeiok [Albemarle Sound]."[25] Lane's plan was to build a sconce—or small fortification—at that location as part of a chain of sconces leading to the Chesapeake where he believed there was "a better harborough" and where King Menatonon reported there was a "greate quantitie of Pearle."[26] Lane added:

> And so I would haue holden this course of insconsing euery two dayes march, vntill I had bene arriued at the Bay [Chesapeake] or Port hee [Menatonon] spake of: which finding to bee worth the possession, I would there haue raised a maine fort, both for the defence of the harborough, and our shipping also, and would haue reduced our whole habitation from Roanoak and from the harborough and port there (which by proofe is very naught) vnto this other before mentioned....[27]

Lane's plan, which never materialized, was to build a series of sconces starting at the fort symbol location and ending at the Chesapeake where he would have built a "maine fort" and then moved the "whole habitation from Roanoke" to the new location at the Chesapeake.

The fort symbol location was never intended to be a future settlement site. White may have drawn the fort symbol in 1585 to designate Lane's intention to build the first of a series of sconces there. The fort symbol was subsequently covered with a patch—the traditional method of making map corrections—because Lane cut short the 1585–86 expedition and the sconces were never built. In that regard it should also be noted that there is a second, larger patch on the Virginea Pars map in addition to the one covering the fort symbol. The purpose of that second patch was the same as the first, to make corrections to the earlier draft. The second patch was added to correct errors in the previously drawn configuration of the coastline and the placement of Indian villages on the mainland south of Roanoke. The patch over the fort symbol was applied for the same reason: to correct—in this case eliminate—the drawing of a structure which was contemplated, but never built.

Perhaps the most logical challenges to the fort symbol theory (and the

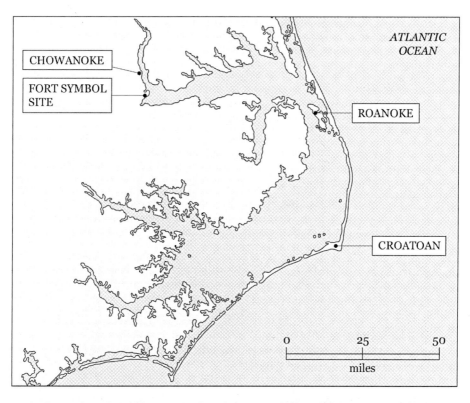

The "Chowanoke" and "fort-symbol" theories are further challenged by the messages left by the Lost Colonists themselves, directing John White *south* to Croatoan from Roanoke (courtesy Michael Gayle).

Chowanoke theory) were the messages the colonists themselves left at Roanoke. The "CRO" and "CROATOAN" inscriptions seem obviously intended to direct White to Croatoan upon his anticipated return in 1588. Croatoan, however, was about fifty miles south of Roanoke. As the map above illustrates, it would have made little practical sense to send White some fifty miles south to Croatoan if the colony had actually settled at the present-day Bertie County or Chowanoke locations at the western end of Albemarle Sound, more than 100 miles from Croatoan. The messages left by the colonists themselves seem to suggest that the 1587 colony headed southward from Roanoke down Pamlico Sound to a destination on the mainland across from Croatoan, not westward across Albemarle Sound to the fort symbol location.

One of the arguments usually cited to support the fort symbol theory— as well as the Chesapeake and Chowanoke theories—has to do with John White's notations that the colony intended "to remoue from Roanoak 50 miles into the maine."[28] A number of news articles based on the First Colony

Foundation/British Museum announcement in May of 2012 suggested that White's fifty-mile reference supported the conclusion that the colony intended to move to the fort symbol location in present-day Bertie County, which would have been about a fifty or sixty mile voyage from Roanoke west across Albemarle Sound.

White made two separate statements regarding the colonists' intention to relocate to the mainland fifty miles from Roanoke. The first was written in 1587, after returning to England, and the second was written after White's failed voyage to find the colonists in 1590. The fact that White used that precise "50-mile" distance on two separate occasions would seem to indicate that the fifty mile designation *did* have a unique significance.

It is clear, though, that White did not know where the colony would decide to go after he left Roanoke in 1587, and he did not know where he might look for them when he returned in 1590 (until, of course, he located the CRO and CROATOAN carved inscriptions). Therefore, since the colony's relocation intentions had not been decided until after White departed, he could not have been designating any specific location by his "fifty mile" references, including the fort symbol location in present-day Bertie County. As iterated previously, it was because he did not know where the settlement would be eventually located that White and the colonists devised the carved-message system so that upon his return White would learn "the name of the place where they should be seated."[29]

The specific fifty-mile designation, then, may have represented something else entirely. Author Lee Miller suggested that the "fifty mile" phraseology might have indicated a jurisdictional limitation, such as the precise fifty mile radius from Jamestown within which the colonists were granted governance in 1607.[30] If that were the case, Miller theorized, maybe "White's colonists felt that they had no rights within that fifty-mile zone" of Roanoke Island.[31] It was reasonably supposed, then, that this interpretation would support the notion that the colony went to the present-day Bertie County site because it was just beyond the fifty mile radius from Roanoke. This reasoning, by the way, would automatically eliminate Parramore's Weapemeoc theory as well as Dasamonguepeuk and the Alligator River for their proximity to Roanoke.

It is very possible that White's fifty-mile designation referred to an understood jurisdictional limitation, as Miller proposed. A specific fifty-mile jurisdiction was indeed included in the comprehensive and detailed 1606 First Virginia Charter, which set out the rules for establishing the Jamestown colony. That fifty miles, however, was a specific *north-south* jurisdiction only. As the charter stated, the colony's authority extended "for the space of fifty like English Miles, all alongst the said Coasts of Virginia."[32] The *east-west* jurisdiction, however, had different parameters: the Jamestown colony was granted rights for all lands from the settlement "directly into the main Land by the Space of one hundred like English Miles" and also to "all the Islands within one hundred Miles" of the shore.[33] In that case the fifty mile argument for the fort patch location to the west of Roanoke would be irrelevant.

Raleigh's charter, granted by Queen Elizabeth on March 5, 1584, was virtually identical to the Letters Patent that had been granted to Sir Humphrey Gilbert in 1578. They both promised exclusive control over all lands "within the space of two hundreth leagues,"[34] or about 600 miles. This was the only jurisdictional limitation mentioned in the Gilbert and Raleigh charters, and it was intended to define the broad territorial claims of the two charters, not English settlements within each charter's territorial claim. Gilbert had already claimed Newfoundland and all land within 200 leagues for the queen in 1583. As suggested earlier, Raleigh's colonization opportunities were thereby restricted to an area no farther north than about 36–37° north latitude, or 200 leagues from the southern limit of the Newfoundland claim. Consequently, once Raleigh established his claim in "Virginia" (Roanoke is 35°53'N) in 1584, England would then control the entire Atlantic coast from Newfoundland to the Spanish settlements in the south.

Although Raleigh's charter did not specifically mention it, there may have been an implied fifty mile limitation separating settlements *within* a larger territorial claim, and then codified in later charters such as the First Virginia Charter in 1606. As mentioned, however, if that were the case then White's fifty mile references would have applied to a north-south restriction only, as it would later be clearly specified in the 1606 First Virginia Charter. It is worth recalling that the original settlement location was supposed to be at the Chesapeake, about fifty miles *north* of Roanoke, which was intended to remain an English possession governed by the newly Christianized and titled Lord Manteo. Once the originally intended Chesapeake location had been eliminated, the most advantageous and logical option may have been fifty miles to the *south* of Roanoke, to the mainland beyond Secotan territory in present-day Carteret, Pamlico, or southern Beaufort Counties.

The discovery of the fort symbol, however, seemed sufficiently compelling at the time to initiate an archaeological investigation at the Bertie County site. In October of 2012 the First Colony Foundation began its archaeological work on the north side of the confluence of Salmon Creek and the Chowan River in Bertie County, identified as Site 31BR246. In March 2014, the FCF published the results of its archaeological investigation in a comprehensive sixty-nine page report and concluded that the Bertie County site was clearly not where the Lost Colony had relocated.[35]

# 5

# *The Colonists Select a Mainland Settlement Site*
## October–November 1587

The situation facing the colonists at Roanoke during the late summer and fall of 1587 may have been somewhat discouraging, but certainly not critical by any means. Their original Chesapeake plan had been altered, and, as previously proposed, was virtually eliminated because the Spanish knew of their intention to settle there and were conducting searches for them. Yet there was no talk of abandoning the entire colonization project. On the contrary, the colonists clearly had the intention of selecting a new settlement site somewhere on the mainland, but the location of that site had not been decided by the time White left for England on August 27. In the meantime the colonists repaired and fortified Lane's old settlement at Roanoke, and they would spend the winter there.

Furthermore, since it now seems likely that Edward Spicer in the flyboat *did* acquire the necessary cargo in the West Indies during the week or so following his rendezvous with the *Lyon* on June 21, the colonists would have had an adequate store of food and supplies. Finally, White had sailed for England and was sure to return the following spring or summer with fresh supplies and additional colonists. The prospects were not nearly as dim as most authors propose, at least not yet.

Another factor, generally ignored, is the role that Manteo would have played at this time. As already noted, Raleigh's original plan seems to have intended the territory of Roanoke and Dasamonguepeuk to be a satellite possession, associated with the main colony at the Chesapeake and enlarging his territorial possessions. Manteo had already been baptized into the Church of England and was now "Lord of Roanoke and Dasamonguepeuk," a title he would have taken seriously. It can be reasonably expected that he would assume that position once the colonists had vacated Roanoke and relocated to their settlement site elsewhere. Until that time Manteo would likely have been a frequent and welcome presence at Roanoke, and his knowledge of the geography and tribes to the south was undoubtedly helpful to the Assistants in the selection of the new settlement location. A group of Manteo's Croatoans may have begun preparations for the occupation of Roanoke and Dasamonguepeuk at this time. It will be recalled that some of the Croatoans had already occupied Dasamonguepeuk prior to August 9, when White launched the unfortunate attack there and mistook the Croatoans for the followers of Wingina/Pemisapan. Those hostile Indians, fearing retaliation for the murder of George Howe, had abandoned Dasamonguepeuk shortly after the killing. It is unlikely that they would return as long as an English presence remained at nearby Roanoke.

The search for the new settlement location on the mainland was probably pursued in earnest during the month or two following White's departure, and a number of considerations would have factored into their final selection. The Cittie of Ralegh was originally intended to be a self-sustaining agricultural colony at the Chesapeake Bay, but the change of venue would not have altered the agricultural nature or intentions of the colony. Fertile soil and potential farmland would have been required, but those could be found at any number of locations on the mainland. What was *not* readily available on the mainland was accessibility. That paramount concern had logistical and geographical implications which would have significantly narrowed the colonists' choices for their permanent mainland settlement site. Their survival as a viable colony depended upon their anticipated regular contact *with*, and periodic supplies *from*, England. Obviously this could only be accomplished if their mainland settlement location was *accessible* for re-supply.

Accessibility to a settlement site on the mainland depended entirely on its proximity to one of the inlets along the barrier islands. Nearly all of the existing inlets along the coast, however, were too shallow to allow access to the sounds in 1587, a problem which the English had experienced since the first Roanoke voyage in 1584. If the 1587 colony were to flourish—or even survive—on the mainland, its proximity to a *navigable* inlet would be critical.

To be sure, there were other concerns on the minds of the colonists regarding the selection of a viable settlement site in 1587–88. Among those would have been the dual threats posed by Spanish ships patrolling the coast and hostile native Indian tribes. The former concern, though, does little to reveal their eventual settlement site since there were numerous mainland locations which would offer concealment beyond the barrier islands. The latter concern would certainly have eliminated lands controlled by hostile tribes as possible settlement locations, and that will be addressed later in this chapter.

**Portion of Theodor de Bry's 1590 engraving from John White's 1585–86 map showing the inlets along the Outer Banks.**

The identification of viable inlets, then, would have been an essential step in determining a potential location for the settlement on the mainland. The map above, a portion of Theodor de Bry's engraving from John White's 1585–86 hand-drawn map, illustrates what White's 1587 colonists would have understood about the barrier islands along the coast of present-day North Carolina (north is to the right).

The Chesapeake Bay, not shown here but located beyond the map's border to the right, would have provided a good harbor and access to the mainland, as it eventually did in 1607 when the Jamestown colony was established. As already noted, however, the Chesapeake was not a viable option in 1587 because the Spanish were well aware of Raleigh's plan to establish a colony there and were actively searching for it. The Spanish, in fact, made two attempts during this time period to find the colony at the Chesapeake, the first in May 1587, and the second in June 1588. With the Chesapeake eliminated as a settlement possibility for the 1587 colonists, their search for potential navigable inlets would have focused on the barrier islands depicted above. A closer view of the White/de Bry map shows a number of inlets, but we know from the early accounts that most of these were far too shallow to be of any use.

The inlet situated at Hatorask (not to be confused with Hatteras) had been known as Port Ferdinando and was the main access to Roanoke from 1584 to 1590 when White finally returned. The Hatorask/Port Ferdinando inlet, however, reached a maximum depth of just twelve feet only at high tide and was very narrow, ranging from just eighteen to thirty feet wide.[1] Between 1584 and 1587 this inlet proved to be just barely adequate, navigable only by shallow-drafting vessels up to the size of a pinnace for the movement of colonists, supplies, and equipment from the larger ships anchored offshore. In his account of the 1585–6 voyage, Lane complained several times about the access to Roanoke, noting that "the harborough and port there ... by proofe is very naught."[2] If the seas were not calm, even small boats had problems at the Hatorask inlet: In August 1590, a boat with eleven men overturned while attempting to navigate the inlet in strong winds, drowning Edward Spicer and six others.

Immediately north of Hatorask is a minor inlet, unnamed on the map but called Port Lane by White, but this was far too small and shallow and does not seem capable of use by anything larger than a small oared boat. The inlet at Trinety harbor also seems to have had very limited use (more on Trinety harbor below). The colonists would have been well aware that access to their new mainland settlement would require a better inlet than Hatorask, which was probably only manageable at all because Roanoke was situated very close to the inlet itself.

From Hatorask down to Cape Fear at the far left on the map, there are three sizable inlets shown, two of which appear to be considerably wider than Hatorask. The first of the three inlets is located at the north end of the island of Croatoan, separating it from Paquiwoc. The second and narrowest is at the south end of Croatoan. The third and largest inlet is located at the north end of the island of Wokokon.

The inlets situated at both ends of Croatoan would have been eliminated from consideration because the early documents show that the Roanoke voyagers, who were always on the lookout for better access to Pamlico and Albemarle Sounds, paid little or no attention to them between 1584 and 1590. Depth soundings, in fact, were taken at the northern Croatoan inlet by sailors on the 1590 voyage, but no entry was attempted. The Wokokon inlet, however, was an entirely different story.

The English took note of the Wokokon inlet during the first Roanoke voyage in 1584, and on the second voyage the following year Sir Richard Grenville made a planned stop there. On June 26, 1585, Grenville's large flagship, the *Tyger*, attempted to enter the Wokokon inlet but missed the main channel and ran aground in the process. The importance of this incident is that it must have been understood at that time that the channel in the Wokokon inlet was suitable enough for a ship the size of the *Tyger* which was "seven score tunnes" (140 tuns).[3] Since there is no evidence that the Hatorask/Port Ferdinando inlet at Roanoke could accommodate vessels any larger than a pinnace (generally in the 30 tun range), there can be no doubt that the Wokokon inlet was far superior.

On July 11, 1585, Grenville and a party of at least sixty men entered the Wokokon inlet and spent eight days exploring Pamlico Sound. This excursion is remembered mainly for the series of drawings John White produced at

Pomeioc and Secota, as well as the controversy about the silver cup and the unfortunate destruction of Aquascogoc. The focus on White's drawings and the incident at Aquascogoc, however, have distracted attention from the probable purpose of this lengthy detour. As mentioned previously, the main reasons for Grenville's excursion through Pamlico Sound may have been to search out alternative settlement locations. According to Quinn, the colonization plan in 1585 was to have taken place in two stages, the first of which was the Grenville/Lane colony which settled at Roanoke. The second stage, led by Amias Preston and Bernard Drake, was to follow a month or two after the first. Quinn suggested that Grenville may have been scouting out a settlement location for the Preston-Drake group. Grenville, however, was unaware that, just before its departure from England in June 1585, the Preston-Drake expedition was ordered to proceed to Newfoundland instead, to warn English ships about heightened Spanish aggression.[4]

In any case, Grenville's activities at Wokokon between June 26 and July 21, 1585, particularly his exploration of the Pamlico Sound mainland, could certainly have had an influence on the 1587 colony's settlement decisions. Grenville obviously considered this excursion important, since it delayed his eventual arrival at Roanoke by nearly a month. If he was seeking alternative settlement locations for his colonists in 1585 or for the colony expected later that summer, then the information gathered during his excursion to the mainland could have played an important role in the ultimate settlement decisions made by White's colony two years later.

It is worth repeating that the key to the survival of a permanent settlement on the mainland was its accessibility for re-supply via a navigable inlet. The Wokokon inlet was undoubtedly the gateway to the mainland south of Roanoke *in 1585*, but the barrier island inlets are notoriously unstable. A single storm a year or two later could have altered the coast significantly. The barrier islands shift continually and inlets tend to migrate southward. Storms, tides, and the volume of water discharged into the sounds from the many rivers constantly create new inlets and close others. Hurricanes and storm surges have a dramatic impact on the barrier islands and can open or close inlets in a matter of hours. It is clear that Wokokon was *the* superior inlet along the Outer Banks in 1585, but was the Wokokon inlet one of these erratic, changeable inlets which might not have provided a reliable access two or three years later?

Fortunately, the history of the barrier island inlets is well established.[5] Presently there are just six active inlets between Cape Lookout and the Virginia state line: Oregon, Hatteras, Ocracoke, New Old Drum, New Drum, and Ophelia. Five of these six currently active inlets have had erratic histories:

1. Oregon inlet was opened by a hurricane in 1846 near the site of a previous inlet (Gun or Gunt) which closed in 1798. Gunt was the successor to the earlier Hatorask/Port Ferdinando inlet known to the Roanoke voyagers. Between 1846 and 1989, Oregon inlet migrated approximately two miles south of its original location.

2. Hatteras (again, not to be confused with Hatorask) inlet opened during the same hurricane that opened Oregon Inlet in September of 1846.

3. Drum inlet initially opened about 1899, but then closed naturally by 1919. It was then reopened during a major hurricane in 1933. By 1971, the inlet had nearly closed again, and the U.S. Army Corps of Engineers dredged open New Drum inlet several miles to the southwest.

4. In 1999, Hurricane Dennis reopened Drum inlet, which is now referred to as New-Old Drum inlet.

5. In 2005, Hurricane Ophelia opened an inlet southwest of New Drum inlet. Currently Ophelia inlet is expanding, and has nearly merged with New Drum inlet.

6. By contrast, the Ocracoke Inlet—known to the Roanoke voyagers as Wokokon inlet—has remained stable throughout the centuries.[6]

The rarity of this phenomenon can be illustrated by advances in modern geophysical science. Ground-penetrating radar has provided data which allows for the identification and dates of *all* inlets, including those that existed when the Lost Colonists were deciding on a mainland settlement location in 1587–88. The map on the following page illustrates the opening dates of the six currently active inlets as well as the opening/closing dates of the eight inlets (in bold) that existed in 1585.[7]

There are two relevant points to be noted here. The first is that the 1585 inlet locations identified by radar correspond quite accurately with those depicted on White's 1585–86 map. The map identifies the modern names of eight inlets which existed during the Roanoke voyages: Old Currituck, Roanoke, Gunt, Chacandepeco, Ocracoke, Swash, South Core Banks 1, and South Core Banks 2. What appear to be inlets on the White/de Bry map at Trinety harbor and the next breach farther north on White's map may have been shoals, with Trinety "harbor" simply indicating a deep water anchorage just offshore. Quinn suggested that Trinety harbor could have served more as an "outlet" for the waters of Albemarle Sound and that it "could conceivably have closed up over the period between September 1585 and June 1586...."[8] Notice that no inlet existed between Old Currituck and Roanoke inlets in 1585. Furthermore, White's Virginea Pars map does not depict an opening at the Trinety Harbor location, another indication that whatever breach existed there was probably only a shoal.

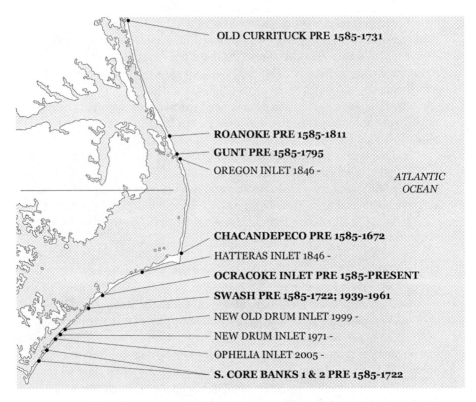

OLD CURRITUCK PRE 1585-1731

ROANOKE PRE 1585-1811
GUNT PRE 1585-1795
OREGON INLET 1846 -

*ATLANTIC*
*OCEAN*

CHACANDEPECO PRE 1585-1672
HATTERAS INLET 1846 -
OCRACOKE INLET PRE 1585-PRESENT
SWASH PRE 1585-1722; 1939-1961
NEW OLD DRUM INLET 1999 -
NEW DRUM INLET 1971 -
OPHELIA INLET 2005 -
S. CORE BANKS 1 & 2 PRE 1585-1722

**Locations and opening dates of the six current inlets and the opening and closing dates of the eight inlets that existed when the Lost Colonists were selecting a mainland settlement site (courtesy Michael Gayle).**

As illustrated on the map on the following page, Hatorask became Gunt inlet, which had migrated southward and closed in 1795. The inlet between Croatoan and Paquiwoc was called Chacandepeco, meaning "shallows"[9] and closed in 1672. Wokokon is present-day Ocracoke. (The name evolved gradually from Wokokon or Wococon to Wococock, then Ocacock, then to Ocracock, and finally to Ocracoke.[10]) The remaining pre–1585 inlets—Old Currituck (closed in 1731), Swash (closed in 1722, opened again in 1939 and closed in 1961), South Core Banks 1, and South Core Banks 2 (both closed in 1722)—are shown on White's map, but are noticeably smaller and must have been considered to be insignificant. The more important point to be made is that of all the inlets identified, both pre–1585 *and* current, the Ocracoke/Wokokon inlet is the *only one* that has existed continually from before 1585 to the present day.

Recent scientific studies have determined that the Wokokon/Ocracoke Inlet is located over an ancient river valley that drained the Pamlico Sound

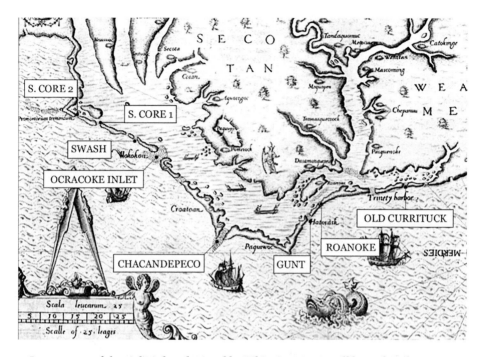

**Later names of the eight inlets depicted by White in 1585–86; all later closed except Ocracoke.**

basin during the last Ice Age, some 20,000 years ago. It is believed that "the occurrence of this river valley beneath the [Wokokon/Ocracoke] inlet accounts for its stability and longevity."[11] Throughout recorded history the Wokokon/ Ocracoke inlet has offered the best navigable route for private and commercial vessels. In fact, prior to the opening of the Oregon and Hatteras Inlets during the hurricane in 1846, the only permanent option for ships traveling to the mainland ports of Bath, Edenton, Washington, and New Bern was the Ocracoke Inlet, which was designated an official port of entry in 1715.[12]

It is worth noting that John Lawson described all the inlets during his 1700–1701 exploration of North Carolina and wrote the following commentary in his *A New Voyage to Carolina*: "Some of their Channels admit only of Sloops, Brigantines, small Barks, and Ketches; and such are *Currituck*, *Ronoak*, and up the Sound above *Hatteras*: Whilst others can receive Ships of Burden, as *Ocacock* [Ocracoke] … *Ocacock* is the best Inlet and Harbour yet in this Country; and has 13 Foot at Low-water upon the Bar. There are two Channels; one is but narrow, and lies close aboard the South Cape; the other in the Middle, *viz.* between the Middle Ground, and the South Shoar, and is above half a Mile wide."[13]

There are a number of old maps illustrating the continual importance and dependability of the Wokokon/Ocracoke inlet. One of these is Henry Mouzon's 1775 *An Accurate Map of North and South Carolina*, on which there is a passage marked by a dotted line which proceeds from the Atlantic through the Wokokon/Ocracoke inlet (called Occacoke Inlet on the map) directly to the mouth of the Neuse River. That passageway through the Wokokon/Ocracoke inlet is marked "A Good Channel," the only inlet so marked on the Outer Banks.

The important conclusion to be drawn here is that the stability and longevity of the Wokokon/Ocracoke inlet have been well-established for well over four centuries, and is unique among *all* the past and present inlets along the Outer Banks. It is a virtual certainty that the Wokokon inlet was the most navigable entry along the Outer Banks in both 1585 as well as 1587–88, when White's colonists were considering settlement options. Again, the *survival* of the mainland colony depended on periodic resupply from England, and *access* to the mainland colony depended upon a navigable inlet. Since Wokokon was undoubtedly the most navigable inlet along the Outer Banks, it follows that the colonists' choice for their mainland settlement location may very well have been as close as practically possible to that inlet across Pamlico Sound.

That same reasoning—the need for, and proximity to, an accessible inlet—further challenges the Lost Colony settlement theories discussed earlier. Both the Chowanoke and the fort symbol locations were not easily accessible. It would have been necessary to use the Hatorask inlet in order to attempt to re-supply a colony at either of those location. As mentioned, Trinety harbor, the closer of the two to the entrance to Albemarle Sound, was likely nothing more than a shoal and would have been virtually useless for resupplying a location far to the west of Roanoke. Hatorask inlet was deeper, but narrow, and was located just south of Roanoke, which would have required navigating some fifteen miles of shallows surrounding the island just to reach the entrance to Albemarle Sound. And then from there everything had to be ferried fifty to sixty miles farther westward across the sound, a lengthy effort requiring multiple trips and an inordinate amount of time. It would have made little sense for the colonists, who depended upon routine re-supply for their survival as a viable English colony, to select a mainland settlement location that would make that resupply extremely difficult, if not virtually impossible.

Likewise, any other theories that suggest a settlement site at places such as Weapemeoc, Dasamonguepeuk, or the Alligator River would be somewhat challenged. All of these locations, although not as distant from Roanoke as Chowanoke or the fort symbol site, would have been more difficult to resupply than Roanoke, requiring the use of the same problematic Hatorask inlet and then necessitating, in multiple trips, navigating the same shallows surrounding Roanoke Island. Furthermore, as noted earlier, since White's colony evidently planned to relocate at least fifty miles from Roanoke, these locations must be eliminated from consideration. Finally, a settlement site at any of these areas surrounding Roanoke would have been particularly vulnerable to attack by the existing hostile tribes.

As mentioned earlier, the threat posed by native Indian hostilities was another significant concern and must be factored in at this point. If White's colony decided that the Wokokon inlet would provide the best access for resupplying their settlement, it follows that the search for that settlement site should begin on the mainland areas of Pamlico Sound near the inlet. What is known from the early accounts about Indian-English relations, however, may help narrow down that mainland area somewhat.

During the span of the Roanoke voyages, between 1584 and 1587, the English had the most frequent contact with the Secotan tribal group, whose large territory, ruled by the weroance Wingina, extended from Albemarle Sound all the way to the Pamlico River. As reviewed previously, however, by 1587 the Secotans were openly hostile towards the English. A series of deadly plots had been hatched and violent clashes occurred during the 1585–86 Grenville/Lane colonization attempt which led to Lane's attack at Dasamonguepeuk and the beheading Wingina/Pemisapan in 1586. On August 1, 1587, not long after White's colony arrived, George Howe was killed by Wingina's followers.

The map on the following page depicts the territories controlled by the various tribes at the time White's colony was considering mainland settlement possibilities. For the reasons just mentioned, it would have been extremely dangerous and foolhardy to attempt to establish a settlement anywhere in the large hostile area marked "Secotan" on the map. It is evident that once the large hostile Secotan territory is eliminated as a possible settlement location, the remaining option is the area south of the Pamlico River where the Pomouik, Neuse and Coree dwelt. That area would include present-day Carteret and Pamlico counties, as well as the southern portions of Beaufort and Craven counties.

As will be seen in a later chapter, there is some evidence to suggest that by 1587–88 the Croatoans may have had an association with their neighbors, the Corees, who dwelt on the peninsula south of the Neuse River and along the coast. It is believed that the Corees, in turn, were allied with the Neusioks on the lower Neuse River particularly on the south side, in present-day Craven and Carteret Counties. It is known from the 1584 Amadas-Barlowe account that the Neusioks were allied with the Pomouiks in "mortall warre" with the Secotan tribes north of the Pamlico River.

Little is known about the Coree tribe, but they very likely had some contact with their coastal neighbors, the Croatoans, and may have been

**Tribal territories accessible via the Wokokon inlet in 1587–88 (courtesy Michael Gayle).**

affiliated with them to some extent. If the Corees were related to the Neusioks, as many believe, and the Neusioks were allied with the Pomouiks, as seems certain, then by 1587–88 the opportunity may have existed for a beneficial partnership among those four tribes and the colonists. The Neusioks, Pomouiks, Corees, Croatoans, *and* the 1587 colony all would have shared a common enemy: the hostile Secotan tribes north of the Pamlico River. There is also some evidence, to be discussed later, indicating that the Corees had knowledge of, and possibly contact with, the Lost Colony. It is also worth mentioning here—and this too will be discussed in a later chapter—that in 1608 the Paspahegh chief reported to John Smith that at Panawicke (Pomouik on the map above) there had once been "many men ... apparelled."[14]

It seems possible that, with the help of Manteo, an arrangement could have been made for the colony to settle on one of the two peninsulas north or south of the Neuse River. Geographically that area would have been uniquely positioned to satisfy *all* of the colony's concerns in 1587–88. It was shielded from Spanish ships in the Atlantic and also removed from the hostile

Secotan tribes. It was also located more than fifty miles to the south of Roanoke, fulfilling the fifty-mile restriction discussed earlier. Most importantly, it was accessible for future re-supply via the Wokokon inlet, the *only* proven navigable channel in Pamlico Sound. The colonists very likely had already selected their settlement site on the mainland by the time John White finally arrived at England on November 5, 1587, after a more than two month voyage.

# 6

## *Pivotal Events in England and Virginia*
### January–June 1588

Unfortunately for the colonists in Virginia, England's war with Spain had reached a critical point by 1587, and an attack by Spain's "Invincible Armada," a term used derisively after the fact in English references, seemed imminent. Raleigh's entire colonization effort had, in fact, been somewhat overshadowed by the Anglo-Spanish war which started two years earlier, when England joined the Protestant provinces of the Netherlands in their rebellion against Spain, and King Philip II ordered the seizure of all English ships in Spanish ports. A series of events followed which would deflect national focus from the Virginia colonists to the immediate threat from Spain. Queen Elizabeth had replied to the seizure of English ships with her letters of reprisal "to take and arrest all ships and merchandises they [English privateers] might find at sea or elsewhere, belonging to the subjects of that king [Philip II]."[1] Elizabeth also "equipped a fleet of twenty-five sail of ships," and employed them under command of Sir Francis Drake, "the fittest person in her dominions, by reason of his success and experience in sundry actions."[2] This was the previously mentioned "Great Expedition" during which Drake raided Santo Domingo, Cartagena, and St. Augustine, before sailing on to Roanoke and evacuating Lane and his colonists in 1586. Drake's expedition did considerable damage to Spanish colonial holdings, but may have hastened Philip's plans for an assault on England by the Armada.

Fearing an imminent invasion, Elizabeth again dispatched Drake in April of 1587—less than a month before White's colony sailed for the Chesapeake—to conduct a raid on Spanish ships at Cádiz in an effort to stall the invasion. On April 19 Drake entered the harbor of Cádiz and engaged a number of ships so successfully that "The whole number of ships that we burnt, sunk or brought away, amounted to 30 at the least, and by our estimation to be the burden of 10,000 tons." The entire raid "was achieved in one day and two nights, to the great astonishment of the king of Spain."[3] Drake's raid not only destroyed and damaged many Spanish ships, but also much of the supplies, provisions, and equipment being readied in preparation for the Armada's assault. This raid significantly delayed the launching of the Armada, giving the English time to prepare their own naval defenses, and on October 9 Elizabeth issued a general stay, prohibiting ships from leaving English ports.[4]

This was the state of affairs that John White encountered upon his return to England in November. Shortly thereafter, he informed Raleigh about the aborted Chesapeake plan and, according to White, Raleigh...

> ... forthwith appointed a Pinnesse to be sent thither with all such necessaries as he understood they stood in need of: and also wrote his letters unto them, wherein among other matters he comforted them with the promise, that with all convenient speed he would prepare a good supply of shipping and men with sufficient of all things needful, which he intended, God willing, should be with them to Summer following. Which Pinnesse and fleet were accordingly prepared in the West Country at Bideford under the charge of Sir Richard Grenville.[5]

This passage is somewhat unclear. White must have known about the general shipping prohibition issued by the queen on October 9, yet he claimed that both Raleigh and Grenville quickly went about preparing ships for a transatlantic voyage to resupply the colonists in Virginia. It has been supposed that both White and Grenville may have been under the impression that Raleigh's influence with the queen would exempt them from the October 9 sailing prohibition, but that argument does not seem very persuasive. Both Raleigh and Grenville would have been preoccupied with the imminent invasion by Spain, and one wonders just how much attention they could have devoted to White and the colonists at that particular time.

Raleigh had been granted a vast estate of 42,000 acres in Ireland the previous year, and he was focused on business there, including "a commitment to settle the province with reliable Englishmen."[6] In November, the same month White returned to England, Raleigh was appointed by the queen to her council of war, joining Grenville and Lane among others, in the preparations for the defense of the kingdom. Throughout 1588 and 1589 Raleigh's attention was focused elsewhere than on the Virginia colony, and in early March of 1589, in fact, he assigned his interest in Virginia to a group of London merchants headed by Thomas Smythe, who would be instrumental in forming the Virginia Company nearly two decades later.[7]

Grenville, although he also apparently spent some time in Ireland, *was* preparing a fleet at Bideford. Given England's war footing at that time, however, it seems highly unlikely that he could have been doing so for the exclusive benefit of the colonists in Virginia. Quinn suggested that the purpose of the Grenville fleet may have been a "diversionary attack across the Atlantic," similar to Drake's expedition in 1585–86, and thereby intended to forestall Spain's invasion.[8] A stopover at Virginia would have been possible afterwards, just as Drake had done. This scenario is also somewhat problematic, however, because the colonists would have departed from Roanoke to parts unknown long before the fleet arrived, and it is doubtful that Grenville would have been willing or able to spend much time searching for them. Regarding White's reference to the pinnace Raleigh supposedly "forthwith appointed" to sail for Virginia, a solo transatlantic voyage in midwinter was rare, and there are no known documents indicating that such a voyage took place. Furthermore, author and former mayor of Bideford Andrew Powell confirms that the Bideford port books contain no listings of departures in late 1587 and early 1588.[9]

Whatever Grenville's actual intentions were, towards the end of March 1588, his fleet was ready, according to White, awaiting only favorable winds:

> This fleet now being in readiness only staying but for a fair wind to put to sea, at the same time there was spread throughout all England such report of the wonderful preparation and invincible fleets made by the King of Spain joined with the power of the pope for the invading of England, that most of the ships of war then in a readiness in any haven in England were stayed for service at home: And Sir Richard Grenville was personally commanded not to depart....[10]

White's passage is fairly accurate, although the general shipping prohibition had been enacted more than five months before Grenville's fleet was recalled. On March 31 Grenville received orders from the Privy Council to bring his fleet to Plymouth to assist Sir Francis Drake in the defense of the kingdom against the now imminent Spanish attack. Grenville, by the way, would never see the Virginia coast again. He was mortally wounded in 1591 fighting aboard his single ship The Revenge against a superior Spanish fleet.

Although, as White wrote, "the voyage for Virginia by these means ... [was] thus disappointed," he "notwithstanding labored for the relief of the planters so earnestly," that he managed to obtain the use of two small pinnaces of 30 and 25 tuns respectively, the Brave and the Roe. They set sail for Roanoke on April 22 with "15 planters and all their provision with certain relief for those that wintered in the Country."[11] According to the testimony of Pedro Diaz, the previously mentioned Spanish pilot who had been captured by Grenville in 1586 and then piloted the Brave in 1588, the colonists consisted of seven men and four women.[12] This was not the first time that the numbers in the Diaz account were contradicted by those in Hakluyt. It will be recalled that, according to the account in Hakluyt, when Grenville arrived belatedly at Roanoke in 1586 only to find that Lane and the first colony had abandoned the island, he left fifteen men there to maintain Raleigh's claim. Diaz, however, said that Grenville left eleven men at Roanoke. Author James Horn wrote that there were "seven men, four women, and four children aboard the *Brave* and the *Roe*,"[13] but, since his source was not cited, the four children may have been an assumption based on the difference in the totals between the White and Diaz accounts. According to Quinn there were eleven men and four women,[14] again an apparent compromise between the White and Diaz accounts. Whatever the actual number of colonists, it is interesting to note that, in spite of the fact that the original Chesapeake destination had been altered, White was still able to enlist any colonists at all for a transatlantic voyage aboard two small vessels to an unknown location in Virginia. Their willingness to participate in such a risky venture could suggest that most of these new colonists were spouses or relatives who had stayed behind in England until the colony was established.

Neither the *Brave* nor the *Roe* made it very far. The day after their departure the two English vessels began privateering raids, the *Roe* in particular chasing and overtaking several smaller vessels, during which the *Brave* lost contact with the *Roe*. The *Brave*, with White aboard, had several minor skirmishes between April 23 and the 26th, and on May 6 the *Brave* was attacked by a larger French ship. A battle ensued and "continued without ceasing one hour and a half,"[15] culminating in the surrender of the *Brave*. The French looted the English vessel, and all the provisions and supplies intended for the colonists in Virginia were lost. The *Brave* was forced to limp back to Bideford and arrived there on May 22. Once again White demonstrated that he had no influence or control over the decisions made aboard ship and blamed the "mariners" for the failure to reach Roanoke. As White put it, "On this occasion, God justly punished our former thievery of our evil disposed mariners, we were of force constrained to break off our intended voyage for the relief of our colony left the year before in Virginia."[16] The *Roe* also aborted the mission shortly thereafter "without performing our intended voyage for the relief of the planters in Virginia, which thereby were not a little distressed."[17]

In the meantime, whatever lingering disappointment may still have remained regarding their situation at Roanoke, the colonists probably greeted the new year of 1588 with renewed confidence. They had no reason to doubt that supply ships were being prepared in England, and they were hopeful that White and the supplies could arrive perhaps as early as June. They could look forward to a better settlement site on the mainland, and plans for their relocation by spring were undoubtedly being drawn up. If a few of the colonists were ready to give up on the entire venture, they could look forward to boarding the ships in August, as soon as they were ready to return to England.

As discussed previously, unlike the earlier Grenville-Lane colonization effort, White's colony had a completely different composition and purpose. The English had learned first-hand in 1585–86 that dependence for food upon the native tribes was an invitation to disaster. Raleigh realized that for land in Virginia to be successfully settled and developed, agriculture was the key. The 1587 colony included women and children and had been organized for agricultural self-sufficiency. Although the colonists had originally intended to establish the "Cittie of Ralegh" at the Chesapeake, the unexpected turn of events would not have changed the make-up of the colony. The continuance of the colony would still have depended on agriculture, and therefore their departure from Roanoke would very likely have been timed to correspond with the local native agricultural cycles.

For the Carolina Algonquians, planting was done from April through June so that a corn harvest was available from early summer through October.[18] Since the colonists would likely have followed this known traditional agricultural pattern, they needed to be at the new location in time to re-assemble the "houses taken downe" which they transported from Roanoke,[19] and to prepare their fields in time for the first planting. The move from Roanoke to the mainland probably took place in stages utilizing the pinnace, perhaps commencing in early 1588, but it had to have been accomplished by the first day of spring in late March, and certainly prior to the first planting in April. The colonists, therefore, could not have waited for White's expected return to Roanoke in June or July, and it is doubtful that they would have left a few colonists behind at Roanoke for fear they would meet the same fate at the hands of hostile Indians as the small contingent left by Grenville the previous year.

The colonists departed from Roanoke in an orderly manner and without duress, as was indicated by the absence of the prearranged cross symbol above the CRO and CROATOAN carved messages they left behind for White "if they should happen to be distressed."[20] Those two carved messages were intended to direct White about fifty miles south to friendly Croatoan, but, as noted, the colonists never intended to establish a permanent settlement on the Outer Banks. Instead they probably placed an outpost on Croatoan to await White's expected arrival a few months later, when he would then have been escorted to the mainland settlement, the location of which may have been, as suggested, across Pamlico Sound somewhere on the mainland west of present-day Ocracoke Inlet.

An event occurred in June 1588, which provides us with two significant clues pertaining to the colonists' departure from Roanoke and their resettlement location. These clues come not from an English source, but from the Spanish account of the voyage of Vincente Gonzalez. As discussed earlier, by 1586 the Spanish were well aware of Raleigh's plans to establish a settlement specifically at the Chesapeake Bay, and King Philip II ordered the governor of La Florida to locate the English colony. Governor Pedro Menéndez Marques sailed for the Chesapeake with three vessels in May of 1587, at the same time White and his colony were en route to the same intended destination. Menéndez Marques stopped at Santa Elena and perhaps other ports along the way, and learned from the natives that they had no knowledge of an English settlement.[21] This was accurate information at the time, because Drake had evacuated Lane's colony from Roanoke the previous year, and White's colonists had not yet arrived. Menéndez Marques made it as far as the Chesapeake, but was driven back to Havana by a storm as he attempted to enter the bay.

In early June of 1588 the governor dispatched Vincente Gonzalez and a crew of thirty men in two ships to Bahia de Santa Maria (Chesapeake Bay) to locate the English colony and also to search for a strait within the bay which was rumored to be a possible water route to the Pacific, which the Spanish referred to as the South Sea. It was believed that the English settlement was located near the shore of this strait.[22] Gonzalez was a logical choice for this expedition because he was quite familiar with the Chesapeake Bay. In 1570 he piloted the Jesuit missionaries and the Indian Paquiquineo to what would later be called the James River. In 1571 he returned to the Chesapeake in an attempt to resupply the Jesuits, and in 1572 he sailed to the Chesapeake again in a punitive raid to punish the Indians who had killed the Jesuits the previous year.[23] Gonzalez sailed north from St. Augustine on June 7, stopping at Santa Elena and perhaps Cape Fear, and entered Chesapeake Bay during the third week in June. He spent a week exploring the western shore of the bay but found no trace of the English or the strait leading to the Pacific.

The day after Gonzalez left Chesapeake Bay on June 29, he made a remarkable, though accidental, discovery. A fierce storm rolled in and rather than risk being buffeted and blown off course, Gonzalez decided to seek shelter beyond the barrier islands and entered a shallow inlet which was almost certainly Port Ferdinando, or Hatorask as the English called it. Beyond the inlet to the north Gonzalez saw an area of thick woods, which he mistook for part of the mainland. He had, in fact, inadvertently stumbled upon Roanoke Island. Gonzalez found it uninhabited, but he did discover English well casings, an abandoned slipway for boats, and the remains of other items which indicated that a large settlement had been located there.[24]

The 1588 Gonzalez voyage is often overlooked, but there is very useful information about the Lost Colony to be concluded from the account, which was not published until about 1617 as part of a larger volume on Spanish colonial missions.[25] In the first place the accidental discovery of Roanoke by Gonzalez provides verification that the colonists had departed from Roanoke prior to June of 1588. This is a helpful piece of evidence because it supports the aforementioned proposal that the colony could not wait for White's arrival, which would have been expected perhaps by early summer, if all went well. As noted, agricultural cycles would have required that they be established at the new mainland location by late March in order to be ready for the first spring planting.

The second and perhaps more significant implication of the Gonzalez voyage was the failure to find any trace of an English presence during his week-long search of the Chesapeake. Since we know that he was also ordered to search for the strait which was thought to lead to the South Sea, and given his familiarity with the Chesapeake, it seems likely that his investigation of the bay and the various rivers that empty into it must have been fairly thorough. This provides convincing, first-hand evidence that White's colonists did *not* relocate to the Chesapeake, their originally intended settlement location, when they vacated Roanoke, and of course it refutes Quinn's theory that the Lost Colonists relocated there. It also supports the conclusion suggested previously, that by the spring and summer of 1587 the Chesapeake had become an impossible settlement option for White's colonists and it remained so in 1588.

All of this lends credence to the larger thesis that the centuries-old institutionalized assumption of Fernandez-as-villain is mistaken, and it supports the earlier proposal that Simon Fernandez had good reason for aborting the original settlement location at the Chesapeake. If Fernandez were the despicable character he has been portrayed, and the colonists continued to view the Chesapeake as a safe and viable site in 1587–88, there is no reason why they would not have relocated there.

With the additional information provided by the Gonzalez voyage, an overall narrative can be reasonably reconstructed concerning the activities of the colonists during the first half of 1588: The colonists would have expected White to return to Roanoke with supplies and additional settlers perhaps by June of 1588. They knew full well that due to the long winter storm season Virginia-bound voyages traditionally left England in April and took nearly three months to make the circuitous trip via the West Indies to the present day Carolina coast. The 1587 colonists themselves departed Plymouth on April 26 and arrived at Roanoke on July 22. The previous England-Virginia voyages had followed the same calendar pattern. As indicated by the account of the Gonzalez voyage, the 1587 colony did not wait for White's expected return and obviously had vacated Roanoke before Gonzalez arrived in the third week of June 1588.

We know from White's 1590 account that the colonists had "taken down" their dwellings at Roanoke, presumably to be transported and reassembled at the new settlement location. Just prior to their departure from Roanoke, in March as suggested, the colonists left behind the prearranged carved messages instructing White to proceed southward to Croatoan, where Manteo's mother and the friendly Croatoans dwelt. The absence of the telltale distress symbol cross accompanying the inscriptions indicated that the colony's move from Roanoke was conducted in an orderly manner. Gonzalez's search of the Chesapeake in June demonstrated that the colonists did *not* relocate to the Chesapeake after leaving Roanoke. Nor do the inscriptions or the evidence suggest, as examined earlier, that they relocated far to the west at Chowanoke or present-day Bertie County.

Three factors—the location of the only viable inlet at Wokokon; the territories occupied by hostile Secotan tribes; and the directions left at Roanoke by the colonists themselves—all argue for a mainland settlement site to the south of Roanoke. While Gonzalez was searching the Chesapeake in June, it is likely that the colonists were well established and perhaps harvesting their first corn crop at their settlement on the mainland. Just across Pamlico Sound a handful of colonists were at an outpost at Croatoan waiting expectantly for White's return.

# 7

## The Legend of the CORA Tree
## and the Outpost at Croatoan
### July–September 1588

By July of 1588 the colonists had been settled in at their new mainland location for several months. If all had gone reasonably well, they would have been enjoying the fruits of their first harvest and making preparations for the arrival of White and the supply ships, which were expected any day. Across the sound at Croatoan the handful of colonists manning the outpost were expectantly scanning the ocean to the south for any sign of the English ships, while keeping a wary eye out for Spanish vessels that might be patrolling the coast. As mentioned, the two Gonzalez ships had passed that way in search of the English colony in mid–June on the way to the Chesapeake, and then again in early July on the return trip to St. Augustine. It is very likely that these ships were observed by the English colonists stationed at Croatoan, particularly in mid–June, since it is known that Gonzalez was instructed to take latitude readings and map the coast on his way to the Chesapeake.[1]

By September, when White still had not arrived, it would have been painfully clear to the colonists on the mainland that he was not likely to return that year. There would have been little chance of a transatlantic supply fleet arriving in the fall, and there would have been no reason to maintain an outpost at Croatoan during the winter. At some point, then, the English outpost would have been abandoned, at least temporarily. Although the colonists' situation took a dramatic turn for the worse when White failed to return—and a discussion of their condition and options will follow in the next chapter—a detour will be taken here to examine an old legend involving the Lost Colonists that still circulates among the locals on Hatteras Island.

There is no shortage of wondrous tales and folklore on the Outer Banks, most of which tell of pirates, witches, and spirits of other notables who once frequented the barrier islands. Two of these legends involve the Lost Colony. The first of these is a whimsical tale about Virginia Dare, John White's granddaughter, who, as the legend goes, was transformed into a white doe by a native Indian sorcerer. The second legend concerns an ancient live oak on Hatteras Island. Still discernable is the very old four-letter inscription "CORA" carved into the trunk of what has come to be known as the "CORA tree." In 2006 an article by author and Hatteras native, Scott Dawson, appeared in the *Outer Banks Sentinel* suggesting that the fabled live oak on Hatteras held a second message from White's Lost Colony.[2] Not surprisingly there is another, more fanciful, legend about the CORA tree, popularized by author Charles Harry Whedbee,[3] telling of a witch named Cora who disappeared when a bolt of lightning struck the tree she was tied to, leaving the word CORA emblazoned in the trunk.

It will be recalled that, prior to John White's departure from Roanoke in 1587, he and his colonists had agreed on a system of communications, "a secret token agreed vpon betweene them and me at my last departure from them, which was, that in any wayes they should not faile to write or carue on the trees or posts of the dores the name of the place where they should be seated."[4] As per that arrangement, the colonists left the inscription "CRO" carved into a tree and the full word "CROATOAN" carved into a post at the entry to the abandoned settlement.

Image of the still-discernible CORA inscription on the ancient live oak at Frisco (photograph by Roberta Estes, 2009).

White also instructed the colonists to use the messaging system and distress symbol "in any of those places,"[5] seemingly indicating that it was not intended to be used exclusively at Roanoke, but anywhere the colonists might be. Moreover, as White explained, the secret agreement was compulsory, as indicated by the instruction "that in any wayes they should not faile" to use this method of communication. When White did not arrive by September, and the outpost was abandoned, could they have left behind a similar message at Croatoan—another link to their whereabouts—just as they had previously done when they left Roanoke?

The *Sentinel* article theorized that the CORA inscription was left by Lost Colonists who vacated Croatoan and dwelt among the Coree or Coranine Indians near the Neuse River. If that were the case, of course, the CORA inscription would represent *the* most important clue in the more than four-centuries-old search for the Lost Colony. Nevertheless, possibly because of its association with the fanciful and popular Cora-witch legend, or perhaps because it simply seems improbable, the CORA tree has been generally ignored in the body of Lost Colony literature. It is also possible that it has remained just beyond the peripheral vision of most Lost Colony authors because it does not conform to their mainstream theories about where the colonists relocated after leaving Roanoke. The CORA tree hypothesis does happen to be compatible with the argument proposed in the previous chapters—that the colonists relocated to the mainland south of Roanoke somewhere directly across Pamlico Sound from the Wokokon inlet. That argument, however, stands upon its own merits and in no way depends on the CORA tree, which may either be a legitimate Lost Colony clue or just another fanciful fable.

The most immediate challenge to its legitimacy is the age of the tree itself. In order for the CORA tree to have any possible connection whatsoever to the Lost Colony, it obviously must have stood there long before the Roanoke voyages. The larger point to be considered in this regard is the age of the CORA tree's habitat itself in the ever-changing Outer Banks environment.

It is estimated that the location and extent of the maritime forests on the barrier islands were well-established approximately 5,000 years ago.[6] It is difficult to determine precisely how much of the Outer Banks was originally forested five millennia ago, but it is certain that the unique maritime forests were far more extensive than today. Today there are just remnants of those original forests on the barrier islands where ancient trees have indeed stood for many centuries. Fortunately, the largest of these remaining forests is Buxton Woods[7] on present-day Hatteras Island, where the CORA tree is located.

The CORA tree itself is one of the many southern live oaks (*Quercus virginiana*) native to the southeastern United States. The southern live oak has a deep tap-root that anchors it when young and develops into an extensive and widespread root system. This, along with its low center of gravity and other factors, makes the southern live oak resistant to strong sustained winds of hurricane force. Southern live oaks are also impervious to the salt spray of a coastal environment.[8] These hardy trees are fast growing at first and may reach their maximum trunk diameter within 70 years, after which their growth rate slows with age.[9] According to the National Wildlife Federation "the oldest live oaks in the country are estimated to be between several hundred to over a thousand years old."[10]

Among the oldest existing southern live oaks are the "Seven Sisters Oak" in Mandeville, Louisiana, estimated to be 1,500 years old[11]; the "Angel Oak" on John's Island in South Carolina, also said to be 1,500 years old[12]; and the "Goose Island Oak" near Lamar, Texas, estimated by the Texas Forest Service to be over 1,000 years old.[13] It should be noted, however, that live oak age estimates are not universally shared within the scientific community. Dr. Kim Coder of the University of Georgia wrote, "The largest [live oak] trees of the native range, especially along the Atlantic coast … [have] a maximum expected lifespan of 500 years…. Many large live oaks are not as old as people believe."[14]

The *Sentinel* article refers to the CORA tree as "a 1,000-year-old water oak," but offers no evidence for that claim. Charles Whedbee wrote, "botanists estimate [the CORA tree] must be at least a thousand years old," and noted that "there are other live oaks in that forest … which almost certainly are as old." Whedbee, however, wrote these statements as part of his introduction to the Cora-witch fiction, and the botanists he referenced are not identified.

In 2009 the Lost Colony Research Group attempted to determine the actual age of the tree. A dendrologist was employed to take a core sample in an effort to establish the tree's age through tree ring analysis. Unfortunately, the CORA tree's trunk is completely split and partially hollow, the combined result of a lightning strike and a decay column—sometimes found in older live oaks[15]—and consequently a valid core sample could not be obtained. The actual age of the tree could not be scientifically verified, but there seems to be little doubt that the CORA tree is certainly centuries old. Given the National Wildlife Federation's estimate of seventy years for a live oak to reach its maximum trunk diameter, and assuming for a moment that the inscription was carved at about the time the tree reached that maximum diameter, the CORA tree's current age would have to be about 500 years. It seems possible, then, that the CORA tree could have been well-established in the maritime forest of present-day Hatteras by 1588, when the colonists abandoned the outpost at Croatoan. Whether or not the inscription was carved at that time, however, is another question entirely.

Native villages were positioned on the sound side of the barrier islands, which provided better protection from the elements and a canopy for shelter in the maritime forest. It is widely accepted in archaeological circles that the principal native Indian village on Croatoan in the late 16th century was located at the H1 Cape Creek Archaeological Site near the present-day community of Buxton,[16] but there was also a village at present-day Frisco, where the CORA tree is situated. That area is still called "Indian Town" by the locals today.

Frisco would have been an ideal choice for an outpost to allow for an early sighting of ships sailing up the coast along the Outer Banks. On the ocean side at Frisco there is an elevated bluff, the highest point in the area, and an excellent position from which to sight and identify any ship approaching along the usual route from the south. It would have made an ideal spot for a lookout position awaiting White's return. The Indian village at Frisco was on the sound side in the maritime forest and could have provided convenient, nightly shelter for the contingent of colonists watching for White's return. The village was not only about a quarter mile walk to the oceanfront bluff, but it also would have offered easy access from the mainland settlement across Pamlico Sound for periodic re-supply and relief of the colonists at a lookout station.

There *is* some hard, though limited, evidence to suggest the possibility of a Lost Colony-Frisco connection. Archaeologist William G. Haag noted that a local resident recovered a number of coins and "a counter" at the H7 Archaeological Frisco Dune Site.[17] "Counters" or jetons were coin-like tokens used particularly in England during the 16th and early 17th centuries in conjunction with a counting board or cloth for making mathematical calculations. At that time most of these counters were made in Nuremburg by a wide variety of manufacturers and sold in sets to the English market. The counters were made of thin malleable metal, hand produced with a hammer and dies, and each manufacturer had his own designs and inscriptions imprinted on each side.[18]

In 1950 three counters were also found in the archeological digs at Fort Raleigh on Roanoke Island. What it particularly remarkable about this find is that two of the three counters found at Roanoke are identical to the one found at the Hatteras site. Not only do all three have the same designs, markings, and wording, but the three bear identical irregularities, indicating that all three were stamped by the same die.[19] Although this is not conclusive evidence, it presents the possibility that the owner of this particular set of counters at Roanoke later spent time at the Frisco Dune site. Of course it is possible that this Englishman was a member of the 1585–86 colony and not the Lost Colony, but it seems more likely that the three identical counters would have belonged to one of the 1587 Lost Colonists. There is no indication in the accounts of the 1585–86 colony that an outpost or a presence of any kind was ever established at Frisco, nor does there seem to have been a reason to do so. The 1587 colonists, on the other hand, had good reason to establish a lookout position specifically at Frisco, across the sound from the mainland settlement, as they waited for White's return with the supply ships in the summer of 1588.

As mentioned earlier, the colonists were instructed to "write or carue on the trees or posts of the dores the name of the place where they should be seated...." White found the first "CRO" message carved into a tree as he approached the old settlement at Roanoke in 1590. At the entrance to the settlement he discovered "CROATOAN" carved into one of the posts. White also wrote that the CRO carving was discovered on the approach to the settlement "vpon a tree" and done in "faire Romane letters." The full CROATOAN inscription was found shortly thereafter on one of the "postes at the right side of the entrance" to the fortified settlement. That post "had the barke taken off, and 5 foote from the ground in fayre Capitall letters was grauen CROATOAN."[20]

The placement and form of the CORA inscription correspond with what little is known about the CRO carving at Roanoke. Both were carved "vpon a tree" and were written in "faire Romane letters." White provided slightly more detail about the CROATOAN message found on the entry post. That carving was placed five feet from the ground and again written in "fayre Capitall letters."

In February 2014, members of the Lost Colony Research Group took measurements of the message on the CORA tree. The inscription itself is five feet six inches from the base of the tree at ground level. The letters in the CORA inscription measure four inches in height and the entire word is seventeen inches in length.[21] It goes without saying that the messages—especially the abbreviated carving on the approach to the Roanoke settlement—had to be large and conspicuous enough to assure that White would notice them upon his return. A seventeen-inch-long inscription containing four letters, each four inches tall, would certainly seem to meet that requirement. From what can be ascertained, the physical characteristics of both the CRO and CORA inscriptions appear to be very similar.

Assuming for a moment that the CORA tree inscription is a legitimate message left by the 1587 colonists, it is likely that the same methodology used at Roanoke would have been repeated at Croatoan. The CRO inscription on the tree at Roanoke was an abbreviated form of the CROATOAN inscription on the entry post at the fort. It is possible, then, that the CORA inscription left on the tree at Croatoan was also an abbreviated form of a more complete message, perhaps left on a post originally located near the CORA tree in the Indian village at present-day Frisco. If so, then CORA could be an abbreviated form of CORANINE, as suggested in the Dawson article.

Coranine was the name of the territory, the tribe, and probably the principal village of the Coree or Coranine tribe, who once occupied the peninsula and coastal area south of the Neuse River in present-day Carteret and southern Craven counties. As will be noted later, they may have ranged even farther south along the coast. At some point prior to the outbreak of the Tuscarora War in 1711, they may also have occupied a village called Core Town near the site of present-day New Bern.

Another potential problem with the CORA tree–Coranine connection, however, is the fact that in 1588 the Coree/Coranine tribe was known to the English only as the "Cwareuuock," as illustrated on the portion of the 1590 White/de Bry map below. The word was later spelled "Cawruuock" on John Smith's 1624 map.

"Cwareuuock," located on the peninsula south of the Neuse River on the White–de Bry map.

Since there are no records indicating that any of the Roanoke voyagers ever visited the Cwareuuock, it is almost certain that White learned about the tribe and its territory from the Algonquian Manteo, in which case "Cwareuuock" was a phonetic transcription of what the Croatoans called that tribe. Linguist Blair Rudes wrote that "-euuock" ("-uuok") was an Algonquian suffix that translates as "people of" and therefore the name means "people of the Cwar (Cawr)."[22] As was common in the 16th century, White used formal English spelling on maps including the classical digraph "double-u" (uu), which was written as "w" in less formal text (this topic will also have relevance in a later chapter). Considering the fact that Elizabethan spelling was notoriously inconsistent, it is conceivable that "Cwareuuock" may have been pronounced "corahwock" in 1588. Blair Rudes suggested that "Cwareuuock" was pronounced "kwarewok,"[23] either one of which might account for the abbreviated CORA inscription.

The question of the CORA tree aside, there is some independent evidence suggesting that the Coree/Coranine Indians were at least familiar with the Lost Colonists and perhaps had contact with them. There are those who believe that the Hatteras (Croatoan), Corees, and Neusioks may already have been intermixed to some degree by the time of the arrival of the English and that elements of these three groups had contact with the Lost Colony after 1587.[24] Some also claim an ancestral connection to this mixed Croatoan/Coree/colonist group, but, like most assertions of this sort, they are based entirely on early Carolina legends and old family or native traditions, which may or may not have some basis in historical accuracy. Nevertheless, as suggested earlier, it is conceivable that there could have been interaction or even alliances among the Croatoans, Corees, Neusioks … and the 1587 colonists.

A more acknowledged Coree–Lost Colony connection is found in John Lawson's *A New Voyage to Carolina*. During his 1700–01 expedition through Carolina, Lawson learned that his Indian Guide, Enoe-Will, was a Coree by birth and lived as a boy perhaps fifty or so years earlier on the coast near the mouth of the Neuse River. Enoe-Will expressed an interest in a book Lawson had and knew that the English "whom he loved … extraordinary well" could "talk in that Book, and make paper speak, which they call our way of writing."[25]

Enoe-Will was also familiar with Christianity. He declined Lawson's offer to become a Christian himself, admitting "their [the English] Ways to be very good for those that … had been brought up therein. But as for himself, he was too much in years to think of a change, esteeming it not proper for Old People to admit of such an Alteration." He did, however, offer to place his fourteen-year-old son under Lawson's tutelage.[26] Some conclude that Enoe-Will's familiarity with reading and writing as well as Christianity must have been acquired about 1650 when he was a very young Coree boy living near the mouth of the Neuse River. Since there were no English settlements in that area at that time, it is thought that the only contact Enoe-Will and the Corees could have had with reading, writing, and Christianity would have been from traditions retained by admixed descendants of White's 1587 colony.

A more direct reference suggesting familiarity or possible contact between the Coree and the Lost Colony can be found in James Sprunt's 1896 *Tales and Traditions of the Lower Cape Fear*. Sprunt wrote, "The Cape Fear Coree Indians told the English settlers of the Yeamans colony in 1669 [actually 1664–7] that their lost kindred of the Roanoke Colony, including Virginia Dare, the first white child born in America, had been adopted by the once powerful Hatteras tribe and had become amalgamated with the children of the wilderness."[27]

Sprunt's mention of the "Yeamans colony" is a reference to a settlement at the Cape Fear River established by English settlers from Barbados, probably in May of 1664.[28] Sir John Yeamans was appointed governor of the colony. It is known that these settlers purchased a thirty-two square mile tract of land on the Cape Fear River from the local Indians, whom Sprunt identified as "Cape Fear *Coree*." The name "Cape Fear" Indians, though, did not indicate a particular tribe, per se. It was simply the name given by the English to the natives living in the area of the Cape Fear River. Like the Coree/Coranine, little is known about them. If these Indians were actually part of the Coree tribe, then the range of Coree territory must have extended much farther south than is generally recognized. In any event, if Sprunt's claim is essentially true, it would seem that the Indians in the Cape Fear area—whoever they were—apparently knew particular details about the assimilation of the Lost Colonists.

It is unfortunate that so little is known about the Coree/Coranine, a tribe that very well could have had connections with the 1587 Lost Colony. Even the Coree/Coranine language affiliation has defied positive identification. Some theorize that because of their proximity to the Iroquoian Tuscarora to the north and west, and their alliance with that tribe in the Tuscarora War, the Coree/Coranine may have spoken an Iroquoian dialect. However, there were also known Algonquian tribes, such as the Machapunga and Pamlico, who were allied with the Tuscarora in the war. Others hold that the Coree or Coranine were Algonquian since they occupied coastal territory that was historically Carolina Algonquian. As noted above, the word "Coree" itself may be derived from the plural Algonquian word transcribed phonetically as "Cwareuuock" on the Mercator/Hondius and White/de Bry Maps.[29]

Finally, Blair Rudes noted that the ethnic identity of the Coree is a complete mystery and that the few known Coree words were neither Algonquian nor Iroquoian,[30] perhaps suggesting that their language could have been a linguistic blend understood to some extent by the surrounding tribes, including the Croatoans. Much of the obscurity surrounding the Coree/Coranine derives from the fact that the area south of the Pamlico River remained largely unknown and unexplored for a century after the Roanoke voyages. Settlement did not begin at the upper reaches of the Pamlico River until at least 100 years after White's 1590 voyage, and it was not until the early 1700s that settlement started in present-day Craven and Carteret counties, traditional lands of the Coree/Coranine.

Likewise, early maps of that area are of little or no help. For virtually all of the 17th century the most influential map of present-day North Carolina was the *Virginiae Item et Floridae*, first published in 1606 by the London firm of Mercator/Hondius. The *"Virginiae"* portion of that map, however, was nothing more than a close rendition of the 1590 White/de Bry map. Consequently informative maps of the territory occupied by the Coree/Coranine, present-day Craven and Carteret counties, did not appear until the first explorers and settlers arrived in the early 18th century.

It was not until John Lawson's expedition in 1700–01 that further information about the Coree/Coranine came to light. During his 600-mile trek through Carolina, Lawson kept a journal in which he recorded the many native Indian tribes he encountered. Included in Lawson's *A New Voyage to Carolina* was his "Map of Carolina" which provided the most detailed information to date about the territory of the Coree/Coranine Indians.

Lawson's map identified three locations as "Coranine." The first is an area located at the north end of the peninsula just below the mouth of the Neuse River. The second is the Coranine Sound, separating the mainland from the barrier islands. The sound still bears the name Core Sound, and the barrier islands extending from Ocracoke Inlet to Cape Lookout are known today as the Core Banks. The third is the Coranine River, which was called the Newport River by the early 18th century.

A related point of interest on Lawson's map is the Weetock River just south of the Coranine. Weetock, like Coranine, is the name of both the river as well as the tribe that occupied the area. The Weetock River is the present-day White Oak River where the village of Swansboro is located. Local historical tradition traces the origins of Swansboro to an abandoned Algonquian site.[31] If that tradition is accurate, the close proximity of an Algonquian tribe to the immediate south of Coree territory as well as the Algonquian Croatoans along the barrier islands to the north further suggests that the Coree/Coranine were at least affiliated in some way with their neighboring Algonquians.

Lawson assigned two villages to the Coree/Coranine Indians in 1701: Coranine and Raruta. He also mentioned that the Coranine Indians "dwell near Cape Lookout" and "on the Sand Banks" as well as "a Branch of the Neuse River."[32] Lawson's reference to the Sand Banks is supported by the archaeological record suggesting that the Coree established temporary hunting and fishing camps on the Outer Banks,[33] strong evidence that the Coree

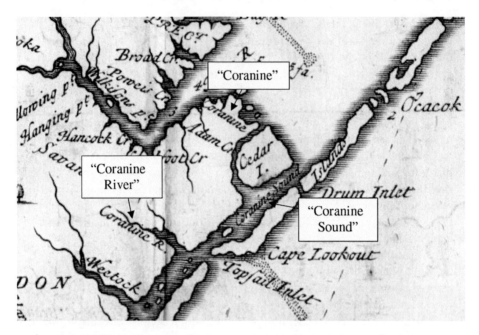

**Detail from John Lawson's 1709 "Map of Carolina" showing Coranine locations.**

were likely associated with the Croatoans. Charles Paul, in his 1965 thesis on the origins of Beaufort, North Carolina, stated that one of these villages named by Lawson "was located on the north side of the Straits of Core Sound which separates Harkers Island from the mainland, a location not more than seven miles east of the present site of Beaufort nor more than eight miles north of Cape Lookout. The other village was located on the west side of Newport [Coranine] River, but the exact spot cannot be given."[34] All of these Coree locations—the villages of Coranine and Raruta, Cape Lookout, the Sand Banks—were located in what is now Carteret County.

The Coranine location only vaguely described by Lawson as on "a Branch of the Neuse River," is not known. Lawson's conversation with the Coree Indian Enoe-Will seems to place that particular branch close to the mouth of the Neuse. It should also be noted that by the time of the Tuscarora War in 1711 there was, as referred to earlier, a large native Indian village called by Christopher de Graffenried "Core Town," which was located north of New Bern.[35] This would place a portion of the Coree/Coranine territory in present-day northern Craven County at the outbreak of the Tuscarora War, but the location there may have been fairly recent in 1711. Coastal tribes had been gradually pushed inland by the influx of white settlers over the previous decade. What was called "Core Town" by 1711 may have been the inland site where the Coree/Coranine had relocated after being driven from their traditionally coastal territories. This would also account for their closer proximity to, and association with, the Tuscarora during the war.

Further complicating matters is White's placement of "Cwareuuock" on the northern shore of the Neuse River. Although the map is geographically imprecise, a Coree/Coranine presence there would extend the Coree territory into present-day Pamlico County. However, Grenville's (and White's) 1585 excursion into Pamlico Sound—on which that portion of the map was based—did not reach the Neuse, and consequently the Cwareuuock location may be an imprecise approximation based on information related to White by Manteo and the Croatoans.

Nevertheless, from all that is known with any degree of certainty, when the Lost Colony left Roanoke, the Coree/Coranine occupied the peninsula and coastal areas south of the Neuse River in present-day Carteret County. The White/ de Bry map suggests that the Coree/Coranine may have occupied an area just north of the Neuse as well, although that is less certain. If the Coree/Coranine retreated inland at the beginning of the 18th century, as seems historically accurate, then the later Core Town site described by de Graffenried is most likely unrelated to the earlier Coranine territorial locations, and therefore irrelevant to any connection the colonists may have had with them when they departed from Roanoke in 1588. It is clear, however, that the Coree/Coranine had previously occupied the coastal areas, and were temporary visitors to Outer Banks. A settlement location on the peninsula south of the mouth of the Neuse in Coree territory may have been seen as a mutually beneficial arrangement for all parties involved: the Coree/Coranine, the Croatoans, and the colonists.

It has already been proposed that the Lost Colony initially settled on the mainland to the south of Roanoke and west of the Wokokon inlet, and present-day Carteret County is certainly one possibility. As Henry Mouzon noted on his *An Accurate Map of North and South Carolina*, there was "a good channel" leading directly from the Wokokon/Ocracoke inlet all the way to the mouth of the Neuse River.

The CORA tree "theory" is also associated with a resettlement location in present-day Carteret County, but that must be viewed as a separate hypothesis altogether. As interesting and compelling as that hypothesis may seem, the final verdict on the plausibility of the CORA tree premise will be made by science. The CORA tree will remain an enigma until scientific dating of the tree—and particularly its inscription—can affirm or refute its connection to the Lost Colony.

Regardless of exactly where that settlement was located, what is certain is that by the end of September 1588, the colonists were faced with an existential crisis. Their survival, certainly as an English colony at least, depended upon regular contact and resupply from England ... but White had failed to return as promised.

# 8

## A Critical Gamble at Sea
### September 1588–August 1589

It would be difficult to gauge the level of desperation that pervaded the mainland settlement as autumn approached in 1588 and all hope for White's return had evaporated. The colonists would have considered the possibility that White and the supply ships had been lost in a storm, or perhaps were captured or destroyed by the Spanish. As mentioned, it is very likely that the lookouts at Croatoan would have seen the Gonzalez ship on its way to the Chesapeake just a few months earlier, and they must have wondered if White and the supply ships could have fallen into the hands of the Spanish. That prospect would have been a particularly bitter one for at least a few of the colonists, since the new settlers White was supposed to bring almost certainly included relatives and spouses, initially left behind in England until the settlement was established. It is not known how many new colonists planned to sail with Grenville's fleet had it not been recalled, but, as mentioned, White wrote that there were fifteen settlers (eleven according to Diaz) who sailed on the failed voyage of the *Brave* and the *Roe* in 1588. In any event the situation had dramatically changed by late summer of 1588 as the colonists came to the stark realization that they were isolated and abandoned.

White's failure to return left the entire colony in a critical situation. Their continuing existence, certainly as a viable English colony, depended upon the arrival of periodic supply fleets, the first and most crucial of which was more than two months overdue. Cut off from England, they would now be forced to sustain themselves for at least another year, with supplies and materials running low and perhaps becoming increasingly dependent on the native tribes. Their only prospect—a very uncertain one—was that English ships might possibly arrive the following year. Given these circumstances and their now dim prospects in "Virginia," the colonists would almost certainly have turned to the one remaining option available to them of reconnecting with England: their seaworthy pinnace.

We know from White's accounts that the 1587 colony was in possession of several small boats plus a pinnace which was capable of ocean travel. The pinnace was nowhere to be seen when White finally returned in 1590, in spite of the fact that he searched the shore of Roanoke "to see if we could find any of their botes or Pinnesse, but we could perceiue no signe of them."[1] The pinnace White searched for was the same one commanded by Captain Edward Stafford and had already made the 1587 voyage, as part of the three-vessel group including the flagship *Lyon* and the unnamed flyboat captained by Edward Spicer. Pinnaces, though relatively small vessels, were frequently utilized for ocean crossings, usually—but not always—accompanied by larger ships. White's failed attempt to reach the colony in 1588, for example, consisted of just two pinnaces, the *Brave* of 30 tun capacity and the *Roe* of 25 tuns. In 1579, it will also be recalled, Gilbert sent the diminutive 8 tun *Squirrel* and a small crew under the command of Simon Fernandez on a solo reconnaissance voyage across the Atlantic. The *Squirrel* is referred to as a pinnace, but it was even smaller, more in the range of a frigate, which was lighter and faster and usually rated at about 10 tuns. The frigate designation would also account for its remarkably quick three-month round trip voyage to Newfoundland and back.

Faced with the reality of their abandonment in the fall of 1588, most of the colonists must have been discouraged enough with their prospects in Virginia that they would have been anxious to attempt a voyage, regardless of the risk involved, which might bring them home to England. The possibility of a successful voyage home would have seemed far more alluring than the certainty of abandonment. Yet to be decided, however, was who would go and who would be left behind, since the pinnace could not accommodate everyone.

The capacity of a pinnace or any 16th century vessel was estimated by its "tunnage," the volume (not weight) of its cargo-carrying capacity. The term is derived from a "tun," which was a large cask of wine containing 252 gallons.[2] Since the *Brave* was rated at 30 tuns, and the *Roe* at 25 tuns, for example, they had the capacity of carrying thirty and twenty-five of these large casks respectively. By comparison, the aforementioned *Lyon* was rated at 120 tuns. It should be noted, too, that although "tons" was often substituted for "tuns" by later writers, as in the excerpt below, tunnage and the later term "tonnage"—based on weight and displacement—are not synonymous.[3]

Unfortunately, the pinnace that remained with the 1587 colony was neither named nor described in terms of tunnage in any of the accounts, so its size and capacity are unknown. Furthermore, vessels referred to as "pinnaces" varied considerably. According to the papers of the Navy Records Society of Great Britain,

> The "pinnace" in the English Service [in 1585–7] … were of two classes—decked and undecked—or, as we should now say, first and second class. The former were always counted as independent units of a fleet; the latter were attached to, and even carried, by the larger ships. They ranged generally from 20 to 60 tons [tuns].[4]

The key consideration relating to the abandoned colonists, however, would have been the vessel's *passenger* capacity for a trans-ocean voyage, and tunnage does not say much in that regard. The following two voyages, for example, illustrate the range of tunnage/passenger variables of very early 17th century trans-ocean fleets.[5]

　　1. Martin Pring's 1603 voyage from England to present-day Maine and New Hampshire consisted of two vessels: The *Speedwell*, rated at 50 tuns, carried thirty men. The *Discoverer*, at 26 tuns, carried thirteen men.

　　2. The 1607 voyage that established the Jamestown settlement consisted of three vessels: The *Susan Constant*, rated at 100 tuns, carried seventy-one persons. The *Godspeed*, rated at 40 tuns, carried fifty-two persons. The *Discovery* (a pinnace), at 20 tuns, carried twenty-one persons.

　　The 1603 two-vessel Pring fleet carried an average of one man per 1.77 tuns, the remaining space used primarily for the considerable food stores, supplies, and equipment necessary for a lengthy trans-ocean voyage. On the other hand, the 1607 Jamestown fleet was more crowded, carrying an average of one person per 1.1 tuns. Of all the individual vessels involved in both voyages, the *Godspeed* carried one person per .76 tun, the largest proportion of people per tun of the five vessels mentioned. It is probable, then, that the *Susan Constant* and the *Discovery* carried most of the food stores and supplies. Using the *Godspeed*'s most crowded passenger calculator (one person per .76 tun), a 30 tun vessel might be capable of carrying about forty persons with a minimum store of food and necessities.

　　As noted, the pinnace in the possession of the 1587 colony was not named nor its tunnage mentioned, but White made three references to it which are instructive. The first was on July 1, 1587, at St. John's Island where White organized a party to go ashore for salt. He wrote, "The Gouernour … appointed thirty shot, tenne pikes, and ten targets, to man the Pinnesse."[6] The second was on July 22 at Hatorask as White prepared to go to Roanoke to look for the small group of men Grenville had left there the previous year and "the Gouernour went aboord the pinnesse accompanied with fortie of his best men."[7] The third reference occurred on July 30 when "Master Stafford, captain of the pinnace, and twenty of our men passed by water to the Island of Croatoan."[8] The 1587 pinnace, then, could apparently accommodate 40 to perhaps 50 persons on short day trips requiring little or no room for provisions. A solo trans-ocean voyage would have to carry far more food stores and supplies and proportionately fewer colonists.

Given these references and the earlier examples, it seems reasonable to estimate the total volume capacity of the 1587 colony's pinnace at about 30 to 35 tuns. If the average passenger capacity of the Jamestown fleet (one person per 1.1 tun) is applied, the estimated capacity of the 1587 pinnace on a trans-ocean voyage comes to between twenty-seven and thirty-two persons. It is immediately evident, then, that the pinnace available to the 1587 colony, while certainly capable of an ocean voyage, could transport not quite a third of the colony, which it seems fair to say probably consisted of at least 100 people by the fall of 1588.

The twenty-seven to thirty-two passengers would have had to include an experienced crew with the nautical expertise to manage an ocean voyage. It is known that Edward Stafford, captain of the pinnace on the voyage to Roanoke in 1587, was not among the list of colonists who remained at Roanoke, but there must have been crew members among the Lost Colonists. Author Andrew Powell addressed this point in his chapter discussing the makeup of the 1587 colony.

> The high number of single men may have resulted from some of them, perhaps up to twenty-five or so, being crew members of the pinnace. The concept of these men being crew members or mariners is not so far-fetched as it may seem. If we go back a moment to Hakluyt's Discourse, we will find that it contains a clear instruction that the colony should have "pinnaces with expert Seamen." It is therefore highly improbable that the colony would have been left an empty pinnace without an experienced crew to sail her.[9]

The crew that was left at Roanoke with the pinnace was most likely made up of the same able seamen who had sailed her *to* Roanoke under Captain Stafford, and these same sailors would most likely have been among the most anxious to depart. It would seem, then, that the colony had a qualified crew capable of an ocean voyage, but it is also clear that the pinnace could only transport between twenty-seven and thirty-two persons, including the crew, on an extended trans-ocean voyage.

Could the 1587 colonists have considered building an additional vessel or vessels in order to transport most, if not the entire colony? That possibility is not as unlikely as it may seem at first, and there are several contemporary instances of such an occurrence. On the way to Roanoke in 1585, Grenville's men stopped at Moskito Bay on St. John's Island in the Caribbean and constructed a fortification there. Grenville had lost one pinnace during the Atlantic crossing and, "we began to build a new pinnesse within the Fort, with the timber that wee then felled in the country."[10] Grenville's 1585 fleet at Moskito Bay consisted of six vessels (excluding the lost pinnace) and would have carried enough spare rigging, sails, casks of pitch and tar, etc., all the required materials for outfitting another vessel should the necessity arise. In addition, Grenville's combined ships' complements would have included skilled shipwrights, carpenters, sawyers, and laborers to accomplish the task.

A more remarkable example had occurred in 1562–63, when Jean Ribaut left about twenty-four soldiers at the new French settlement of Charlesfort on present-day Parris Island, South Carolina. Ribault departed in June of 1562, leaving no vessel behind at the settlement, and promised to return in six months with additional supplies and colonists. When he reached France, however, the country was embroiled in a civil war. Ribault ended up in England, where he spent two years in prison. In the meantime, after Ribault failed to return to Charlesfort as promised, the abandoned men decided to build a boat and try to sail to France. It is noteworthy that there were no sailors or shipwrights among the stranded Frenchmen, but they managed to build a vessel with makeshift sails and set off across the Atlantic. Although they eventually resorted to cannibalism by drawing lots, the emaciated survivors actually completed the 3,500 mile voyage and were finally rescued by an English vessel.[11]

The best and most comparable example occurred in 1609, when the *Sea Venture*, flagship of the so-called "third supply" to Jamestown, was separated from the fleet during a hurricane and was grounded on a reef off Bermuda. The 153 castaways made it ashore and would spend the next nine months stranded there. The decision was made to construct a pinnace capable of transporting perhaps half of the settlers to Jamestown, after which the plan was to send a vessel back to Bermuda and rescue the remaining castaways. Construction on the pinnace began on August 28. It is significant, however, that a major controversy arose about who would be left behind, a situation that may well have troubled the Lost Colonists in 1588. For the castaways at Bermuda it was feared that the more elite among them would take the skilled workmen and the best mariners and sail to safety, leaving the rest behind perhaps forever.[12] The stranded Lost Colonists, of course, could only speculate about White's failure to return as promised, but, as proposed earlier, they knew that the Spanish were searching for them at the Chesapeake Bay and they very likely had observed the Spanish ship captained by Vincente Gonzalez as he slowly made his way north along the coast the previous June. The Lost Colonists must have considered the possibility that White and the supply ships were lost to the Spanish, and—like the stranded colonists at Bermuda— they must have been distressed about the likelihood that those who were not chosen to sail with the pinnace would be abandoned forever.

To resolve the problem at Bermuda it was finally agreed that they would build two pinnaces, the aptly named *Deliverance* and *Patience*, which eventually transported about 140 of the castaways to Jamestown (several had died at Bermuda and a few were intentionally left behind). The construction of the *Deliverance* in particular was an extraordinary feat. She was reported to have a capacity of 70 to 80 tuns and, with a keel of 40 feet and a beam of 19 feet, was nearly half the length of the *Sea Venture*. The *Patience* was smaller, with a keel of 29 feet and a beam of about 15 feet.[13] Both vessels made the 600 mile voyage to Jamestown in about three weeks without incident. Fortunately for the castaways at Bermuda, they had access to the wrecked *Sea Venture*, which they dismantled. The oak beams, sails, rigging, and some of the oak boards from the *Sea Venture* were all salvaged and reused for the construction of the *Deliverance*. Ropes from the wreck were shredded, pounded into the seams, and covered with the pitch and tar from the barrels which were also recovered. The smaller *Patience* was constructed entirely of native wood, mostly cedar, using wooden pegs and perhaps part of the rigging and sails from the *Sea Venture*.

Were the 1587 colonists capable of building a similar sea-worthy vessel? On the plus side timber was plentiful, and we know from White's accounts that there must have been carpenters and sawyers among the colonists, because the dwellings left by Lane's colony the previous year were repaired by the colonists in 1587 and new ones were constructed. We also know that they subsequently erected "a high palisado of great trees, with cortynes and flankers very Fortlike" around the settlement at Roanoke. It is not known for certain whether the colonists had a shipwright among them, a specialized carpenter with shipbuilding and repair capabilities. However, in addition to the "expert seamen" listed by Hakluyt in his 1584 *Discourse of Western Planting*, he also instructed that colonization voyages be equipped with "shipwrights in some number to be employed on the timber. Oarmakers, and makers of cable and cordage." Given the fact that a seaworthy pinnace and crew were left with the 1587 colony, it is more than likely that a shipwright was among them as well.

Somewhat more problematic would have been the availability of essential shipbuilding materials—cables, lines, and sails for the rigging as well as oakum, tar, and pitch for caulking—which were available to both Grenville's fleet and, to some extent, the castaways at Bermuda. The pinnace that was left with the colony was intended to be utilized for local navigation and exploration, but a solo trans-ocean voyage was probably not anticipated. Nevertheless, the pinnace would have been supplied with some spare rigging and maintenance material, and they probably had the "makers of cable and cordage" whom Hakluyt had recommended. Oak and cedar were certainly plentiful, as was pine, from which a tar-resin could be made. The inexperienced Frenchmen at Charlesfort had sealed the seams of their clumsy vessel with pine resin and Spanish moss. As mentioned, the *Patience* was constructed entirely of native Bermudian lumber and held together with wood pegs.

There was another important factor to consider: the route. When White failed to return in 1588, the colonists understood, of course, that they were now isolated and cut off from England, but their most pressing objective would have been to reestablish contact with English *ships*, not necessarily with *England* per se. A return Roanoke-to-England voyage following the circuitous southern route across the Atlantic by way of the Caribbean would not only be long and arduous, but it would also risk exposure to the Spanish, whom the colonists likely blamed for White's failure to return. Direct voyages to the east across the Atlantic were not yet commonplace, and a 3,500 mile voyage due east would have been seen as extremely risky. There was a shorter and safer way to contact English ships. About 1,200 miles to the north of Croatoan were England's long-established cod fishing waters. A pinnace—or two—could reach those fishing routes in perhaps six weeks.

A northern heading to the cod fisheries would have had a number of advantages. In the first place it would keep the vessel or vessels close enough to the Atlantic coast to search out a safe harbor in case of bad weather and also provide access to fresh water and provisions. Secondly, it would virtually eliminate any chance of discovery by Spanish ships on patrol from St. Augustine, and also preclude a dangerous trip through the Spanish Caribbean. Thirdly, English ships had been frequenting the well-known and well-established fishing routes near Newfoundland for many decades. The English had been engaged in North Atlantic cod fishing since shortly after Cabot's discovery of "new founde land" in 1497, and that territory had become an English possession in 1583 when Raleigh's half-brother, Sir Humphrey Gilbert, claimed the land in the name of Queen Elizabeth. The colonists would have been well aware of the annual English activity to the north. Finally, the shorter voyage along the accessible coast would require less cargo space for provisions and correspondingly more room for colonists. A *single* 30 to 35 tun pinnace could carry more than forty persons and limited provisions on such a voyage.

Bideford was the primary English port engaged in fishing the Newfoundland waters from the 16th to the mid–18th centuries.[14] This is particularly noteworthy because from 1585 to 1588 both Bideford and its renowned resident, Sir Richard Grenville, were deeply involved with the Roanoke voyages. Grenville, of course, led the 1585 voyage to Roanoke and in 1586 sailed from Bideford to resupply the colony. Grenville also had a hand in recruiting colonists both in London and Bideford for the 1587 voyage. Given Bideford's strong association with the Newfoundland fisheries as well as Grenville's prominent role in the colonization effort, it seems certain that a great many of the 1587 colonists, and certainly the Bideford crew members among them, would have been very familiar with these Newfoundland fisheries to the north.

Furthermore, a number of voyages had already been made from the vicinity of Roanoke to Newfoundland. George Raymond, captain of the *Red Lion* and part of the Grenville-Lane expedition to Roanoke, had sailed from Croatoan to Newfoundland in the summer of 1585. In June of 1586 several of Drake's ships sailed on to Newfoundland after the evacuation of Lane's colony from Roanoke. Later in 1586 some of Grenville's belated supply ships, intended for Lane's colony at Roanoke, headed to Newfoundland after learning from a native Indian that Lane's colony had departed with Drake.[15]

Two decades later the disgruntled Jamestown colonists would also try to sail to Newfoundland, as the colony's prospects appeared dim. The Jamestown colony was failing for a variety of reasons and a number of settlers were planning to escape to Newfoundland in the pinnace. John Smith became president of the council in September of 1608, and he instituted a strict work policy—his "order for the drones" as he called it—aimed at the laziest of the colonists.

> But dreame no longer of this vaine hope [for food] from Powhatan, not that I will longer forbeare to force you, from your Idlenesse, and punish you if you rayle. But if I finde any more runners for Newfoundland with the Pinnace, let him assuredly looke to ariue at the Gallows.[16]

When the Bermuda castaways finally arrived at Jamestown aboard the *Deliverance* and *Patience*, they found only sixty pitiful colonists left alive after the previous winter's "starving time." It was decided to abandon Jamestown and sail to Newfoundland. William Strachey wrote about the decision:

> It soon then appeared most fit, by a general approbation, that to preserve and save all from starving, there could be no readier course thought on than to abandon the country, and accommodating themselves the best that they might in the present pinnaces then in the road, namely in the *Discovery* and the *Virginia*, and in the two brought from and builded at the Bermudas, the *Deliverance* and the *Patience*, with all speed convenient to make for the New found Land, where, being the fishing time, they might meet with many English ships into which happily they might disperse most of the company.[17]

The four vessels were loaded up and had actually sailed down the James River to Point Comfort on their way to Newfoundland, when the newly appointed Governor Lord De La Warr arrived with more colonists and supplies, and everyone returned to Jamestown.

Newfoundland would have been the most logical destination for the abandoned colonists in 1588. In the 16th century "New-found-land" was used to describe the shoreline from Labrador as far south as the present-day Gulf of Maine.[18] English fishing fleets would naturally follow the codfish migrations, which would range from the polar current at Labrador during the summer southward to the Gulf of Maine in the fall,[19] putting the potential contact with English ships less than 1,200 miles north of Croatoan.

There would have been some debate about the timing of the voyage, and this would have had a direct bearing on the Lost Colonists' decision about building a second pinnace. Since the Newfoundland cod fishing season generally ran from May through October, by the time they had given up all hope of White's return—perhaps by late August—it would probably have been too late to attempt a voyage that year. A voyage to Newfoundland would take well over a month, and they could not risk arriving at Newfoundland after the English fishing fleet had already headed back to England. In addition it would have taken a considerable amount of time to properly outfit the pinnace and gather all the necessary stores and supplies for the voyage. Consequently, they most likely could not sail until the following spring, in which case contact with the fishing fleet could be expected by early summer.

That being the case, there is an even greater likelihood that an additional vessel would have been built during the six or seven month delay until spring. They had the time and probably the means, and certainly the widespread fear of permanent abandonment was incentive enough to build another pinnace. The colonists stranded at Bermuda started work on the 70–80 tun *Deliverance* on August 28 and the ship was finished in March. She remained at anchor until the second pinnace was completed. The construction of the smaller *Patience* was probably started by October, and was certainly finished in April. Using the construction of the *Patience* as a guide, then, it would conceivably have taken the Lost Colonists six months to build a similar vessel. Both the original pinnace and the newly-built vessel would have been ready to sail for Newfoundland in the spring of 1589.

The probability of a second vessel necessitates a reassessment of the number of Lost Colonists who could have attempted the voyage to Newfoundland. The two ships built at Bermuda had a combined capacity of about 105 tuns, the stated 70–80 tun *Deliverance* and an estimated 30 tun *Patience*. Since nearly 140 colonists were transported to Jamestown on the two vessels, the result was a one person per .75 tun ratio, very close to the fairly crowded one person per .76 tun ratio of the previously mentioned *Godspeed*. As mentioned, an excursion northward along the coast would require less cargo space than a transatlantic voyage. Using the passenger per tun ratio of the Bermuda colonists (one person per .75 tun), two 30 tun pinnaces would be capable of transporting eighty persons. Two 35 tun vessels could carry about ninety-two people, nearly all of the estimated 100 remaining Lost Colonists in 1588–89. Although these numbers and estimates are largely hypothetical, they present the strong possibility that by the early summer of 1589 only a small handful of Lost Colonists at most may have been left in "Virginia." If all went well, the vessel or vessels would have hoped to make contact with the English ships at Newfoundland during the summer of 1589.

Of course, all apparently did *not* go well. The pinnace or pinnaces were not seen again, nor were any of the colonists who may have been left behind.

# 9

## The Great Hurricane
## and the Final Collapse
## of the Colony
### September 1589

It is not uncommon for important clues about the Lost Colony to turn up in Spanish documents rather than English sources, where they would normally be expected. It was the Spanish letters cited earlier, for example, that revealed Spain's awareness of Raleigh's plans to colonize the Chesapeake, which led in turn to Simon Fernandez's likely decision to alter the colony's original destination. The Spanish account of the Vincente Gonzalez voyage, also discussed previously, provided the evidence that the 1587 English colony had vacated Roanoke prior to June of 1588, and that they had not relocated to the Chesapeake.

Similarly, nothing is known from English sources about turbulent storm events that could have affected the 1587 colonists during the three-year span from August of 1587, when John White left Roanoke, through August of 1590, when he was finally able to return. What little *is* known about Atlantic storms during all the Roanoke voyages comes from the few references in the accounts of 1586, 1587, and 1590: In 1586 an early season storm of June 13–16 prevented the evacuation of Ralph Lane's colony from Roanoke by Sir Francis Drake, who, according to Lane, "had in that storme sustained more perill of wracke than in all his former most honourable actions against the Spanyards."[1] On August 21, 1587, a storm forced Simon Fernandez to cut the ship's cables and delayed John White's departure from Roanoke for six days.[2] Again, in August of 1590 a storm broke anchor cables and apparently prevented White and Captain Cooke from sailing the short distance from Roanoke to Croatoan.[3]

Although storms certainly occur frequently along the coast of present-day North Carolina, most of them are not "hurricanes" per se, which must attain sustained winds of between 74 to 95 mph to be classified even as a minor Category 1 hurricane.[4] The weather events in the aforementioned Roanoke accounts may have been tropical depressions, having sustained winds of less than 39 mph, or tropical storms, with winds higher than 39 mph,[5] which occur more frequently than hurricanes. Nevertheless, both minor (Category 1–2) and major (Category 3–5) hurricanes do strike the Carolinas regularly. Based on an analysis of 126 years of hurricane data and storm paths, AccuWeather recently reported that Cape Hatteras is one of the most vulnerable U.S. locations, with a 15 percent probability of a hurricane strike in any given year.[6] According to the Hurricane Research Division of the National Oceanic and Atmospheric Administration (NOAA), fifty hurricanes affected North Carolina between 1851 and 2014,[7] averaging one every 3.26 years. Based on probabilities alone, there is a good chance that a hurricane could have struck during the three year period during which the 1587 colony seems to have disappeared.

Other than the Lost Colonists themselves, there was no English presence in "Virginia" between 1587 and 1590, but the Spanish maintained a continual presence farther south, and detailed records of their activities are preserved at the Archivo General de Indias in Seville, Spain. The Archivo General contains 44,000 bundles, each with 1,500–2,000 manuscript pages, and continues to reveal new information about the Spanish colonial period. Fortunately, some of that information contains references and notations about Atlantic hurricanes, and weather researchers have been sorting through the Spanish documents for half a century. In 2005 a meteorological research team reported seventy previously unrecorded references to hurricanes occurring between the 16th and the 19th centuries.[8] Although this research was undertaken to complete preexisting storm chronologies and cyclone tracks, several of their 16th century discoveries will prove relevant here.

It should be noted, though, that there are a few problems with the original manuscript records in the Archivo General. Some are incomplete or fragmentary while others may not yet have been examined. Another factor is the geographic origin of the Spanish reports. The northernmost Spanish settlement in the 1580s was located at Santa Elena on what is now Parris Island, South Carolina (built on the site of Ribault's 1562 Charlesfort), but that settlement was abandoned in 1587 after Drake's raid convinced the Spanish to consolidate their strength farther south. Consequently, the Spanish colonial storm references from mid–1587 through 1590 describe hurricanes reported farther south in St. Augustine and the Caribbean. Nevertheless, since several of the reports—particularly in 1589—are probably separate accounts of the same storm event obtained from various Spanish sources at different locations, it is possible to "track" the path of that particular hurricane as it moved across the Caribbean and then turned northward up the Florida coast.

The following is a summary of all the meteorological research conducted at the Archivo General concerning reports of hurricanes that occurred between 1587 and 1590.[9] Asterisks represent hurricanes that either *could have*, or—in the case of the September 1589, hurricane—*did* turn north towards the Carolinas:

### 1587

No hurricane reports for 1587.

### 1588

| September | *A very strong hurricane struck near Havana, Cuba; few details reported (unrecorded prior to 2005). |
|---|---|
| November | Landfall near Cartagena de Indias in Colombia (unrecorded prior to 2005). |

### 1589

| August | *Hurricane struck the Leeward Islands (northern islands of the Lesser Antilles, just east of Puerto Rico); few details (unrecorded prior to 2005). |
|---|---|
| September | *A large Spanish treasure fleet departed from Havana on September 9 and had just entered Old Bahama Channel when a hurricane struck sinking four large ships. It has been noted that "the location of the sinking [of one of these ships] 'in about 30 degrees of latitude,' suggests that the term 'Bahama Channel' in various sources may refer to the northern extension of the Straits of Florida…" and indicates that the following three reports "may originate in different recollections of the same storm event" (unrecorded prior to 2005).[10] |
| ? | *(Month not stated, but clearly the same event as above.) A Spanish ship carrying sugar and hides from Puerto Rico joined the aforementioned fleet in Havana. A hurricane struck about 50 leagues from the Old Bahama Channel accompanied by fierce northeasterly wind lasting four days. On the first day ten carracks sank. |
| ? | *(Month not stated, but very possibly the same event as above.) Hurricane passed Cape Canaveral; no details (unrecorded prior to 2005). |
| ? | *(Month unknown, but probably the same event as above.) One of the ships under the command of Martín Pérez de Olazábal was wrecked during a hurricane off Cape Canaveral. Vessels from St. Augustine assisted four severely damaged ships and rescued forty crewmen from the ship lost at Cape Canaveral. |

### 1590

| November | A strong hurricane struck a Spanish flotilla at Vera Cruz, sinking four ships and damaging another. |
|---|---|

Two of the above hurricane accounts can be safely eliminated from consideration here because it is highly improbable that they could have affected the Carolinas: The November 1588, hurricane made landfall near Cartagena de Indias in Colombia, South America, probably too far south to be a likely factor. The November 1590 hurricane can be excluded for two reasons: Its location was Vera Cruz, too far west into the Gulf of Mexico, and it also occurred three months too late for the August 1587–August 1590 timeframe during which the colony disappeared.

Assuming, then, that the last four entries for 1589 are separate references to the same September hurricane, as seems likely, there were three hurricanes that *could possibly* have taken a path to the Carolinas between August of 1587 and August of 1590. All three of these occurred in the twelve-month period between September of 1588 and September of 1589 and, as noted, are marked with an asterisk above. Unfortunately very few details were reported about either the strong hurricane that struck Cuba in September 1588, or the one that struck the Leeward Islands in August 1589. It is possible, however, that one or both of these could have turned northward, following a typical Atlantic track, and had an impact on the Carolinas and the English colony. Due to the lack of additional information, though, little else can be said about them.

Much more can be established about the track of the September 1589 hurricane. From the four reports of that event, it appears that the Spanish fleet's first encounter with the outer bands of the hurricane occurred on September 9, about 150 miles ("50 leagues") east-northeast of Havana, probably about 100 miles or so from the Bahamas. Since hurricanes in the northern hemisphere rotate counter-clockwise, the "fierce northeasterly wind" would place the center of this storm considerably farther to the east-southeast, perhaps just north of the present-day Dominican Republic on September 9. This hurricane was clearly moving west-northwest towards southern Florida and then had to have tracked northward if, as indicated in the final two Spanish reports, it was soon located off Cape Canaveral.

The future track of this September 1589 hurricane, then, is reasonably predictable. It appears to have followed the same historical path of many known hurricanes which have moved through the Caribbean and turned northward up the east coast of Florida to strike the Carolinas. This track along the east coast tends to follow the Gulf Stream, which provides a source of thermal energy and helps maintain a hurricane's strength.[11] As demonstrated in the following illustration based on data from the National Oceanic and Atmospheric Administration as well as the National Weather Service, Hurricane Floyd followed a very similar track through the Caribbean and then up the Florida coast on September 13, 14, and 15, 1999, as had the September 1589 hurricane.[12]

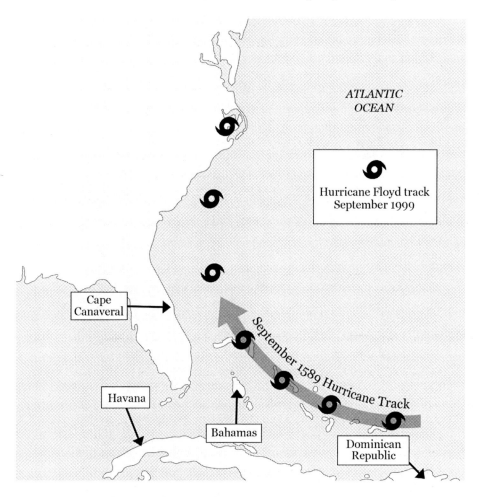

The position and track of the September 1589 hurricane corresponded with Hurricane Floyd's, Sept. 13–16, 1999 (courtesy Michael Gayle).

Hurricane Floyd, one of the worst to strike North Carolina, followed a historical path up the Atlantic coast, tracking the Gulf Stream, and made landfall at Cape Fear on September 16, 1999. Based on the Spanish reports, the reconstructed 1,000 mile path of the 1589 hurricane—from about the Dominican Republic to Cape Canaveral—was almost identical to that of Floyd on September 13, 14, and 15. Hurricanes traveling westward through the Caribbean either turn in a northward direction and curve toward the eastern coast of the U.S., like Floyd, or stay on a north-westward track and enter the Gulf of Mexico.[13] Consequently, once the 1589 hurricane turned northward along the Florida coast, it likely followed the same thermal Gulf

Stream track and made landfall somewhere along the Carolina coast, perhaps in the same general area as Floyd, on or about September 13, 1589.

From the reports in the Archivo General, then, there were three hurricanes which could possibly have turned northward and affected the Carolinas between August of 1587 and August of 1590. All three possibilities occurred between September of 1588 and September of 1589. One of these three, the September 1589 event, can be reliably tracked through the Caribbean and then northward past Cape Canaveral, following the Gulf Stream hurricane path, and very likely struck the Carolinas. This hurricane could have had serious consequences for any Lost Colonists who may have remained behind in 1588, when the pinnace or pinnaces sailed north, as proposed earlier.

It will be helpful at this point to understand the specific effects of a hurricane and how they could have impacted the remaining Lost Colonists. As defined by the National Oceanic and Atmospheric Administration and other meteorological sources, there are various factors which contribute to the destruction and loss of life in a hurricane. Strong winds, of course, are associated with all hurricanes and can cause extensive damage, but "the greatest threat to life actually comes … in the form of storm surge … water from the ocean that is pushed toward the shore by the force of the winds swirling around the hurricane."[14] Most flood-related deaths are caused by drowning, of course, but the death count increases dramatically when water levels rise rapidly, as they do from a storm or tidal surge. Hurricane Katrina, for example, caused at least 1,500 deaths in 2005, attributed mostly to the surge that accompanied the storm. According to the American Meteorological Society's study of the fifty-nine Atlantic hurricanes that occurred from 1963 to 2012, about half of all hurricane-related deaths were caused by storm surge, whereas hurricane winds only accounted for 5 to 10 percent of fatalities. Moreover, the strength of the hurricanes when they made landfall was not necessarily related to the fatality rate. Of the ten most deadly storms during that forty-nine year period, only three were considered major hurricanes, i.e., Category 3 or higher. Six of the ten most deadly were just Category 1 hurricanes, or tropical storms, when they made landfall.[15] Regardless of its strength at landfall, the 1589 hurricane could have had dire consequences for any colonists who remained either at Croatoan or the mainland settlement to the west.

While a storm surge is the abnormal rise in seawater level caused primarily by a storm's winds pushing water onshore, "a storm tide" is the total rise of seawater resulting from the *combination* of storm surge *and* the astronomical tide.[16] When a storm surge occurs at normal high tide, the effects are even more devastating. If a storm tide accompanied the 1589 hurricane, the results would have been immediate and catastrophic. The previously mentioned Hurricane Floyd had diminished from a category 4 to just a minor category 2 hurricane when it made landfall near Cape Fear in 1999, yet the storm surge along the North Carolina coast was estimated at nine to ten feet. Most of the fifty-six deaths attributed to Floyd were due to the surge.[17] By way of comparison, Hurricane Hazel made landfall at the North Carolina–South Carolina border as a category 4 on October 15, 1954. A storm surge of more than twelve feet inundated the coast, but reached as high as eighteen feet at Calabash, North Carolina, where the storm surge coincided with the time of the lunar high tide.[18] It would not have taken a surge nearly as great as these to wipe away the mainland settlement and cause considerable fatalities among any Lost Colonists who may have been left behind the previous year.

A few words should be added here about the settlement's vulnerability to a storm surge. As proposed, by late March of 1588 the new settlement was established on the mainland, and by May a small contingent of colonists waited for White at an outpost on Croatoan and would then have led him to the settlement site upon his expected arrival perhaps as early as June. The mainland site must have been readily accessible via a good, navigable inlet—Wokokon—to facilitate what was expected to be periodic supply ships from England. As discussed, that site may well have been located west of the Wokokon/Ocracoke inlet in present-day Carteret, Craven, Pamlico, or the southern part of Beaufort County.

Note the surge levels at those counties and the surrounding areas on the following storm tide map based on the models provided by the National Oceanic and Atmospheric Administration.[19] As illustrated by the shaded areas, the maximum storm tide levels resulting from a so-called minor Category 2 hurricane would inundate the coastal parts of all the aforementioned counties with a surge of seven to nine feet, which would have effectively destroyed a new settlement at any of those locations. In fact the entire area from the northernmost reaches of the Pungo River all the way south to Cape Lookout and beyond, as well as the Outer Banks, would be similarly inundated.

The impact from a Category 4 hurricane would have been even more devastating. Such an event could produce a surge reaching as high as fifteen feet well up the Neuse River in Craven County some twenty miles above New Bern. The same surge levels could be reached as far as thirty-five miles up the Pamlico River. A surge of twenty feet would inundate the coastal areas of Beaufort, Pamlico, Craven, and Carteret Counties, all of which were potential settlement sites in 1588. A Category 4 surge would have been calamitous for the colonists and their new mainland settlement if it was located anywhere near these coastal areas or along the rivers farther inland.

There is one irony concerning the 1589 hurricane and the Lost Colonists, and that has to do with a passage in John White's account of his return voyage to Roanoke. When White returned to the original settlement site in 1590, it

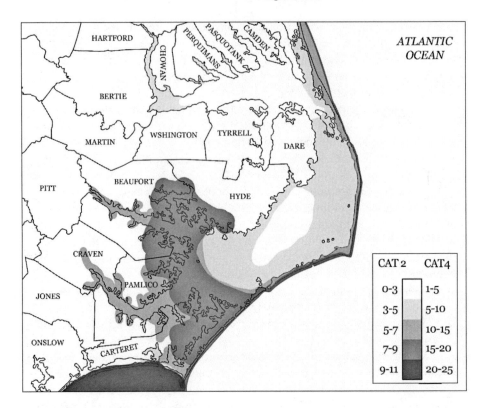

**Maximum storm surge levels from Category 2 and 4 hurricanes (courtesy Michael Gayle).**

of course had long been abandoned, and as mentioned he "found the place very strongly enclosed with a high palisado of great trees, with cortynes and flankers very Fortlike."[20] It might seem, then, that if a hurricane and storm surge struck in 1589 and eradicated the new settlement on the mainland, how could the original palisade enclosure at Roanoke—constructed in 1587—still be standing in 1590?

The answer to that question depends entirely on the Roanoke settlement's vulnerability to a tidal surge, and that in turn depends on the settlement's exact location on the island in 1587. As illustrated on the map above, Category 2 and 4 surges may reach as high as nine to twenty feet respectively, more than enough to wipe away a settlement and cause any number of fatalities along the Outer Banks and the coastal mainland of southern Pamlico Sound. Note, however, the following close-ups of Roanoke Island based on data taken from the same NOAA maps.

The shaded area surrounding and mostly covering Roanoke represents five to ten foot maximum surge elevations in Category 2 and Category 4

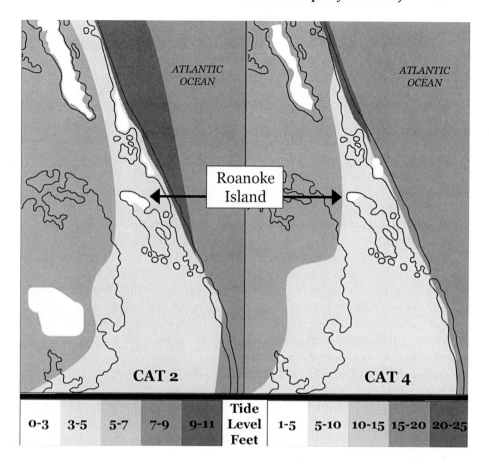

| 0-3 | 3-5 | 5-7 | 7-9 | 9-11 | Tide Level Feet | 1-5 | 5-10 | 10-15 | 15-20 | 20-25 |

**Category 2 and 4 hurricane surge models show little impact on the north end of Roanoke Island where the fortified settlement was located (courtesy Michael Gayle).**

storm tides respectively. In both models, however, there are elevated areas at the northern end of the island that are affected far less by either storm tide. The Fort Raleigh National Historic Site, which claims to preserve the location of the 1587 Colony, is located at the extreme north end of the island, well within that less affected zone. Erosion over the centuries may have erased part of the original site, leading to some debate today about its precise location, but there is no doubt that the 1587 settlement was located somewhere at the northern end of the island.

John White wrote that the original settlement was located "round about the North point of the Iland" and was clearly at some elevation since to approach the settlement site he "entered vp the sandy banke."[21] A Category 2 or 4 storm tide in 1589 would probably not have affected the old palisade built of "great trees" very much at all, and would account for the fact that it was still standing when White returned in 1590. Ironically, the mainland settlement may have been eradicated by a surge that inundated Carteret, Craven, Pamlico, and Beaufort Counties, while leaving their original settlement at Roanoke virtually unscathed.

Finally, the potential 1589 hurricane and surge must be juxtaposed with the other critical event that probably impacted the Lost Colony after John White's failure to return as expected in the summer of 1588: the likely decision to utilize their seaworthy pinnace—and perhaps build a second vessel—in an effort to make contact with other English ships about 1,200 miles to the north at Newfoundland. A single 30–35 tun pinnace might carry forty to forty-five persons on a northward voyage along the coast, leaving about fifty-five to sixty colonists behind. If the colonists built a second pinnace, it is probable that they did so in order to accommodate everyone who wished to go, like the castaways at Bermuda would later insist. Perhaps there were a few who decided to take their chances among the Croatoans. There is a chance, then, that there may have been anywhere from just a few to as many as sixty remaining colonists *before* the hurricane struck in September of 1589.

The death toll from a seven to thirteen foot surge is impossible to calculate, but the percentage could have been quite high. Assuming a 50 percent fatality rate—a conservative estimate considering that such a surge would have inundated Croatoan and completely swept away the mainland settlement—the number of surviving colonists may have been as few as one or two to as many as thirty immediately following the hurricane of 1589. There could very possibly have been additional deaths among the survivors afterwards, from injury, illness, and malnutrition from inadequate or spoiled food caused by the storm.

Any attempt to describe the psychology of the surviving colonists after the 1589 hurricane would be highly conjectural; nevertheless, work *has* been done in recent decades to understand the specific psychological effects of floods on survivors. Interestingly, it has been found that a survivor's dislocation and the loss of personal possessions after a flood may undermine his sense of attachment and self-identity.[22] Whether or not this condition has any relevance to whatever colonists may have survived the hurricane surge in 1589 cannot be known with any degree of certainty, of course, but the event would most likely have accelerated the assimilation of any survivors into the native Indian society.

A hurricane strike and surge in September of 1589 would have initiated a rapid and decisive physical collapse of the colony. The immediate results would have been the inundation and eradication of the mainland settlement. A seven to thirteen foot surge would have swept away the wooden dwellings which had been disassembled and transported from Roanoke, along with equipment, supplies, and personal belongings. Iron and brass items like tools and "Falkons [or falconets, very light cannon capable of firing a 1-pound ball] and small Ordinance which were left with them [in 1587],"[23] and which they removed upon vacating Roanoke, would have been buried under tons of silt. Their powder supply would have been ruined and, if any of their matchlock muskets remained, they would have been useless. The surge would have destroyed the corn crop and ruined existing food stores. Whatever livestock the colonists may have possessed would have perished. Everything would have been swept away.

Such an event could provide a logical explanation for a number of unanswered questions surrounding the fate of the Lost Colony. In the first place it would explain how an entire English settlement could seemingly disappear without a trace left behind, and it would account for the failure of archaeological efforts to locate that site, which would have been literally wiped away. Also, many Lost Colony theorists have assumed that a very gradual, even generational, integration of the English colonists with the native Indian tribes took place. In actuality the number of colonists who survived the surge may have been quite small, and, without the bare essentials, they would have integrated very quickly—regardless of the psychological effect mentioned above—with elements of the remaining Croatoan or another tribe. Under this scenario, after September 1589, the English colony and the mainland settlement ceased to exist.

# 10

## The "Legend of the Coharie" and the Hurricane's Aftermath
### October 1589–January 1590

There are any number of oral traditions and family histories in southeastern North Carolina that claim an ancestral connection to the 1587 Lost Colonists. One of the most interesting of these is a little known oral narrative which had been passed down for many generations in Sampson County and was finally transcribed by local historian Ernest M. Bullard in about 1950 as the "Legend of the Coharie." What is fascinating about this particular legend is that it directly associates a powerful hurricane with the fate of the 1587 colony ... long before there was any documentary evidence whatsoever that such a storm had actually occurred.

This remarkable narrative traces—in considerable detail—the migration and ancestry of a mixed group of surviving Lost Colonists and Croatoan Indians and their descendants from shortly after the hurricane to their 19th century location in Sampson County, North Carolina, where their bloodlines are said to be mixed with the tribe known today as the Coharie Indians. The legend speaks of a "tremendous tidal wave" which forced the surviving group of Indians and colonists farther inland and had "salted the earth where they first settled so that it would not grow corn." This account of a substantial storm surge is unique among oral histories dealing with the Lost Colony. The following is the first part of the legend dealing with the hurricane and its aftermath. To use Bullard's introductory line, "Only this much of truth I know to be; I tell the tale as 'twas told to me."

> About the end of the year 1588 or early in the year 1589 the remnant of the Lost Colony which had taken up their abode with Manteo on Croatoan Island, the place of Manteo's birth, accompanied by Manteo and all that survived a tremendous tidal wave left the island for the mainland beyond the sound to the west.
> One of the colonists making this sojourn was young George Howe, whose father

George Howe, Sr., was slain by the Indians on Roanoak Island on July 28, 1587. These migrants of whites and Indians, it is believed, landed in what is now Carteret or Pamlico County, because, so goes the legend, they tried early the next year, probably 1589, to ascend the "Neus" River farther inland in order to reach higher land on which they could grow Indian corn, for the tidal wave had salted the earth where they first settled so that it would not grow corn. Many of the colonists grew sick for lack of bread to eat with sea foods and game which were abundant.

Before they could get settled on a desirable location they were attacked by an unfriendly tribe and a few of the migrants were wounded.[1]

It is interesting to note that the legend does not speak of a hurricane per se, but rather of "a tremendous tidal wave," which would have accompanied a hurricane. "Tidal wave" was probably the common term used by Ernest Bullard in 1950 for what is technically called "storm surge" today, although "tidal wave" may actually be more accurate in this instance. As mentioned in the previous chapter, a "storm tide"—the simultaneous occurrence of a storm surge and the astronomical tide—is even more devastating than a storm surge.

The details contained in the legend regarding the aftereffects of the tidal wave are remarkably consistent the modern NOAA surge models, and of course those models did not exist when Bullard transcribed the legend. The saline contamination of the soil is a particularly interesting and credible detail in the narrative. A storm tide of seven to thirteen feet, as illustrated in the Category 2–4 surge, would have "salted the earth" in a vast coastal area, including present-day Carteret, Pamlico, and Beaufort Counties, as well as other potential mainland settlement locations in the surrounding areas. Croatoan/Hatteras, too, would have been inundated and contaminated. Tidal surges result in increased levels of both sodium and chloride, both of which are toxic to crop plants such as corn, the main food source for both the colonists and the Indians.[2] Depending on rainfall and soil factors, salt levels may gradually reduce to tolerable levels within a year's period of time, but "on soils with high water tables, it may take several years for salt levels to drop to acceptable levels."[3]

As mentioned previously, Indian corn planting was done from April through June so that a corn harvest was available from early summer through October. A September 1589 hurricane and surge would not only have spoiled the fall harvest and the remainder of the summer stores, but also contaminated the soil for at least the next nine months, eliminating the 1590 planting season as well. Given the total impact of a storm tide in 1589, the migration westward "to reach higher land on which they could grow Indian corn" seems plausible.

Saline floodwaters can also have a delayed effect on drinking water. The U.S. Geological Survey compared the quality of water pumped and distributed to customers by the CHWA (Cape Hatteras Water Association) before and after Hurricane Emily in 1993. Before Emily the chloride content of water distributed to customers was 40 to 45 milligrams per liter. During the three months after Emily the chloride content rose slowly but steadily to a maximum of 280 to 285 milligrams per liter, as the salt water infiltrated the production zones of the wells.[4] Croatoan and the flooded coastal mainland may very well have remained barren and uninhabitable for an extended time period after the hurricane of September 1589.

The legend also tells of an interesting secondary effect of the storm surge and the loss of crops and existing food stores. According to the legend, "Many of the colonists grew sick for lack of bread to eat with sea foods and game which were abundant." Both the colonists and native Algonquians were dependent on the previously mentioned agricultural cycle. It is entirely conceivable that the survivors of the hurricane and surge, both colonists and native Croatoans alike, would have had little choice but to abandon the sterile areas on the Outer Banks and seek arable land farther west of the flooded coastal mainland. It seems equally credible that a sudden dietary change, presumably from mostly grain-based to exclusively shellfish and wild game, would have had a negative reaction among the colonists. As noted in the previous chapter, death can occur among hurricane surge survivors from the effects of injury, illness, and malnutrition from inadequate or spoiled food.

The legend claims that "the remnant of the Lost Colony," accompanied by Manteo and other Croatoan survivors, migrated west from Croatoan "about the end of the year 1588 or early in the year 1589." This, though, would place the occurrence of the tidal wave in 1588 rather than 1589. There were three hurricanes cited in the previous chapter which could have impacted the colony between September of 1588 and September of 1589. One of these was the powerful hurricane that struck Cuba in September 1588. As mentioned, there were few details relating to this event in the Spanish archives, but it very well could have followed the same track as the hurricane in 1589, in which case the colony may have been struck by two consecutive hurricanes and surges, first in September of 1588 and then in September of 1589. The Atlantic hurricane season technically runs from June 1 until November 30, but on the Outer Banks the majority of hurricanes or tropical cyclones have historically arrived in late August or September.[5] If the 1588 hurricane recorded briefly in the Archivo General actually struck present-day North Carolina, it would place the collapse of the colony only six months after the colonists left Roanoke and established their new settlement on the mainland.

On the other hand it is evident that the legend, in its present transcribed form, contains a number of historical details and references which could not have been part of the original oral tradition. These historical details are associated with the general narrative, but clearly were added either by Ernest

Bullard, as historian, or perhaps by someone earlier in order to augment the legend's narrative. One of these additions is probably the name of George Howe, Sr., along with the exact date of his death at the hands of hostile Indians at Roanoke on July 28, 1587. Another is the mention of his son, "young George Howe," and of course the names of Carteret and Pamlico Counties. All of these are historically accurate details, the Howe references coming directly from White's account of the 1587 voyage, but these would have been later attachments, inserted into what could have been only a very general oral tradition if it had survived for centuries. It is likewise implausible that the precise "end of the year 1588 or early in the year 1589" reference could have been passed down over the centuries as part of the oral tradition.

It is possible that the oral tradition could have referenced the effects of a great storm that occurred sometime after the colonists resettled, and that Bullard or someone earlier added that specific timeframe to the transcription as a logical estimate. It should be noted once again that the 1588 and 1589 hurricanes were not part of the historical record until their recent discovery in the Spanish archives. When Bullard first heard the legend in 1892 and transcribed it in 1950, there was no knowledge whatsoever of an Atlantic hurricane in either 1588 or 1589, and it is the unique reference to a hurricane or "tidal wave" that makes the legend intriguing. In the final analysis, whether the storm struck in 1588 or 1589, or whether storms struck in September of *both* years is largely inconsequential, since the outcome would have been the same. The mainland settlement would have been wiped away, the colony would have ceased to exist, and whatever survivors there were would have been forced farther inland in search of arable land.

The legend goes on to assert that the combined group of tidal wave survivors—including Manteo, some of his native Croatoans, and some colonists—attempted to ascend the Neuse River in search of unspoiled land to grow corn. As cited above as one of the examples of Bullard's augmentations, he added that "what is now Carteret or Pamlico County ... [was] where they first settled." Carteret County was also mentioned in connection with the Lost Colony by Hamilton McMillan (1837–1916), North Carolina assemblyman and advocate for the Lumbee tribe in Robeson County. McMillan had recorded an oral tradition among the Lumbees, which—like the Bullard legend but with far less detail—claimed a direct ancestral connection to the Hatteras/Croatoan tribe and the Lost Colonists. McMillan wrote, "After the English colony became incorporated with the [Hatteras] tribe, they began to emigrate westward.... The line of emigration extended westward from what is now Carteret County."[6]

The Bullard and Hamilton reference to either a temporary settlement or emigration point in present-day Carteret County supports the suggestion made earlier that the Croatoans, and by association the Lost Colonists, could have interacted or at least had contact with the Coree tribe. As mentioned, at the time of the Roanoke voyages the Coree/Coranine occupied the peninsula and coastal areas south of the Neuse River in present-day Carteret County. This would in turn support the belief that at least part of the tribe which eventually became known as the Coharie had ancestral links to both the Coree as well as the Neusiok, who dwelt on the south side of the lower Neuse River in present-day Carteret and Craven counties. The actual "Coharie" name did not come into existence until about a century later.

The Coharie-Coree connection could also explain a potential linguistic question not addressed in the "Legend of the Coharie" or elsewhere, namely that of the language affiliation of the Indians in this Lost Colony/Indian group. Manteo and his small tribe from Croatoan, the only Indians mentioned in the legend as accompanying the group of Lost Colonists traveling inland, were Algonquians. James Mooney proposed that, since the Neusiok were allied with the Algonquian Pomouik (Pamlico) in 1584, the Neusiok may also have been Algonquian,[7] but Mooney's conclusion is generally disputed. Most ethnologists now hold that the Neusioks (and possibly but not definitely the Coree), from which the present-day Coharie tribal council officially claims descent,[8] were Iroquoian. Consequently, for the Coharie tribe to be linear descendants of colonists and Croatoans, as the legend claims, *and also* descendants of the Neusioks, as the tribal council claims, there had to have been an infusion of Iroquoian blood at some point. Present-day Carteret County would have been a logical place for that admixture to occur.

It is not stated how far the group traveled up the Neuse River, but according to the legend, "Before they could get settled on a desirable location they were attacked by an unfriendly tribe and a few of the migrants were wounded." This part of the narrative is also historically consistent, at least with what is known of the late 16th century tribes. The "unfriendly tribe" would almost certainly have been the Tuscarora, known to the English as Mongoaks, who occupied the upper Neuse at that time and were frequently at war with the tribes closer to the coast.

The exact origin of the "Legend of the Coharie" is unclear. Ernest Bullard wrote that it was first told to him about 1892, and added that it had been passed down "by word of mouth for more than three hundred years before one word of it was ever put into writing." The legend is not widely known today outside the Bullard extended family and Sampson County, but it is probable that it was passed down orally prior to 1892 in the Hall family line. Ernest Bullard wrote, "on top of a knoll overlooking the lowland of Big Swamp in the western part of what was known at the time (1779) as 'The Territory' of Duplin County [the western part of Duplin County became Sampson County in 1784] there stood a small log cabin belonging to Enoch Hall. According to the legend Hall was "said to have been a lineal descendant from

George Howe of the 'Lost Colony,' the name having been changed from Howe to Haw, then to Hall." George Howe, as mentioned, was killed shortly after White and the colonists arrived at Roanoke in July of 1587. His son, George Howe, Jr., was listed among the colonists and—according to the legend—is purported to be the ancestral link to Enoch Hall and the Hall descendants in Sampson County centuries later.

The legend, therefore, seems to have been passed down in the Hall family line at least until 1892, when Ernest Bullard first heard it. There is a genealogical connection between the Bullards and the Halls which might explain Bullard's access to the legend. W. Stephen Lee, grandson of Ernest Bullard, reports that one of Ernest Bullard's great aunts, Lucy Bullard Hall, was married to Everett Hall, son of Enoch Hall, who himself was the son of another Enoch Hall.[9] It has always been common practice to recount old stories and traditions when extended families occasionally gather from near and far for such events as wakes and weddings. Lucy Bullard Hall died in 1892, the same year the legend was related to Ernest Bullard. It is possible that young Ernest Bullard first heard the legend from one of his Hall relatives when the Bullard and Hall families assembled for Lucy's funeral.

Ernest Bullard was a member of the Sampson County Historical Society, an indication of his interest in local history. W. Stephen Lee believes his grandfather transcribed the "Legend of the Coharie" after his retirement, and that it was published at that time by the historical society. The story was reprinted in "Pitch 'n' Tar," a series of publications for a high school oral history project conducted by Matilda West and her students in Roseboro in the late 1960s or early 1970s.[10] Most recently the legend was reprinted in the January 2014 issue of "Huckleberry Historian," the quarterly journal of the Sampson County Historical Society.

No discussion of the "Legend of the Coharie" would be complete without further mention of Hamilton McMillan and the Lumbee tribe. In 1892, when Ernest Bullard first heard the Coharie Legend, a great deal of attention was being paid to the above-referenced booklet which had been published by Hamilton McMillan just four years earlier. McMillan had recorded the Lumbee oral tradition which—like Bullard's legend—claimed a direct ancestral connection to the Hatteras/Croatan tribe and the Lost Colonists. McMillan wrote that he first learned of the Lumbee connection to the Lost Colony in 1864, when he heard an old Indian named George Lowrie state that his tribal ancestors included English colonists from Roanoke. McMillan's subsequent investigations and interviews in Robeson confirmed that there was a tradition connecting some portion of the Lumbee tribe and the 1587 colony at Roanoke. McMillan's arguments, in fact, led directly to North Carolina's recognition of the Lumbee tribe, initially called "Croatan Indians."

That same oral tradition is found among the closely related Coharie

tribe in Sampson County. Coharie tribal member Enoch Emanuel wrote the
following about 1913 when he was approximately 70 years old:

> The mixed race of people living in Sampson County are sure that the statements
> given to us by our ancestors concerning our origin are true. We have only asked for
> Indian prestige, while we know in our veins also flows the blood of our white ances-
> tors. We have always been told by our fathers and mothers that we were mixed with
> the lost colony of the Roanoke. We therefore are a mixture of Governor White's col-
> ony and the original Indians.[11]

More than a half century later another analysis of Coharie traditions was
done by Don A. Grady for his 1981 master's thesis on the oral folk history of
the Coharie tribe. Grady interviewed ten descendants of the tribe and wrote,
"Perhaps the most important tradition is that of the tribe's origin. They believe
very strongly that they are the descendants of a coastal tribe of Indians and
the Lost Colony."[12]

After McMillan's success with the Lumbee tribe, efforts were undertaken
in Sampson County to do for the Coharie what had been done for the Lumbee
in Robeson. In 1914 Special Indian Agent O.M. McPherson was directed to
investigate the Indians of Robeson and the surrounding counties, and in early
1915 he presented his "Report on the Condition and Tribal Rights of the Indians of Robeson and Adjoining Counties."[13] In his report McPherson included
213 Sampson County Indians as part of the Croatan tribe (which by 1913 was
called "Cherokee Indians of Robeson County"). McPherson's report relied
heavily on the previous work done by McMillan. In 1916 Coharie advocate
George Edwin Butler (1868–1941) used the same arguments in his successful
appeal for separate schools for the Coharie in Sampson County.[14]

It might seem from all of this that Ernest Bullard, like his contemporaries
McPherson and Butler, may have been directly influenced by McMillan's earlier work, and that the "Legend of the Coharie" could essentially be an adaptation of McMillan's 1888 publication. That does not seem to be the case.
Other than its thematic link to the Lost Colony, Bullard's legend bears virtually no resemblance whatsoever to the narrative in McMillan's publication.

In the first place the Bullard Legend begins with the tidal wave and its
aftereffects, events which were unknown to McMillan, McPherson, Butler,
or anyone else. The legend also provides a far more detailed and coherent
chronology of events from the occurrence of the tidal wave to about 1690–
1700, when the descendants of the mixed Colonist-Indian group supposedly
reached Sampson County, as will be seen later. The Lumbee oral tradition,
as recorded by McMillan, recalls a direct connection to the Croatoan [Hat-
teras] tribe and the Lost Colony, but provides virtually no information on
the century that transpired afterwards, when the Lumbees were said to have
eventually settled in Robeson County.

Secondly, the "Legend of the Coharie" consists essentially of two separate, interrelated narratives. The first is the aforementioned chronological and geographical account about survivors of John White's English colony and a group of Croatoan Indians. Woven into that broader narrative, however, is the male lineage of two specific individuals: George Howe, Jr., son of the English colonist killed at Roanoke on July 28, 1587, and an unnamed daughter of Manteo, leader of the tribe at Croatoan. McMillan's version, as stated, is a much more general account of Lumbee origins, reconstructed from interviews he conducted long after the tribe had developed into the heterogeneous group that it remains today. By McMillan's time the "Lumbees" were already comprised of a blend of tribal elements and traditions including Hatteras, Cherokee, Cheraw, Tuscarora, Mattamuskeet, and perhaps others. McMillan offers no explicit narrative whatsoever about specific individuals or events between 1587 and 1711.

In addition, from what can be determined it seems that the "Legend of the Coharie" was passed down along Enoch Hall's ancestral bloodline and was not known outside the Hall family until it was finally recorded by Ernest Bullard, "...as 'twas told to me." This may account for the fact that McMillan, McPherson, and Butler were apparently unaware of the Howe-Hall oral family history. As mentioned, McMillan's investigations were focused on Robeson County and the Lumbee tribe. Both McPherson and Butler borrowed liberally from McMillan and, since McMillan's arguments had been successful, possibly did not see the need to explore alternate oral histories in Sampson County.

Thirdly, it should be noted that, unlike the Bullard Legend, the McMillan, McPherson, and Butler accounts all had a political agenda, i.e., tribal recognition of the Lumbee and the Coharie by the state of North Carolina. These unclassified admixed "Indians" in Robeson, Sampson, and surrounding counties had been designated "free persons of color" in 1835, and were thereby prevented from attending schools for whites, a prohibition they would resent until McMillan entered the scene. McMillan spent a number of years compiling enough evidence to persuade the state that the Lumbee ancestry could be traced back to the 1587 colony at Roanoke and the Croatoan (Hatteras) tribe. His arguments were aimed at—and directly brought about—North Carolina's official recognition of the "Croatan" tribe and its right to a separate school system. The Bullard Legend is a family oral history and had no such political agenda.

Finally, neither Bullard's "Legend of the Coharie," nor McMillan's account of Lumbee origins, should be seen as a comprehensive history of tribal ancestry. Lumbees Adolph Dial and David Eliades described the Lumbee tribe as a community consisting of "remnants both of the 'Lost Colony' and several Indian tribes of which the Hatteras and various Eastern Siouan peoples were the most prominent."[15] McMillan's account focuses exclusively on the Croatoan

(Hatteras)—Lost Colony connection, but in truth that tradition is retained by just one segment of the Lumbee tribe. Similarly, the Bullard legend should not be viewed as the complete history of the present-day Coharie tribe. Nevertheless, as Ernest Bullard put it, the Lost Colony—Hatteras descendants who "have lived and are now living in Sampson County" are a part of that story.

A few words should be added about the reliability of oral traditions in general and the "Legend of the Coharie" in particular. Since writing was unknown to the native Indian tribes until after the arrival of the Europeans, it is obvious that the oral histories concerning tribal origins cannot be substantiated by traditional documentary methods. Nevertheless, they certainly should not be viewed as historically unreliable and dismissed out of hand. Helen Rountree wrote that individual public recitations of personal exploits by young individual Powhatan tribesmen were often exaggerated,[16] but the same should not be assumed about the oral histories of the tribes as a whole. These traditions represent centuries-old memories of tribal origins and identities, and the oral histories of some major tribes date back more than a thousand years.

As stated above, however, the "Legend of the Coharie" is both a tribal history *and* an account of the role played by George Howe, Jr., and his descendants in the eventual settlement of the Coharie tribe in present-day Sampson County. As such, it is impossible to tell exactly where the Howe-Hall lineage portion of the "Legend of the Coharie" fits on the sliding scale of historical reliability. Furthermore, as noted, the version of the legend that has existed since 1950 must be seen as an annotated and enhanced adaptation of the oral history in its original form, which certainly lacked many of the details added by Bullard in his transcription.

In the final analysis, though, the legend's version of the aftereffects of the hurricane is compatible with the proposal offered earlier regarding the location of the Lost Colonists' mainland settlement and its vulnerability to a tidal surge. The migration farther inland to find terrain uncontaminated by the surge, the effects of the sudden dietary change on the surviving colonists, and the encounter with a hostile tribe as they ascended the Neuse are all credible elements within the narrative. And again, perhaps the most remarkable element that contributes reliability to the legend is its unique account of a tidal surge from a hurricane whose occurrence would not be confirmed until its recent discovery in the Spanish archives.

# 11

## John White's Final Voyage; Roanoke and Croatoan Abandoned
### February–October 1590

By February of 1590 plans seemed to be finally in place to resupply the colony in Virginia. In a letter written in 1593 to chronicler Richard Hakluyt describing the events of 1590, John White wrote, "About the end of Februarie in the yeare of our redemption 1590 … there were at the time aforesaid three ships absolutely determined to goe for the West Indies, at the speciall charges of M. Iohn Wattes of London Marchant … for the supplies and reliefes of the planters in Virginia."[1] Once again, however, history seemed to repeat itself for the hapless White, because "when they were fully furnished, and in readinesse to make their departure, a generall stay was commanded of all ships thorowout England. Which so soone as I heard, I presently (as I thought it most requisite) acquainted Sir Walter Ralegh therewith."[2] Through Raleigh's intercession, White wrote, a license was obtained "for those three ships to proceede on with their determined voyage" and it was agreed that they "should take in, and transport a conuenient number of passengers, with their furnitures and necessaries to be landed in Virginia."[3]

When White arrived at the docks with his colonists and supplies, however, Abraham Cooke (sometimes spelled Cocke), captain of the flagship *Hopewell*, would only allow White to board. As White put it, "I was by the owner and Commanders of the ships denied to haue any passengers, or any thing els transported in any of the said ships, sauing only my selfe and my chest; no not so much as a boy to attend vpon me."[4] With no opportunity to complain to Raleigh, and, after receiving the captain's assurance that they would make a stop at Roanoke and look for the 1587 colony, White acquiesced and went aboard. It is not clear what White could have expected to accomplish by sailing without any of the sorely needed supplies or additional colonists, other than perhaps to satisfy his own curiosity about the fate of the colonists, who had by then been abandoned for three years.

Here again White seems to have misunderstood what was happening around him. Although John Watts was a London merchant, as White stated, he was better known as a principal in one of the most powerful privateering syndicates in London at that time.[5] Watts certainly was "determined to goe for the West Indies," but the primary objective of the voyage was the capture of Spanish prize ships, not the resupply of the colony in Virginia, as White seemed to think initially. Whatever arrangement White thought had been made regarding the transportation of supplies and additional colonists, neither Captain Cooke nor "the chiefe Commanders" nor "the owner of the said ships" seemed to have any knowledge of it. It was only because of White's "great sute, and earnest intreatie" that Cooke permitted him to board the *Hopewell* at all.

Although White doesn't mention what was happening on the national scene, neither colonization in general nor the 1587 colony in particular was on anyone's mind—except for White's—at that time. The "generall stay" was brought about after England had suffered a major defeat at sea just a few months earlier in 1589. The victory over the Spanish Armada did not turn out to be the crushing blow to Spain that was originally thought, and England did not emerge as a great naval and colonial power at that time. In an attempt to land that crushing blow, Queen Elizabeth assembled a "Counter Armada" in 1589 in a bold attempt to destroy the remaining Spanish fleet which was then being refitted at Santander and San Sebastian in northern Spain. As one historian wrote:

> A successful strike against the stationary Spanish squadrons would have had history-making consequences. Deprived of the core of his Atlantic fleet, Philip not only would have been impaired in his capacity to wage war in Europe; he also would have lost his capacity to effectively guard and secure his New World Empire. The Americas would have been rapidly opened to competitors, and Spain's own uncertain grip on its New World possessions would have been pried free. Argentina and Peru may have become the first colonies of the British Empire. Spanish colonies in North America would have been stillborn as the English and French were finally free to exploit their frustrated ambitions in the 16th century. The Spanish treasure galleons still lingered as a mouth-watering prize, and a major precious metals transport was moving into Iberian waters in 1589.[6]

Although the English fleet was led by two proven naval commanders, Sir Francis Drake and Sir John Norris, the operation was a disaster. The reasons for the defeat of the "English Armada" need not concern us here, but the results are relevant. Spain would re-emerge with a more powerful navy, better capable of both thwarting English privateers and transporting treasure safely from America.[7] England, on the other hand, emerged militarily and financially weaker, and colonization would not be attempted again for nearly two decades.

Thus it was, then, that on March 20, 1590, after an absence of nearly three years, John White finally sailed from England aboard the *Hopewell* in a belated effort to re-establish contact with his abandoned colony. The *Hopewell* was accompanied by the *John Evangelist*, and the *Little John*, and would later be joined by the *Moonlight* and another pinnace. After several successful privateering encounters with Spanish ships in the Caribbean, Cooke headed northward, as promised, to try to make contact with the colony left at Roanoke in 1587. By August 15 they were anchored off Hatorask, and the next morning White, Cooke, and Edward Spicer set out with a party of men in boats towards Roanoke. It is worth pointing out here that they did *not* sail directly to the Chesapeake, a further indication that White must have known that the colonists would not have relocated there. Encouraged at first by columns of smoke rising from Roanoke and Kenricks Mount to the south, they spent the day investigating the sources of the smoke, which turned out to be naturally caused brushfires. The search at Roanoke would wait until the next morning.

In the afternoon of August 17, however, one of the two boats overturned while trying to navigate the inlet at Hatorask, drowning seven of the eleven on board. One of the drowned men was Edward Spicer, captain of the flyboat on the 1587 voyage. The nineteen remaining men rowed on to Roanoke, but darkness prevented them from searching effectively and "we overshot the place a quarter of a mile." At daybreak on the 18th White, Captain Cooke, and the rest of the crewmen, searched the island and finally arrived at the deserted settlement at the north end of Roanoke where the colony was left three years earlier. White made a number of observations and discoveries there. He noted that the dwellings had been disassembled, an indication that the colonists had moved them to the new settlement location for re-assembly, and that a strong palisade surrounded the abandoned settlement, obviously constructed after his departure in August of 1587. He also found that the colonists had taken their smaller ordnance with them, but left behind heavy armament and other items too difficult to transport. The most important discoveries made by White, of course, were the two carved messages left by the colony directing him to Croatoan. As mentioned previously, these messages are the only undisputed primary source evidence we have from the Lost Colony after August 27, 1587.

White's reaction to these messages merits closer examination. It is somewhat curious that White appears to have concluded from the messages that his colony was permanently *settled at Croatoan* in 1590. He wrote that the carved messages were meant "to signifie the place, where I should find the planters seated," and again that the carvings indicated "the name of the place where they should be seated."[8] He later wrote that "I greatly ioyed that I had safely found a certaine token of their safe being at Croatoan."[9] The next morning, White wrote, he attempted to "…goe for the place at Croatoan, where our planters were."[10] There can be little doubt that White intended his account to convey his assurance that the 1587 colony was settled "at Croatoan which is the place where Manteo was borne, and the Sauages of the Iland our friends."[11]

According to White's account of the 1590 voyage, stormy weather, broken anchor cables, and a shortage of fresh water prevented the *Hopewell* from making the stop at Croatoan. White claimed unconvincingly that it was initially agreed to sail to the Caribbean, spend the winter there, and then return to Croatoan in the spring of 1591. That idea was soon abandoned, however, and they eventually sailed back to England, arriving on October 24. We are led to believe—and it is widely accepted—that, had it not been for the various mishaps, John White would have made the short trip to Croatoan and been reunited with his colonists.

White, of course, had no knowledge of the critical events that had occurred in 1588 and 1589, or that his colony had probably already ceased to exist. He *must have been* aware, however, that *Croatoan was deserted* in 1590 … despite his unwavering assurance that his colony was safely settled there.

This conclusion is supported, once again, by the details contained in White's own account of the 1590 voyage. As was the case with his version of the 1587 voyage, White's credibility as narrator is dubious here too. Virtually all of the historical interest in White's 1590 return voyage to Roanoke has been focused on August 18 and 19 when White discovered the carvings left by his colony and then failed to reach Croatoan. Little or no attention has been paid to the less sensational but equally important events that occurred between August 12 and August 16, *before* White and the fleet reached Roanoke. During that time there was certainly one, probably two, and perhaps three opportunities for any colonists on Croatoan to communicate, either by signal fire, shot, or even direct personal contact, with the English ships *Hopewell* and *Moonlight*.

The first opportunity occurred on August 12 as the English ships made their way from Wokokon along the barrier islands northward toward Croatoan on their way to Roanoke. White wrote that they first anchored near Wokokon on August 9 and "on the 12 in the morning we departed from thence and toward night we came to an anker at the Northeast end of the Iland of Croatoan."[12] If any colonists had been on Croatoan in 1590, they would likely have been aware of English or Spanish ships' sails heading northward on the usual route up the present-day Carolina coast. In the case of an English ship approaching, signal fires would have been lit and initial contact probably made on August 12. No signals of any kind were detected as the ships sailed slowly northward along the coast of Croatoan.

The best opportunity for contact occurred later on August 12 and also on the 13th when the English ships actually anchored at Croatoan. As the ships were passing Croatoan, the English observed a breach or channel at the north end of the island and decided to anchor there. (This was the same shallow inlet referred to earlier that was unnamed in 1590, but was later called Chacandepeco and closed in 1672.) They remained at that position through the night of the 12th and on the following morning, August 13, they sent smaller boats "to sound ouer this breach: This breach is in 35. degr. and a halfe, *and lyeth at the very Northeast point of Croatoan*"[13] (italics added). They spent the morning taking a number of depth soundings at this channel "whereas goeth a fret out of the maine Sea into the inner waters, which part the Ilandes and the maine land."[14] They found a "great diversity of soundings" in this channel where the smaller boats would have come very close to the Croatoan shoreline. It is impossible to think that the English could have been anchored at this location from the 12th to the 13th and undertaken these sounding activities without the knowledge of anyone—native or colonist—on Croatoan, particularly near the north end of the island.

As shown on the White/de Bry map, there *was*, in fact, a Croatoan village at the north end of the island during that time period. John White drew his map during the 1585 Grenville-Lane expedition, and it was published in 1590 by Theodor de Bry. White, who had first-hand knowledge of Croatoan, placed three distinct Indian towns there. Two of these were in the central portion of the island and the third was located very near the northern tip, not far from the point where the ships were anchored and very close to the "breach" where the smaller boats would have been taking and calling out soundings. Since White had no information about the whereabouts of his colonists at this point, one wonders why he did not attempt to visit the nearby and familiar Croatoan village during this delay, unless of course he already realized that the island must have been abandoned.

The activities of the English ships would have either been directly observed by anyone there, or communicated quickly from the nearby village to any remaining colonists—or Croatoans—elsewhere on the island. If any colonists were at Croatoan on August 12 and 13, they surely would have made direct contact at that time with the ships in some manner. On August 18 when White found the "Croatoan" messages at Roanoke, he must have understood that the colony could *not* have been at Croatoan five days earlier, despite the assurances he gave in his account.

Three days after the soundings were taken at the breach at Croatoan, there was even another possible opportunity for contact by any colonists or friendly Indians at Croatoan. On the morning of August 16, White, along with Captains Cooke and Spicer and others, manned two boats and headed for Roanoke as the *Hopewell* fired off "2 Minions and a Falkon" to announce their arrival. Before they were half way there, however, they saw smoke "to the Southwest of Kindrikers mountes"[15] and decided to venture there first, even though it was a much greater distance. They were disappointed to find that the smoke was not from a man-made fire after all, and "Being thus wearied with this iourney we returned to the harbour where we left our boates ... [and] deferred our going to Roanoak vntill the next morning."[16]

This potential contact opportunity on August 16 depends on the actual location of Kindrikers mountes to the south of Roanoke. Kindrikers mountes, also called Kenricks mount, was, in the late 16th century, a large conspicuous sand dune situated along the narrow barrier island chain well south of Roanoke. Due to the changing configuration of the Outer Banks over the centuries, its exact location is not precisely known today. General consensus locates Kindrikers mountes at what is called Wimble Shoals just offshore from present-day Rodanthe, which is located about half way between Roanoke and Hatteras/Croatoan.

If White was on a southerly course to the vicinity of present day Rodanthe to locate the origin of the smoke, as his account indicates, he would have been heading towards Croatoan along the eastern shore of Pamlico Sound. Any colonists or friendly Indians on Croatoan who, for whatever reason, missed the direct contact opportunities on August 12 and 13, would have now been heading northward towards Roanoke in an attempt to intercept the English ships. These colonists and/or Indians would have either met White's group heading south on August 16, or else would have reached Roanoke and met the English there before August 19, when the English ships finally departed. No such encounter ever occurred.

It should also be noted that the 30–35 tun pinnace in possession of the 1587 Lost Colony was nowhere to be found during the week of August 12–19, 1590. White specifically mentioned that "we could perceiue no signe of them [the pinnace or the smaller boats]" on the 18th when they searched Roanoke and "along by the water side."[17] There was also no sign of the pinnace on the 12th and 13th when the *Hopewell* and *Moonlight* were anchored off Croatoan. Given the absence of the pinnace and the fact that nothing ever came of the several contact opportunities between August 12 and 19, it must have been evident to White that neither the pinnace, nor his colony, nor *anyone* for that matter, could have been on Croatoan at that time. The evidence points decidedly to the conclusion already discussed in an earlier chapter, that Croatoan was abandoned by both colonists as well as the Croatoan tribe in September of 1589, and that it was still abandoned in August of 1590 when White returned.

White must have been keenly aware of this dilemma when he found the

"Croatoan" carvings at Roanoke, but he gave no hint of it in his journal. On the contrary, as previously noted, only five days after taking the soundings at Croatoan and just one day after the excursion to Kindrikers mountes, he wrote that he "greatly ioyed that I had safely found a certaine token of their safe being at Croatoan." Given the contact opportunities at Croatoan and Kindrikers mountes over the previous four days, especially the proximity of the soundings location to the Croatoan village indicated on White's own maps, not to mention the colony's expressed intention to settle at a location on the mainland and not the barrier islands, it is difficult to understand the seemingly unwavering assurance expressed in his published account that his colony was safe at Croatoan in 1590.

Unless White was afflicted with a severe case of wishful thinking, there is one logical explanation for White's insistence—despite his awareness of all the evidence to the contrary—that the colony was safe at Croatoan in 1590: the preservation of Raleigh's 1584 Charter. As mentioned earlier, the charters granted by English sovereigns provided the legal entitlement for colonizing the New World, but they were contingent upon actually establishing colonies and otherwise expired after a set term of years. Raleigh's charter, granted by Queen Elizabeth and issued on March 25, 1584, was titled:

THE LETTERS PATENTS, GRANTED BY THE QUEENES MAIESTIE
TO M. WALTER RALEGH NOW KNIGHT, FOR THE DISCOVERING AND
PLANTING OF NEW LANDS AND COUNTRIES, TO CONTINUE THE SPACE
OF 6. YEERES AND NO MORE.[18]

The charter, portions of which are excerpted here, conferred...

to our trustie and welbeloued seruant Walter Ralegh, Esquire, and to his heires and assignes ... free libertie and licence ... to discouer, search, finde out, and view such remote, heathen and barbarous lands, countreis, and territories, not actually possessed of any Christian Prince, nor inhabited by Christian People ... [to] goe or trauaile thither to inhabite or remaine, there to build and fortifie ... [to] haue, take, and leade in the saide voyage, and trauaile thitherward, or to inhabit there with him, or them, and euery or any of them, such and so many of our subiects as shall willingly accompanie him or them.... And further that the said Walter Ralegh ... shall haue, holde, occupie, and enioye to him, his heires and assignes ... all the soile of all such landes, territories, and Countreis, so to bee discouered and possessed ... where the saide Walter Ralegh, his heires, or assignes, or any of them, or his, or their or any of their associates or company, shall within six yeeres (next ensuing) make their dwellings or abidings....[19] (Underlining added.)

The "six yeeres" limitation of this charter would commence on the "next ensuing" year giving Raleigh a total of seven years to establish a permanent settlement. Unless such a permanent colony was established, his charter would expire in 1591. It will be recalled that Raleigh certainly wasted no time in this effort. On April 27, 1584, he sent the Amadas/Barlowe expedition followed by the 1585 Grenville/Lane colonization effort at Roanoke. It should be noted, by the way, that for the expressed purpose of perpetuating Raleigh's Roanoke claim, Grenville left the contingent of men there upon his return in 1586 when he discovered that Lane and the 1585 colonists had unexpectedly abandoned the island. Establishing and maintaining a continuing territorial claim was of vital importance to the terms of Raleigh's charter.

The year 1587 should have been a banner one for Raleigh's colonization efforts. If all had gone according to plan, Raleigh would have had two permanent domains in the New World. The first of these was the original claim at Roanoke. On August 13, 1587, "by the commandement of Sir Walter Ralegh," the loyal Croatoan Indian Manteo was baptized into the Church of England and appointed Lord of Roanoke and Dasamonguepeuk "in reward of his faithfull seruices."[20] This was more than just a meaningless gesture of generosity. Manteo became a titled baron, an English peer, and lord of the realm of Roanoke and Dasamonguepeuk, thereby becoming one of Raleigh's "assigne[e]s" in accordance with the provisions in the royal charter. Raleigh's second and more important domain in the New World, the "Cittie of Ralegh," was originally intended to be located at the Chesapeake Bay in 1587.

By the time White was finally able to return in 1590, Raleigh's colonization efforts had virtually crumbled, and consequently his royal charter was in jeopardy of expiring. The Chesapeake location had been eliminated in 1587 because the Spanish were searching there for the English at that time. The whereabouts of the colony was unknown. Roanoke had been abandoned, not only by the 1587 colony, but also by the Indians, including Lord Manteo, whose titled domain included Roanoke. Despite the messages left at Roanoke, it was evident that by 1590 Croatoan had also been abandoned. For the moment it appeared that Raleigh had no territorial claim whatsoever in the New World, without which his 1584 charter would soon expire.

The only way to prevent the expiration of that charter was to provide evidence of the survival and location of the 1587 colony, neither of which had been determined by the 1590 voyage. To the contrary, as explained above, White must have realized that the colony could not have been at Croatoan in the summer of 1590, and yet his account states in no uncertain terms that the colony was indeed alive and well at that location. It is quite plausible, then, that White's account intentionally misrepresented the significance of the "CROATOAN" carvings to provide evidence of the colony's continued existence and location, thereby preventing the termination of Raleigh's charter.

It is unclear when, and actually by whom, this deception would have been conceived and incorporated into White's account, but Raleigh certainly could have had a hand in it. The final draft of White's account of the 1590 voyage was obviously completed after his return to England and almost certainly after reporting directly to Raleigh. It is not inconceivable that Raleigh either personally edited, or directed the editing of, the final published version of the account for the purpose of extending his charter and preserving his rights and interests in Virginia. Had the truth been known, Raleigh's charter would have expired, since the colony had already ceased to exist. As proposed, at least part of the Lost Colonists had made a failed attempt to reach Newfoundland in 1588 or 1589, and possibly just a few of the remaining colonists survived the hurricane of September 1589. The mainland settlement had been eradicated and the planting fields on the Outer Banks had been contaminated. The few Lost Colonist survivors, along with some of the coastal Indians, were somewhere on the mainland in the summer of 1590.

A somewhat subtle point to be made about the account itself, written *after* the voyage, is its subdued tone, its lack of urgency regarding the colonists. As mentioned above, virtually all of the interest in this voyage has been focused on White's commentary regarding the events of just four days, from the morning of August 16 to the 19th, but this needs to be put into some perspective. The 1590 voyage lasted seven months, from March 20 until October 24. For the first five months—from March 20 until August 15, when the *Hopewell* finally anchored off Hatorask at Roanoke—White's account is taken up entirely with the details of their travels through the Canaries, the first landfall at Dominica, and the many encounters with various ships as they wound their way through the Caribbean. It seems odd that White made no mention whatsoever of the colonists at all, neither his intention to locate them nor his expectations about finding them, during the entire first half of the account, until the evening of August 15, when they mistook smoke "in the Ile Raonoak neere the place where I left our Colony in the yeere 1587."[21] His apparent indifference may have been a reflection of his true belief that the colonists were *not* at Croatoan and were indeed lost.

White's claim regarding the agreement to winter in the Caribbean and return to Croatoan in the spring of 1591 is also rather impassive. According to White, Captain Cooke and the entire crew of the *Hopewell* agreed on August 19 to sail either to Hispaniola, St. John, or Trinidad, and "returne to visit our countreymen at Virginia"[22] after spending the winter in the Caribbean. The master of the *Moonlight*, however, informed Captain Cooke that he was unable to accompany them due to the *Moonlight's* poor condition and would sail directly to England. Cooke then "set his course for Trynidad," as planned, "which course we kept two dayes."[23] The colonists were *never mentioned again* in the account. On August 28 the winds changed, and White wrote, "wee were driuen to change our first determination for Trynidad, and stoode for the Ilands of Açores [Azores],"[24] some 2,500 miles northwest of the Caribbean. On September 19 they arrived at Flores in the Azores, where White described in great detail the various English ships and men-of-war assembled there and the Spanish prizes they had seized in the Caribbean.

They remained with the English fleet for a week, during which White's account described the meetings with some of the captains and their plans to intercept the Spanish treasure ships returning from the Caribbean. On September 27 "wee tooke our leaue of the Admirall and the whole fleete," and soon set sail for England, where on October 24 "we came in safetie, God be thanked, to an anker at Plymmouth."[25]

After the brief reference to the colonists on August 19 when the *Hopewell* left Roanoke, White's account did not include another word about them. Nothing else was mentioned regarding the plan to return to Croatoan in the spring, and no regret or concern about the colonists was noted in his account. As suggested, perhaps White's indifferent attitude may be taken as a further indication that he knew no one awaited him at Croatoan in August of 1590.

As mentioned above, most Lost Colony authors and historians have focused exclusively on just the morning of August 16 to August 19 of the seven-month voyage, and have assumed one of two scenarios. The first and less plausible of the two is that the Lost Colonists relocated from Roanoke directly to Croatoan, and that White would have been reunited with them if only he had sailed there in 1590. This theory ignores all the previously discussed reasons that Croatoan could *not* have been their relocation destination in 1587–88. The second scenario is that the Lost Colonists split into two groups, the primary group going on to the mainland settlement location, and the smaller group going to Croatoan to await White's return. Quinn, for example, postulated that the main group relocated to their originally intended destination at the Chesapeake—a theory flawed in itself—while a smaller group waited for White at Croatoan. As discussed earlier, there were likely a few colonists waiting for White at Croatoan in 1588, but all theories that have the main group of colonists settled far to the west or north of Roanoke seem highly improbable.

John White never ventured to Virginia again. The last record of his thoughts about his colonists were contained in the letter sent by him to Richard Hakluyt in 1593: "Thus committing the reliefe of my discomfortable company the planters in Virginia, to the merciful help of the Almighty, whom I most humbly beseech to helpe and comfort them, according to his most holy will and their good desire, I take my leaue."[26]

# 12

# Raleigh and Guiana;
# Rumors of Survivors
# 1594–1606

For about a decade after White failed to find his colony in 1590, there were no known attempts by the English to locate the Lost Colony, nor was there any serious discussion about further colonization in Virginia. Raleigh fell out of favor with Queen Elizabeth in 1591 after he secretly married Elizabeth Throckmorton, one of the queen's ladies-in-waiting, who were not permitted to marry without the queen's consent. Furthermore, "Bess" Throckmorton had the audacity to marry Raleigh, the queen's court favorite. Once the marriage was discovered, both Raleigh and his wife were imprisoned in the Tower of London for a time, in 1592. Although Raleigh was released from the Tower in August (his wife was not released until December) he remained out of favor with the queen for several years afterwards.

It was during this time that Raleigh's concern about the 1587 colony seems to have waned, at least temporarily, and was replaced with an obsession about the fabled legend of El Dorado and thoughts of establishing an English colony in South America. The El Dorado legend pre-dated the arrival of the Spanish and told of a fabulously rich tribe somewhere in the mountains of Guiana, where there was said to be so much gold that the natives covered their chief with it. The Spanish, who called the gilded king "El Dorado," had sent out a number of expeditions in search of the legendary kingdom of gold, but failed to locate it. Raleigh's research into the legend convinced him that El Dorado was located near the source of the Caroni River in Guiana. He believed that an English colony could be established there which would challenge Spain's dominance in the region. He also very likely hoped that a quest for potential riches and an English foothold in South America would rehabilitate his reputation and standing in the court of Queen Elizabeth. In 1595 he led the first of two expeditions to Guiana, but it produced little other than his exaggerated account, "The Discovery of Guiana," published in 1596.

There is one reference to the Lost Colony in his Guiana account. Raleigh wrote that at one point during his voyage some Spaniards came aboard and

> ... those poor soldiers having been many years without wine, a few draughts made them merry, in which mood they vaunted of Guiana and the riches thereof ... but [I] bred in them an opinion that *I was bound* only *for the relief of those English which I had planted in Virginia*, whereof the bruit was come among them; *which I had performed in my return, if extremity of weather had not forced me from the said coast*[1] [emphasis added].

The italicized portion of this quote has been used by some to demonstrate Raleigh's continued interest in the 1587 colonists and his intention to resupply them personally in 1596, but that conclusion is inaccurate. The full context of Raleigh's passage clearly indicates that his intention to sail "for the relief of those English which I had planted in Virginia" was just a deception to explain his presence in those waters. Just how serious Raleigh was about searching for the colonists on his return trip is highly questionable. He had assembled a fleet of five ships for the Guiana expedition, which would seem to indicate that he had the resources, but not the resolve, to launch a serious search for the Lost Colony. Six years later Raleigh would focus briefly on Virginia and the colonists one last time, as will be seen below, but once he was back in the Tower in 1603 he continued to fund several expeditions to Guiana, a further indication that, after 1603 at any rate, his interests were no longer involved with the abandoned colonists. In a letter dated January 9, 1610, John Chamberlain wrote to his friend Sir Dudley Carleton, clerk of the Privy Council, "Sir Walter Raleigh hath a ship come from Guiana, richly laden, they say with gold ore,"[2] but the rumors of gold would turn out to be baseless. Raleigh would make one more voyage to Guiana in 1616. The riches of El Dorado never materialized and his last voyage resulted in the death of Raleigh's son in Guiana and, due to his men's violation of a peace treaty with Spain, Raleigh's execution in 1618.

By the time of Raleigh's first Guiana venture in 1595, White's colonists had been missing for eight years. As proposed, at least thirty-five to forty and perhaps as many as eighty-five to ninety of them may have disappeared in the pinnace or pinnaces in 1588 or 1589 in a failed attempt to reach Newfoundland. Perhaps half or more of those who remained at the mainland settlement would likely have drowned when the hurricane surge inundated Croatoan and swept the mainland settlement away in September of 1589. It is conceivable that there were only a few colonists alive by 1590. The surge survivors, both colonists and natives alike, would have been forced to abandon the Outer Banks and the coastal mainland as well. As demonstrated in the previous chapter, Croatoan was still deserted in August of 1590, when White finally returned.

The aftermath of the hurricane and surge would have presented additional difficulties, to say the least, for the handful of English survivors, who may have been at different locations before the surge struck. As far as can be reasonably reconstructed, by the early summer of 1588 there would have been colonists at two locations. The majority of them were already situated at the nearby mainland settlement somewhere directly across from the Wokokon inlet. A much smaller group was at Croatoan, perhaps at an outpost near present-day Frisco, waiting for White's return. There would have been no need to man the outpost after White failed to appear by summer's end in 1588, and many—if not most—of the colonists would likely have given up on the colonization venture at that point. As proposed, the plans to sail to Newfoundland would likely soon have been conceived, raising the question of whether to build another pinnace.

The number and location of the remaining Lost Colonists in September of 1589 depends largely on the existence of that second pinnace. If the colonists decided to build a second vessel—a realistic possibility—then the few colonists who may have remained behind would almost certainly have moved to Croatoan. Some of these colonists could have survived a hurricane surge on the high bluffs at Frisco. If just the original pinnace was used in the attempt to reach Newfoundland, and sixty or so colonists remained behind, they may have still occupied the mainland settlement when the hurricane and surge struck. If any of these survived, they would have been driven to higher ground somewhere farther inland.

Shortly after the hurricane surge, therefore, the relatively few English survivors could have been scattered at distant locations. Those on the Outer Banks would have remained with the friendly Croatoans, while the mainland survivors may have been hopelessly separated and eventually integrated with other coastal tribal groups. The surviving colonists and Indians at Croatoan would have migrated to the mainland, at least temporarily, until their fields on the Outer Banks could be planted again. What became of this mixed group is open to speculation. Some may have migrated up the Neuse River, as the "Legend of the Coharie" claims, and then continued along the coast to the south. Any surviving Lost Colonists in this group would have become well integrated with the Croatoans, and in time there could have been mixed offspring among them. Eventually a number of Croatoans would return to the Outer Banks. Perhaps a few of them were young, first generation mixed offspring, ancestors of those Hatteras Indians who a century later would tell John Lawson about their ancestral claims to Raleigh's colonists.

It is certainly possible that a few of the original adult Lost Colony hurricane survivors were still alive by 1600. If any of the eleven original English children survived the 1589 surge, they would most likely be alive by 1600 and now be grown to young adulthood. If the two-year-olds, Virginia Dare and the unnamed Harvie child, did not perish with those on the pinnace, it seems doubtful that they could have lived through the hurricane surge. If they did survive, they would have been thirteen years old by 1600. Any of the eleven original children who still lived would now have spent half their lives in Virginia, and through integration with the native peoples, their English "identities" would have been significantly erased. It is also very possible that, after more than a decade of integration, there could have been admixed English/ Indian offspring from them as well. Given the matriarchal structure of many Algonquian tribes, including the Croatoans, these mixed offspring would be raised as native tribal members by the women.

According to the "Legend of the Coharie" a few of those original surviving colonists had lived through the 1589 tidal surge and the sickness that ensued, as well as the skirmish with the Tuscarora along the Neuse River. The legend names young George Howe, Jr., whose father had been killed by Indians at Roanoke on July 28, 1587, as a prominent survivor. George Howe, Jr., would have been in his twenties by 1600. This small group of surviving colonists and Indians, the legend claims, dwelt along the mainland coast south of the Neuse–Coree territory—for a number of years and slowly migrated southward towards Cape Fear. As discussed previously, there is reason to believe that the colonists' mainland settlement in 1588 was located in present-day Carteret, Pamlico, or Beaufort counties. A Croatoan/Coree alliance would have provided a safe corridor through Coree territory for the migrating group and also could explain James Sprunt's observation that the Cape Fear Coree had knowledge of the colonists more than two generations later.

Events occurred in 1602 and 1603 which could provide support, however slight, for the scenario that the Indians at Cape Fear may have known about the surviving Lost Colonists and what happened to them. By about 1600 Raleigh's attention had returned at least temporarily to Virginia. He may have been planning another expedition to America at this time, but nothing apparently came of it until 1602, when he dispatched Samuel Mace on a voyage to America with a twofold mission. The primary mission seems to have been commercial. Mace was to collect enough natural commodities such as sassafras and china root as well as whatever marketable items could be obtained through trade with the local Indians to make the expedition commercially profitable. Mace was also instructed to proceed farther up the coast towards Hatarask, the inlet at Roanoke, to locate possible survivors of the 1587 colony, who had by that time been missing for fifteen years.

Mace apparently sailed up the Atlantic coast to a point "fortie leagues to the Southwestward of Hatorask, in thirtie-foure degrees or thereabout,"[3] which would indicate that he reached Cape Fear. (The town of Southport, North Carolina, near the mouth of the Cape Fear River, is located at 33.9244 degrees north latitude.) Interestingly, Mace spent an entire month in that area accumulating the marketable plants, as well as commodities traded from the Indians to cover Raleigh's expenses for the voyage, but he made no attempt to continue north, as instructed, in search of survivors of the 1587 colony. According to what little information is available, bad weather was said to have been the reason for his failure to search farther north.

It is not known whether Samuel Mace brought back any information concerning the Lost Colonists from his 1602 voyage, but the following year Raleigh commissioned two ships commanded by Bartholomew Gilbert and Samuel Mace with the expressed intention of searching for the 1587 colonists. Gilbert apparently went ashore near the entrance to the Chesapeake, but was attacked and killed by Indians, and the remainder of his crew, consisting of just eleven men, returned to England in September. Nothing is known about the 1603 Samuel Mace voyage. Queen Elizabeth had died on March 24, 1603, and by the time Mace returned to England, Raleigh had been arrested for treason and had been imprisoned in the Tower of London since July 19. The Gilbert-Mace voyage was the last that Raleigh commissioned to Virginia.

Quinn speculated that Mace's 1603 voyage may have turned up valuable information concerning the survivors of the 1587 colony and their whereabouts. His hypothesis was based on the circulation of printed material in London at about this time containing references to survivors of the colony "weakly planted" among the Indians and producing mixed English-Indian offspring. The first reference was in George Weymouth's treatise to King James I which advocated the establishment of towns in America "in those parts thereof which long have been in possession of our English nation ... but weakly planted with the English and they more weakly defended from the invasions of the heathen amongst whom they dwell."[4]

The second reference was the play *Eastward Hoe,* written about 1604, which contained the following lines about settling in America: "A whole Country of English is there ... bred by those that were left there.... They have married with the Indians and make them bring forth as beautiful faces as any have in England...."[5] Quinn logically concluded that these two references would have made no sense either to King James or to London audiences unless information about Lost Colonists dwelling among the Indians had been widely circulated previously.

Quinn decided that Mace must have obtained the information during the 1603 voyage, about which—as mentioned—nothing is known. It is important to recall, however, that Quinn was a firm believer in the theory—now refuted—that all or most of the 1587 colony settled at the Chesapeake Bay after abandoning Roanoke. Therefore, Quinn incorrectly assumed that the information about the colonists could not have been acquired during the

1602 voyage, since it is known that Mace ventured no farther north than Cape Fear, some 240 miles short of the Chesapeake Bay.

It is suggested here that the information about survivors and offspring may have come from Mace's 1602 voyage. During the month Mace spent in the Cape Fear area, it is certain that he traded and interacted with the coastal Indians, possibly Sprunt's Corees, and could have learned from them that survivors of the English colony and their mixed offspring were living among a group of Hatteras Indians. Perhaps Mace even returned with stories about the "beautiful faces ... bred by those that were left there" fifteen years earlier. This conclusion might also provide a plausible explanation for the fact that Mace spent an entire month in the Cape Fear area in 1602 and made no attempt to venture farther north in search of the colonists. If he learned that nothing remained of the 1587 colony but admixed offspring, he may have decided that any further search was pointless.

In 1605 another reference to the Lost Colony surfaced from an unusual Anglo-French commercial venture, which was commissioned to establish trade contacts along the entire Atlantic coast from the Spanish-claimed territories to present-day Maine. The expedition was backed by a merchant in London, Pierre Beauvoir, and led by John Jerome and Bertrand Rocque. It consisted of two vessels, the *Castor and Pollux* and a pinnace, and a mixed English and French crew. There was also a physician/herbalist aboard to examine and collect medicinal herbs. They were instructed to proceed to Trinidad to acquire tobacco and then sail up the Atlantic coast to Croatoan where it was hoped they could make contact with some of the 1587 colonists, who might assist them in finding medicinal plants and especially milkweed, which was believed to be a valuable source of textile fiber.[6]

The intended stopover at Croatoan seems to indicate that in 1605 it was thought that some of the 1587 colonists were still alive and that they—or information about them—could be found at Croatoan. The source of their evidence about the Lost Colonists and Croatoan is not known, however, and it is possible that it came from White's account of his 1590 voyage, which by this time had been published by Hakluyt. As shown previously, Croatoan was uninhabited in 1590 as a result of the effects of the hurricane the previous year, but it is almost a certainty that Croatoan would have been reoccupied again by 1605. Whether any of the 1587 colonists could have been among those occupants is impossible to say.

The *Castor and Pollux* sailed on to St. Helena Sound—formerly Santa Elena—and began trading with the Indians there, while the pinnace lagged behind and was attacked by Indians at Guale, present-day Cumberland Island, Georgia. Captain Jerome and his pilot were killed, two others captured, and the remaining four escaped aboard the pinnace and caught up to Rocque at St. Helena Sound. The Spanish, however, had been alerted to their presence and in March, Spanish ships under Francisco Fernández de Écija captured the *Castor and Pollux* and the pinnace in St. Helena Sound and imprisoned the crew. Three of the captives, including Rocque, were interrogated and they told the Spanish that they did not know how many Englishmen might be found at Croatoan, but that they were sent by another Englishman named Walter Raleigh and came to settle fifteen (actually eighteen) years ago.[7]

Based on the information obtained from the interrogations, Florida Governor Pedro de Ybarra dispatched Francisco Fernández de Écija to search for the English alleged to be at Croatoan. His search of the coast started at Santa Elena near present-day Parris Island in Port Royal Sound, South Carolina. From there he proceeded northward perhaps as far as Cape Fear, but he was unable to continue and turned back to St. Augustine.

With the death of Queen Elizabeth, Raleigh's fortunes changed dramatically. Accused of plotting against the new monarch, James I, Raleigh was tried and convicted of treason and would spend the next thirteen years in the Tower. His rights of discovery in Virginia reverted to the crown, but some of his former friends, particularly Thomas Smyth and Richard Hakluyt, would be associated with what was to become the first permanent English colony in America. London and Bristol merchants and investors, including Smyth and Hakluyt, petitioned and were granted a royal charter to colonize between 34 and 41 degrees north latitude, which was referred to as "South Virginia." A Plymouth group, including Humphrey Gilbert's sons and Raleigh's adversary John Popham, who had presided as chief justice over the treason trial, received a charter for the territory between 38 and 45 north latitude, known as "North Virginia." The Plymouth Company got a head start and attempted to establish a trading settlement on the Kennebec River in present-day Maine, but it soon failed. Nothing further was accomplished by the Plymouth Company until 1620 when the permanent colony was settled at present-day Plymouth, Massachusetts. In late 1606 the London Company sent three ships and more than 100 colonists to South Virginia under the command of Christopher Newport and Bartholomew Gosnold, and they would established a permanent settlement on the James River.

The Spanish had been worried about an English settlement to the north for two decades, and they had conducted a number of unsuccessful searches for it. Francisco Fernández de Écija, who had searched for English colonists in 1605, would finally locate the English colony. That would not happen until several years later, however, and the colony he discovered was Jamestown.

# 13

# John Smith's A True Relation and the "Zúñiga Map" 1607–1608

It was not until the Jamestown settlement was established in 1607, a full twenty years after John White bade farewell to his colonists at Roanoke, that the next serious attempts were undertaken by the English to find out what happened to the 1587 colony. The Jamestown leaders had been instructed to acquire information about the Lost Colonists, and these efforts resulted in some tantalizing—but misunderstood—reports about the colonists' location and fate. The most definitive revelations were reported by two sources: Captain John Smith, one of the principals among the 104 original colonists who established the Jamestown settlement on May 16, 1607, and William Strachey, who would become Secretary of the Jamestown colony in 1610. Unfortunately, both Smith and Strachey thoroughly misinterpreted the information they obtained, and their errors would obstruct any real progress in the search for the truth about the Lost Colony for more than four centuries.

Smith had been a controversial figure during the voyage to the Chesapeake, where he arrived in shackles and accused of mutiny. However, the London-based Virginia Company, which sponsored the colonization expedition through a charter obtained from King James I, had enough faith in Smith's abilities to name him in a sealed letter as one of the seven council members to govern the Jamestown colony. There is little doubt that Smith proved to be an effective leader without whom the colony might not have survived. On September 10, 1607, Smith and other council members voted Edward Maria Wingfield out of office as president of the colony, and installed John Ratcliff in his place. Smith was made cape merchant, responsible for obtaining food from the Indians through trade, negotiations, or coercion if necessary.

It was during an early encounter with these Powhatan Indians that Smith heard what he believed to be the first news about the Lost Colonists. In December of 1607 Smith and two others were attacked by natives led by Opechancanough, younger brother of Wahunsunacock, as they traveled up the Chickahominy River, a northern tributary of the James River. Smith was spared, possibly because the Indians believed he was an important weroance or chief, but the other Englishmen were slain. The Indians conducted Smith to the village of Rasawrack, where he was fed and treated quite well by Opechancanough, who told Smith "what he knew of the dominions" and "of certaine men cloathed at a place called Ocanahonan, cloathed like me."[1] These, Smith concluded, could be none other than the lost 1587 colonists.

Smith was then taken to the village of Werowocomoco, the political center of the Powhatan chiefdom, where Wahunsunacock, whom the English would thereafter call "Powhatan," resided. Wahunsunacock also related some remarkable information to Smith about distant places where "there were people with short Coates, and Sleeves to the Elbowes, that passed that way in Shippes like ours.... The people cloathed at Ocamahowan, he also confirmed.... He described a countrie called Anone, where they have abundance of Brasse, and houses walled as ours."[2] Shortly after Smith's return to Jamestown in early January 1608, he and Captain Newport "agreed with the king of Paspahegh, to conduct two of our men to a place called Panawicke beyond Roonok, where he reported many men to be apparelled."[3] Smith recorded all these experiences, as well as the information he had obtained, in a lengthy letter which would later be published without his authorization under the title of *A True Relation*.

In July of 1608 a packet containing Smith's letter arrived from Jamestown "to a worshipfull friend" in England. The letter contained Smith's account of the first year of the Jamestown colony, including his month-long captivity in December and January, and the supposed references to the 1587 colonists. The narrative was accompanied by a roughly drawn and geographically confusing map of the regions surrounding Jamestown. Three notations on this map—which has come to be called the "Zúñiga Map" after the Spanish ambassador who managed to obtain it—contained references to the information Smith had learned about the lost 1587 colonists, and these have given rise to considerable speculation about the colonists' whereabouts ever since the map was rediscovered and finally published in 1890.

Although John Smith probably did not actually draw the map, he clearly had a role in its production, since it illustrated his movements during his captivity in 1607–08 and identified many of the Indian villages he mentioned in his account. The map, along with Smith's manuscript, came to England aboard the *Phoenix* with Captains Francis Nelson and John Martin in June 1608. The map and manuscript generated considerable excitement in London, but not, it seems, because of the potential Lost Colony references. About a month earlier Christopher Newport had arrived in England with the first delivery of letters and reports from the fledgling settlement of Jamestown. These first reports were not particularly encouraging. The lukewarm attitude in London about the new colony is illustrated by a letter from Sir Dudley Carleton, to John Chamberlain, in which he summarized the content of the letters from Jamestown:

> They write much commendations of the air and the soil and the commodities of it; but silver and gold have they none, and they cannot yet be at peace with the inhabitants of the countrie. They have fortified themselfs and built a small towne which they call Jamestowne, and so they date theyr letters, but the towne me thincks hath no gracefull name....[4]

That perception changed quickly after the arrival of the *Phoenix*. Martin, who most likely drew the map, brought news about a gold mine he had heard about from the Powhatan Indians. The mine was to be found far up the James River,[5] which is drawn in detail and highlighted on the Zúñiga Map, and is perhaps a good indication that Martin was its author. The primary importance of the map, at least in the eyes of Newport and Martin, was apparently not the possible references to the Lost Colony, but rather the gold which was four or five days up the James into the territory of the Monacans. Adding to the allure of the upper James River was the possibility that the elusive passage to the South Sea could also be found there. Smith had written in his letter "that within 4 or 5 daies journey of the falles was a great turning of salt water." These developments hastened Newport's return to Jamestown, loaded with gifts for Powhatan, who hopefully would be persuaded to provide guides in the exploration up the James River.

As soon as Newport arrived at Jamestown, Smith met with Chief Powhatan to arrange for the presentation of Newport's gifts and the accompanying ceremony which was tantamount to a coronation. Smith was highly critical of the entire arrangement, and—in a sign that he, at least, had not forgotten about the Lost Colonists—wondered "How, or why, Captaine Newport obtained such a private commission as not to returne without a lumpe of gold, a certainty of the south sea or one of the lost company of Sir Walter Rawley I know not."[6] Smith was particularly annoyed with the never-ending talk about gold, especially coming from those who "would rather starve and rot with idlenes, then be perswaded to do anything for their owne reliefe without constraint." At one point he remarked, "The worst mischiefe was our gilded refiners, with their golden promises, made all men their slaves with hope of recompense. There was no talke, no hope, no worke, but dig gold, wash gold, refine gold, load gold...."[7] The promise of gold was never realized, and, regarding the passage to the South Sea, Smith would later record Chief Powhatan as saying, "But for any salt water beyond the mountaines, the relations you have had from my people are false. Powhatans answer."[8]

In August Smith's letter was submitted for publication in London and titled *A True Relation*, the first account of the new Virginia colony. Martin's intriguing map, however, fell into the hands of the Spanish ambassador to England, Don Pedro de Zúñiga, who maintained an extensive spy network in England and apparently had a "confidential person" in the Virginia Council. Zúñiga had been warning King Philip III since January 1607, about the English plans to establish a colony in Virginia. Once the colony was settled in May, he persistently tried to encourage King Philip to "up-root" it. In one letter he urged the king to "command that such a bad project should be up-rooted now while it can be done so easily." Again in December Zúñiga wrote, "Will your majesty give orders that measures be taken in time; because now it will be very easy, and quite difficult afterwards, when they have taken root, and if they are punished in the beginning, the result will be that no more will go there."[9]

The so-called Zúñiga Map was sent to King Philip, and it eventually made its way into the royal archives located in Simancas in the province of Valladolid, Spain. It remained there unnoticed until historian Alexander Brown (1843–1906) discovered it while in Spain researching for his book, *Genesis of the United States*, which was published in 1890. The most detailed and accurate feature of the Zúñiga Map is naturally the area surrounding Jamestown, including the James River, since this territory was the first to be explored by the English settlers. The map becomes increasingly unintelligible as the distance from Jamestown increases. ⎮

All three of the Lost Colony notations are located on the most problematic part of the map, the area south of Jamestown, where the geography is vague and inaccurate. There is not even consensus among scholars, in fact, as to the identities of the rivers depicted there. The author's close rendition of the southern quadrant of the Zúñiga Map, re-oriented on a north-south axis, is shown below. Included are the names of the more important locations (with their original spellings) as they appeared on the map, although as stated the overall geography depicted south of Jamestown is confusing and unreliable. The three names with the asterisks are directly associated with the Lost Colonists, and those three—indicated by the letters A, B, and C—were accompanied by handwritten notations on the original map which related to the colonists. The word "Warraskoyack" did not appear on the original Zúñiga Map, but has been added here for reference purposes because it is the name of the location associated with notation "C." Those three notations are of particular importance, for they are the basis for the fascination with the Zúñiga Map on the following page, at least as it pertains to the Lost Colony.

The notation for "A," which was written next to "Pakrakanick" on the original map, was "Here remayneth 4 men clothed that came from Roonock to Ocanahawan."

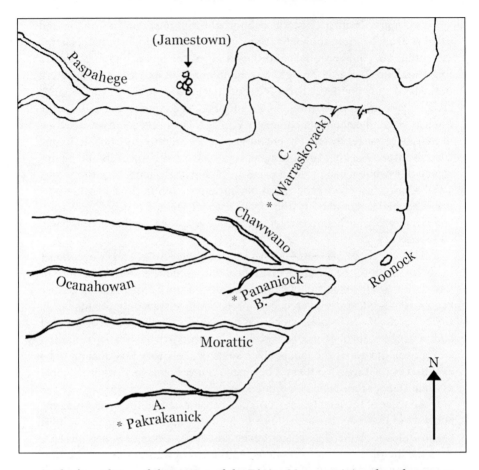

Author's rendition of the portion of the Zúñiga Map containing the references to the Lost Colony. The * indicates direct association with the Lost Colonists; the A, B and C are explained in the text.

The notation for "B," written next to "Pananiock" was, "Here the King of Paspahegh reported our men to be and wants to go."

The notation for "C," written next to "Warraskoyack" was, "Here [the king of] Paspahegh and 2 of our own men landed to go to Pananiock."

The first observation to be made is that Smith's influence on the production of the map was quite extensive. As mentioned, the original drawing illustrates his movements during his captivity in December and January. Moreover, most of the details in the map notations, in fact, were borrowed directly from passages in Smith's *A True Relation*. This offers an advantage for research purposes, because the map was clearly intended to illustrate passages found in Smith's text. Consequently, the confusing notations found on the Zúñiga Map can be compared with the information in *A True Relation*, upon which the map was based.

Notation "A," for example, is a summary of the two passages in Smith's *A True Relation*, the first of which described the information he obtained during his captivity by Opechancanough in December of 1607: "What he [Opechancanough] knew of the Dominions he spared not to acquaint me with, as of certaine men cloathed at a place called Ocanahonan, cloathed like me." Shortly thereafter in the text Smith related the information he received when Opechancanough delivered him to Chief Powhatan at Werawocomoco: "Many Kingdomes hee [Powhatan] described to me…. The people clothed at Ocanahowan, he alsoe confirmed." However, the number of "men cloathed"— "four" on the Zúñiga Map—is not mentioned in *A True Relation*. Pakrakanick, too, while noted on the Zúñiga Map, is not mentioned in *A True Relation*.

Notation "B" is a summary of the arrangement Smith and probably Captain Newport had made with the Paspahegh chief in January of 1608. As cited earlier in *A True Relation*, "We had agreed with the king of Paspahegh to conduct two of our men to a place called Panawicke, beyond Roanoke, where he reported many men to be apparelled." There is a slight discrepancy, however, between this passage in *A True Relation* and the notation on the Zúñiga Map. The former names the place where the "apparelled" men were as "Panawicke," but the latter refers to it as "Pananiock." Panawicke/Pananiock, an important reference, will be addressed separately in a later chapter.

Notation "C" simply identifies the starting point, Warraskoyack, for the planned expedition to Pananiock (or Panawicke). This trip, however, never took place, as is explained in *A True Relation*: "Wee landed him [the Paspahegh chief] at Warraskoyack, where playing the villaine, and deluding us for rewards, [he] returned within three or foure dayes after without going further."[10]

These 1608 references on the Zúñiga Map and in Smith's *True Relation* were the first tantalizing allusions seeming to suggest that some of John White's Lost Colonists were still alive at locations which have continued to defy accurate identification.

# 14

## The "Men Cloathed" at Ocanahonan and Pakrakanick
### 1607–1608

### The Second Institutionalized *Assumption*

There are three locations on the Zúñiga Map with possible connections to the Lost Colonists: Ocanahowan/Ocanahonan; Pakrakanick; and Pananiock/Panawicke. Regarding the first two, Ocanahonan and Pakrakanick, the following would summarize what was understood about those locations and the existence of Lost Colonists in June 1608, when Smith's letter and the map were sent to England: The "men cloathed," presumably John White's 1587 colonists, had traveled from Roanoke to a place called Ocanahonan, and then continued on to Pakrakanick some distance farther south.

It will be useful to keep in mind that the *source of all the information* on the Zúñiga Map and in Smith's *A True Relation* supposedly relating to the Lost Colony was the Powhatan Indians. It is certainly possible that the Powhatans had heard about clothed men who were rumored to be at distant places called Ocanahonan and Pakrakanick, well beyond Powhatan territory. It is far less likely that they would have been able to identify them as English or as having dwelt originally at Roanoke, and it is virtually impossible to believe that they could have known them to be members of 1587 colony specifically. It is far more reasonable to infer that the latter conclusions—the clothed men were English, they originally came from Roanoke, and they were members of the 1587 colony—were simply assumptions made by Smith, who, as one of the Jamestown leaders, had been instructed to search out information about the missing colonists. Those conclusions will prove to be completely mistaken, and together they represent the second institutionalized assumption cited in the Preface.

It is obvious that the geography of the Zúñiga Map is woefully inaccurate

134

and confusing, particularly south of Jamestown, and that has led to a variety of opinions about their possible locations. Looking at the illustration of the Zúñiga Map, it would appear that the first major waterway to the immediate south of the James River could be a poorly drawn continuum made up of Albemarle Sound, the Chowan, and the Roanoke Rivers, particularly since "Chawwano" is indicated as one of its branches. However, this is contradicted by another large river farther south labeled "Morattic" [Moratoc], which was what the Roanoke River was called at that time.

It is evident that whoever drew the Zúñiga Map—and Smith too since he clearly had a hand in its production—knew little of the geography to the south. They also evidently did not have available to them a copy of the 1590 White/de Bry Map, which offered a distorted view of the Chesapeake Bay and its adjoining areas, but had fairly reliably portrayed what the Zúñiga Map did not, i.e., the tributary rivers of Albemarle and Pamlico sounds. It appears that most of what they did know was related to them by the Powhatan Indians, who themselves had only a limited knowledge of significant events and places beyond their own territorial boundaries.

Historians have claimed an assortment of locations for Ocanahonan and Pakrakanick. Alexander Brown, the discoverer of the Zúñiga Map, concluded that Ocanahonan was on the upper Pamlico or Tar River and that Pakrakanick was "probably on the Neuse River, near Sampson County."[1] Stephen Weeks claimed that Pakrakanick was "on the upper waters of the Neuse" and that Ocanahonan was on the south side of the Roanoke River.[2] Samuel A'Court Ashe placed Pakrakanick "on the Tar or upper Pamlico River" and Ocanahonan on the upper Chowan or Nottoway.[3] Philip Barbour placed Ocanahonan "near the modern Virginia–North Carolina boundary, west of the Chowan River."[4] All of these locations, as varied as they may be, share one common thread. They all place Ocanahonan and Pakrakanick somewhere at or near the fall line separating the Carolina coastal plain and the Piedmont plateau.

It is proposed here that Ocanahonan and Pakrakanick were located considerably farther *west* in present-day North Carolina than has previously been thought, and that this more westerly geographic location—a critical factor—will explain what the Powhatans were actually relating to Smith and Strachey, and at the same time will refute Strachey's later claims about Lost Colony survivors. Ocanahonan, the evidence will show, was located far to the west of the fall line and well into the Carolina Piedmont. Pakrakanick was farther south from there.

Evidence to support this conclusion can be found in several sources. In 1609 the Virginia Company provided information about the location of Ocanahonan and Pakrakanick in their instructions to Sir Thomas Gates, the newly appointed governor of Jamestown. Those instructions, though somewhat confusing, did clearly state that the first leg of the journey from Jamestown to Ocanahonan was to "goe by Indian guides from Jame's forte to *Winocke* by water...."[5] "Winocke" and its many spelling variations will help to identify the route to Ocanahonan. Some of the known variations of "Winocke" include Wyanoke, Wainock, Haynokes, Oenock, Anock, Aeno, Anone, Anoeg, Enoke, and Enoe.[6]

The Winocke tribe, long extinct, dwelt in the Piedmont region of Virginia and North Carolina. The name first appears in the historical record as "Anone" in Smith's *A True Relation* cited earlier: "After good deliberation, hee [Powhatan] began to describe mee the Countreys beyond the Falles.... Beyond them he described people with short Coates, and Sleeves to the Elbowes, that passed that way in Shippes like ours.... The people cloathed at Ocanahonan he also confirmed, and the Southerly Countries also ... he described a countrie called Anone, where they have abundance of Brasse, and houses walled as ours."[7]

Smith's "Anone" is undoubtedly what Strachey would later call "Anoeg." Strachey wrote that the Anoeg, "whose howses are built as ours," dwelt to the southwest of Powhatan territory "ten daies distant from us...." Strachey also wrote about a servant of Powhatan with the interesting name of "Weinock"—itself a variation of "Winocke"—who often traveled to Anoeg, which "stands at the foote of the mountains," and he "could repeat many words of their language."[8] By these accounts it seems clear that Anone/Anoeg was located well "beyond the Falles" and "at the foote of the mountains," which would be the Blue Ridge/Appalachian Mountains.

Strachey also wrote, "at Peccarecamek and Ochanahoen the people have howses built with stone walles, and one story above another." That line is actually part of a larger passage describing the country far west of the fall line in the foothills of the Blue Ridge Mountains. Here is the entire passage:

> From the falls [of the James] our men have heretofore marched (as the river led them) about forty or fifty miles ... all along from the north, by a sowth-west lyne ... are those mountains; from them fall certaine brooks, which after come to be the five principall navigable rivers [James, York, Rappahannock, Potomoc, and the Patuxent Rivers] ... These waters wash from the rocks such glistening tinctures.... Sure it is that some minerals have ben there found.... This high land is, in all likelyhoods, a pleasant tract, and the mowld fruictfill, especially what may lye so-ward; where, at Peccarecamek and Ochanahoen, by relation of Machumps, the people have howses built with stone walles, and one story above another....[9]

In this passage Strachey was accurately describing the Piedmont region of Virginia, which stretches westward "from the falls" (of the James River in this case) across the rolling terrain to the foot of the Blue Ridge Mountains. "Our men" traveled west from the falls to the foothills of the mountains, far enough to conclude that "the five principall navigable rivers" are formed from "certaine brooks" in those mountains. Strachey wrote that Ocanahonan and Pakrakanick "lye so-ward" from "this high land," that is, somewhere southward from the foothills of the Blue Ridge Mountains in Virginia. This area is far west of the fall line and well into the Carolina Piedmont.

John Lederer's expeditions in 1669 and 1670 will confirm the location of Smith's and Strachey's Anone/Anoeg, and can provide additional clues to the approximate whereabouts of Ocanahonan. Lederer made three expeditions to the Appalachian Mountains and became the first known European to see beyond the Blue Ridge Mountains. During the second expedition, illustrated by Lederer's dotted line on the map below, he visited the Indian town of "Oenock," a known variation of "Anone/Anoeg" and "Winocke," the location indicated in the Virginia Council's instructions sixty years earlier as the first leg of the journey from Jamestown to Ocanahonan. The Indian village of Oenock is indicated on the Lederer map below at the foot of the Blue Ridge Mountains, just south of the Virginia-Carolina border (north again is to the right).[10]

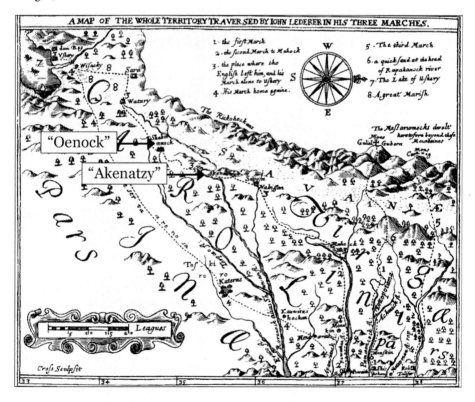

Lederer's second expedition southwest through the Piedmont to the Blue Ridge Mountains; Oenock and Akenatzy are indicated.

Lederer's previous stop had been at Akenatzy [Occaneechi]—also highlighted on the map—an Indian village in southern Virginia on an island at the junction of the Dan and Roanoke Rivers. The Indian Trading Path is sometimes called the "Occaneechi Path" after this small but important tribe, and was a 500 mile corridor of trails extending from present-day Petersburg, Virginia, to Augusta, Georgia. The Occaneechi acted as middlemen in trading arrangements with the interior tribes.[11] Weinock, the previously mentioned servant of Powhatan who made frequent trips to Anoeg, would likely have used part of the Occaneechi Path.

Lederer left Akenatzy on June 14, "pursuing a South-southwest course," but although Oenock was "not in a direct line above thirty odde miles distant from Akenatzy, yet the Ways were such, and obliged me to go far about, that I reached not *Oenock* until the sixteenth."[12] Since the Occaneechi village at the junction of the Dan and Roanoke Rivers was perhaps ten miles north of the Carolina border, "Winock/Oenock" can be reliably located about twenty miles (as the crow flies) into North Carolina to the southwest of Akenatzy.

From there to Ocanahonan, though, the Council's instructions read only "From thence [Winock] to Manqueock."[13] By "Manqueock" the Council may have been referring to "Mongoack," the tribe Ralph Lane heard about in 1585–86 and described as "another kinde of Sauages, dwelling more to the Westward of the said Riuer [Moratoc/Roanoke]."[14] John White placed the Mongoack south or southwest of the Moratoc River, which would put them somewhere south (left) of Oenock on the Lederer Map.

From there, however, the Virginia Council's instructions became indecipherable other than to say that Ocanahonan was south from Manqueock, and that Pakrakanick was beyond Ocanahonan. It is evident from these references, at least, that Ocanahonan and Pakrakanick were south or perhaps south-southwest of Winocke/Oenock and Manqueock/Mongoack respectively. The specific sites of Ocanahonan and Pakrakanick will prove to be less important, however, than the fact that they were located a considerable distance west of the Carolina fall line. The documentary evidence demonstrates that Ocanahonan and Pakrakanick were located somewhere towards the western portion of the North Carolina Piedmont region, and this will be a key factor in identifying the "men cloathed" and the "howses built as ours."

The location of Ocanahonan and Pakrakanick well into the Carolina Piedmont puts a new light on the information Smith and Strachey obtained from the Powhatans and suggests a very different conclusion about the "men clothed" there: they were *not Englishmen.*

Long before the first Roanoke voyage in 1584, Spanish and French explorers had been venturing through what is now North and South Carolina. By 1526 Lucas Vázquez de Ayllón had explored the Cape Fear River and established the short-lived settlement of San Miguel de Gualdape, probably at the mouth of the Pee Dee River. In 1540 Hernando de Soto explored present-day Georgia and South Carolina and reached the Appalachian Mountains of North Carolina. As mentioned earlier, in 1562 Jean Ribault built Charlesfort, named after French King Charles IX, on what is now Parris Island, South Carolina.

The most fascinating expeditions—and the most illuminating for the topic at hand—were led by Spanish explorer Juan Pardo, who led two excursions through the Piedmont of present-day North Carolina to the Appalachian Mountains between December of 1566 and March of 1568. After reinforcing the village of Santa Elena by constructing Fort San Felipe in 1566 (at the site of the abandoned French Charlesfort), Pardo led an expedition of 125 men northward into the Piedmont of present-day North Carolina, stopping at many villages along the way. In January 1567, the Spaniards reached Joara, the thriving Indian center of commerce. With the consent of the principal chief, Joara Mico, they built Fort San Juan, the first European settlement in the interior of North Carolina, predating Raleigh's first Roanoke voyage by seventeen years. Because of its favorable location at the foot of the Appalachian Mountains and its nearby salt mines, Joara was in its day a major Indian crossroads and trading center. With Pardo's military backing, Joara Mico extended his regional dominance even further.

Pardo expanded Spanish sovereignty as well, retaining his base at Joara and claiming additional territory for Spain. He constructed several forts in the Piedmont, as well as southward toward Santa Elena, which was hoped at the time would become the capital town of the Spanish territories in La Florida. Pardo's plan was to establish part of an inland route that would eventually reach Zacatecas, Mexico, by which the Spanish could transport the precious metals they hoped to find, without the threats posed by French and English ships along the coast.

What is particularly revealing is that along his route from Santa Elena into the present-day Carolina Piedmont, Pardo's men *taught the natives how to build wooden houses and grainaries* to be used exclusively by the Spanish. Each house was to be kept supplied with corn by the local chiefs or caciques, and the Indians were strictly prohibited from entering these houses without permission from the Spanish. Those villages that could not provide the requisite amount of corn would be obliged to supply deerskins and, lacking that, salt. As directed, the Indians built these houses at various locations, which served as chain of way stations for the Spanish. If necessary, some of the corn could be transported southward to resupply the fort and settlement at Santa Elena.

Another very notable and relevant fact is that the houses built by the Indians for the Spanish were *elevated*, and the storage rooms for corn were built on the second story.[15] The narrator of the Pardo expeditions wrote of "elevated houses" and "two elevated rooms" and "a good new wooden house and inside it an elevated room with a certain quantity of maize" and "a new house of wood with a large elevated room full of maize which the cacique had built by the command of the captain for the service of His Majesty."[16] The diagram below shows the names and approximate locations of the many villages along the route of Pardo's expeditions[17] where houses with elevated rooms were built by the Indians for the Spanish.

What Machumps related regarding the existence of "howses built as ours … and one story above another" at faraway places to the south would have been especially enticing to Strachey. The same kind of two-story houses with

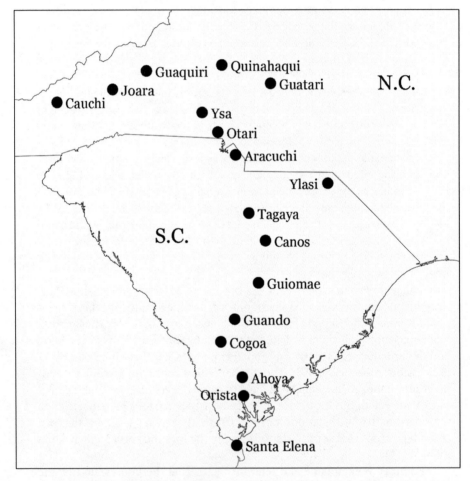

**Locations of the villages where Indians built houses with elevated storerooms for Pardo's Spaniards (courtesy Michael Gayle).**

corn lofts were built at Jamestown after the arrival of Sir Thomas Gates and his Bermuda castaways, including Strachey, in 1610. Ralph Hamor wrote of Jamestown, "The Towne [Jamestown] it selfe by the care and prouidence of Sir Thomas Gates ... is reduced into a hansome forme, and hath in it two faire rowes of howses, all of framed Timber, two stories, and an vpper Garret, or Corne loft high."[18] It is easy to understand how Strachey would have jumped to the hasty conclusion that the clothed people who taught the Indians to build these structures must have been Raleigh's Lost Colonists. Machumps' description was quite accurate; the Indians *were* taught to build two-story buildings with elevated lofts for maize. They were taught, however, by Pardo's Spaniards and not by any Englishmen.

When word of a possible French attack at Santa Elena reached Pardo at the end of February 1567, he started back to Santa Elena and arrived in early March. Six months later Pardo and a force of about 100 men headed back to the North Carolina Piedmont, and during the journey they were fed from the storehouses the Indians had built for them. Pardo stopped at Tacoe (near present-day Asheville) and at Cauchi (near Marshall) before traveling into East Tennessee, where he found some of his men besieged by Indians. During Pardo's absence the Indians had turned against the Spanish garrisons, and Pardo eventually returned to Santa Elena. By 1568 the Spanish had vacated the Carolina Piedmont.

Stories about these strange intruders and their activities in the present-day Carolinas spread far and wide over the Indian trading routes and were the source of all the fragments of information told to the Jamestown colonists about "men cloathed," "howses built as ours," and "people with short Coates and Sleeves to the Elbowes" at places to the south called Ocanahonan and Pakrakanick. It is now evident that it was the Spanish, not the English, who taught the Indians to build those houses with second-story granaries.

There are other clues as well which demonstrate both the impact of the Spanish on the Siouan Piedmont tribes and the extent to which the Spanish presence had become part of the native oral traditions. In a 1654 letter from Francis Yeardley to John Ferrar of the Virginia Company, Yeardley wrote that a Tuscarora Indian had described "a great nation called the Haynokes (the previously discussed Winocke), who had valiantly resisted the Spaniards' further northern progress."[19] Obviously, nearly a century later, memories of Pardo and his men were even known among the Tuscarora, the Iroquoian tribe that dwelt on the inner Coastal Plain east of the fall line.

During Lederer's visit to Oenock he "took particular notice of small Wheels serving for this purpose [counting] among the *Oenocks*, because I have heard that the *Mexicans* use the same,"[20] another indication of Spanish influence to the north of the Carolina Piedmont. The Oenocks also planted "an abundance of Grain" according to Lederer, and had storehouses which were large enough to "supply all the adjacent parts."[21] In 1916 Frederick Olds, a colleague of Samuel A'Court Ashe and "father" of the North Carolina Museum of History, wrote that the Eno/Winocke were allied with the Siouan tribes and "had well-built houses and barns, in which they stored grain and other supplies."[22]

There is clear evidence of Spanish influence as far north as the Indian village of Sara, perhaps 60 miles from the Virginia border (see Lederer's map). Upon leaving Oenoke, Lederer traveled fifty-four miles to the southwest along the east slope of the mountains, passing Shakor and Watary until he reached Sara. "Sara," Lederer wrote, "is not far distant from the Mountains, which here lose their height, and change their course and name: for they run due West, and receive from the Spaniards the name of *Suala*."[23] The historical record is clear: It was these Spaniards—not a handful of imagined Englishmen—whose influence prevailed throughout the Piedmont of North Carolina in the 16th and 17th centuries.

There is one reference in the Jamestown accounts indicating that the English had concluded that Ocanahonan was indeed a Spanish settlement. On page 110 of Smith's 1624 *Generall Historie* he made mention of "Ocanahowan ... where they report are Spaniards inhabiting." Smith's line was borrowed from Hamor's *A True Discourse*, which had been published in 1615 and included a report about five Jamestown mutineers who attempted to escape to a "Spanish plantation" at "Ocanahoen." This may well explain why all of Smith's references to the "men cloathed" and two-story dwellings at Ocanahonan and Pakrakanick in his *True Relation*, the source of so much earlier speculation about the Lost Colonists, were completely absent from his later *Generall Historie*.

All of this points convincingly to the conclusion that Ocanahonan and Pakrakanick are completely irrelevant to the Lost Colony or its fate. The Powhatan Indians were not relating old stories of *Englishmen* who had gone from Ocanahonan to Pakrakanick, but of *Spaniards* and their activities through the Carolina Piedmont. And of course they certainly had not originally come "from Roonock" as the author of the Zúñiga Map inaccurately assumed.

Cartographer John Speed's 1676 map is included below for reference purposes. This map, based heavily on Lederer's 1669–70 expeditions and Ogilby's 1674 map, was one of the earliest attempts to map the Carolina interior. While not geographically perfect, Speed's map was the most accurate to date. Inserts for Jamestown, the fall line of the James River, Oenock, Akanatzy, Sara, and the Cape Fear River have been added to show their relative locations.

As mentioned earlier, Powhatan's servant "Weinock" often traveled to Oenock, where "howses are built as ours" and which, according to Strachey,

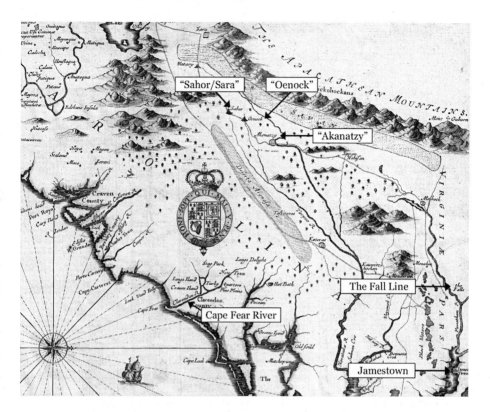

"Sahor/Sara"    "Oenock"    "Akanatzy"    The Fall Line    Cape Fear River    Jamestown

**The locations of Ocanahonan and Pakrakanick would have been near the foot of the mountains south of Oenock and west of the Cape Fear River on this portion of John Speed's 1676 "Map of Carolina."**

was "ten daies distant from us." According to the map's legend (not shown here) Weinock's trip from the falls to Oenock would have covered about 240 miles, or twenty-four miles per day, a seemingly realistic estimate for an Indian travelling over familiar routes. Again, this map uses the contemporary English compass orientation, so Ocanahonan and Pakrakanick would have been located "at the foote of the mountains," as Strachey noted, some distance to the left of Oenock. Note also the location of Oenock in relation to the Cape Fear River, which was called Clarendon River at that time. Since we know that Ocanahonan and Pakrakanick were south (left) of Oeneok at the foot of the mountains, that would seem to place them some distance west (up) from the Cape Fear River and well into the present-day North-South Carolina Piedmont where Pardo led his expeditions between 1566 and 1568.

The Jamestown-era references to Ocanahonan and Pakrakanick had everything to do with the Spanish, and nothing whatsoever to do with the English. Opechancanough, Wahunsunacock, and Machumps told the Jamestown colonists stories they had heard of clothed men and oddly built houses at distant places called Ocanahonan and Pakrakanick. It was only Smith's imagination that suggested the clothed men were English and remnants of the 1587 Lost Colony. That erroneous conclusion represents the 2nd institutionalized assumption which has impeded Lost Colony theory for more than 400 years. Likewise, Strachey's claim that it was the Lost Colonists who taught the Indians to build European-style houses was nothing but an extension of Smith's baseless conjecture. Ocanahonan and Pakrakanick are completely irrelevant to the Lost Colony narrative.

# 15

# The "Men Apparalled" at Pananiock/Panawicke
# 1607–1608

Although Smith and Strachey misinterpreted the information related to them by the Powhatans about the "cloathed men" at Ocanahonan and Pakrakanick, which had no relevance at all to the 1587 Lost Colonists, the same cannot be said of Pananiock and Panawicke. There is a good chance that the report of "apparelled" men at Pananiock and Panawicke may have been a legitimate reference to the 1587 colonists. Pananiock and Panawicke, it will be seen, were two names for the same place, and its location had been known to the English since 1584.

As previously cited, notations "B" and "C" on the Zúñiga Map both refer to Pananiock. Notation "B," written next to "Pananiock" was, "Here the King of Paspahegh [Wowinchopunck] reported our men to be and wants to go." As already mentioned, Notation "B" parallels a passage in Smith's *A True Relation* regarding an arrangement made with the Paspahegh chief in January of 1608: "We [Smith and probably Newport] had agreed with the king of Paspahegh to conduct two of our men to a place called Panawicke, beyond Roanoke, where he reported many men to be apparelled."[1] Also mentioned in the previous chapter is the discrepancy between the location of the "appareled" men in *A True Relation*—Panawicke—and that on the Zúñiga Map—Pananiock. It is clear from the context of these passages that both names refer to the place to which the Paspahegh chief had agreed to guide the English, and therefore "Pananiock" on the Zúñiga Map undoubtedly refers to the same location as Smith's "Panawicke" in his *True Relation*.

Notation "C," written next to "Warraskoyack" reads, "Here [the king of] Paspahegh and 2 of our own men landed to go to Pananiock." Notation "C" simply identifies the starting point, Warraskoyack bordering the James River, for the planned expedition to Pananiock (or Panawicke). For reasons that are not clear—according to Smith, the Paspahegh king [Wowinchopunck] was a "villaine ... deluding us for rewards"—the trip was never completed. As mentioned, Wowinchopunck "returned within three or foure dayes after without going further." As will be seen below, the failure to complete the trip to Pananiock may have been a missed opportunity to learn about the Lost Colonists.

As to the location of Pananiock, it would seem from Smith's brief reference alone that Pananiock had to be somewhere to the south of Roanoke. Smith wrote in *A True Relation* that Pananiock (Panawicke) was located "beyond Roonok, where he [the Paspahegh chief, Wowinchopunck] reported many men to be apparelled." Since Smith was writing about Pananiock/Panawicke from his location at Jamestown, it would seem that "beyond Roonok" was intended to mean that the location of Pananiock/Panawicke was *beyond Roanoke from Jamestown*, that is, somewhere *to the south of Roanoke*. The Zúñiga Map, as confusing as it may be, seems to corroborate that much at least.

Nevertheless, for more than a century various opinions have been put forward asserting other locations for Pananiock. As far back as 1890 Stephen B. Weeks declared in his published paper that Pananiock "is the name given to the territory known to the earlier explorers as Dasamonguepeuk,"[2] which was the village on the coastal mainland immediately west of Roanoke.

Samuel A'Court Ashe, in his 1908 *History of North Carolina*, wrote that Pananiock was located near the mouth of the Moratoc and Chowan Rivers at the western end of present-day Albemarle Sound. Although it is difficult to see how the placement of Pananiock on the Zúñiga Map could support such a location, Ashe wrote, "The Indian account [as he referred to the Zúñiga Map] places Pananiock, where White's colony settled, between the Moratoc and Chowan Rivers...."[3] Ashe's interpretation seems to have been based largely upon Ralph Lane's description of the area as "goodly highlands," and, since it was "substantially 'fifty miles into the interior,'" Ashe apparently determined that Pananiock must have been located there. It should be noted that Ashe was a proponent of the previously mentioned theory that the 1587 colonists relocated to the Chowan River in present-day Bertie County, which in turn laid the groundwork used to support the fort symbol theory discussed earlier.

More recently Lee Miller made a similar assertion, claiming that the precise location of Panawioc (Pananiock) "appears on the Zúñiga Map on Cashie Creek, Bertie County."[4] Miller added to this claim by declaring that "Panawioc" is an Algonquian word which translates as *Place of Foreigners*, an apt name for a site where they *reported our men to be*."[5]

Each of these assertions about the location of Pananiock conformed to each proponent's theory about the Lost Colony, but they are challenged by well-established documentary evidence to the contrary. Virginia scholar Lyon Gardiner Tyler, editor of the *Narratives of Early Virginia*, had noted in 1907 that Panawicke was "The Panauuaioc of Hakluyt and of DeBry's map."[6] Philip Barbour, in his *The Complete Works of John Smith* also recognized that "Panawick ('Panawaioc,' etc.) appears on Theodore de Bry's map of North Carolina (based on John White's map)."[7] Tyler's and Barbour's references to Hakluyt and de Bry are accurate. Evidence from the White/de Bry map and from a passage in Hakluyt's *Principal Navigations* make it clear that a) it had been fairly well established that Panawicke and Panauuaioc were names for the same place, b) the English knew of this place as early as 1584, and c) they knew it was located between the Neuse and Pamlico Rivers.

Portion of the 1590 White–de Bry Map showing the location of "Panauuaiock."

The English first learned of that location during the Amadas/Barlowe reconnaissance voyage in 1584. The account of that voyage was published a few years later by Hakluyt and clearly places Pananuaioc between the Pamlico and Neuse Rivers: "Adioyning to this countrey aforesaid called Secotan beginneth a countrey called Pomouik 'or Pananuaioc' ... belonging to another king whom they call Piamacum, and this king is in league with the next king adioyning towards the setting of the Sunne, and the countrey Newsiok, situate vpon a goodly riuer called Neus."[8]

There can be no doubt that Pananuaioc and Panauuaioc were names for the same place and that its location was somewhere between the present-day Pamlico and Neuse Rivers, although, as Barbour noted, its precise location has not been determined. On the portion of the White/de Bry Map above, for example, Panauuaiock may refer to the name of a particular Indian town or village, as illustrated by the circle, but it could also refer to the tribe and territory, or "countrey" as the area between the two rivers was called in the Amadas-Barlowe account. This tribe would later be known as the Pamlico Indians.

It is important to note here that "Panauuaiock" and its variations, "Panawicke," "Pananiock," and "Pomouik" must *not* be confused, as Hamilton McMillan did,[9] with the village of "Pomeiock," which White visited and sketched in 1585. Both Panauuaiock and Pomeiock are shown on the White/de Bry map above at two different locations entirely, with Pomeiock placed near present-day Lake Mattamuskeet.

Obviously, most of the confusion regarding 16th and 17th century English place-names has to do with the variety of spelling inconsistencies found in the different source documents. As mentioned earlier, for example, there was a contradiction between the name "Pananiock" used on the Zúñiga Map and the name "Panawicke" used in A *True Relation,* but they both clearly refer to the same place. Spelling discrepancies were plentiful in the Roanoke and Jamestown accounts, particularly when it came to place-names, which were mostly Anglicized forms of Algonquian words. English spelling, of course, had not yet been standardized, resulting in various forms of the same word, found even within the same text, penned by the same author. Fortunately, in the case of Pananiock and Panawicke the spelling variations were *not* simply arbitrary. Both of these words very likely underwent a discernable spelling transition during the transcription process, and that process can further demonstrate linguistically that Pananiock, Panawicke, and Panauuaiock were identical locations.

In 16th and 17th century English orthography, the classical digraph "double-u" (uu), from which our "w" derives its name, was still being used on *formal* documents and maps, such as the White/de Bry, even though the letter "w" had been used in informal writing for quite some time. When words with the "double-u" digraph were copied from these maps, the "double-u" was usually transcribed as the more common and concise letter "w" and then often mistaken for letters with similar strokes as the word was subsequently recopied. As Jonathan Culpeper put it in his *History of English*, "The problem with double <u> was legibility. The characters <u, uu , i, n, m> were all written with straight down-strokes or 'minims' and were thus in danger of being confused."[10]

Consequently, Smith's "Panawicke" and the Zúñiga Map's "Pananiock," as they were written in 1608, can easily be seen as later versions of the "Panauuaiock," which appeared on the White/de Bry "Americae pars, Nunc Virginia" map published by de Bry in 1590. Substituting the original double-u digraph, "Panawicke" becomes "Panauuicke" and "Pananiock" becomes "Panauuock," or perhaps at some point "Panauiock," all of which closely resemble the original "Panauuaiock" on the de Bry map. This transition from the double-u digraph demonstrates that Panauuaiock, Pananuaioc, Pananiock, and Panawicke are all variations of names designating the same location, the area between the present-day Pamlico and Neuse Rivers.

The documentary and linguistic evidence disputes the aforementioned opinions about Pananiock's location, and also casts doubt on Millers's suggestion that the translation of the Algonquian "Panawioc" as "Place of Foreigners" was "an apt name for a site where they *reported our men to be.*" A connection to the 1587 colonists in the meaning of the word "Panawioc" would only make sense if the location received its Algonquian name *after* "our men"—i.e., the "foreigners"—arrived there. However, both the name and general location of Panawioc/Pananiock had been known to the English in its earlier spelling—Pananuaioc—about a quarter century before the Zúñiga Map was produced, and several years before White's colony ever arrived at Roanoke. It would also seem probable that the name must have been in use among the Algonquians long before the English ever arrived, certainly before the Amadas-Barlowe voyage in 1584, when it was first mentioned. It is difficult, then, to see how the *meaning* of the word "Panawioc" could relate in any way to the Lost Colonists.

John Smith's own map on the following page of "Ould Virginia" in his *Generall Historie* also illustrates Pananaioc. The map is not perfect (the villages of Secota and Setuoc—"Setuook" on the White/de Bry—have been incorrectly switched), but it does place Panawioc/Pananiock between the Neuse and Pamlico Rivers, where it was known to be from 1584 through the Jamestown years. Smith's *Generall Historie* was not published until 1624, but it is clear that Pananaioc *and* its general location were well known.

The Zúñiga Map's reference to "our men" at Panawioc could very possibly be connected to Englishmen who had been in that area previously, if not to the Lost Colonists themselves. In July of 1585 Grenville and a party of about forty

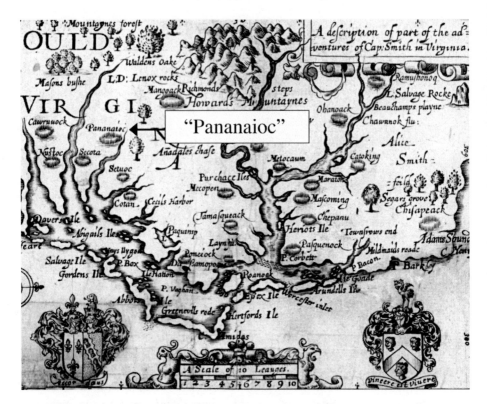

"Pananaioc"

John Smith's map of "Ould Virginia" from his *Generall Historie* (published in 1624) showing the location of Pananaioc (Panauuaiock).

men explored Pamlico Sound before continuing on to Roanoke. It is not known exactly how far south they traveled, but they went at least far enough to discover the native Indian village of Secotan on the Pamlico River, where they "were well entertained there of the Sauages."[11] Ralph Lane also reported that he explored "from the Island of Roanoak ... into the South..." as far as Secota, "being by estimation fourescore [eighty] miles distant from Roanoak."[12]

Furthermore, the 1587 Lost Colonists must have explored this region during their search for a suitable mainland settlement site. As noted earlier, the area between the present-day Pamlico and Neuse Rivers is directly across Pamlico Sound from Ocracoke/Wokokon inlet, which had very likely influenced the colonists' choice of their mainland settlement site in 1588. As discussed previously, those potential settlement locations on the mainland can reasonably be narrowed down to the area south of the Pamlico River where the Pomouik, Neusiok, and Cwareuuock dwelt in 1588. That area would include present-day Pamlico County and the southern portion of Beaufort County, where Panawioc appears to have been located.

It is also possible that surviving colonists traveled to Panawioc from their mainland settlement after the hurricane surge in 1589. That mainland settlement, as previously suggested, may have been located in the aforementioned counties or on the peninsula just south of the Neuse in present-day Carteret County. The hurricane surge would have driven the surviving colonists and Croatoans farther inland, and they could have joined with the Pomouik/Panawioc/Pananiock tribe. Of course by early 1608 when Smith was recording the information about the men "apparalled" at Panawioc/Pananiock, the Lost Colony had been missing for more than two decades. Even if Wowinchopunck's information actually was a legitimate Lost Colony clue, it almost certainly was not current, just as the information about "men cloathed" at Ocanahonan and Pakrakanick was many decades old. At best it can probably be concluded that "our men" may have been at Pananiock at some point in the past, but one can only speculate about whether or not any signs of the colonists still remained there in 1608. What is certainly true is that—other than the English who were involved in the Roanoke voyages—there were no known Europeans in the area of Pananiock from 1584 to 1608, when Smith's *A True Relation* and the Zúñiga Map were composed.

It is curious that the planned trip to Pananiock never took place, considering that its location was known, at least generally, and that Pananiock was the place where "the King of Paspahegh reported our men to be...." An agreement had been made by Smith and possibly Newport with Wowinchopunck "to conduct two of our men" to Panawicke (Pananiock), which was "beyond Roonok." The trip began at Warraskoyack, where the Pagan River empties into the James. What happened next is not clear. All we know is what Smith wrote about the king of Paspahegh, that he, "playing the villaine, and deluding us for rewards, returned within three or foure dayes after, without going further," and Panawicke/Pananiock was not mentioned again.

Relations with Wowinchopunck and his Paspahegh tribe were never good. To begin with, the English established their new colony of Jamestown in Paspahegh territory, about six miles south of their main village, and this was seen by the Paspahegh as an unwarranted encroachment. Ten days after the arrival of the English Wowinchopunck sent two messengers with the promise of a deer, which twenty Paspahegh Indians delivered a few days later. However, they were clearly feigning friendship in order to scout the settlement, because six days later the Paspahegh attacked Jamestown with 200 fighters. As time passed, Smith traded for corn on several occasions with the Paspahegh, but their dealings were always marked with suspicion, and he considered them a "churlish and trecherous nation." He also learned from other surrounding tribes "that Paspahegh and Chickahammania did hate us, and intended some mischief."

It is possible that Smith dismissed the entire story about surviving colonists at Pananiock as nothing more than a deception engineered by the villainous Paspahegh king for no other reason than to gain "rewards" from the English. On the other hand we don't know the identities of the "two of our men" who apparently accompanied Wowinchopunck, and we know absolutely nothing about what may have occurred during the "three or foure dayes" that they were gone. We also don't know Wowinchopunck's true motive for abandoning the search, but, based on the poor relations with the English at Jamestown in 1608, he may not have been very anxious for them to make contact with more potentially troublesome Englishmen rumored to be—or to have been—at Pananiock.

The Paspahegh tribe's seemingly instinctive animosity towards the English at Jamestown may also have been rooted in their decades-old experience with Europeans. Paquiquineo, a young native Indian who was taken by the Spanish—it is not clear whether he was abducted or went voluntarily—near the York or James River in 1561, was believed to have been the son of the Paspahegh chief. Paquiquineo spent nine years in Spain and Mexico, during which he was eventually baptized and took the name of his sponsor, Don Luís de Velasco. After convincing the Spanish that he would help establish a Christian mission in Ajacán, which he called his old tribe's territory, Paquiquineo and a group of eight Jesuits landed at the James River in 1570 and in short time established a settlement probably closer to the York River. Paquiquineo soon deserted the Jesuits and, after returning to his Indian family, reverted to his tribal customs. When three of the Jesuits came to the village for food in early 1571, Paquiquineo killed them and then led an assault on the mission, killing the remaining Jesuits except for a boy named Alonso de Olmos. After Spaniards on a resupply ship learned that the Jesuits had been murdered, a punitive expedition was sent to the James River in 1572. A number of Paquiquineo's tribesmen were killed or captured and eight were hanged, one for each of the Jesuits, from the ship's spars. The Spaniards rescued young Alonso de Olmos, but Paquiquineo was never found.

Jesuit authors Clifford M. Lewis and Albert J. Loomie proposed that Paquiquineo was directly related to Powhatan and his brother Opechancanough, perhaps being their uncle, which would establish his status as a chief's son and future tribal leader.[13] Colonial historian Carl Bridenbaugh suggested that Paquiquineo actually was Powhatan's brother, Opechancanough, who led the Powhatan chiefdom after his brother's death and orchestrated the massacre of the English colonists in 1622.[14] That does not seem possible, partly because Paquiquineo would have been about seventy-five in 1622. Furthermore, Bridenbaugh's suggestion is effectively challenged by Smith's interaction with Opechancanough in December of 1607, when Smith was captured by him "with 200 men." According to Smith, Opechancanough "tooke great delight in understanding the manner of our ships" and "I presented him with a compasse diall, describing by my best meanes the use therof, whereat he so amazedly admired, as he suffered me to proceed in a discourse of the roundnes of the earth, the course of the sunne, moone, starres and plannets."[15] Paquiquineo, having lived and traveled among the Spaniards for nine years in Spain and Mexico, would not have been mystified or amazed by English ships or a compass dial.

Nevertheless, Paquiquineo would have been about sixty years old in 1607, and certainly could still have been alive. In any case, his experiences with the Jesuits and the Spaniards' retribution in 1572 would have left a lasting impression on the Paspahegh tribe regarding Europeans. To the Paspahegh, the lesson of Paquiquineo's story would have been that Europeans bring nothing but trouble and must be avoided at all costs and actively resisted if necessary. Avoidance was not possible, since the English had planted themselves in Paspahegh territory, and consequently resistance was the only option. That belief might account for their initial and seemingly natural hostility towards the English, and it could explain why Wowinchopunck did not complete the journey to Pananiock. It would have been unwise and dangerous for the Paspahegh to have the Jamestown colonists make contact with other kinsmen to the south.

Unfortunately for the Paspahegh, the lesson of Paquiquineo's story would prove to be all too true. In August of 1610 the new and ruthless Jamestown governor, Lord De la Warr, ordered an attack on the main Paspahegh town, during which the village was destroyed, the crops ruined, and most of the Paspahegh were killed. In the aftermath, one of Wowinchopunck's wives and her children were also brutally killed. Wowinchopunck was killed the following February, by which time the Paspahegh tribe had virtually disappeared.

It should be emphasized here that the false assumptions about Lost Colonists at Ocanahonan and Pakrakanick were *not* found in the information that the Powhatans related from their collective memories and oral traditions. The mistakes were entirely due to Smith's and others' misinterpretation of that information. There were, in fact, "men cloathed" and "people with short Coates, and Sleeves to the Elbowes," and "houses walled as ours," and structures "one story above another" at distant places with strange names like Ocanahonan. It was Smith and later Strachey, not the Powhatans, who misinterpreted that information and jumped to the erroneous conclusion that the "clothed men" were Lost Colonists. It is very possible, then, that there were also "many men … apparelled" at Pananiock at some point in time. Wowinchopunck may have had good reasons for abandoning the search, and, as suggested above, Smith may have subsequently rejected the story of appareled men at Pananiock because he considered the "churlish and treacherous" Paspahegh—and their reports—to be untrustworthy.

Smith would later dispatch two other searches to find "the lost company of Sir Walter Rawley," but it is not surprising that they found nothing, since they were sent where the 1587 colonists had never been. Michael Sicklemore and two guides searched Chowanoke, "but found little hope and lesse certaintie of them were left by Sir Walter Raleigh." Nathaniel Powell and Anas Todkill were guided far west to the Mangoag (Mongoack), possibly in search of Ocanahonan, "but nothing could they learne but they were all dead." Unfortunately, the most promising location—Pananiock—was never searched. One cannot help but wonder what an expedition there might have turned up.

# 16

# John Smith and the
# Powhatan-Slaughter Myth
## 1608–1609

## The Third Institutionalized Assumption

In early 1609 the Royal Council in England received the shocking word from Jamestown that Wahunsunacock, Chief Powhatan, had slaughtered the 1587 colonists. There is some question as to the source of this stunning news, but the evidence indicates that it had to have come from John Smith. Quinn believed that the information must have arrived in the form of a letter from Smith, now lost .[1] Christopher Newport had reached Jamestown with the so-called "second supply" in early October of 1608, and he returned to England in late December or early January with a Powhatan Indian named Machumps, brother of Winganuske, one of Powhatan's many wives, as well as a second Indian named Namontack. Since the news of the slaughter was not known in England before 1609, it almost certainly must have been brought aboard the *Mary Margaret* on the aforementioned voyage to England captained by Newport.

It has been suggested that the news of the slaughter came from William Strachey via a conversation with Machumps,[2] the Powhatan Indian mentioned above, after his arrival in England with Newport, but that is not at all likely. There is no evidence that Strachey had any contact with Machumps until after the departure of the *Sea Venture* on June 2, 1609. Strachey signed on with the Virginia Company for the "third supply" to Jamestown, where he hoped to become a chronicler and perhaps secretary of the new colony, but that hope would not be realized until May of 1610. The post of Colonial Secretary had been held by Gabriel Archer since 1607, except for Mathew Scribner's brief stint in 1608–9 during Archer's trip to England, and it was for that reason that Strachey could only enlist with the Virginia Company as a planter.[3] It was partly because the position was not available, by the way, that Strachey's good friend, the poet John Donne, lost interest in the Virginia venture. As noted, the first Secretary of the Jamestown Colony was Archer, who held the post—with the exception of the interlude above—until his death in the winter of 1609–1610 during the "starving time." Despite the reference to Strachey as "The First Secretary of the Colony" on the title page of the Hakluyt Society's publication of *The Historie*, Strachey was not appointed to that post until June 13 of 1610, several weeks after the *Sea Venture's* shipwrecked company finally arrived at Jamestown.

Moreover, Strachey spent most of the winter of 1608–9 and into the spring with his wife and sons at his father-in-law's estate in Crowhurst, some fifty miles from London. London's periodic plagues had struck again in the summer of 1608 and persisted through May of 1609, closing theaters and sending those who could afford it out of London to the countryside.[4] There would have been no incentive to return to London until the *Sea Venture* was prepared to depart for Jamestown. It is unlikely that Strachey could have had any access to or contact with Machumps until it was time to board the *Sea Venture*, which he did three days before the ship weighed anchors and cruised down the Thames River. The Privy Council had been informed about the slaughter long before then and had already prepared written instructions for the new governor, Thomas Gates, regarding the slaughter. Strachey would have had opportunities for conversation with Machumps after the *Sea Venture's* wreck at Bermuda in July 1609, but there is no mention at all of Machumps in Strachey's *A True Reportory*, an account of the time period between June of 1609 to about mid–July of 1610. *A True Reportory* is a detailed account of the time spent on Bermuda, including the shipwreck and hurricane, which some believe Shakespeare used as a background for *The Tempest*. All that can be said with reasonable certainty is that Strachey's interviews with Machumps occurred at Jamestown between May of 1610 and the summer of 1611, and that he recorded the additional Lost Colony slaughter details at that time.

It is far more likely that John Smith informed the Council about the slaughter via a letter or report, which Christopher Newport delivered after his return to England in December or January of 1608–9. It is evident from the 1609 instructions to Governor Gates that Smith was in good standing with the king's Virginia Council members and that they had been in contact with him previously: "To this command [regarding the defense of Jamestown and the placement of future forts] wee desire Captain Smyth may be allotted aswell for his earnest desire as the greate confidence & trust that we haue in his care & diligence."[5] It is also clear that Smith was the source of the information in the Council's instructions alleged to be about the Lost Colony. Both Ocanahonan and Pakrakanick from Smith's 1607–08 *A True Relation* letter and the Zúñiga Map are mentioned in the 1609 instructions as "Ocona-hoen" and "Peccarecamicke." The Council's instructions also contained the 1607–08 reference from the Zúñiga Map about the "4 men clothed [at Pakrakanick] that came from Roonock to Ocanahawan." In the 1609 instructions the line read, "Peccarecamicke where you shall finde foure of the english aliue, left by Sir Walter Rawley which escaped from the slaughter of Powhaton...." This is the first known record mentioning the slaughter of the Lost Colonists by Chief Powhatan and, like the other references in the instructions, it must also have come from Smith. The other bit of news included in the instructions was that the slaughter occurred "vpon the first arrivall of our Colonie," i.e., about or just prior to May of 1607.[6]

Smith had a number of conversations with Powhatan on a variety of topics, including "peace and warre." It is probable that Smith learned about the alleged slaughter from Powhatan during one of these talks. Interestingly, Smith made no mention whatsoever of the Powhatan–Lost Colony slaughter story in his own published works, but there was probably a practical reason for that. The Virginia Company, which blatantly promoted the wonders and benefits of their Jamestown venture, closely monitored and edited what was published. News of an English slaughter by Chief Powhatan would hardly attract potential settlers and investors. Smith, however, *did* inform his friend and chronicler, Samuel Purchas, about the conversation he had with Chief Powhatan. This Powhatan-Smith conversation was noted years later by Purchas, who had been recording the personal narratives of sailors returning to England and added their accounts to a collection of manuscripts left to him by Richard Hakluyt, who had died in 1616. Purchas published *Hakluytus Posthumus or Purchas His Pilgrimes* in 1625, and it contained the following marginal notation regarding the fate of White's 1587 colony: "Powhatan confessed that hee had bin at the murther of that Colonie and shewed to Cap. Smith a Musket barrell and a brasse Morter, and certaine peeces of Iron which had bin theirs."[7]

In the spring of 1609 Smith's dreadful news about the slaughter prompted the Council to take action. The situation was complicated, however, by the fact that just months earlier the Council had recognized that Powhatan's cooperation was necessary for the success of the colony, and had instructed Newport to conduct an elaborate coronation of Powhatan in order to ensure the chief's allegiance and assistance. The council now decided "if you finde it not best to make him [Powhatan] your prisoner yet you must make him your tributary..." and as for Powhatan's priests, who had persuaded him to carry out the slaughter, "we pronounce it not crueltie nor breache of Charity to deale more sharpely with them and to proceed even to death with these murtherers...."[8]

As it turned out, the instructions for dealing with Powhatan and his priests did not reach Jamestown in a timely manner. Governor Thomas Gates was aboard the aforementioned *Sea Venture*, the flagship of the "third supply" for Jamestown, when a hurricane struck. As already discussed, the *Sea Venture* was separated from the rest of the fleet and driven onto a reef off Bermuda in July 1609. The Council's instructions would have been carried with Gates aboard the *Sea Venture*. By the time the instructions finally reached Jamestown ten months later, in May of 1610, the colony was on the verge of collapse and the retribution against Chief Powhatan was never carried out.

Of course once the Council officially acknowledged the reported slaughter of the 1587 colony, the original Lost Colony narrative had to be altered. It will be recalled that in early January of 1608 Smith had returned to Jamestown after his captivity by Opechancanough and Wahunsunacock with the news about "men cloathed" at Ocanahonan and Pakrakanick, who Smith incorrectly assumed were Raleigh's Lost Colonists. That information, coupled with the Zúñiga Map, provided the earliest narrative concerning the whereabouts of the colonists: The "men cloathed," presumed to be the 1587 colonists, went "from Roonock to Ocanahawan" and then farther south to Pakrakanick where there "remayneth 4 men clothed."

This initial chronology is interesting in light of the fact that the Council had not yet received the news that the Lost Colony had been slaughtered by Powhatan. If the "men clothed" were part of the 1587 Roanoke colony and had traveled from Roanoke to Ocanahonan, quite far from Powhatan's domain, and then continued from Ocanahonan to Pakrakanick even farther to the south of Ocanahonan, there was no place in that sequence for them to have been part of a slaughter conducted by Powhatan far to the north. Consequently, the narrative—already fatally flawed since the "men cloathed" at Ocanahonan and Pakrakanick were Spaniards, not Lost Colonists—had to be changed. The new but equally flawed narrative naturally assumed that the slaughter of the Lost Colonists must have occurred between the departure from Roanoke and the arrival at Ocanahonan, and the "cloathed men" must have been *survivors* of the slaughter.

Versions of that same chronology have evolved and continue to be promoted today, resulting in the previously mentioned claims placing the location of Ocanahonan and Pakrakanick—as well as survivors of the slaughter—at the upper Pamlico, Tar, Neuse, Roanoke, Chowan, or Nottoway Rivers. Virtually all serious mainstream theories about the Lost Colony are grounded in this Powhatan–Lost Colony slaughter scenario, which can be traced back to an erroneous interpretation provided by Smith regarding information  he obtained from Chief Powhatan about a slaughter. Powhatan's slaughter of the 1587 colony has remained a cornerstone of Lost Colony theory, and it represents the third flawed institutionalized assumption outlined in the Preface. Like the Fernandez-as-villain error, the Powhatan–Lost Colony slaughter myth has obstructed the search for the Lost Colony for four centuries.

The entire version of the Powhatan–Lost Colony slaughter account must be viewed with a great deal of skepticism. In the first place, we do not even have Smith's own words regarding what he may have heard from Powhatan. We are left only with an assumption made by Smith and the fragmentary Samuel Purchas version of what Smith told him about a conversation he supposedly had with the chief. From a historical-source standpoint this cannot be considered reliable.

As is true of *all* the Jamestown references and claims about the Lost Colony, it is important to recognize that they are *secondary*—or in the case of Purchas even *tertiary*—English interpretations derived exclusively from Powhatan Indians who related recent and past memories from their oral tradition. The 17th century journals and accounts of Smith, Strachey, and the Jamestown principals—while *primary Jamestown* sources—cannot be considered *primary Lost Colony* sources and should not be treated as such. The only undisputed primary source "records" from the Lost Colony after August of 1587 are the two messages the colonists themselves carved into the tree and entrance post at Roanoke.

The tendency, though, has been to rely on these early 17th century Jamestown interpretations as unimpeachable primary Lost Colony documents, rather than as the less reliable secondary and tertiary sources they actually are. This is an important distinction, of course. Any historical research which equates primary with secondary and even tertiary sources runs the risk of perpetuating someone's subjective, and often inaccurate, interpretation of events. As already seen, such was the case with both Smith and then Strachey when they misidentified Powhatan's "men cloathed" at Ocanahonan and Pakrakanick as Lost Colonists.

In that instance, as previously discussed, it was reasonable to believe that the Powhatan oral tradition did indeed contain stories of clothed men and two-story dwellings at distant places called Ocanahonan and Pakrakanick, and those stories can now be verified by the historical account of the Pardo expedition. It was impossible to believe, however, that the Powhatans could have identified the clothed men as English or that they had been specifically part of the 1587 colony. Those conclusions were merely unfounded assumptions made by John Smith and later compounded by William Strachey.

This is not to say that the Lost Colony references in the Jamestown accounts are completely irrelevant. On the contrary, aside from the carvings left at Roanoke—and barring new archaeological findings—they are the *only* versions we have of the actual Powhatan oral tradition allegedly connected to the Lost Colony. Yet *versions* they are, English interpretations of the fragments of essentially accurate information related by the native Powhatans. Smith's vulnerability to interpretive error has already been demonstrated, and once again he misinterpreted the information he received from Powhatan, and made the same erroneous assumption he had made previously: The clothed men at Ocanahonan and Pakrakanick must be Raleigh's Lost Colonists, he inaccurately concluded, and likewise the victims of Powhatan's slaughter—who may have had "certaine peeces of Iron"—must be the Lost Colonists as well.

The question of sources has been stressed here because it represents— even more so than the Ocanahonan/Pakrakanick misinterpretation—the most obvious problem with the Powhatan–Lost Colony slaughter story. In the case of the Ocanahonan and Pakrakanick references, we at least have Smith's own account of what Opechancanough and Wahunsunacock told him and the context of those conversations. Additionally, that information was corroborated by the notations on the Zúñiga Map, to which Smith was a contributor. Yet that information was completely misinterpreted and in reality had nothing at all to do with the 1587 colonists. In the case of the Powhatan– Lost Colony slaughter, we do not even have a single word from Smith about what Powhatan supposedly related to him concerning the slaughter. All we know of that conversation, or "confession" as Purchase put it, is the brief notation he recorded some seventeen years after the conversation took place. Characterizing whatever was said as a "confession" also seems quite overstated. It is difficult to believe that Chief Powhatan, who was well aware of the dangers posed by the English and their superior weaponry, would knowingly incur their wrath and retribution by admitting to having massacred an entire colony of their countrymen.

Although Powhatan's assumed slaughter of the 1587 colonists was dreadful news to the English, it must also be seen in its proper context and from Powhatan's viewpoint. As Strachey would note later, the supposed slaughter of the Lost Colonists coincided with just one of the many massacres Powhatan had conducted over the prior decade, during which he successfully expanded his chiefdom by conquest whenever necessary. He massacred the Payankatank tribe in 1608, the Chesapeake tribe in 1607, and undoubtedly a number of others before the arrival of the Jamestown settlers. He would have had no qualms about discussing such slaughters with Smith, and in fact he may well have boasted about them. If, as will be explained later, a handful of white people had also been killed during one of these intertribal massacres, it would have been little more than a curiosity to Powhatan.

Chief Powhatan's "Musket barrell and a brasse Morter, and certaine peeces of Iron," provide no proof of a slaughter in themselves and certainly not of an entire English colony. They could have come to him in a variety of ways. More importantly, they provide no evidence whatsoever that these items had once belonged specifically to White's 1587 colony. How could Smith—or Powhatan for that matter—have determined that these few metal items "had bin theirs," as Purchas reported? Certainly if Smith had more credible proof—details of the slaughter or any evidence at all concerning the original owners of these items or the identities or location of those apparently slain by Powhatan—he would have provided it to Purchas. If the slaughter of the Lost Colony occurred about the time the Jamestown colonists first arrived—"vpon the first arrival of our Colonie," as the Council's instructions noted—then surely more convincing evidence would have been available.

Once again, just as it is impossible to believe that Powhatan could have identified the clothed men at Ocanahonan and Pakrakanick as 1587 Lost Colonists, it is equally impossible to believe that he could have told Smith that he was responsible specifically for the extermination of the 1587 colony. Smith, hearing about a slaughter and seeing the few metal objects displayed, jumped once more to a hasty conclusion, this time that Powhatan's victims must have been White's Lost Colonists. Smith subsequently relayed this startling news via Christopher Newport to the Virginia Council, and the myth of the Powhatan slaughter of the Lost Colony was born. Ironically—and this will be seen in a later chapter—Powhatan *was* likely involved with a slaughter of sorts, and there may well have been a few Englishmen among the victims, but they were not members of the 1587 Lost Colony.

Smith's overall reliability as a narrator is also a factor to be considered, as demonstrated by the differences between the accounts of his captivity in *A True Relation*, written in 1608, as opposed to that of *The Generall Historie*, written in 1624. In the former, Chief Powhatan's daughter, Pocahontas, is mentioned only in passing, but in the latter she is the central figure in a harrowing ordeal from which Smith only barely escaped due to her intervention. (The debate over the Pocahontas question has been thoroughly explored by Philip Barbour in his *Complete Works of Captain John Smith*.[9])

It is also possible that Smith misunderstood a common native Algonquian cultural ritual that he may have undergone in December of 1608. Seth Mallios wrote in his *The Deadly Politics of Giving*, "While Smith often exaggerated in his texts … what is known is that the details of his Powhatan abduction, tour, and rescue parallel adoption rituals practiced in a variety of Algonquian cultures."[10] In either case—misunderstood or embellished—this episode questions Smith's reliability as an accurate narrator of Powhatan/Algonquian motivations and events.

He may also have misunderstood the cultural implications of native Indian hospitality which required pleasant and compliant responses to an adopted outsider such as himself. This was the same cultural phenomenon that confounded the Jesuits in Newfoundland as they attempted to convert the Algonquian Mi'kmaqs, who viewed conversion as "a superficial courtesy rather than an eternal commitment."[11] The same tradition was misunderstood by Lewis and Clarke 200 years later when they questioned the Mandans, whose answers were designed to please them rather than provide factual information.[12] Perhaps like the Mandans and the Mi'kmaqs, Powhatan was observing ritual obligations requiring him to reply to his virtual son's questions in the same manner, cordially but not accurately, allowing Smith to believe whatever he wanted to hear about the fate of the Lost Colony.

Smith had a natural inclination towards exaggeration. In his *Generall Historie*'s version of the Roanoke voyages, for example, he mentioned several times that Grenville left "50" men to maintain possession of Roanoke after Drake had evacuated Lane and the 1585–86 military colony. Hakluyt had recorded the number as fifteen. Likewise, Smith wrote that the number of Indians attacking this contingent was 300, but in Hakluyt's account it had been thirty. This embellishment is all the more remarkable since Smith's account of the Roanoke years was copied, sometimes verbatim, directly *from* Hakluyt.

Smith was certainly a talented and effective leader, without whom the Jamestown colony probably would not have survived. His absence from Jamestown after his injury from a gunpowder mishap demonstrates how important he was. Following his departure to England in October 1609, Jamestown nearly collapsed, and when the shipwrecked *Sea Venture* company finally arrived in May of 1610, only sixty starving colonists were left alive out of perhaps 500 or more, though the numbers vary. Smith did, however, have the tendency to exaggerate and portray himself as the protagonist in the Jamestown drama, as demonstrated by the aforementioned version of the Pocahontas episode. In fact if his 1608 *A True Relation* account is at all accurate—and it was written shortly after the fact—Smith seems to have been feasted and treated quite well by his captors, and was apparently befriended by Powhatan, who claimed that he would forever regard him as his own son if Smith reciprocated his friendship. Given his tendency towards embellishment, it is likely that Smith instinctively exaggerated Powhatan's reference to a slaughter, convincing himself that he had discovered the long-sought answer to the Lost Colony's fate, and at the same time fulfilled the Council's directive to acquire information about "the lost company of Sir Walter Rawley."

There is no credible evidence to support Smith's assumption that the Lost Colonists were slaughtered at the hands of Chief Powhatan. Like the erroneous supposition that 1587 colonists were the "cloathed men" at Ocanahonan and Pakrakanick, the centuries-old Powhatan–Lost Colony slaughter myth was based entirely on another mistaken interpretation of information provided by Powhatan in 1608. That error was later compounded by the fragmentary details about the "slaughter" that William Strachey would add after he became Secretary of the Jamestown Colony in 1610. Strachey's information came from one or more conversations with the aforementioned Machumps between 1610 and 1611 and would add a few more confusing details to Smith's earlier version of the slaughter. Those additional details, supposedly about the Lost Colony, were included in Strachey's *Historie of Travaile Into Virginia Britannia*. Based entirely on the fragmentary references from Smith, via Purchas, and Strachey, a misguided tale was woven about the fate of the Lost Colony at the hands of Chief Powhatan, and versions of that story have persisted for over 400 years.

# 17

## The Francisco Fernández de Écija Reconnaissance 1609

Between 1587 and 1605 there had been no fewer than a dozen attempts, either planned or actually carried out, to locate the Lost Colony. Only two, and possibly three, of those attempts—the Vincente Gonzalez expedition to the Chesapeake in 1588, John White's voyage to Roanoke in 1590, and possibly Samuel Mace's voyage to Cape Fear in 1602—would produce any evidence at all concerning the location of the 1587 English colony. The Gonzalez and White voyages provided important information about where the Lost Colony was *not* located: As discussed in previous chapters, in June of 1588 the Lost Colonists were not at Roanoke or the Chesapeake, and in 1590 neither they nor the Croatoans were at Roanoke or Croatoan. The 1602 Mace voyage may have acquired information from the Cape Fear Indians about survivors of the 1589 hurricane and possibly admixed offspring.

By early 1607 the Spanish were once again concerned about renewed English plans for a colony in Virginia. On January 24 Spanish Ambassador Don Pedro de Zúñiga wrote to King Philip III about what he was able to learn about the English plans, and on March 8 the king replied that he had consulted with his council about what steps should be taken to prevent the English from colonizing North America.[1] King Philip took no action, however, and, as previously mentioned, once Jamestown was established Zúñiga strongly urged King Philip to "up-root" the fledgling settlement even though the initial English reports from Virginia were disappointing. In September Zúñiga sent the king either the original or a copy of the Martin/Smith map of South Virginia accompanied by a report on Virginia, which may have been a copy of Smith's *A True Relation*.[2] On November 8, 1608, Zúñiga wrote yet again to the king, saying, "it is very important Your Majesty should command that an end be put to these things done in Virginia; because it is a matter of great importance—and they propose (as I understand) to send as many as 1,500 men there; and they hope that 12,000 will be gotten together there in time."[3]

King Philip finally sent orders to Pedro de Ybarra, governor of Florida, instructing him to send a ship to the north and explore "the bays and ports which are in Virginia and its coasts" and discover "what English have gone there and with what designs and if they have established and fortified themselves in any part and with what people and forces."[4] He was to search the coast, sailing only by day and keeping always on the lookout, up to latitude 37° 30' (Chesapeake Bay) where it was suspected the English may be planning to fortify themselves, and "likewise visit the isles in the Bay where people were found in the year 1586, when privateer Francis Drake took them with him on his way back to England," a clear reference to Roanoke.[5] He was also instructed to search the coast northward from the Chesapeake Bay to 44° 30' north latitude, where a second English colony was rumored to be located. This was a reference to the previously mentioned Plymouth Company's attempt to establish a trading settlement on the Kennebec River in present-day Maine, then called North Virginia. The Spanish did not yet know that the settlement attempt had been abandoned.

Thus in June of 1609, more than two decades after the 1587 colony was left at Roanoke, the Spanish would send out another search for the English, who were known to have settled once again in the territory which the English called "Virginia." Although this reconnaissance was focused on finding the 1607 English colony, the details of the account inadvertently provided a few additional clues about the 1587 Lost Colony. On June 26, 1609, Governor Pedro de Ybarra sent <u>Francisco Fernández de Écija</u> from St. Augustine in the pinnace *La Asuncion de Christo* with twenty-three sailors and soldiers and an Indian woman from Santa Elena to serve as interpreter. Among his crew was Ensign Juan de Santiago, who had sailed with Vincente Gonzalez on the expedition to the Chesapeake, and inadvertently to Roanoke, in 1588. On July 8 Écija reached the Rio Jordan, either the present-day Santee River or Winyah Bay, and he remained there for a week gathering information about the English from the local Indians. At this time he also ransomed a Frenchman named Juan Corbe, who had been held captive for many years by an unnamed "cacique of those regions," and who Écija hoped would be an additional source of information about the English.

The Indians provided Écija with information about Jamestown, which they referred to as "Guandape," a very old Indian town believed to have been located near the Jamestown site. In 1526 Lucas Vázquez de Ayllón and 600 Spanish settlers had made their way up a major river in the Chesapeake, said to be the present-day James River, and landed at the Indian town of Guandape, which Ayllón christened San Miguel de Guandape. In less than a year disease and hostile Indians reduced their numbers to less than 200 and the Spanish abandoned the settlement in the spring of 1527. In any case, the Indians at Rio Jordon were able to provide Écija with an astonishingly detailed and accurate description of Guandape, or Jamestown. "An Indian chieftain and others" told Écija that four days' journey northward there was a

> settlement of the English in a village which is called Guandape, lying beside a river which runs into the sea, and it is on an island surrounded by water, which on one side is joined to the mainland, and that ordinarily there are ships in that port, and three months ago seven departed from it … and in the harbor there remained always some on guard, and every day many others came and went, up the coast to the northward, and that they had made a fort but that it was of wood, and they had made a league with the neighboring caciques … and they entertained them much and gave them clothes and tools and ordered them to sow grain, although the English themselves did not occupy themselves with this but with their fortification.[6]

After receiving this remarkable intelligence, Écija then resumed his slow reconnaissance northward and rounded Cape San Roman (Cape Fear) on July 17. By the time he was off the Cape of Trafalgar (probably Cape Lookout) on July 18, Écija's pinnace was "dressed in her false colors" to disguise her as a vessel from Amsterdam. On July 19 Écija anchored off the Cape of Engano (probably Hatteras) and the next morning they came to a bar, "where the English, as we heard … had been in previous times." There is some confusion about this location, but the chronology and geography suggest that it was Croatoan. Also, it will be recalled that in 1605 Écija had captured Bertrand Rocque, captain of the *Castor and Pollux*, who told the Spanish that part of his mission included a stop at Croatoan, where he hoped to contact some of the 1587 English colonists.

At Croatoan Écija witnessed an interesting occurrence. The Spanish saw "signals made by means of smoke" and a small group of Indians appeared on the beach and began drumming and shouting to the ship. When the Spanish called back, the Indians became fearful and ran back from the beach and then started playing on what Écija thought were flutes.[7] A similar event occurred later when the Spanish were near Roanoke. Smoke signals were seen inland followed by Indians appearing on the beach and shouting to the ship. Once again when the Spanish called back, the Indians retreated, but soon a few Indians reappeared playing what the Spanish described as pipes or flutes perhaps played in a European style.[8]

On July 24 Écija arrived at the Bay of Jacan (Chesapeake) where an English ship (possibly Samuel Argall's ship, the *Mary and John*) blocked the entrance to the bay. Fearing that *La Asuncion de Christo* would be trapped in the bay, Écija withdrew and returned to Rio Jordan to gather additional information about the English, whose presence at the Chesapeake had now been established.

Back at the Rio Jordan the Indians confirmed everything they had said earlier, and Écija learned

> that alongside the wooden fort they had cast much stone into the water, mid-leg deep, and that they brought it in boats, and that there were many women and children who went about through the fields and houses of the neighboring Indians, and that from the Rio Jordan to the settlement by a straight path overland it was little more than fifty leagues ... from there to the place where the English are fortifying themselves, and the Frenchman whom they rescued declared that from the Indians of the town in which he was kept captive, who frequently went and came to the settlement of the English, he had learned that they had built a wooden fort and a town made of the same and had two large ships with guns, guarding the fortlike castles, and two others as guards and sentinels of the bar, in addition to those that went and came, and that every year a ship came from England laden with provisions and munitions.[9]

Since an English "league" was generally considered to be about three miles, it might appear at first that there was an error in the stated distance from Rio Jordan to Guandape/Jamestown as "little more than fifty leagues," which would put Jamestown only about 150 miles from Rio Jordon, far too close. In the early years of the 17th century, however, the English and the Spanish "league" differed. The Spanish "league of the degree" (Legua de por grado) was equivalent to 4.88 miles.[10] Fifty leagues, then, would be 244 miles and a "little more" by a "straight path overland" and would be closer to the actual 300 miles separating the two locations. Having verified the English presence at Guandape/Jamestown, and having gathered all the information he could about the settlement there, Écija returned to St. Augustine.

There are two areas of interest in the account with possible relevance to the Lost Colony. The first involves an inference drawn from Écija's mission and the intelligence he gathered during the week of July 8–15, 1609. It is important to note here that, although the Spanish knew about the Jamestown colony in "Virginia," they did not know exactly where that settlement was located, or whether the English might be found at more than one location. It was only after stopping at Rio Jordan on July 8 that Écija was able to gather the remarkably detailed information from the natives about the English who had settled at Guandape/Jamestown far to the north. It is interesting that he did not search—as instructed—"the isles in the Bay where people were found in the year 1586." Écija may have been told that there were no English anywhere except Guandape, or he may have concluded that, since the Indians at Rio Jordan were able to provide such detailed information about Guandape/Jamestown, they would surely have known if there were any English in the vicinity of Roanoke or Croatoan, which were even closer to Rio Jordan than Guandape.

The native Indians in this area had always been unusually well-informed

about English settlements to the north. It will be recalled that Pedro Menéndez Marques stopped near Santa Elena during his search for the English colony in May of 1587. The Indians told Menéndez Marques that there were no
English anywhere, an accurate assessment in May 1587. Lane had abandoned
Roanoke on June 19, 1586, and White would not arrive until July 22, 1587.

The Indians Écija questioned at Rio Jordon obviously had extensive
knowledge of the English presence about 300 miles to the north, and they
would also have known if English settlers dwelt elsewhere. They probably
would also have known if there were English captives held among other tribes,
as was the case with the Frenchman whom the Spanish called Juan Corbe. It
seems reasonable to conclude from this alone, then, that the 1587 colony no
longer existed as a recognizable English entity by 1609. Consequently, if any
of White's original colonists were still alive twenty-two years after their disappearance, they must have been very few in number and had been thoroughly assimilated by one or more of the tribes for many years. Likewise, if
any of the eleven English children at Roanoke still survived in 1609, they
must also have completely shed their "Englishness" over that time period.

What these Rio Jordan Indians apparently knew in 1609—that there
were no other Englishmen than those at Jamestown—supports what has been
proposed previously: a) that whatever portion of the 1587 colony remained
after the potential failed voyage to Newfoundland had long since collapsed
as a result of the 1589 hurricane surge; b) that no semblance of the colony
remained thereafter; and c) that the few survivors were quickly assimilated
by the neighboring tribes. This would also challenge the long held claim, first
proposed by Hamilton McMillan in the late 19th century, that the 1587
colonists and their descendants retained their Elizabethan English identity,
habits, speech, and many surnames down through the centuries where they
supposedly could still be found in Robeson and surrounding counties.

The second, and more interesting, area of relevance to the Lost Colony
in the Écija account is the series of events that occurred between July 17 and
July 24.

As referred to above, there is a minor toponymic problem associated
with Écija's voyage up the coast, and it is often difficult to match the place-
names from the early 17th century Spanish accounts with their modern coun-
terparts. As noted, for example, the location of the Spanish "Rio Jordan,"
where Écija spent the week of July 8–15, is generally believed to be the Peedee
River or nearby Winyah Bay, but it has even been assumed to be as far south
as Port Royal Sound near Beaufort, but that is refuted by the Spanish league
measurements above. The map below, using the Spanish references,[11] illustrates the probable chronology and locations of Écija's movements between
July 17, when he rounded Cape San Roman (Cape Fear) and July 24, when
he approached the Bay of Jacan (Chesapeake).

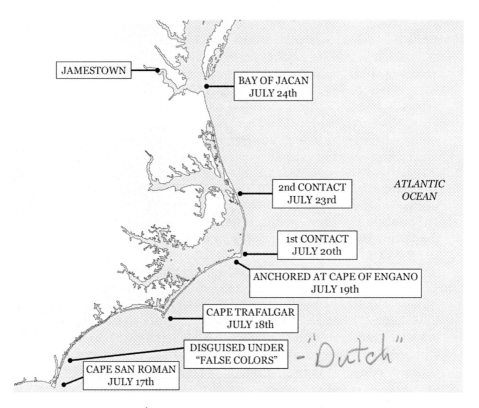

**Chronological map of Écija's reconnaissance, July 17–24, 1609 (courtesy Michael Gayle).**

The sequence begins with Écija's decision to disguise his ship's Spanish identity by sailing under the "false colors" of a Dutch ship from Amsterdam. That decision was probably made after Écija learned from the Indians at Rio Jordan that many ships "came and went" in the English harbor. The actual identity switch occurred on July 17 or 18, before reaching Cape Hatteras, and Écija's obvious intention was to advance northward unmolested by whatever English ships might be in the area. Écija knew that the English would not be alarmed at the sight of a flag flown by a ship from the Netherlands. England had been allied with the Netherlands since 1577, and in 1584 Queen Elizabeth sent 7,000 troops to help the Dutch in their fight for independence from Spain. Écija's ruse, however, seems to have fooled the local Indians as well. Of particular interest is the perception and reaction of the Indians at Croatoan (first contact July 20) and Roanoke (second contact July 23) when they saw Écija's vessel sailing slowly just offshore.

It does not seem likely that the typical Croatoan/Hatteras Indian in 1609 would have been capable of recognizing the "colors" flown by a Dutch ship.

Manteo, on the other hand, the thoroughly Anglicized Croatoan, had sailed across the Atlantic on four occasions: the 1584 Amadas/Barlow return trip to England, the 1585 Grenville/Lane voyage to Roanoke, the 1586 Lane/Drake return voyage to England, and the 1587 voyage to Roanoke with John White. During these many trans-ocean voyages, as well as his time spent in England, Manteo would have seen any number of "foreign" ships, and he probably would have become familiar with the "colors" of many. Whether Manteo was present or even alive in 1609, however, is unknown.

Perhaps the most realistic estimation about the Indians' perception of Écija's "colors" is simply that they recognized that the ship was not—or at least *appeared* not to be—*Spanish.* That alone would account for their fearful reaction when the replies from the ship came back in the Spanish language. The mistaken identity may also account for the unusually determined effort the Indians made to contact what they probably thought was an English ship … because they may *not* have seen one in many years.

With the exception of Captain Cooke and John White, who failed to reach Croatoan in 1590, there were no known English expeditions that had contact with either Croatoan or Roanoke after 1587. The 1604–05 Anglo-French expedition led by Jerome and Rocque had intended to stop at Croatoan, but had only made it as far as present-day South Carolina before being captured by the Spanish. Furthermore, although a few unsuccessful inland attempts were made in 1608 by the Jamestown settlers to find survivors of the 1587 Lost Colony, no vessels were ever sent from Jamestown to search Roanoke or Croatoan. The one reference in the Jamestown chronicles regarding English ships at Croatoan was part of a ruse by Edward Maria Wingfield, president of the colony, to deceive the Indians: "7 or 8 Indians presented the President a dear from Pamaonke [Pamaunkey] a wyrouance, desiring our friendshipp. They enquired after our shipping; wch the President said was gon to Croutoon [Croatoan]. They fear much our shipps; and therefore he would not haue them think it farr from us."[12]

Wingfield had good reason to be wary of the local tribespeople. This incident occurred on July 3, 1607, less than two months after the English established "James Fort" and only about a week after Captain Newport sailed for England. A similar visit and offer of a deer had been made by Paspahegh Indians on May 14, and less than a week later the Paspahegh attacked the settlement. In this passage Wingfield was trying to convince the Indians that Newport's ship was close by, when in fact he was well on his way to England. There was no English ship at Croatoan.

Moreover, from the very first voyage to Jamestown in 1607, ships from England had avoided the old route of the earlier Roanoke expeditions which took them along the coast near Cape Fear, Croatoan, and Roanoke. George Percy, one of the original Jamestown settlers and future president of the colony, provided the most detailed account of the 1607 voyage: The ships *did* make the traditional stop at Dominica in the Caribbean, and replenished supplies at several islands, but upon reaching Puerto Rico they veered directly north instead of following the old north-westerly heading which continued to the Bahama island chain and then north along the coast to Cape Fear.

Once they left Puerto Rico, the 1607 Jamestown voyagers remained far out to sea and did not make landfall again until they "descried the Land of Virginia [and] the same day wee entred into the Bay of Chesupioc directly."[13] After Jamestown was established, ships from England started following an even more direct course across the Atlantic, avoiding the Caribbean altogether by sailing west from the Azores to Bermuda and then west again from there directly to the mouth of the Chesapeake.

It is very possible, then, that the Indians at Croatoan and Roanoke had not seen an English ship draw near those locations for two decades, not until what *appeared* to be an English vessel approached Croatoan on July 20, 1609. A twenty-two year wait would explain their enthusiastic attempt to make contact with Écija's disguised ship. One is reminded of John Lawson's comment about images of "Sir Walter Raleigh's Ship" that these Croatoan/Hatteras Indians still imagined a century later.[14]

It is significant, too, that when the Indians called out to the ship on both July 20 and 23 and the replies came back in Spanish, they immediately retreated in fear. It is logical to conclude that if the Indians thought Écija's ship was English, then they would have expected the replies to be in English, and it follows, then, that they had some familiarity with the English language in 1609. Although Manteo in particular had interacted with all the Roanoke voyages, the Indians' determined effort more than two decades later to contact what they thought was an English ship, as well as their apparent ability to distinguish between English and Spanish, suggests perhaps a more recent affiliation with Englishmen. It also raises the possibility that these Indians may have had some important information to impart about the 1587 English colonists.

That possibility is further supported by what immediately followed the Indians' initial retreat on both occasions. They began playing musical tunes upon—what to Écija sounded like—pipes or flutes. This highly unusual activity, somewhat confusing to the Spanish, could have been an attempt to mimic *English* tunes and intended to identify *themselves* as friends and companions of the English. The ability to imitate English tunes in 1609 is additional evidence of a past association with English colonists. Interestingly, John White had used a similar musical tactic in 1590 when he tried to announce his arrival to his colony, thought to be at Roanoke: As they rowed towards the island the men "sounded with a trumpet a Call, and afterwardes many familiar English tunes and Songs."[15]

Since the second attempt to contact Écija's ship was made on the beach opposite Roanoke, it is possible that by 1609 the Croatoan tribe had also occupied Roanoke and perhaps Dasamonguepeuk as well. John Lawson wrote in his 1709 *A New Voyage to Carolina* that the Croatoans, by his time called Hatteras Indians, "either then lived on *Ronoak*-Island, or much frequented it."[16] Manteo, it will be recalled, "by the commandement of Sir Walter Ralegh, was christened in Roanoak, and called Lord thereof, and of Dasamonguepeuk, in reward of his faithfull seruices."[17] A few 17th century maps also had the Dasamonguepeuk location labeled "Croatoan."

It is tempting to theorize from this that some of the original colonists may have been alive and in the vicinity of Croatoan or Roanoke on July 20 and 23, 1609, but that is improbable. An equally enticing but still unlikely scenario is that one or two of the eleven English children from Roanoke—the original nine plus Virginia Dare and the Harvie child—now grown to adulthood, may have dwelt among the Croatoans. It is more likely that mixed descendants of the colonists and Indians could have been among those attempting to contact Écija's ship. What is certain is that the Spanish regarded these peculiar contacts at Croatoan and Roanoke as curiosities, not vital to their mission, and whatever first-hand information these Indians may have possessed about the 1587 colony was lost forever.

At the same time Écija was searching for the English in July of 1609, John Smith and the Jamestown colonists were awaiting the arrival of the flagship of the "third supply," which carried the instructions for the punishment of Chief Powhatan and his priests for his supposed slaughter of the 1587 colony. The *Sea Venture* was wrecked off Bermuda and the planned retribution was not carried out. Up to this time three searches for the Lost Colonists had been conducted from Jamestown, but, as noted, the most promising one to Pananiock "returned within three or foure dayes after, without going further." It is ironic that, based on the Indian reaction to Écija's ship at Croatoan and Roanoke, credible information about the plight of the Lost Colonists may have been readily available not very far to the south of Jamestown.

# 18

# William Strachey and the "Slaughter at Roanoke" 1609–1611

## The Fourth Institutionalized Assumption

On July 29, 1609, having been separated from the rest of the "third supply" and about to be sunk in a hurricane, the *Sea Venture*—with William Strachey aboard—was intentionally grounded on a reef off what would later be called St. George's on the Bermuda archipelago. All passengers managed to make it ashore, and in the next few days they were able to salvage most everything of importance and usefulness from the wrecked ship. As it turned out Bermuda provided an abundance of natural food sources—fresh water, wild hogs, fish, fowl, sea turtles—and perhaps most important, the archipelago was uninhabited, eliminating the ever-present threat of hostile Indians that plagued Jamestown.

Lookouts were stationed on the higher dunes and signal fires prepared, but no ships were sighted. Fortunately there were at least two shipwrights among the stranded colonists, and on August 28 Richard Frobisher began work on the construction of a pinnace. As mentioned previously in reference to the 1587 colony's likely attempt to sail to Newfoundland, some objections were raised in 1609, particularly by a number of the more disgruntled colonists who feared they would be left behind. Consequently it was agreed that a second pinnace would be built so that all the colonists could make the 600-mile voyage to Jamestown. On May 2 the *Deliverance* and *Patience* sailed from Bermuda and arrived in just nineteen days at Point Comfort, a peninsula in the Chesapeake about thirty-five miles downriver from the colony at Jamestown. Upon their arrival at Jamestown they found a disheartening sight:

Viewing the fort, we found the palisadoes torn down, the ports open, the gates from off the hinges, and empty houses, which (the) owners' death had taken from them, rent up and burnt, rather than the dwellers would step into the woods a stone's cast

173

off from them to fetch other firewood. And it is true the Indian killed as fast without, if our men stirred but beyond the bounds of their block¬house, as famine and pestilence did within, with many more particu¬larities of their sufferances brought upon them by their own disor¬ders the last year than I have heart to express.... In this desolation and misery our governor found the condition and state of the colony.[1]

It was soon decided that the situation at Jamestown was hopeless and that there was no other option left but to abandon the settlement and sail for the Newfoundland fisheries. On June 7 all the colonists headed down the James River aboard the four ships, the *Discovery*, the *Virginia*, the *Deliverance*, and the *Patience*, and it looked briefly like Jamestown would take its place among the failed English settlements. Before they reached Point Comfort, however, new governor Lord De La Warr arrived with 150 new colonists and much-needed supplies and everyone returned to Jamestown. De La Warr immediately instituted a reconstruction program, repairing and rebuilding Jamestown and erecting two more forts at the mouth of the James River. On June 13, 1610, he organized a governing council and made several key appointments, including "William Strachei, esquire, secretary and recorder." More than a year after William Strachey had left London, he finally became Secretary of the Jamestown Colony.

Strachey's early endeavors as Secretary, in addition to recording official business, were devoted to writing and revising the final draft of his *True Reportory*, an account of the hurricane and the subsequent events at Bermuda. Eventually his attention turned to what would be his major work, *The Historie of Travaile Into Virginia Britannia*. Two of Strachey's Indian sources were Kemps and the aforementioned Machumps, and it was particularly from the latter that Strachey obtained a few perplexing bits and pieces of information about Powhatan's alleged slaughter of the Lost Colony and possible English survivors. Strachey remained at Jamestown for a little more than a year, returning to England in September of 1611 and completing his *Historie* in 1612. Strachey's *Historie* did not have an immediate impact on the established Powhatan–Lost Colony slaughter scenario which had been reported by John Smith to the Council in 1609, however, because Strachey's manuscript remained unpublished for 237 years. In addition to Strachey's own, there were only two copies of the manuscripts known to exist by 1849, one dedicated to Sir Francis Bacon and the other to Sir Allen Apsley.[2]

The Virginia Company may have declined to publish both Strachey's *True Reportory* and his *Historie* because of his descriptions of discontent and mutinous activity at Bermuda and his occasionally unflattering portrayals of the leadership at Jamestown. He was also highly critical of the selection of the site for the settlement which he believed was

seated in somewhat an unwholesome and sickly air, by reason it is in a marish ground, low, flat to the river, and hath no fresh water springs serving the town but what we drew from a well six or seven fathom deep, fed by the brackish river oozing into it; from whence I verily believe the chief causes have proceeded of many diseases and sicknesses which have happened to our people, who are indeed strangely afflicted with fluxes and agues; and every particular season, by the relation of the old inhabitants, hath his particular infirmity too; all which, if it had been our fortunes to have seated upon some hill accommodated with fresh springs and clear air, as do the natives of the country, we might have, I believe, well escaped.[3]

Strachey's *Historie* also competed with John Smith's *The Proceedings and Accidents of the English Colony in Virginia,* which was published in 1612. It is interesting to note that Smith's *Proceedings* made no mention of Powhatan's slaughter, whereas Strachey's account did contain the troubling slaughter references. The Virginia Company may have rejected Strachey's *Historie* precisely because of those references, which would hardly encourage new settlers and investors had the dreadful news been made public. The Virginia Company did, in fact, publish a propaganda pamphlet later that year praising the wondrous benefits that could be had by those who would venture to Jamestown, but neglecting to mention, of course, the reported slaughter of an English colony. Strachey's *Historie* was eventually published by the Hakluyt Society in 1849, by which time the fate of White's Lost Colonists had been firmly rooted in the flawed Powhatan slaughter scenario for nearly two and a half centuries. The task of reconciling Strachey's seemingly confusing statements with the established, but mistaken, Lost Colony doctrine was left to later authors and historians, who have struggled with it ever since.

As proposed earlier, the Powhatan–Lost Colony slaughter story was a myth based entirely on John Smith's misinterpretation of a statement apparently made by Chief Powhatan concerning a slaughter that had nothing to do with the 1587 colony. The publication of Strachey's *Historie* provided more details supposedly connected with the fate of the 1587 colony, but those details only further confused the long-standing and already misguided Powhatan–Lost Colony slaughter story. The failure to explain Strachey's references satisfactorily has resulted in attempts by 19th and 20th century authors and historians either to sidestep or slant those references in order to have them comply with preconceived, long-standing theories about the colony's fate. While these efforts resulted in many of the most widely accepted Lost Colony theories, virtually all have been based on a key distortion of Strachey's assertion that the slaughter of the 1587 colony happened "at Roanoke." That distortion, now generally glossed over, represents the fourth and final institutionalized assumption cited in the Preface.

Since all serious theories regarding the fate of the Lost Colony must ultimately confront the troublesome references in Strachey's *Historie,* they are cited here:

Excerpt #1: ...the men, women, and childrene of the first plantation at Roanoak were by practize and commandement of Powhatan (he himself perswaded thereunto by his priests) miserably slaughtered, without any offence given him either by the first planted (who twenty and od yeares had peaceably lyved intermixt with those salvages, and were out of his territory)....[4]

Excerpt #2: ...Powhatan hath slaughtered so many of our nation without offence given, and such as were seated far from him, and in the territory of those weroances which did in no sort depend on him or acknowledge him....[5]

Excerpt #3: It is not long since that his priests told him how that from the Chesapeack Bay a nation should arise which should dissolve and give end to his empire, for which, not many yeares since ... he destroyed and put to the sword all such who might lye under any doubtful construccion of the said prophesie, as all the inhabitants, the weroance and his subjects of that provinve, and so remaine all the Chessiopeians at this daye, and for this cause, extinct.[6]

Excerpt #4: ...at Peccarecamek and Ochanahoen, by relation of Machumps, the people have howses built with stone walles, and one story above another, so taught them by those Englishe whoe escaped the slaughter at Roanoak, at what tyme this our colony under the conduct of Captain Newport, landed within Chesapeake Bay, where the people breed up tame turkeis about their howses, and take apes [metal] in the mountains, and where, at Ritanoe, the weroance Eyanoco preserved seven of the English alive—fower men, two boyes, and one yonge mayde (who escaped and fled up the river of Chanoke), to beat his copper of which he hath certaine mynes at the said Ritanoc, as also at Pamawauk are said to be store of salt stones.[7]

Excerpt #5: ...southwest to Anoeg ... whose howses are built as ours, ten daies distant from us....[8]

Excerpt #6: ...he [Powhatan] doth often send unto us to temporize with us, awaiting perhaps a fit opportunity (inflamed by his furious and bloudy priests) to offer us a tast of the same cuppe which he made our poore countrymen drink of at Roanoak....[9]

Excerpt #7: ...and thus we will commune and entreate with them [the Powhatans], truck, and barter, our commodityes for theirs, and theirs for ours ... in all love and friendship, untill, for our good purposes toward them, we shall find them practize violence or treason against us (as they have done to our other colony at Roanoak).[10]

All of the serious past and present narratives about the fate of the Lost Colony have been based on Smith's earlier references and these passages from Strachey, and they all are variations of the following scenario: The 1587 Roanoke colonists had been living peacefully for more than twenty years among a group of Indians, presumably the Chesapeake tribe beyond Powhatan's domain, when they were massacred. Powhatan himself directed the slaughter because of prophesies by his priests about a danger that would arise from the Chesapeake Bay, and the slaughter took place about the same time that Christopher Newport arrived at the Chesapeake Bay with the Jamestown colony on April 26, 1607. Powhatan exterminated the Chesapeake Indians and the 1587 colonists. Finally, and most perplexing, Strachey claimed that the slaughter of the colonists occurred "at Roanoke" and that several colonists survived "the slaughter at Roanoke" and escaped to various places he called Peccarecamek (Pakrakanick) and Ochanahoen (Ocanahonan), and perhaps Anoeg, where they taught the Indians how to build English-style houses.

One of the most notable historians to tackle Strachey's Lost Colony references was the previously cited David Beers Quinn (1909–2002). His overall efforts, particularly on the Roanoke voyages, provided an unparalleled body of work which set the standard for late–20th century Lost Colony research. Quinn was not without his critics however. Among those was his contemporary, North Carolina historian Thomas C. Parramore (1932–2004). Both Quinn and Parramore grappled with William Strachey's difficult references, and their conclusions represent divergent schools of thought in Lost Colony theory. Their work has influenced virtually every author and historian in this field over many decades, and it is fair to say that effectively all serious Lost Colony theories today have been inspired in one way or another by the analyses of Quinn and Parramore. Since mainstream Lost Colony theory owes so much to the earlier work by these two historians, it will be helpful to see just how they explained Strachey's references.

Quinn approached Strachey's *Historie* as an essentially credible source and believed Strachey to be "thoroughly reliable and conscientious in what he wrote."[11] Quinn acknowledged that it would have been impossible for Strachey to verify everything he wrote, but that Strachey's statements "were based on the best information he could obtain."[12] As mentioned previously, Quinn was a proponent of the now-refuted theory that most of the 1587 colonists must have traveled north to the Chesapeake, their original destination, where they apparently settled among, and intermixed with, the Chesapeake Indians.

This scenario was compatible with excerpts 2 and 3 above, since the Chesapeake tribe inhabited the area to the east, just beyond Powhatan's domain, and did not pay homage to him.[13] Quinn speculated that the colonists may have settled among the Chesapeake Indians about fifteen miles along the Elizabeth River at Skicoac, where Englishmen—possibly including John White—had received a cordial reception during the previous 1585–86 Grenville-Lane expedition. There, Quinn proposed, the colonists lived and intermixed with the Indians for "twenty and od yeares," as Strachey wrote, until April of 1607, when Powhatan ordered their slaughter. Quinn was incorrect, however, when he wrote, "Strachey alone indicates when the Lost Colonists were killed...."[14] The Council's 1609 instructions to Gates, written more than two years before Strachey started his *Historie*, noted that the slaughter happened "upon the first arrival of our [Jamestown] Colonie." In any case, to support his theory Quinn used the previously cited notation from Samuel Purchas regarding the so-called "confession" Chief Powhatan made to Smith about his slaughter of the Lost Colony. For Quinn this piece of evidence was not only corroborated by Strachey's assertions, but it also seemed to validate his own Lost Colony "Chesapeake" theory.

Thomas Parramore and his followers have taken a much more critical view of Strachey's *Historie* and consequently of Quinn's theory as well. Whereas Quinn generally attempted to accommodate Strachey's Roanoke colony references, Parramore essentially claimed that Strachey simply had it all wrong. If the Chesapeake Indians were extinct, as Strachey claimed in the third excerpt above, "who was it, then," Parramore asked, "that attacked Newport and his party near Lynnhaven Bay in April 1607?"[15] Although Strachey wrote that it was Powhatan's custom to re-inhabit conquered areas with loyal tribesmen, Parramore remained unconvinced. He went on to say that Ensign Thomas Willoughby, "not Powhatan," most likely caused the extinction of the Chesapeake Indians during a raid twenty years later in 1627.[16]

Parramore concluded that Strachey's account of the extinction of the "Chessiopeians," as well as Quinn's Chesapeake theory, was "flawed" for other reasons as well. Such a sensational event as the eradication of an entire tribe along with the Lost Colony would certainly have been widely known and easily confirmed by the Jamestown settlers, especially if it occurred about the same time as the arrival of the English in 1607. In order to keep such a major catastrophe secret, Parramore continued, it would have required an improbable cover-up of immense proportions.[17]

To further support his criticism of both Strachey and Quinn, Parramore cited the expedition by Vincente Gonzalez to the Chesapeake Bay. As mentioned previously, Gonzalez searched for the English colony in 1588 and found no trace of it, convincing evidence that the 1587 colony had not relocated there. As to the Samuel Purchas notation regarding Powhatan's confession to John Smith, Parramore found Powhatan's evidence, "a few pieces of iron ... unimpressive" and the entire confession a probable empty boast "to overawe Jamestown settlers."[18] Parramore also pointed out, and Quinn acknowledged, that no 16th century English remains, tools, or instruments have been discovered in the present-day Norfolk area which could prove that the Lost Colony had settled there. Other than the Chesapeake extinction argument, Parramore's criticism was well founded. From this point on, however, his arguments became increasingly unconvincing.

The most confounding puzzle in Strachey's Lost Colony references was his contention that the colonists were slaughtered "*at Roanoak*" (see excerpts 1, 4, 6, and 7). This startling phrase clearly repudiates all variations of current and past Lost Colony theories that involve a slaughter. This was indeed a mystifying detail, presumably obtained from Machumps, and Strachey made the assertion on three or four occasions in his *Historie*. Strachey's claim that the slaughter of the Lost Colony occurred "at Roanoke" has defied logical explanation. Clearly no slaughter of the Lost Colony had occurred at Roanoke during its brief occupation there in 1587–88, as was evident from John White's account of his return to Roanoke in 1590. White found no indications that any slaughter had occurred there; on the contrary, everything pointed to a well-planned and orderly departure by the colonists. There is no evidence, other than Strachey's statements, that White's Lost Colonists were slaughtered at Roanoke.

Yet those problematic "at Roanoak" phrases—particularly those in excerpts 4, 6, and 7—stood as plain as day and presented a formidable hurdle to all Lost Colony theories. It was absolutely necessary for historians to confront and explain Strachey's troublesome phrases. Parramore used John White's 1590 account to begin his assault on the notion that the slaughter occurred at Roanoke:

> We can rule out a slaughter or slow death of the colonists on Roanoke Island. White saw no sign of any such disaster and the signal CROATOAN was not accompanied by the cross-mark that would have indicated that the colonists left in distress. It seems clear that they had moved....[19]

This argument, though, was not enough. If, as the various scenarios of today's mainstream theories continue to claim, the attack on White's colonists occurred at some location other than Roanoke, it was vital that these troublesome "slaughter at Roanoke" phrases be completely repudiated. Both Quinn and Parramore attempted to explain the "at Roanoak" phrases by claiming that Strachey must have meant something other than what his phrases literally indicated. In explaining his own theory, Quinn at least admitted that his Chesapeake paradigm only made sense "*assuming* that 'at Roanoak' and, elsewhere, 'of Roanoak' meant not Roanoke Island but the settlers of the Roanoke colony."[20] By his own admission Quinn recognized that his Chesapeake theory rested entirely on the weak assumption that "at Roanoke" was not a reference to a location, but actually meant the colonists themselves.

Parramore took it a step further. He countered both Strachey and Quinn with the supposition that "at Roanoak" *did* really mean a location, but not a specific one. According to Parramore, Strachey's use of "at Roanoke" actually meant the vague area surrounding Albemarle Sound. This claim would now permit the massacre to have occurred anywhere in that huge area *other than* Roanoke Island or the Chesapeake: "There is also Strachey's fragile authority for the massacre occurring 'at Roanoke,' the common Virginia expression for the Albemarle Sound area, which places the scene well south of Chesapeake country."[21]

Parramore attempted to support his remarkable claim with a footnote citation of an obscure and inaccurate annotation in the mid–17th century Court Records of Lower Norfolk County, Virginia, edited and republished by Alice Granbery Walter in 1978. The entire passage reads exactly as follows. (Walter's editorial annotations are in parentheses):

> Know all men by these presents that I Thomas Ward of Lynhaven in the County of Lower Norff: Chirurgeon did by the Command of Capt: Thomas Willowghby serve in an expedition against the Indians to Yawopyn als (alias?) Rawanoake (Roanoke?) as Chirurgeon to the whole company and did divers Cures upon severall men in the sais service....[22]

Parramore's entire assertion, then, is based on the assumption that "Yawopyn" was synonymous with "Rawanoake" in this single 1645 passage, but even that is uncertain. "Alia" and "Als" were sometimes used for "alias," but usually in 17th and 18th century wills to indicate name changes through marriage or adoption, rarely for locations. Also confusing is the probability that the event cited here was the Willoughby expedition against the Chesapeake, not the Yeopim, Indians. Parramore's claim is also challenged by Francis Yeardley's use of the word Roanoke several years later. Yeardley (also of Lynnhaven like the "Chirurgeon" Ward) sponsored an expedition "to rhoanoke" to acquire land, and his men went specifically to Roanoke Island, where the Indians showed them the remains of Lane's fort. Finally, whatever was meant by this one edited court record has no bearing on what Strachey meant by "Roanoak" nearly thirty-five years earlier.

This vague territorial claim about "Roanoke" was also repeated by one of Parramore's associates, author F. Roy Johnson, who collaborated with Parramore on *The Lost Colony in Fact and Legend*, when he wrote that "To the Englishmen at Jamestown, Roanoke was the vague vast country to the south which had been visited by Raleigh's explorers; it extended westward from the Atlantic to near the head of Albemarle Sound."[23] Years later (2001) Parramore would challenge Quinn directly on this point:

> Quinn is among those historians who misconstrue the term 'at Roanoak,' where Strachey insists, the colonists were killed. But seventeenth-century Virginians used the name "Roanoak" to signify the region bordering what some early maps call the "Sea of Roanoak," modern Albemarle and Currituck Sound. When, for example, Virginia fur trader and explorer Nathaniel Batts met Quaker founder George Fox on the lower Chowan River in 1672, Batts boasted of having formerly served as "governor of Roanoak," the thinly settled area on the northern sounds that in 1663 became Carolina. It was this region, not Roanoke Island specifically, that that Strachey almost certainly was referring to in his remarks on the Lost Colony's fate.[24]

This was Parramore's final attempt to challenge Quinn and put Strachey's perplexing "at Roanoke" phrases to rest. Once again, however, there are a number of problems with Parramore's "evidence." This time Parramore supported his interpretation of "at Roanoak" with a single reference made by George Fox about Nathaniel Batts in 1672, when "Batts boasted of having formerly served as 'governor of Roanoak,' the thinly settled area on the northern sounds that in 1663 became Carolina." This is rather misleading. Parramore's evidence is taken from George Fox's journal wherein Fox mentions meeting a number of people, including Batts, at Hugh Smith's house near the Maco-comock River in 1672. Fox wrote,

> ... the people of other professions came to see us ... and many of them received us gladly. Amongst others came Nathaniel Batts, who had been governor of Roan-Oak; he went by the name of Captain Batts, and had been a rude, desperate man. He asked me about a woman in Cumberland, who, he said, he was told, had been healed by our prayers, and laying on of hands....[25]

Whatever was meant by "governor of Roan-Oak" in this passage is certainly not clear, particularly since no other record of, or reference to, this title exists. It is probable, however, that Batts assumed that title in 1653 when he went to Roanoke Island under the sponsorship of Francis Yeardley and purchased large tracts of land from the chief of the Roanoke Indians there.

What *is* clear is that Parramore essentially used his own unsubstantiated claim as an appositive, a noun phrase or clause that renames or provides more information about the noun preceding it: 'Roanoak.' There is nothing in the original Fox passage that identifies "Roan-Oak" as "the thinly settled area on the northern sounds that in 1663 became Carolina." These are entirely Parramore's words, not Fox's. Consequently, the credibility of Parramore's claim about the meaning of "Roanoak" is dependent on nothing more than *his own* inserted claim itself, which does not appear in the Fox journal. Parramore's argument, then, is an example of the previously mentioned logical fallacy of "repeated assertion." In this case his evidence is simply his own repeated claim regarding the vague definition of Roanoke. Like his previous example, Parramore's reference to the Fox-Batts encounter offers no convincing evidence for his claim. It is also worth repeating that whatever was meant by "Roan-Oak" here would seem to have little or no bearing on what Strachey meant by "Roanoak" well over a half century earlier in 1610 and 1611.

Another of Parramore's contemporaries, fellow North Carolina historian William S. Powell, offered a somewhat ambiguous explanation for the broad geographical interpretation of Roanoke when he wrote, "In order to distinguish between the new colony of Virginia centered in Jamestown and Raleigh's Virginia, the name Roanoke was frequently used for the older area. John Smith's map of 1624 called the region 'Ould Virginia,' while at a later time the terms South Virginia and the Southern Plantation were applied."[26]

Powell footnoted this passage citing as evidence a reference to a single Virginia Company's notation of an exploration conducted "to the Southward to Roanocke" by Marmaduke Rayner in 1620. The complete original line containing that phrase in the records of the Virginia Company is, "Ther was also read vnto the Company a Relaçon of three seuerall Voyadges made this last

Suṁer one to the Southward to Roanocke made by mr Marmaduk Rayner."[27] In the first place the account of Rayner's voyage has been lost, as Powell acknowledged, and so no record exists to tell us precisely where he went. Powell's interpretation, therefore, rests entirely on the assumption that Rayner either did not visit Roanoke Island on his voyage or did not sail from Jamestown towards Roanoke Island. The phrase "Southward to Roanocke" does not mean that the broad area of "Raleigh's Virginia" was *called* "Roanoke," but rather that Marmaduke Rayner explored the area from Jamestown in the direction of, or towards, or as far as Roanoke Island. A similar phrase with a similar meaning was used by the Reverend Patrick Copland in 1622 when he wrote about Jamestown council member John Pory's exploration from Jamestown, "Maister Pory deserves good incouragement for his painefull discoveries *to the southward, as far as Choanoack*"[28] (emphasis added). This does not mean that the entire area "to the southward" was called "Choanoack," nor does "to the Southward to Roanocke" mean that the entire area was called "Roanocke."

Powell also cited page twenty-eight of Strachey's *Historie* to support his claim that the term "South Virginia" was used "at a later time," about 1624 and afterwards, but that during the early years of "the new colony of Virginia centered in Jamestown ... the name Roanoke was frequently used." Page twenty-eight of Strachey's *Historie*, however, written during his tenure as Secretary in 1610–1611, reads,

> Now concerning the low land, or Virginia ... yt may well enough be divided into South Virginia and North Virginia, the Chesapoack Bay and Powhatan River parting these twoo.... North Virginia lyeth on the North side of Powhatan, or the first river within the Chesapeak Bay (which we have called the King's River) up to the Falls.[29]

Strachey used the term "South Virginia" on three occasions in his *Historie*, each time referring to the area south of the James River as opposed to the area north of the James which he called "North Virginia." Strachey used the name "Roanoke" many more times, but *not*, as Powell implied, to indicate "the older area" of "Raleigh's Virginia." It is clear from the text that Strachey, who was writing in 1610 and 1611 at Jamestown and was the author of the "slaughter at Roanoke" phrase, used "South Virginia"—not "Roanoke"—to indicate the area south of the James River. As will be seen later, when Strachey used the word "Roanoke," he was specifically indicating Roanoke Island.

As Powell acknowledged, Strachey's contemporary John Smith did not refer to the general area visited by Raleigh's explorers as Roanoke, but rather as "Ould Virginia," as it is so indicated on the map in his *Generall Historie*. Smith used the word "Roonok" twice in his 1607–08 *A True Relation* and both times the word indicated no other place than Roanoke Island. The same word—"Roonok"—was used on the Zúñiga Map, which accompanied Smith's letter to England, to specifically label Roanoke Island.

Powell also cited William Bullock's 1649 booklet, *Virginia Impartially examined,* written to encourage new settlement in Virginia and less dependency on tobacco as the primary crop. The booklet only mentions "Roanock" a few times, the first of which is "the rich and healthfull Countries of Roanock, the now plantations of Virginia and Mary-land"[30] The most definitive reference to "Roanock" is the following:

> To speak first of the most Southerly Climat, viz. from the degree of 34 to 36, the Aire is extream pleasant & wholsome, as it was found by M. Ralph Laine, M. Heriot and others, who with their Company sat down upon the Island of *Roanock*, which is a little to the Southward of that place in *Virginia*, where now the *English* are planted....[31]

In describing the "Naturall Commodities" to be found in Virginia, Bullock wrote, "In *Roanock* they found Silk-wormes bigger then Walnuts, and were informed by the *Indians*, that higher in the Countrey there were abundance, and bigger."[32] There is little here to support the assertion that "Roanoke" was the common expression for the Albemarle Sound area, and none whatsoever that this is *what Strachey meant* by "at Roanoke" four decades earlier.

It is possible that the notion of "Roanoke" as a vague geographic area could have been conceived in the late 19th century by another North Carolina author, Lumbee advocate Hamilton McMillan. McMillan, mentioned previously, was a North Carolina legislator who championed the cause of the Lumbee Indians of Robeson County in their effort to gain official tribal status in the state. His 1888 publication of *Sir Walter Raleigh's Lost Colony* was written in support of the Lumbee claim that at least some of their tribe was descended from Croatoan Indians who integrated with White's Lost Colonists sometime after 1587.

According to McMillan, Lumbee tradition holds that "their ancestors came from 'Roanoke in Virginia.' By Virginia, they mean territory occupied by the tribe in the vicinity of Pamlico Sound."[33] Croatoan, Hamilton wrote, was the "principal seat" of the tribe, but the name also referred to their territory, which "once embraced portions, at least, of the present counties of Carteret, Jones and Craven."[34] McMillan essentially claimed that the terms "Virginia," "Croatoan," and "Roanoke" were more or less interchangeable to the Lumbees. As he put it, "The tribe once lived in Roanoke in Virginia, as they persist in calling Eastern North Carolina. The name Roanoke is applied to the country around Pamlico Sound...."[35] It is worth noting that Parramore was unquestionably familiar with McMillan's geographic assertion, since he made specific references to it in his chapter "The Lost Colony and the Tuscaroras."[36]

McMillan's claim that "Virginia," "Croatoan," and "Roanoke" are geographically equivalent is specious in itself, but the credibility of that claim is irrelevant to the central point being made here. What the Lumbees may or may not have meant by "Roanoke" in the late 19th century has no bearing whatsoever on what *Strachey and his contemporaries* meant by *their* use of the word "Roanoke" in the early 17th century. Parramore, who was clearly acquainted with McMillan's claim that Roanoke-Croatoan-Virginia were synonymous, may have embraced the idea and used a similar interpretation to challenge the problematic "at Roanoke" phrase in Strachey's *Historie*. McMillan claimed that to the Lumbees "Roanoke" referred to "the country around Pamlico Sound," and Parramore claimed that to the Jamestown settlers "Roanoke" referred to "the Albemarle Sound area." The similarity between the two interpretations is interesting.

In any case it makes little difference what anyone thought about the meaning of "Roanoke" other than Strachey himself and his Jamestown contemporaries. The fundamental defect with the assertion that "Roanoke" was considered a vast geographic area is that the claim is not supported by relevant sources: local native tradition, historical "Roanoke" usage, or—most importantly—by the contemporary Jamestown chroniclers, including Strachey himself.

To the native peoples there was an important distinction made between the *location* of Roanoke and the territory which the *Roanoke tribe* occupied at various times. According to a Roanoke-Hatteras tribal history source, the original *territory* of the *Roanoac* tribe was limited to Roanoke Island and the nearby eastern shore of the mainland where their capital town, Dasamonguepeuk, was located (near today's Mann's Harbor). That location, although sometimes *inhabited* by the Roanoke tribe, was continually called Dasamonguepeuk, and never Roanoke. From time to time they also occupied the narrow barrier Bodie Island just to the east of Roanoke Island.[37] The Roanoke *tribe* occasionally inhabited these peripheral areas, but the *location* of "Roanoke" was always Roanoke Island. The Roanoke Indians, in fact, called themselves "*the northern people*" because tradition says they lived at the north end of Roanoke Island.[38] The *location* called "Roanoke" always meant Roanoke Island in Indian tradition.

It might be assumed that the existence of locations—other than Roanoke Island—bearing the name of "Roanoke" could lend support to the assumption that "Roanoke" was not considered a specific location to the Jamestown colonists. The "Roanoke" River, for example, flows more than 400 miles from southern Virginia to Albemarle Sound. If one counted the entire river basin, including the land area drained by the Roanoke River and its tributaries, the total area would be vast and vague indeed. That argument, however, rests upon the faulty assumption that the Roanoke River was so called by the early 17th century Jamestown writers and mapmakers.

The present-day Roanoke River has been known by a variety of different names in the course of history, but it was not called "Roanoke" River until the 18th century. At the time of English contact in the late 16th century it was called Moratuc or Moratoc; the Morattico River in 1657; the Noratake River in 1671. There is one early reference to "divers sorts of *Firre, Sivet Cats* up *Roanock* River" in Bullock's aforementioned 1649 *Virginia Impartially examined*, but it is likely that Bullock was referring to the body of water adjacent to Roanoke, present-day Albemarle Sound. The first indisputable reference to the river as "Roanoke" apparently did not appear until 1733 when Edward Moseley wrote the name "Roanoke River" on his map.[39] Other Virginia locations did not bear the name "Roanoke" until much later: Roanoke County in Virginia was so named in 1838 and the town of Roanoke, Virginia, was called "Big Lick" until 1883 when it became an important railroad terminus.[40] All such designations obviously did not come into existence until long after Strachey and his contemporaries were writing. There are a few 17th century examples of the word "Roanoke" used in a descriptive phrase, as in "the sea of Rawnocke,"[41] and probably Bullock's "Roanock River" above, referring to the body of water adjacent to Roanoke (Albemarle Sound), but the word was not used to indicate a location unless it referred specifically to Roanoke Island.

More significantly, Parramore's broad geographical interpretation of "Roanoke," which he claimed was "the common Virginia expression" for the area surrounding Albemarle Sound to the south, is not supported by the early 17th century source documents themselves, *including William Strachey's*. An examination of the contemporary accounts reveals an entirely different picture. Within the six narratives recounting Virginia colonization contained in Hakluyt's *Principal Navigations*, there are thirty-one references to "Roanoke." Three of these are "an Island called Roanoke," "Island of Roanoke," and "Isle of Roanoke." The remaining twenty-eight are phrases such as "at Roanoke," "to Roanoke," "from Roanoke" etc., and *all* clearly signify Roanoke Island.[42] This, of course, is to be expected since the six accounts in Hakluyt narrated events between 1584 and 1590, before Jamestown was founded. Nevertheless, it demonstrates that "Roanoke" continually indicated Roanoke Island since the first arrival of the English in 1584.

After Jamestown was settled in 1607 "Roanoke" continued to indicate Roanoke Island. As mentioned above, Smith's 1607–08 *A True Relation* contains two references to Roanoke (Roonok), and they both clearly indicate Roanoke Island. His *Generall Historie*, published in 1624, contains eight references to Roanoke, all of which also unquestionably refer to the specific location, Roanoke Island.[43] The same is true of Harriot's *Briefe and True Report*: ten references, all indicating Roanoke Island.[44] Even Robert Beverley's later *The History of Virginia*, originally published in 1705, contains fourteen references to Roanoke, nine of which specifically mean Roanoke Island, and the remaining five which refer, not to any location, but to the name (Roenoke) given to pieces of cockle shell used by the Indians as ornaments and currency.[45]

Most importantly, William Strachey himself used the word "Roanoak" on twenty-seven occasions in his *Historie*, including the excerpts cited earlier. An examination of all twenty-seven of Strachey's uses of the word "Roanoke" demonstrates that there is no evidence, contextual or otherwise, that anything other than Roanoke Island was intended on each of these occasions.[46] It is Strachey, after all, as author of the troubling "slaughter at Roanoke" phrases, whose meaning is essential. Of the ninety references to "Roanoke" or its spelling variants used by Hakluyt, Smith, Harriot, Beverely, and Strachey himself, all—with the exception of the five cockle shell names—refer to Roanoke Island. The conclusion is unavoidable: The argument by Parramore and others that Strachey's "Roanoak" must have meant a larger, much more general geographic area than Roanoke Island is convincingly repudiated by the textual evidence. To William Strachey and his Jamestown contemporaries "Roanoke" specifically meant Roanoke Island.

The interpretation of "Roanoke" as the broad area south of Jamestown lives on only through the authority of repeated assertion, the fallacy mentioned above and in the Preface. This particular fallacy has unfortunately led Lost Colony theory hopelessly astray. It has hindered any real progress in Lost Colony research for decades and has resulted in the many misguided theories being promoted today. It has allowed authors and historians to fashion scenarios placing an imagined massacre of the Lost Colony *anywhere* in "the vague vast country to the south ... which extended westward from the Atlantic to near the head of Albemarle Sound."

# 19

# The "Slaughter
at Roanoke" Solved
1610–1611

Lost Colony authors, historians, and devotees have essentially dealt with
Strachey's "slaughter at Roanoke" in one of two ways. The more seriously
focused writers have followed the Parramore school of thought and have
embraced the assumption that when the Jamestown writers used the word
"Roanoke," they were not referring to Roanoke Island, but to a broad area of
territory south of Jamestown. As demonstrated, however, that assumption
was based on an unproven and unchallenged assertion, which is directly contradicted by an examination of the Jamestown writers' use of the word
"Roanoke." Other authors have simply disregarded the "slaughter at Roanoke"
phrase entirely. In either case the result has been, especially in recent decades,
a general devaluation of Strachey as a reliable Lost Colony source. A discred-
ited or ignored William Strachey, after all, has opened the field to an assortment of other theories about the Lost Colony. With Strachey disputed or
ignored and Quinn's Chesapeake theory safely retired, it was possible to place
the Lost Colony at a variety of locations—the Chowan River, the Roanoke
River, Weapemeoc, Cashie Creek in Bertie County—and the slaughter almost
anyplace other than Roanoke Island.

And thus we are left with an assortment of Lost Colony theories today,
all of which are essentially variations of the following broad scenario: The
1587 colony, short of food and supplies, left Roanoke hastily and settled near
or among the Chesapeake, Chowanoke, Weapemeoc, or Croatoan tribes,
where they lived for many years among the local natives. At some time perhaps coinciding with the arrival of the Jamestown settlers in 1607, the Lost
Colonists were slaughtered by the Powhatans or a neighboring tribe some-
place in present-day North Carolina or Virginia, but a handful of colonists
survived the slaughter and were scattered to remote places throughout the land.

187

As demonstrated, however, the textual evidence from the Jamestown chroniclers is more than enough to conclude that when Strachey used the phrase "at Roanoke," he was clearly referring to Roanoke Island. It follows that when he used the phrase "slaughter at Roanoke," he intended it to mean that the slaughter actually happened at Roanoke Island. The phrase is not inexplicable or equivocal, nor is it an archaic reference or a slip of the quill on Strachey's part. He used the identical phrase on several occasions, and each time he wrote precisely what he meant to say.

Strachey was an educated gentleman whose writing skills were very well regarded. He was educated at Cambridge, and he was a familiar figure in literary circles. He regularly attended plays in London and was a shareholder in the Blackfriars Theatre. He was certainly acquainted with London's poets and playwrights, among whom were Thomas Campion, John Donne, Ben Jonson, and William Shakespeare. Strachey was regarded highly enough by his contemporaries to have a poem of his included in Jonson's play *Sejanus His Fall* in 1605. As previously mentioned, many believe that Shakespeare's *The Tempest* was directly influenced by Strachey's *A True Reportory*, his account of the shipwreck of the *Sea Venture* on the islands of Bermuda en route to Jamestown. And of course Strachey's appointment as Secretary of the Jamestown Colony in 1610 was an acknowledgment of his writing skills. Although early 17th century spelling and morphology may have changed over the centuries, English grammar—based largely on Latin—has remained fairly stable. William Strachey was certainly no stranger to proper grammatical usage and syntax.[1]

Further confirmation of this can be provided by an analysis of Strachey's "at Roanoke" phrases. In the problematic excerpts cited in the previous chapter, consider his use of "at," a preposition which indicates specificity, and is used "to show an exact position or particular place."[2] Regarding a slaughter of the colonists, Strachey uses the phrase "at Roanoak" in the four excerpts (nos. 1, 4, 6 and 7):

The first usage is "the men, women, and childrene of the first plantation at Roanoak were ... miserably slaughtered...." In this case "at Roanoak" is an adjective phrase indicating a specific location, but the phrase is modifying the word "plantation" and simply indicates that Roanoke was the specific location of the plantation, *not* that the slaughter necessarily happened there. It does, however, once again clearly indicate that Roanoke meant Roanoke Island and also that the victims of the slaughter were from Roanoke—an important point to be taken up later.

The second, third, and fourth occurrences of "at Roanoak" tell a very different grammatical story. The second occurrence, found in the fourth excerpt, is "those Englishe whoe escaped the slaughter at Roanoak...." Here is another adjective phrase, but this time modifying the key noun "slaughter" and clearly indicating that Roanoke was the specific place where the slaughter happened.

The third occurrence, in excerpt 6, is "the same cuppe which he made our poore countrymen drink of at Roanoak." Here Strachey was speaking figuratively, equating the slaughter to a cup from which the colonists were forced to drink. In this case "at Roanoak" is an adverbial phrase modifying the archaic verb "drink (of)" and telling clearly and specifically *where* "our poore countrymen" were made to drink of that figurative cup: unquestionably the same specific location meaning Roanoke Island. The fourth occurrence, in excerpt 7, is "we shall find them [the Powhatans] practize violence or treason against us (as they have done to our other colony at Roanoak)." Once again "at Roanoak" modifies "our other colony" and indicates the place where the "violence" occurred.

There is no grammatical or contextual evidence that the word "Roanoke," used elsewhere in Strachey's *Historie* and in all the contemporary accounts cited earlier, refers to any other location than Roanoke Island, and it is clear that Strachey intended to say that the slaughter occurred there. R.H. Major of the British Museum, editor of Strachey's *Historie* published in 1849 by the Hakluyt Society, had no doubt about Strachey's use of the word "Roanoak" and wanted the reader to understand as well. Immediately after the word "Roanoak" in the aforementioned passage contained in excerpt 6— "the same cuppe which he made our poore countrymen drink of at Roanoak"—R.H. Major inserted a footnote which reads, "The colony planted by Sir Walter Raleigh, which Powhatan destroyed."[3] The latter part of Major's footnote—"which Powhatan destroyed"—will be addressed below, but suffice it to say for now that his notation clarifies the fact that a slaughter of "our poore countrymen" planted by Raleigh occurred at Roanoke Island.

Finally, there is conclusive verification *in Strachey's own words* that the slaughter indeed happened at Roanoke Island. Aside from a mention of Roanoack (Island) in the introductory notes called "Praemonition to the Reader," the first reference to "the slaughter at Roanoke" in the body of Strachey's *Historie* is found on page twenty-six of the work. That reference is the previously cited excerpt which begins, "at Peccarecamek and Ochanahoen, by relation of Machumps, the people have howses built with stone walles, and one story above another, so taught them by those Englishe whoe escaped the slaughter at Roanoak."[4]

Two pages later, on page twenty-eight, the second mention of Roanoack is found: "in this country [South Virginia] it was that Sir Walter Raleigh planted his two colonies, in the islande aforesaid, called Roanoack."[5] The "islande aforesaid, called Roanoack" is a direct and indisputable reference to the "slaughter at Roanoak," on page twenty-six. There is no other "aforesaid" Roanoke than that one. These are Strachey's first two references to "Roanoak," and he was unquestionably equating the latter with the former. Here is conclusive confirmation from Strachey himself that when he wrote of the "slaughter at Roanoke," he was undoubtedly referring to the specific location of Roanoke Island and was saying that the slaughter occurred there and no place else. Any assertion that Strachey's "Roanoak" must have meant some vast geographical area is clearly mistaken. Consequently, any theory which includes a slaughter occurring any place other than Roanoke Island must also be flawed and must also be reconsidered.

Once it is firmly established that Strachey's "slaughter at Roanoak" indeed refers to a slaughter that occurred at Roanoke Island, the fog begins to lift. There is only one legitimate candidate for the "slaughter" and it cannot be John White's Lost Colony. As mentioned, any notion that the 1587 colony was slaughtered at Roanoke Island is quickly dispelled by the documentary evidence. Parramore was initially right when he cited White's own description upon his return to the island in 1590 in search of his colony. There was no evidence of any "slaughter" or actual Indian attack on the 1587 colony at Roanoke. All indications pointed to the facts that the colonists willingly abandoned the island, that they dismantled and removed transportable parts of their dwellings, that they carried their portable weapons and implements with them, that they took the time to bury cumbersome chests too difficult to transport, and that they left messages intended to direct White to Croatoan.

Yet Strachey insisted that there was a slaughter at Roanoke, and it has now been well established that the slaughter happened at Roanoke Island. There was only one Indian assault known to have occurred at Roanoke Island, but it happened in 1586, the year before White's arrival. The Grenville/Lane military expedition to Roanoke in 1585 had resulted in open hostility between the English and Indians and culminated, on June 1, 1586, with Lane's attack upon the Indians on the mainland and the killing and beheading of their leader Pemisapan. Sir Francis Drake arrived at Roanoke about two weeks later, and Lane decided to accept Drake's offer to transport the colony back to England. In the meantime Sir Richard Grenville was just days away from Roanoke with his supply ships intended for Lane's colony. When Grenville arrived, he found the settlement deserted, but before departing he left a fifteen, or possibly an eighteen, man garrison at Roanoke in order to retain territorial possession for Raleigh. That garrison was later attacked and routed by Pemisapan's followers. This Indian assault was the only significant attack to occur at Roanoke, and the evidence will show that this must have been the event Strachey actually referred to in his *Historie*. The 1587 Lost Colony was not involved at all.

Strachey's own words demonstrate that this is the event he wrote about. Note his previously cited reference to *two* colonies in "Sir Walter Raleigh planted his two colonies, in the island aforesaid, called Roanoack." His reference is historically accurate. There were two attempts at colonization at Roanoke; the first was the Grenville-Lane military colony in 1585–86 and the second was White's 1587 colony. Therefore when Strachey wrote that the colonists, "*of the first plantation* at Roanoak ... were miserably slaughtered," he could only be referring to the 1585–86 colony, which Grenville tried to perpetuate upon his arrival with the re-supply ships in July 1586, by placing and provisioning the contingent of men there.

There is also a potential mathematical reference in the same excerpt to demonstrate that Strachey was describing the 1585–86 colony. Strachey wrote that "the men, women, and childrene of the first plantation at Roanoak were ... miserably slaughtered, (*who twenty and od yeares* had peaceably lyved intermixt with those salvages, and were out of his territory)..." (italics added). "Twenty and od" could be read as "twenty-one" years, but certainly no fewer. Since it was reported that the slaughter took place about the same time that Newport arrived at the Chesapeake in April 1607, simple subtraction would indicate that the victims of the 1607 slaughter had been living with the Indians since 1586, making them likely survivors of Grenville's 1586 contingent, and clearly not White's 1587 colony.

The reference to "men, women, and childrene of the first plantation" is easily explained by the fact that the men from the 1586 contingent had "*lyved intermixt* with those salvages" for twenty-one years and would have had admixed offspring by then. Their offspring, "miserably slaughtered" in 1607 along with their English fathers and Indian mothers as well as the rest of the tribe, would correctly be called "childrene of the first plantation at Roanoak." If any of the admixed children were preserved, as was customary, one of these could very well have been the young boy seen by George Percy along the James River in 1607: "At Port Cotage in our Voyage up the River, we saw a Savage Boy about the age of ten yeeres, who had a head of haire of a perfect yellow and a reasonable white skinne, which is a Miracle amongst all Savages."[6]

In any case, Smith's report of Powhatan's slaughter was not entirely wrong. There certainly could have been a slaughter conducted by Powhatan, and a few Englishmen may have been victims, but they were not Lost Colonists. Quinn's Chesapeake theory may also have been partially accurate. Roanoke colonists *were* possibly killed along with the Chesapeakes in 1607, but they would have been survivors of Grenville's 1586 garrison, not White's 1587 colonists. What, then, is known of Grenville's garrison?

As noted earlier, the actual number of men left by Grenville is disputed. Hakluyt's account said fifteen, but the deposition of Pedro Diaz, the Spanish pilot captured by Richard Grenville in 1585 and pilot for Grenville's relief expedition to Roanoke in 1586, claimed that Grenville left eighteen men on the island. Smith wrote in his *Generall Historie* "that the fiftie men left by Sir *Richard Grenvill*, were suddainly set vpon by three hundred of Secotan, Aquascogoc, and Dassamonpeack."[7] Beverely would also write in 1705 that Grenville "left Fifty Men in the same Island of *Roenoke*, built them Houses necessary, gave them Two Years Provision, and return'd."[8] Beverely's account, however, was probably taken from Smith, who, as noted previously, had a natural tendency to exaggerate. It is probably safe to say that the actual number was somewhere between the fifteen and eighteen indicated by Hakluyt and Diaz.

According to the Croatoan account related to Master Stafford in July of 1587 and recorded by John White, eleven of the fifteen men were at the settlement when the Indians attacked. Two of the Englishmen were killed in the ensuing battle, with a few others wounded, and the men gradually retreated to the water's edge where they managed to escape in a boat and row towards the barrier islands. On the way they picked up the other four men who had been gathering oysters, and they "landed on a little Island on the right hand of our entrance into the harbour of Hatorask, where they remayned a while, but afterward departed, whither as yet we know not."[9]

They must have paused on one of the small islands adjacent to Roanoke, immediately west of the barrier islands, and carefully considered their options. The thirteen remaining men had escaped with their lives, but little else. Several were wounded. They had a few weapons and little food other than the oysters collected by the four who were not present during the attack.

According to author Giles Milton, these fifteen men were soldiers, probably battle-tested in Ireland or in the Netherlands against the Spanish,[10] and this seems to be an accurate assessment. White's account relates how the Indians, pretending friendship, attacked the eleven Englishmen using to "great aduantage" the elements of surprise and the familiar, thickly treed terrain. Outnumbered nearly three to one, the men "were forced to take vp such weapons as came first to hand, and without order to runne forth among the Sauages, with whom they skirmished aboue an howre."[11]

During the course of the battle these nine men were driven to the shoreline where they managed to escape in a small boat. As mentioned, the group eventually rowed to a small island and, as the Croatoans reported, "afterward departed, whither as yet we know not." It is possible, however, to reconstruct a plausible destination: It obviously would have made no sense to row eastward into the Atlantic in a small open boat without provisions. They would not have risked going west, back within reach of the same Indians bent on their destruction. F. Roy Johnson thought they could have traveled some thirty to forty miles south to the village of Pomeiock and eventually integrated with the Indians there.[12] That decision would have been highly unlikely, since they would have chosen to go to a village occupied by Indians who were allied with those who had just attacked them at Roanoke. It was also in an area unlikely to be visited by English ships. If they had gone farther south, they would have approached Croatoan, in which case the Croatoans would surely have been able to report their whereabouts to Stafford.

It is far more likely that they ventured north along the leeward side of the barrier islands, stopping when necessary to rest, tend to the wounded, re-supply fresh water, and gather crabs, oysters, or any other of the available indigenous shellfish. The thirteen may have understood, perhaps from Grenville, that future colonization plans would probably be pointed northward to the Chesapeake Bay area, and concluded that the odds for making contact with English ships were better there. Ironically, White was instructed to stop at Roanoke in 1587 and "take in the aforesaid fifteen men left there by Sir Richard Grenville the yeare before, and so to alter their seat unto the Chesapeake Bay."[13]

A northward journey would take the thirteen survivors up Currituck Sound perhaps to the present Virginia Beach area. They may also have veered to the northwest, avoiding Back Bay, and navigated the interconnected waterways leading to the present Norfolk area and the Elizabeth River. Either route would have enabled them to reach one of the several Chesapeake villages, where they may have been welcomed and assisted, just as Lane's exploratory group had been the previous winter. It is most likely that it was this band of Englishmen who, for "twenty and od yeares had peaceably lyved intermixt with those salvages."

It is essential to note once again that Strachey's sources were Powhatan Algonquians, because it means that their information must be viewed from a Native American perspective and with an understanding of Indian tradition. Algonquian Indian boys learned at an early age that there were few acceptable alternatives to becoming a warrior. Success in war was publicly acclaimed and richly rewarded. "Powhatan men were encouraged to recite accounts of their exploits as hunters and warriors, especially on public occasions with 'royalty' present."[14] At such occasions a line of young warriors formed, and each stepped forward in turn and related stories of the great feats he had performed in battle. Hyperbole was a common thread interwoven in such accounts.[15] The important point here is that, lacking a written language, tribal history and great deeds were transmitted by oral tradition, which—however exaggerated—contained an essential truth.

It is reasonable, then, to see Strachey's account of the "slaughter at Roanoak" as a somewhat exaggerated event containing a core truth, related to him directly by Indians immersed in that same oral tradition. As indicated above, the only known sizable attack involving the killing of colonists at Roanoke took place after the departure of Grenville's re-supply fleet in the summer of 1586 and before the arrival of John White and his colonists in July of 1587. That attack would not have been seen as a minor encounter by the native tribesmen.

The events leading up to this attack apparently involved the largest, most coordinated, well-planned Indian offensive against the English to that point in time. Upon the death of his brother Granganimeo and his father Ensenore, two steady allies of the English, the Indian Wingina changed his name to Pemisapan and set in motion a plan for a major assault against the English at Roanoke Island. According to Ralph Lane, Pemisapan's strategy called for uniting all the tribes in the surrounding area and even the Moratocks and Mongoaks far to the west in a massive armed coalition aimed at destroying the English at Roanoke.[16]

As outlined earlier, on June 1, 1586, Lane's men preempted the Indian assault, attacked the village at Dasamonguepeuk, and killed and beheaded Pemisapan. About two weeks later Sir Frances Drake, following his successful raids on Santo Domingo, Cartagena, and St. Augustine, arrived unexpectedly at Roanoke. At this point Grenville's re-supply ships were overdue; therefore, after consultations with his men and the onset of stormy weather, Lane accepted Drake's offer of transportation back to England. On June 18 Lane and the rest of the first colony left Roanoke with Sir Francis Drake. Nothing is known of the Indian reaction to Lane's attack and the gruesome killing of Pemisapan, but it can be safely surmised that their hatred of the English had reached a boiling point. Lane's men, in fact, were "well aware of the possible results ... were they to remain."[17] That hatred would still have been simmering when Grenville's re-supply finally arrived a short time later, and it would have culminated in the successful attack and rout of the garrison left by Grenville at Roanoke.

From the Indian perspective the assault against the contingent at Roanoke would have represented an important victory as well as retribution, a common and primary motivation for the native Indians, for the killing of their leader Pemisapan. The friendly Croatoans described the encounter: The Englishmen had been attacked "by 30 of the men of Secota, Aquascogoc, and Dasamonguepeuk." This was a well-planned and coordinated attack. The Indians battled bravely, killed two in the process while wounding others, and finally drove the English completely from the island. It was the first and only decisive victory against the English up to that time. It would not take much embellishment to see this event as a major triumph and a complete rout of the English, subsequently taking its appropriate place in native oral tradition, and becoming, as it would be related to Strachey almost a quarter century later, the "slaughter at Roanoak."

All things considered, it seems likely that during his interviews with the Powhatans, Strachey intertwined information, some of it perhaps exaggerated, about two different "slaughters." The first of these took place in 1586 at

Roanoke Island and involved the fifteen-man garrison left by Grenville in order to retain territorial possession for Raleigh. Survivors of this assault made their way north and settled among the Chesapeake Indians at one of their villages. The second slaughter occurred twenty-one years later when Chief Powhatan, upon the advice of his priests, attacked and slaughtered the "Chessiopeians" along with the few surviving men from Grenville's garrison and perhaps some of their mixed offspring. The 1587 Lost Colony was not involved in either of these events.

This scenario, supported by the evidence supplied above, also satisfies the objections cited by Strachey's critics earlier. Parramore's doubt about Strachey's statement that the Chesapeake Indians were "extinct" is answered by the somewhat exaggerated, but essentially true, nature of Indian oral tradition. A near, but not complete, eradication of several Chesapeake villages could easily be retold as "extinction." According to Hakluyt there were thirteen initial survivors of the 1586 assault at Roanoke Island. If a few of them were still alive in 1607 and living among the Indians with their admixed offspring, their demise along with the tribe of Chesapeakes would not have been viewed by the Powhatan Indians as the catastrophic event Parramore imagined. His "massive cover-up" argument was based on the assumed presence of the majority of White's colonists, not two or three of the thirteen Roanoke garrison survivors.

Parramore found Powhatan's evidence, "a few pieces of iron … unimpressive," but Powhatan's limited evidence could be explained by the small number of Englishmen who escaped the 1586 attack with the few implements they were able to salvage during their hasty retreat. This scenario would also explain the fact that no 16th-century English artifacts have been discovered in the present-day Norfolk, Virginia, area. The group was simply too small and too ill-equipped to have left enough archeological evidence besides the few items Powhatan had removed.

The arguments proposed here and in the previous chapter dispute the flawed but often repeated assertion—the fourth institutionalized assumption—that Strachey's use of "Roanoke" referred to a "vague vast country to the south" of Jamestown. A textual examination of the late 16th and early 17th century writers confirms the fact that their use of "Roanoke" invariably meant Roanoke Island. Strachey himself left conclusive evidence in his specific notation that the "slaughter at Roanoke" mentioned on page twenty-six of his *Historie* occurred at Roanoke Island. The only assault conducted by native tribesmen at Roanoke was the successful attack and defeat of the contingent of men left there by Grenville in 1586. The Lost Colony was in no way implicated in either "the slaughter at Roanoke" in 1586 or Powhatan's slaughter of the Chesapeakes in 1607.

# 20

## Lost Colony Clues and Powhatan Oral Tradition
### 1611–1612

By 1612 William Strachey was back in England putting the finishing touches on his *Historie of Travaile Into Virginia Britannia*. John Smith had returned to England in late 1609 and his *Proceedings of the English Colony of Virginia*, an expanded version of his earlier *A True Relation*, was about to be published. The final chapter of the fate of the Lost Colony had also been written, at least in the minds of England's officialdom. Smith's alarming report about the colony's slaughter at the hands of Powhatan had been accepted as gospel by the Virginia Council, although the Virginia Company of London made no mention of it for obvious reasons in its promotional literature. Strachey had followed up with a few more confusing details about the slaughter, but they would not be widely known until 1849, and it did not alter the basic slaughter story. The focus at Jamestown had now turned toward expansion, with new settlements having been established at Henrico and Kecoughtan. By 1612 the book on the 1587 colony was officially closed.

The Powhatan-slaughter report had been adopted by the Council as the official explanation for the fate of the Lost Colony in part because it was provided by Smith, in whose leadership abilities the Council members had previously expressed confidence. The ultimate credibility of the slaughter account, however, was derived largely from the belief that it was based on the testimony of the perpetrators themselves—the Powhatans—but, of course, that was not the case. The myth of the slaughter of the Lost Colony was a consequence of the erroneous assumptions made by Smith and Strachey about the information the Powhatans provided to them.

In retrospect, however, the Powhatans' information per se was actually quite accurate. It is fair to say that native oral traditions, histories, and collective memories contain essential truths. While it is also true that some memories—particularly those that recount great deeds or important events—may be exaggerated, they still contain a basically accurate framework upon which certain adornments may subsequently be attached. This seems to have been the case, for example, with the Powhatans' understanding of the Indian assault and route of the contingent of Englishmen at Roanoke in 1586. The Powhatans were in no way involved with that event, and so the victory could easily have been embellished in the several retellings as a "slaughter" by the time the news reached them.

The Powhatans responded truthfully and accurately to the questions put to them by Smith and Strachey. Opechancanough was correct when he told Smith "of certaine men cloathed at a place called Ocanahonan, cloathed like me." So was Wahunsunacock, Chief Powhatan, when he told Smith about distant places where "there were people with short Coates, and Sleeves to the Elbowes, that passed that way in Shippes like ours.... The people cloathed at Ocamahowan, he also confirmed.... He described a countrie called Anone, where they have abundance of Brasse, and houses walled as ours." This was all accurate information drawn from the collective oral traditions of the tribe.

Opechancanough and Wahunsunacock related exactly what they had heard about strangely apparelled men at distant places far from their domain. As already seen, these references were actually shared memories of stories which were passed on, via Indian trading routes, to the Algonquian tribes about events that had occurred four decades earlier to the south and south-west of Powhatan territory. The Powhatans had no way of further identifying the strange people, but, as already seen, the clothed men were Juan Pardo's Spaniards, whose expeditions in 1566–68 had a lasting and significant impact on the tribes of the western Carolina Piedmont. What Machumps told Strachey about "howses built as ours ... and one story above another" was also accurate, and documented in the Pardo account of the two-story granaries the Spanish taught the Indians to build. So too was what Smith was told about the "abundance of Brasse" at Anone, which Strachey recorded as Anoeg, "whose howses are built as ours." All of this information was true and accurate. The error was in Smith's and Strachey's assumption that the clothed men and other references were related to the Lost Colony.

What Smith heard from Powhatan about a "slaughter" he conducted was also true. It apparently *did* happen in 1607 at about the same time as the arrival of the Jamestown colonists, and the victims were the Chesapeake Indians and perhaps a few Englishmen who had dwelt among them for two decades. Likewise, what Machumps told Strachey about a slaughter at Roanoke was equally true, and it can now be said with confidence that the slaughter *did* occur at no other place than Roanoke Island. The few English victims of Powhatan's 1607 slaughter, as discussed, were not Lost Colonists as Smith erroneously reported to the Virginia Council in 1609, but rather survivors of the contingent left at Roanoke by Grenville in 1586. By the time Strachey arrived at Jamestown in 1610, the Powhatan–Lost Colony slaughter myth had already been officially accepted by the English court. Strachey built on that established slaughter fiction with the few additional details provided by Machumps.

As noted, Strachey's interviews with Machumps produced fragments of information about two "slaughters" that apparently involved Englishmen. The first of these had to have occurred in 1586 at Roanoke, and the second—the same slaughter reported by Smith—most likely happened in 1607 in the southeast area of present-day Virginia involving the Chesapeake tribe and the few Englishmen who dwelt with them. John White's 1587 Lost Colony obviously could not have been part of the 1586 slaughter at Roanoke. Furthermore, if the few English victims of the 1607 slaughter were survivors of the 1586 event, then they also could not have been White's Lost Colonists.

All of this further supports the conclusions reached earlier, that the 1587 colony had ceased to exist after 1589. Many likely perished in a failed attempt to reach Newfoundland and almost all of any remaining colonists would have been victims of the hurricane and surge in 1589. Since the references to European styled houses and clothed men at various locations (with the possible exception of Pananioc) had nothing at all to do with the Lost Colonists, then where else could they have been? Furthermore, if the Lost Colonists were not involved in either of the events reported by Smith and Strachey—the 1586 "slaughter" at Roanoke or the 1607 "slaughter" of the Chesapeake tribe— then what became of them? The early 17th century Powhatan oral traditions contained memories of the 1566–68 Spanish presence in the Piedmont, as well as a victory by their fellow Algonquians over Englishmen at Roanoke in 1586, and of course the more recent slaughter of the Chesapeake tribe in 1607 along with a few of the aforementioned Roanoke survivors who had lived among them for more than twenty years. Noticeably *absent* from the Powhatan oral tradition was any memory whatsoever—with the possible exception of the clothed men at Pananioc—concerning the 1587 Lost Colony.

Everything that the Powhatans related to Smith and Strachey was factually accurate, yet none of it had anything to do with the Lost Colony. It was only Smith's and Strachey's *interpretation* of that information that resulted in the false assumptions about the slaughter of the Lost Colony and the existence of survivors in faraway places. If the Powhatans related complete and accurate information to the English, and if we accept the premise that Indian oral tradition is an essentially valid and complete record of tribal history and memory, then logic dictates the following inescapable conclusion: Whatever happened to the Lost Colony was never part of the Powhatan oral history because the Powhatans had no contact whatsoever with the 1587 colony. This would be perfectly reasonable, of course, if the colony had collapsed decades before Smith and the Jamestown settlers arrived.

As suggested earlier, the ramifications of this conclusion are critical for almost all past and present Lost Colony theories. If the Powhatans were not connected in any way with the fate of White's colony, then obviously the centuries-old Powhatan–Lost Colony slaughter narrative, initiated by Smith, perpetuated by Strachey and Purchas, promoted by Quinn in the 1980s, and still held by many today, is logically impossible. All modifications of that theory must also be mistaken. As reviewed in an earlier chapter, a number of Lost Colony theories claim that White's 1587 colony left Roanoke and settled in a variety of locations including present-day Bertie County, the Chowan River, Dasamonguepeuk, the Alligator River, or Weapemeoc. These theories usually conclude with the Lost Colony being attacked and destroyed by Powhatan's warriors as they ventured northward in an attempt to make contact with the Jamestown settlers. Obviously if the Powhatans were not involved in any way with whatever happened to the Lost Colony, then all scenarios that involve the Powhatans in the Lost Colony's demise are also logically negated.

It is worth pausing here to recall the misunderstood line of inductive argument discussed in the Preface—proving a negative—since the Powhatan slaughter myth is one more in a long line of examples. Some of the most important clues to the Lost Colony mystery have been uncovered by similar instances of "proving" negatives. For example, it can be reasonably concluded that the 1587 colony did not relocate to the fort symbol location in Bertie County because, in addition to the documentary and logistical arguments provided earlier, the First Colony Foundation's physical investigation found no archaeological evidence to indicate that the Lost Colony had settled there. Croatoan is another example. A number of early English artifacts have been found at Hatteras, a known contact location. However, from the contemporary documentary evidence and the extensive archaeological work conducted there, it can be reasonably concluded that the 1587 colony did not resettle at Croatoan upon leaving Roanoke. From the search of the Chesapeake by Vincente Gonzalez in 1588 it can be reasonably concluded that the Lost Colony did not relocate there either. From Francisco Fernández de Écija's interviews with the local Indians at Rio Jordon in 1609 it could be reasonably concluded that no English colony other than the one at Jamestown existed at that time. And like Carl Sagan's previously mentioned dragon, we can reasonably conclude that a Powhatan slaughter of the Lost Colony did not happen because— *if it had*—there would have been legitimate evidence of its occurrence in Powhatan tribal memory.

Since it can now be said that the basic information related by the Powhatans—including the two slaughter events—was essentially accurate, but misinterpreted by Smith and Strachey, then *all* versions of the Powhatan–Lost Colony slaughter scenario are invalid. All of Smith's and Strachey's suppositions (except maybe Pananioc) about the "lost company of Sir Walter Rawley" between 1607 and 1611 can be disregarded, in fact, because they are completely unrelated to the Lost Colony. The 1587 colony was never slaughtered by Powhatan's warriors at the Chesapeake or as they ventured northward to make contact with the newly established Jamestown colony.

Could such an event have occurred elsewhere in the vast Powhatan chiefdom? By the time of the Jamestown settlement in 1607 the Powhatan domain was indeed vast, having expanded to about thirty sub-tribes, each of which paid tribute to Wahunsunacock, Chief Powhatan, as their paramount leader. His realm stretched throughout the inner coastal plain from as far as present-day Washington, D.C., in the north all the way south to perhaps present-day Chesapeake, Virginia, and westward to the fall line. The existence and slaughter of an English colony anywhere in the Powhatan chiefdom would probably not have occurred without Wahunsunacock's sanction and certainly not without his knowledge. Slaughters *were* conducted by Powhatan in 1607 and 1608, such as that of the Chesapeakes and the Payankatanks, and he was not reluctant to speak freely about them. A slaughter of an English colony anywhere in the Powhatan chiefdom would certainly have been part of recent tribal history and would have been related, as were the other slaughters, to Smith and Strachey during their inquiries with the Powhatans.

It is also unlikely that a slaughter of the 1587 Lost Colony could have occurred beyond Powhatan's domain. The territory to the south was occupied by other tribes belonging to the same Algonquian linguistic group, but they were not associated with the Powhatans. At the time of the initial English-Indian contact by the Barlowe-Amadas expedition in 1584, the Algonquians were one of the most populous and widespread native language groups in North America, extending all the way to the province of Quebec. The tribes encountered by the English in 1584, however, represented the southernmost extension of the Algonquian groups along the Atlantic seaboard.[1] Anthropologist Frank Speck, specialist in the Algonquian and Iroquoian peoples, wrote that the Carolina Algonquians were comparatively recent intruders into the region and formed the last offshoot of the general Algonquian migration southward along the Atlantic Coast.[2] It stands to reason, then, that the range of overall Algonquian oral tradition extended at least as far south as the geographic limits of Algonquian migration, which was towards the southern reaches of Pamlico Sound, near the area of the Pamlico and Neuse Rivers.

It is obvious that the account of a specific event in Algonquian oral history would naturally be most detailed and accurately recalled within the tribal community where the event took place or in which its tribal members participated. Symbols woven into beadwork or painted on skins, tangible markers such as "heaps of stones" or branches marking loc. pathways, were used by the Algonquian tribes to commemorate im events.[3] Physical markers such as these would help keep the memory event in sharper focus and also tend to "localize" the oral traditions of a particular tribe.

Yet it is also clear that there was a shared, though less detailed, oral history among chiefdoms in the same overall Algonquian language group. Perhaps an apt metaphor to explain the transmission of oral tradition among tribes within a language group would be the ripple effect in physics, whereby concentric waves expand from the point of origin, gradually diminish, and eventually disappear. As an example, the Algonquian warriors from Secota, Aquascogoc, and Dasamonguepeuk who participated directly in the assault and routing of Grenville's contingent at Roanoke in 1586 would retain clearly defined memories of the planning, details, and perhaps even individual warriors involved in the event. The Powhatans to the north, however, knew of the "slaughter at Roanoke," but had only vague knowledge and virtually no specifics concerning this occurrence.

Moreover, it is also probable that the Powhatans would have known something about the existence of an English colony even in the distant territories of another Indian language group. The Algonquian Powhatans obviously knew of clothed men—who turned out to be Spanish—at Ocanahonan and Pakrakanick in the Siouan Piedmont region, and they would have known of Europeans elsewhere as well. The previously mentioned Indians interviewed by Francisco Fernández de Écija in 1609, almost certainly Siouan, had remarkably detailed information about the English colony at Jamestown, in what was Powhatan/Algonquian territory 300 miles away. The Powhatans would very likely have been similarly informed about another, more recent European presence than the one at Ocanahonan and Pakrakanick four decades earlier. Since the Powhatans had been relating accurate information to Smith and Strachey, there is no reason to doubt that they would have told Smith and Strachey about the existence of another colony or about a major event such as the slaughter of a European colony … if one had occurred.

It has been suggested that the Lost Colony may have met its end at the hands of the Tuscarora,[4] known to the Roanoke voyagers as Mongoacks or Mangoags. This suggestion, though, is another outgrowth of the unlikely theory that the Lost Colony headed west, perhaps to the Chowan, and encountered the Tuscaroras, who dwelt even farther west. There is no evidence that an English colony or any colony of whites was slaughtered there. As already mentioned, in 1654 the Tuscaroras still retained a century-old memory which they related to Francis Yeardley about a conflict with Europeans, but the conflict involved the Haynoke tribe, not the Tuscaroras, and the Europeans were

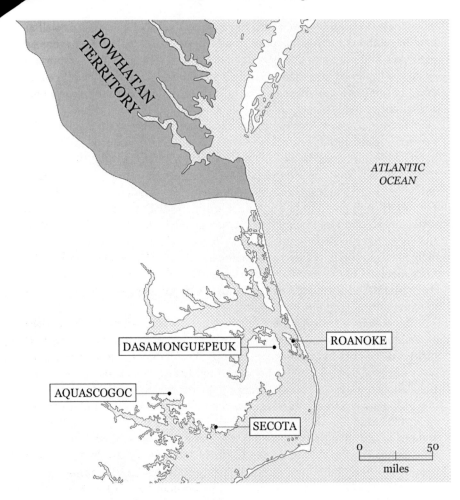

POWHATAN TERRITORY

ATLANTIC OCEAN

DASAMONGUEPEUK

ROANOKE

AQUASCOGOC

SECOTA

0          50
miles

**Locations of the Indian villages that participated in the 1586 assault at Roanoke beyond Powhatan territory (courtesy Michael Gayle).**

the Spanish, not the English. Surely the Tuscaroras would have retained even more vivid memories if they themselves had participated in the slaughter of a colony of Europeans.

The Tuscarora, part of the Iroquoian language group, dwelt along the upper regions of the present day Roanoke, Neuse, Tar, and Pamlico rivers. In the "History of the Tuscarora Indians" portion of his 1881 volume, Tuscarora Chief Elias Johnson spoke of the time "Before the discovery, by Columbus" when the Tuscarora "had many years of enjoyment and peaceful possession of their domain, consisting of six towns on the Roanoke, Neuse, Taw [Tar] and Pamlico Rivers in the [present] State of North Carolina."[5] There is no mention of any massacre of whites prior to the beginning of European settlement near the Pamlico River in the 1690s, which are referred to as "the first colonies." The first reference to contact with whites was the following:

> A little previous to these disorders, it seems that there were some white men, as our tradition states, with long coats and wide brimmed hats, visited several nations of the Indians in that neighborhood, and appeared to be very friendly toward them, wishing them success in everything, and told them that those settlers who were on the borders of their lands and constantly encroaching and committing depredations on the Indians, were not of the government, but were merely squatters, who settled of their own accord, and if they were cut off, there would be none to avenge them, and were advised to do so.[6]

The "disorders" referred to are the capture of John Lawson, his execution, and the coordinated massacre of settlers along Neuse, Pamlico, and Trent Rivers, which initiated the Tuscarora War in 1711.

The previously mentioned "Legend of the Coharie" did speak of a skirmish with a hostile tribe as the mixed group of hurricane survivors ascended the Neuse in what would probably have been 1589. If the event is at all accurate, the hostile tribe could historically have been the Tuscarora, but the 1587 colony had already ceased to exist. There could only have been a few assimilated colonists at most in this mixed group, and in any case the encounter would hardly have been considered a memorable event to the Tuscaroras. In the final analysis there is no evidence at all that the Lost Colony was ever slaughtered by anyone. The evidence *does* indicate that after September of 1589 there was simply no colony left to slaughter. At some time after the summer of 1588 at least part of the colony probably attempted to reach Newfoundland, but failed, and whatever remained of the mainland colony would likely have been swept away in the hurricane surge in September of 1589.

Of all the Smith and Strachey references, the single potentially legitimate clue to the Lost Colony was the previously mentioned "men apparelled" at Pananiock. Unlike Ocanahonan and Pakrakanick, which were located in the Carolina Piedmont and were related to Juan Pardo's excursions, Pananiock was situated between the Neuse and Pamlico Rivers. The only Europeans who could have been near that location in the latter part of the 16th century were the Grenville-Lane colonists of 1585–86 and the 1587 Lost Colonists themselves. Since the raw, uninterpreted information provided by the Powhatans was historically accurate in the other instances, the possibility exists that the references to "men appareled" at Pananiock may have been accurate as well. We do not know for sure whether Lane's 1585–86 colonists explored Pananiock. Grenville's week long excursion through Pamlico Sound in 1585 included visits to several villages, including Secota, and "diuers other places." Ralph Lane reported that exploration from Roanoke had proceeded as far south as Secota, which was just across the Pamlico River from Pananiock territory. It is not clear, though, whether he was referring to Grenville's excursion of Pamlico Sound or to another exploration conducted to that area afterwards.

We also do not know with certainty that the 1587 colonists visited Pananiock, but it is a very likely possibility. As noted previously, the territory of Pananiock would have been a suitable choice for a mainland settlement in 1588. In addition to its geographic accessibility directly across from the Wokokon inlet, the Pomouik/Pananiock tribe had been at "mortall warre" with Wingina and may well have seen the 1587 colonists as welcome allies against a common enemy. Archaeologist William G. Haag made the following remark about the coastal region of the Pamlico River: "If the colonists left Roanoke willingly, this river might be one they would look upon with favor as a new homesite."[7]

Pananiock has already been discussed as a potential Lost Colony location, but not in terms of its credibility as part of Powhatan oral tradition. Since the references to clothed men at Ocanahonan and Pakrakanick have been shown to be historically accurate (but misinterpreted), it is likely that there were also clothed men at Pananiock. If so, it is possible that Wowinchopunck's 1608 claim about clothed men at Pananiock could have been a recollection of the 1587 Lost Colonists. It is worth noting, too, that the Pananiock references appeared in early 1608, *before* Smith learned about the Powhatan "slaughter." Once Smith's misinterpreted slaughter report reached the Council, along with its equally erroneous tale of Lost Colony slaughter survivors at Ocanahonan and Pakrakanick, Pananiock became more or less irrelevant. Attention was exclusively focused on the more distant Ocanahonan and Pakrakanick where there were "men cloathed," and "people with short Coates and Sleeves to the Elbowes" and "howses built with stone walles, and one story above another, so taught them," as Strachey would later write, by those English who escaped the slaughter at Roanoke. The report seemed convincing, and it was quickly concluded that these must be Lost Colonists who managed to survive Powhatan's slaughter.

Overshadowed by Ocanahonan and Pakrakanick, and further diminished perhaps by Smith's distrust of Wowinchopunck, the Pananiock references were unfortunately marginalized. Those references, however, deserve reconsideration. On the Zúñiga Map was the notation "Here the King of Paspahegh reported our men to be and wants to go." Smith's line in *A True Relation* was "We had agreed with the king of Paspahegh to conduct two of our men to a place called Panawicke [Pananiock], beyond Roanoke, where he reported many men to be apparelled." If the presence of these men at Pananiock is accurate, they could have been 1587 colonists, in which case it would represent a significant step forward in the search for the Lost Colony's mainland settlement location. It could either indicate that the colonists relocated to the mainland coastal area specifically between the Neuse and Pamlico Rivers in 1588, or that the survivors of the hurricane surge sought refuge there in 1589. "*Many* men ... appareled" would suggest the former rather than the latter possibility.

The possible presence of colonists at Pananiock, coupled with the fact that the Powhatans had no contact with the 1587 colony, narrows down the earlier proposal that the colonists relocated to the mainland somewhere south of Roanoke in 1588. Parts of Beaufort, Craven, and Pamlico Counties would all overlap into the territory of Pananiock. A settlement location in that area might also help explain the legends and traditions about the Lost Colony which predominate in the southeastern part of North Carolina.

# 21

# *Survival Possibilities*
# 1612–1711

A question not yet adequately addressed is the possibility of Lost Colony survivors into the early 17th century, and the likelihood of admixed descendants in the centuries beyond. It is difficult to make mortality estimates for the original 1587 colony, which presumably numbered 119 originally, excluding murdered George Howe, Sr., and including Virginia Dare and the Harvie child born on August 18 and 19 respectively, shortly after the arrival at Roanoke. What can be said with a fair amount of assurance is that under normal circumstances in England infants had about a 14 percent chance of not surviving a year and about a 30 percent chance of dying before age fifteen.[1] William Strachey wrote that he was godfather to the appropriately named Bermuda Rolfe, the daughter of John and "Goody" (Sarah Hacker) Rolfe, born while the *Sea Venture*'s passengers were stranded at Bermuda. Although food was plentiful and the climate accommodating, the child lived only a few weeks and Goody died shortly after they reached Jamestown. The average life expectancy in Elizabethan England was said to be about forty-two years, but that number is somewhat skewed by the higher infant mortality rate. If we can guess that the adult colonists averaged thirty to thirty-five years of age in 1587 and allow them an extended fifty to fifty-five year lifespan, then they could be expected to live to between 1602 and 1612 under normal circumstances.

These were not normal circumstances, however. A good number of the colonists were likely lost at sea in the failed attempt to reach Newfoundland in either 1588 or 1589. If they decided to build a second pinnace, a plausible scenario, they could not have sailed until 1589, in which case many more of the colonists would have perished, perhaps in the same hurricane that struck the Outer Banks in September and swept away the mainland settlement. That hurricane and surge would have inundated Croatoan and eradicated the coastal mainland settlement, possibly reducing the number of remaining colonists by at least fifty percent. By October 1589, there may have been only a handful or so of the colonists left alive.

By 1612 John White's colony had been missing for a quarter century, and, using the aforementioned estimate, it is questionable that any of the original adult colonists could still be alive. Virginia Dare and the Harvie child would have been twenty-five years old if they survived, but that is an unlikely proposition. If they were among a group that sailed for Newfoundland, they certainly had died, and if they remained behind, they would not likely have survived the hurricane surge as two-year-olds in 1589, assuming they overcame the fourteen percent infant mortality rate in the first place. There were eleven children among the original colonists, possibly between the ages of ten and fifteen. If any of these children survived, they would have been between thirty-five and forty years old in 1612. One of these was said to be the previously mentioned George Howe, Jr., son of George Howe who was killed by Wingina's/Pemisapan's followers shortly after the colony arrived at Roanoke.

According to Ernest Bullard's previously mentioned "Legend of the Coharie," a mixed group of Indians, and one named colonist, George Howe, Jr., began a slow migration southward along the coast, beginning perhaps a year or two after the 1589 hurricane. It is difficult to evaluate much of the post–1589 legend, when the surviving group was said to have changed from its previously fixed agricultural make-up at Croatoan and the mainland settlement to one of a migratory nature. Mooney noted that migratory tribal groups "have short histories and as they seldom stopped long enough in one place to become identified with it, little importance was attached to their wanderings and little was recorded concerning them."[2]

Nevertheless, the legend claims that they eventually settled east of the Cape Fear River, where they lived for a long period, until white settlers began to arrive at the lower Cape Fear. Ernest Bullard suggested that these white settlers may have been the so-called Clarendon Colony, otherwise known as the "Yeamans Colony," established by English settlers from Barbados in 1664. The legend goes on to claim that the admixed descendants of what Bullard refers to as "Manteo's tribe" migrated farther inland "very much desiring peace and tranquility." This passage, however, would appear to contradict the long-standing tradition of the Croatoan/Hatteras Indians regarding their affinity for the English. One would wonder why this group, supposedly including admixed descendants, would withdraw from Englishmen with whom they shared a traditional kinship.

The Clarendon Colony was the last of three groups to arrive at the Cape Fear River between 1663 and 1664. In September 1663, Captain William Hilton had sailed from Barbados to examine the suitability of the Cape Fear River for settlement, and it was Hilton's report that led to the establishment of the

Clarendon Colony the following year. Earlier in 1663, however, a group of settlers from Massachusetts had entered the Cape Fear River and established themselves on the south bank about twenty miles from the river's mouth. Relations with the local Indians quickly turned hostile. It is believed that these New Englanders took a number of Indian children and, under the pretense of teaching them the ways of civilization, sent them north to be sold into slavery. When the local Indians learned of this treachery, they attacked the settlement with such resolve that the New Englanders abandoned the area after only three months and sailed back to Massachusetts.

If the Bullard legend is to be believed, this event could explain the fearful reaction of "Manteo's tribe" to the English and their reason for migrating farther inland at that time. In that case the legend's "colony of white people" may actually have been the Massachusetts settlers, and the migration inland would probably have begun *prior* to the arrival of both Hilton in October of 1663 and the Clarendon Colony in May of 1664. It is also noteworthy that none of the Indians Hilton encountered at the Cape Fear could speak English, and communication had to be accomplished through sign language. Hilton recorded only one word—"bonny"—which a few Indians repeated over and over as an indication of their good intentions, and Mooney regards this as a "reminiscence of previous contact with Spaniards."[3] After more than three generations of migration and assimilation, any surviving descendants of Lost Colonists would by this time have been fundamentally "Indian" in appearance, practice, and language.

At some time after the arrival of white settlers the group is said to have migrated farther and farther inland, apparently following the Cape Fear River, until it reached the confluence of the Deep and Haw Rivers, tributaries of the Cape Fear. An unknown—but apparently considerable—number of years passed during this extended, gradual migration. What follows the arrival at the Deep and Haw Rivers in the Bullard legend is the first reference to a specific genealogical connection between this group and the Lost Colonists, and here the legend is at its weakest. The present-day "Haw" River, we are told, is actually a corruption of "Howe," which the river was originally named in honor of George Howe III, grandson of Manteo. Four Howe generations are identified in the legend. George Howe, Jr. (referred to with the generational suffix "II" in the text) is said to have married one of Manteo's daughters. The "Legend of the Coharie" ends in Sampson County, where in 1779 Enoch Hall, said to be a lineal descendant of George Howe, resided in a small log cabin overlooking the lowland of Big Swamp in what was then called the Territory of Duplin County.

If George Howe, Jr., was about twelve years of age in 1587 when his father was killed, a marriage to Manteo's daughter could perhaps have taken place about 1595, and George Howe III may have been born about 1615, putting him close to fifty years of age at the time the Massachusetts settlement was established in 1663 at the Cape Fear. If, as the legend contends, the "Howe" river was named in his honor, it would mean that at least one admixed descendant of the original 1587 colony still survived with this group after nearly a century, and that he still retained his English surname, a rather implausible consideration.

Furthermore, the legend's account of the naming of the "Howe" River is contradicted by John Lawson, who made the first documented reference to that river in his *A New Voyage to Carolina*, published in 1709. (Lawson's actual 600 mile exploration was undertaken in 1700–1701.) Lawson wrote,

> … with great Difficulty, (by God's Assistance) [we] got safe to the North-side of the famous *Hau*-River, by some called *Reatkin*; the *Indians* differing in the Names of Places, according to their several Nations. It is call'd *Hau*-River, from the *Sissipahau Indians*, who dwell upon this Stream, which is one of the main Branches of *Cape-Fair*.[4]

Little is known about the "Sissipahau" tribe, sometimes called Saxapahaw, other than the possibility that they may have been related to the Shakori, and probably belonged to the Siouan linguistic family. The name "Saxapahaw" is believed to be an anglicized version of the Siouan/Catawban word *"sak'yápha"* meaning "foothill."[5] Their principal settlement appears to have been along the Haw River, perhaps ten miles west of present-day Chapel Hill. The tribe apparently faded from the historical record after 1717, but their name is retained in the small mill town of Saxapahaw and the newly restored Saxapahaw Rivermill area. The Saxapahaw may have been the same tribe spelled "Sauxpa" or "Sauapa" whom the Spanish encountered in 1569 near the Santee River in South Carolina.[6] This tribe may well have migrated to the Haw River long before "Manteo's tribe" could have arrived. Therefore, it is more likely that the "Haw" name was appropriated to suit the "Haw-Howe" tradition, in which case the legend's claim regarding the naming of "Howe River" is simply an embellishment.

There is one recorded incident demonstrating that the Saxapahaw may have had an affinity for the English, at least for a time. In early 1712, as Col. John Barnwell marched his army from South Carolina into North Carolina to assist that colony in the Tuscarora War, he met a sizable group of Saxapahaws who were fleeing from the Tuscaroras. They told Barnwell that sixteen of their people had been killed when they were attacked by the Tuscaroras because they refused to join them in the attack on the English settlers. Barnwell referred to these Saxapahaws as "brave men and good" and persuaded them to join his army.[7] However, the affinity for the English had apparently changed shortly thereafter, since, as John Reed Swanton noted, "They were one of those tribes which joined the confederation against the English in 1715 [the Yamasee War in South Carolina]."[8]

Any attempt to hypothesize about the possible existence and location of Lost Colony descendants in the 17th century must follow, as closely as possible, the movement of the tribes. For nearly a century after Jamestown was established, English expansion extended southward only as far as Albemarle Sound, and little is known about the movements and activities of the tribes farther south with whom any admixed descendants of the Lost Colonists would have most likely dwelt. A number of exploratory expeditions were sent out from Jamestown during the 17th century, but they tended to venture west to the Appalachians or southwest as far as the Chowan and Roanoke Rivers. John Pory led an expedition to the Chowan in 1622, and in 1650 Edward Bland explored the Chowan, Roanoke, and Meherrin Rivers, an area he called "New Brittan." During Pory's trek he reportedly heard from a Tuscarora Indian about an Englishman who dwelt among them, but the "Englishman" would turn out to be the Spaniard that Francis Yeardley would hear about four years later. Finally, John Lederer led three expeditions westward to the Appalachians in 1669 and 1670.

As previously suggested, the yellow-haired "savage boy" observed by George Percy at the James River in 1607 could have been a descendant of one of Grenville's 1586 contingent, but not of a 1587 Lost Colonist. Percy estimated the boy's age to be about ten, so he would have been born about 1597. The 1587 Lost Colony had virtually disappeared eight years earlier and 150 miles to the south or at sea in the pinnace, but the eleven or so surviving members of Grenville's contingent may well have been living among the Chesapeake tribe for about ten years by 1597. Powhatan's "slaughter" of the Chesapeakes apparently occurred just prior to the arrival of the Jamestown settlers, and the boy's presence in Powhatan territory at the James River can be explained by the customary native Indian practice of sparing younger children from other tribes and adopting them as their own.

References in Francis Yeardley's 1654 *Narrative of Excursions into Carolina* are occasionally cited as possible Lost Colony clues, but they are usually taken out of context and actually are not relevant. The first reference is to "Sir Walter Ralegh's fort, from whence I [Yeardley] received a sure token of their being there." The second reference is that the great chief at Roanoke wanted Yeardley to teach his son "to speak out of the book, and to make a writing."[9] It would be incorrect to suspect from these that Yeardley may have obtained something from the old fort at Roanoke that related to the 1587 colony, or that the chief's knowledge of reading and writing might be an echo of previous contact with the Lost Colony. Quinn wrote, "There were Indians on Roanoke Island when Francis Yeardley went there in quest of land in 1653 … but they had nothing to say of how the earlier colonists met their end, except to point out to him the remains of the old fort."[10]

However, Yeardley only funded the "excursions to Carolina," and he did not personally participate, as Quinn wrote. The expedition came about quite by accident. A trader in beaver pelts, the previously mentioned Nathaniel Batts, came to Yeardley to request provisions so that he could search for the sloop which had accidentally left him and "had been gone to Rhoanoke." And so,

> he set forth with three more in company, one being of my family, the others were my neighbours. They entered in at Caratoke, [Currituck] ten leagues to the southward of Cape Henry, and so went to Rhoanoke island; where, or near thereabouts, they found the great commander of those parts with his Indians a hunting, who received them civilly, and shewed them the ruins of Sir Walter Ralegh's fort, from whence I received a sure token of their being there.[11]

In the sometimes misconstrued latter part of that quote, "their" refers to the Indians and the Englishmen looking for the sloop, and has nothing to do with the Lost Colonists. From what we can infer of Yeardley's account, the Indians at Roanoke seemed to know nothing about the history of the fort or its inhabitants.

At some time afterwards the Roanoke chief and a few of his tribesmen were escorted to Yeardley's house at "Linne-Haven," today's Lynnhaven in Virginia Beach...

> where they abode a week, and shewed much civility of behaviour. In the interim of which time, hearing and seeing the children read and write, of his own free voluntary motion he asked me, (after a most solid pause, we two being alone), whether I would take his only son, having but one, and teach him to do as our children, namely is his terms, to speak out of the book, and to make a writing; which motion I most heartily embraced.[12]

The Roanoke chief's interest in having his son taught "to speak out of the book, and to make a writing" was initiated by his observations of English children reading and writing in 1653 at Linne-Haven, and not from a past tribal connection to the Lost Colony. After returning south, Yeardley's men purchased "three great rivers" from the Roanoke king "in the name, and on the behalf, of the commonwealth of England." Later, the Roanoke chief and some of his tribesmen guided Yeardley's men to the west, where they met the "Tuskarorawes emperor" at a hunting camp. It was there that the Tuscarora chief told the Englishmen about a Spaniard who had lived at their main village for seven years. This Spaniard was almost certainly the misidentified "Englishman" who was living among the Tuscarora in 1650 and reported to Edward Bland during his exploration of "New Brittan."

By the time Yeardley was writing in 1654, any surviving admixed descendants of the Lost Colonists—after two or three generations—would have been thoroughly assimilated with the native tribespeople with whom they dwelt. As suggested, therefore, what happened to those descendants and where they might be found depends entirely on the location of the tribes and the events that could have impacted them. From Yeardley's narrative it seems that the Roanoke Indians abandoned the coastal area in 1653 and moved to what must have been a considerable distance inland, since it was near there that the Englishmen met the Tuscarora. Yeardley promised to build the Roanoke king an English styled house at his "new habitation" after the land purchase was completed...

> ... and actual possession was solemnly given them by the great commander, and all the great men of the rest of the provinces, in delivering them a turf of the earth with an arrow shot into it; and so the Indians totally left the lands and rivers to us, retiring to a new habitation, where our people built the great commander a fair house, the which I am to furnish with English utensils and chattels.[13]

It is unfortunate that Yeardley did not provide more information about the "great commander" at Roanoke or about "all the great men of the rest of the provinces." The Hatteras Indians were known to frequent Roanoke, and perhaps "the rest of the provinces" could have included the Outer Banks to the south.

By this time the old tribes encountered by the Roanoke voyagers north of Albemarle Sound were slowly but surely succumbing to the wave of English expansion from Jamestown. The tribe known in the 16th century as the Weapemeoc now consisted of a number of smaller interrelated tribes such as the Yeopim—probably a shortened form of the original "Weapemeoc"— the Pasquatank, Poteskeet, and Perquiman.[14] In 1660 and 1662 the Yeopim king sold some of the land to Nathaniel Batts and George Durant respectively, making these the first "recorded" land deeds in North Carolina. The Yeardley purchase in 1653 was confirmed by the delivery of "a turf of the earth with an arrow shot into it," but apparently never officially recorded. According to Lawson, by about 1700 the Pasquatank were down to just ten fighting men, the Poteskeet thirty, and the Yeopim only "6 people."[15]

The once dominant Chowanoke tribe, ruled by Menatonon during the 1585–86 Grenville-Lane colonization attempt at Roanoke, had dwelt along the Chowan and Meherrin Rivers. It will be recalled that John Smith sent Michael Sicklemore to Chowanoke on a fruitless search for the Lost Colonists in 1607. In 1663 the Chowanoke entered into a "treaty of friendship" with the English, but went to war against the encroaching colonists in 1675. By 1677 the Chowanoke were utterly defeated and removed to a reservation at Bennett's Creek in present-day Gates County. With the defeat of the Chowanokes all the tribes to the immediate north of Albemarle Sound became tributaries of the newly established North Carolina Colony and no longer posed a threat.[16]

Far to the south of Albemarle Sound, where the Lost Colony had relocated, were the Coree, Pamlico, and Hatteras tribes, plus the Machapunga and Bay (or Bear) River tribes who were most likely remnants of the late 16th century Secotans. One of these tribes with whom the Lost Colony may have had contact was the previously mentioned Coree or Coranine, known to the Roanoke colonists as Cwareuuock. This tribe dwelt on the coastal mainland south of the Neuse River and, since they occasionally established hunting and fishing camps on the Outer Banks,[17] they were certainly well known to the Croatoans, and perhaps even the 1587 colonists or any surviving admixed descendants at Hatteras. As suggested earlier, it is possible that the Coree could have been involved, through the intercession of Manteo, in the colonists' selection of a mainland settlement location in 1587–88. Again, according to Sprunt the Corees at Cape Fear in 1665 had knowledge about the Lost Colony. At some point—apparently in the mid 17th century—a portion of the Coree tribe was deceived and destroyed by the Machapunga, a tribe that was most probably part of what had been called the Secotans by the Roanoke voyagers. The event seems to have taken place on the Outer Banks, since Lawson places it "on the Sand-Banks," where the Hatteras dwelt and both the Coree and Machapunga are known to have frequented the barrier islands. Lawson described what happened:

> Another Instance was betwixt the *Machapunga Indians*, and the *Coranine's*, on the Sand-Banks; which was as follows. The *Machapungas* were invited to a Feast, by the *Coranines*; (which two Nations had been a long time at War together, and had lately concluded a Peace.) Thereupon, the *Machapunga Indians* took the Advantage of coming to the *Coranines* Feast, which was to avoid all Suspicion, and their King, who, of a Savage, is a great Politician and very stout, order'd all his Men to carry their *Tamahauks* along with them, hidden under their Match-Coats, which they did; and being acquainted when to fall on, by the Word given, they all (upon this Design) set forward for the Feast, and came to the *Coranine* Town, where they had gotten Victuals, Fruit, and such things as make an *Indian* Entertainment, all ready to make these new Friends welcome, which they did; and, after Dinner, towards the Evening, (as it is customary amongst them) they went to Dancing, all together; so when the *Machapunga* King saw the best Opportunity offer, he gave the Word, and his Men pull'd their *Tamahauks* or Hatchets from under their Match-Coats, and kill'd several, and took the rest Prisoners, except some few that were not present, and about four or five that escap'd. The Prisoners they sold Slaves to the *English*. At the time this was done, those *Indians* had nothing but Bows and Arrows, neither side having Guns.[18]

The fact that these "two Nations had been a long time at War together" could harken back to the "mortall warre" between Wingina's Secotans and the tribes south of the Pamlico River, first reported by Amadas and Barlowe in 1584. The tribes allied against the Secotans at that time were certainly the Pomouiks/Pamlicos, the Neuse, and very likely the Cwareuuocks/Corees, who were adjacent to, and likely affiliated with, the Neuse. Two years before the arrival of the Amadas-Barlowe reconnaissance, a deadly event occurred that was remarkably similar to the aforementioned deception of the Corees:

... about two yeeres past there was a peace made betweene the King Piemacum, and the Lord of Secotan ... but there remaineth a mortall malice in the Secotanes, for many iniuries and slaughters done vpon them by this Piemacum. They inuited diuers men, and thirtie women of the best of his countrey to their towne to a feast: and when they were altogether merry, and praying before their Idol, (which is nothing els but a meer illusion of the deuill) the captaine or Lord of the town came suddenly vpon them, and slewe them euery one, reseruing the women and children.[19]

The location and fate of any possible admixed Lost Colony descendants is, of course, most likely connected to the Hatteras tribe, which is widely accepted to be the later name for what the Roanoke colonists called the Croatoans. As proposed earlier, the Croatoans and whatever Lost Colonists remained after the 1589 hurricane had abandoned the Outer Banks. As must have been the case following previous hurricanes, however, their abandonment was temporary and they would have returned to their towns on the sound side of Hatteras once the fields were again arable. The most notable clues about the English/Croatoan admixed descendants were Lawson's well-known comments in his *New Voyage to Carolina*:

A farther Confirmation of this [the 'infant colonies' at Roanoke] we have from the *Hatteras Indians*, who either then lived on *Ronoack*-Island, or much frequented it. These tell us, that several of their Ancestors were white People, and could talk in a Book, as we do; the Truth of which is confirm'd by gray Eyes being found frequently amongst these *Indians*, and no others. They value themselves extremely for their Affinity to the *English*, and are ready to do them all friendly Offices. It is probable, that this Settlement miscarry'd for want of timely Supplies from *England*; or thro' the Treachery of the Natives, for we may reasonably suppose that the *English* were forced to cohabit with them, for Relief and Conversation; and that in process of Time, they conform'd themselves to the Manners of their *Indian* Relations. And thus we see, how apt Human Nature is to degenerate.

I cannot forbear inserting here, a pleasant Story that passes for an uncontested Truth amongst the Inhabitants of this Place; which is, that the Ship which brought the first Colonies, does often appear amongst them, under Sail, in a gallant Posture, which they call Sir *Walter Raleigh's* Ship, And the truth of this has been affirm'd to me, by Men of the best Credit in the Country.[20]

While it is true that the "gray Eyes" recessive trait is confirmation of European genetic admixture, it has been correctly pointed out that the Lost Colonists were not the only Europeans to have contact with the Croatoan/Hatteras Indians on the Outer Banks. "Many shipwrecked or similarly jettisoned Europeans," Kupperman wrote, "must be added to the famous Lost Colonists of Roanoke, left in 1587, so that hundreds must have joined Indian societies all along the coast."[21] In addition the Englishmen of the 1585–86 Grenville-Lane colony made several visits to Croatoan, some of which were for extended periods. Nevertheless, more than a century later the oral tradition of these Hatteras Indians still retained memories of "the Ship which brought the first Colonies.... Sir *Walter Raleigh's* Ship." Although not conclusive by any means, Lawson's commentary offers the possibility that admixed Croatoan/Lost Colonist descendants *may* have existed about 112 years after the colony collapsed.

The expansion of white settlements in the 17th century brought with it deadly diseases which took a heavy toll on the tribes and, unless the admixture transferred an acquired immunity, would have reduced the chances of survival for the descendants as well. Harriot had remarked in 1585–86 that "within a few dayes after our departure from euery such Towne, the people began to die very fast, and many in short space, in some Townes about twentie, in some fourtie, and in one sixe score, which in trueth was very many in respect of their numbers."[22] In 1696–97 a smallpox epidemic swept down from Virginia and devastated the Carolina tribes. Another tribe with whom the Lost Colonists could have had contact was the Pamlico Indians, particularly if they relocated to Pananoic, where Smith wrote in 1608 "our men" were reported to be. John Archdale noted, "When I was in the North about eleven Years since [1696], I was told then of a great Mortality that fell upon the Pemlicoe Indians."[23]

Lawson told of the Indians at the Santee River who had "lost much of their former Numbers ... most by the Small-pox, which hath often visited them, sweeping away whole Towns."[24] Of the effect on the Indians in general, he wrote,

> formerly it destroy'd whole Towns, without leaving one *Indian* alive in the Village.... The Small-Pox and Rum have made such a Destruction amongst them, that, on good grounds, I do believe, there is not the sixth Savage living within two hundred Miles of all our Settlements, as there were fifty Years ago. These poor Creatures have so many Enemies to destroy them, that it's a wonder one of them is alive near us.[25]

If the admixed descendants of George Howe, Jr., dwelt in the Cape Fear area during the latter part of the 17th century, as the Bullard legend claims, they would have been confronted by another threat, the expansion of the Indian slave trade out of Charles Town. Shortly after Charles Town was founded in 1670 by English colonists from Barbados, settlers to the north of Charles Town on Goose Creek developed a lucrative trade with the adjacent tribes. Soon these traders started exchanging merchandise for Indian slaves, and it was not long before Indians themselves were raiding other villages for captives who would be sold to the slave traders. These slave raids ranged far into North Carolina, and would be one of the principal causes of the Tuscarora War in 1711. Although most of these Indian slaves were shipped to the Caribbean, by 1700 there were 800 Indian slaves in South Carolina.[26] At that time "the most important items shipped out of Charles Town were deer hides and Indian slaves."[27] The actual identity of the Indians who dwelt at the Cape

Fear River is unknown, but Swanton believed they were possibly offshoots of the Waccamaw tribe.

According to one source, the Indians in North Carolina's Coastal Plain numbered approximately 30,000 in 1660, but prior to the start of the Tuscarora War in 1711, "rum, small pox, and intertribal warfare had reduced them to no more than 5,000."[28] By 1700 the Hatteras were reported to have one village named Sandbanks and sixteen fighting men. The Corees had two towns and twenty-five warriors. The Pamlico had one village on an island in the river and fifteen fighting men.[29] Based alone on the dramatic eighty-three percent decline in the population of the Coastal Plains tribes, the probability of Lost Colony/Hatteras admixed descendants surviving into the 18th century would have been greatly reduced.

# 22

# The Search for Descendants
## 18th Century and Beyond

On the slim chance that any admixed descendants of the Lost Colonists *did* survive into the 18th century, 1711 and the succeeding few years would have presented another major obstacle. In the early morning hours of September 22, 1711, a combined force of about 500 Tuscaroras, Corees, Pamlicos, Machapungas, Weetocks, and Bay/Bear River Indians swept down along the Pamlico and Neuse Rivers in a surprise attack that initiated what would afterwards be called the Tuscarora War, the bloodiest Indian war in North Carolina history. The account of this conflict has been well documented and need not be repeated here, other than to look at the effect it had on the tribes in general and particularly those who either may have had contact with, or claimed descent from, the Lost Colonists.

By the time the Tuscarora War was over in 1715, about 2,000 to 3,000 Indians had been enslaved or killed, and, according to David La Vere, "that number could easily be higher."[1] Several tribes, such as the Pamlico, Neuse, Bay or Bear River, and Weetock disappeared altogether from the historical record. By 1716 only seven named tribes remained on the eastern North Carolina Coastal Plain: the Tuscarora, Chowanoke, Poteskeet, Coree, Machapunga, Meherrin, and the Hatteras. All were now tributaries of North Carolina, and eventually they were provided with surveyed reservation tracts, subject to—and supposedly protected by—English law and justice. The Chowanoke and Poteskeet had already been assigned reservations north of Albemarle Sound before the end of the previous century. After the war the remaining Corees and Machapungas were given a reservation at Lake Mattamuskeet, and the Meherrins would have a reservation at the Chowan and Meherrin Rivers in 1729. Most of the remaining hostile Tuscaroras left North Carolina and reunited with the Five Nation Iroquoian Confederacy in New York. Chief Tom Blount's Tuscaroras of the Upper Towns, who had remained neutral and actually aided the English during the war, were assigned a reservation between the Neuse and Pamlico Rivers. In 1717 Chief Blount requested permission to relocate and received a new tract on the Roanoke River which would come to be called Indian Woods. The Hatteras, who turned to North Carolina for protection during the war, did not receive a reservation until 1759, when they were given a 200-acre tract at the south end of Hatteras Island.[2]

As noted previously, from what can be reconstructed about the movements and activities of the Lost Colonists after 1587, the tribes with a reasonable likelihood of contact with them would have been the Panauuaioc (Pamlico), the Cwareuuock (Coree), the unnamed tribe or tribes later to be called Cape Fear Indians, and of course the Croatoan (Hatteras), about whom there is little doubt. As also noted, however, the Pamlicos, who joined with the hostile Tuscaroras against the English, ceased to exist as a tribe by the end of the Tuscarora War. It will be recalled that the Pamlicos had already been reduced by the smallpox epidemic in 1696 to just fifteen fighting men. Furthermore, under a treaty with the English in the early stages of the war, Blount's friendly Tuscaroras agreed to exterminate several of the small hostile tribes, one of these being the Pamlicos.[3] Any who were not killed outright would have been enslaved. If there had been Lost Colony descendants living among the Pamlicos, they would not have survived the war.

The Coree tribe, referred to by Yeardley as "a bloody and barbarous People," was one of those also reduced in numbers by the smallpox epidemic, but they fought aggressively against the English during the war and were still troublesome after they were assigned to the reservation at Lake Mattamuskeet along with the Machapunga. Swanton said that they probably "became extinct" at Mattamuskeet, but La Vere wrote that they apparently left the Machapunga reservation because of irreconcilable differences,[4] a plausible conclusion considering their long adversarial history which included the Machapunga's previously mentioned deception and slaughter of the Coree at the celebration on the Sandbanks. The Corees were certainly among the last holdouts in the war, and remnants of the tribe may have joined other groups. Although affiliations could certainly change over a century, given the Corees' strong antipathy towards the English, it seems unlikely that any Lost Colony descendants who still retained traditions of their mixed origins could have been among them.

The Cape Fear Indians are included in this group of tribes having potential contact with Lost Colony descendants partly because of the "Legend of the Coharie," which places colonist George Howe's descendants in the Cape Fear River area for more than a century. There are also two other sources that put remnants of the Cape Fear Indians at a location supposedly occupied by Lost Colony descendants. One of these is Coharie tribal member and author C.D. Brewington, who wrote that the amalgamated Indians who were found on the Lumber and Coharie Rivers were also found "on the banks of the Cape Fear."[5] Swanton made a similar connection.[6] The so-called Cape Fear Indians are difficult to follow because there were many tribes in the Cape Fear River area, and, since the tribal name of the group referred to by the English as "Cape Fear" is not known, they could have been associated with any of them. Swanton believed the Cape Fears may have been part of the Waccamaw tribe who dwelt near present-day Myrtle Beach. Some of the Indians at the Cape Fear River were recruited by Col. Barnwell on his march north in late 1711 during the early stages of the Tuscarora War. Later the Cape Fears were among the dozen or so groups that attempted to destroy the English in South Carolina at the outset of the Yamassee War in 1715. The Indians at the Cape Fear were driven from the area during that war, and remnants may have joined other tribes in South Carolina. The "Legend of the Coharie" claims that the admixed descendants of the Lost Colony, "very much desiring peace and tranquility," continued to migrate farther inland along the Cape Fear River as white settlements advanced. If true, it would mean that these admixed Indians managed to remain together as a coherent group, apparently undetected and unmolested for more than a century until their eventual arrival in present-day Sampson County.

The Croatoans, of course, had frequent interaction with both the 1585–86 and the 1587 colonies, and consequently the Hatteras tribe is the most likely of all the potential tribes to have had English descendants among them in the 17th century. Regarding the 1585–86 colony, Harriot mentioned that "they [the Indians] noted also that we had no women among vs, neither that we did care for any of theirs."[7] If Harriot's statement was accurate, it would strengthen the probability that any admixed English/Croatoan offspring would have been descendants of the 1587 colony. Those chances are enhanced considerably by the likelihood that any Lost Colony survivors after 1589 would have quickly integrated with the Croatoans.

There are few references to the Hatteras tribe in the North Carolina colonial records, but it is clear that the Hatteras struggled during and after the Tuscarora War. In late May 1714, the Hatteras sought help from the English military commander, Col. Thomas Boyd, who reported the problem to the Governor's Council. The minutes of the Council for May 29 read:

> Whereas report has been made to this board that ye Hatteress Indyans have lately made their Escape from ye Enemy Indyans and are now at Coll Boyds house It is ordered By this Board that the afsd Coll Boyd Doe supply the Said Indyans wth Corne for their Subsistance untill they can returne to their owne habitations againe....[8]

The identity of the "Enemy Indyans" is not mentioned, but La Vere noted logically that they were probably Machapungas, which would place the Hatteras at Lake Mattamuskeet prior to their "escape."[9] As mentioned above, the

Machapungas were provided with a reservation at Lake Mattamuskeet and Hatteras Indians are known to have been there in later years. In any case it is clear that these Hatteras were not at "their owne habitations" on the Outer Banks in 1714 and that they were not faring well. In March of the following year the Hatteras made another appeal to the Council, which reported, "Upon Petition of the Hatterass Indyans praying Some Small reliefe from ye Country for their services being reduced to great poverty."[10] Although they are still mentioned as a tribe by the Council in 1731, another source claimed that "by 1733 there were only six or eight Indians living at Hatteras and these lived among the English."[11] In May of 1761 the Hatteras are mentioned in a letter written by Alexander Stewart to Philip Bearcroft about his March trip to "Altamuskeet [Mattamuskeet] in Hyde County."

> ... I likewise with pleasure inform the Society, that the few remains of the Altamus-keet, Hatteras & Roanoke Indians ... appeared mostly at the chapel & seemed fond of hearing the *Word* of the true God & of being admitted into the church of our Lord Jesus Christ. 2 men & 3 women & 2 children were baptized by me.[12]

In another letter Stewart wrote, "the remains of the Attamuskeet, Roanoke and Hatteras Indians, live mostly along that coast, mixed with the white inhabitants."[13] The Hatteras had virtually disappeared by the 1780s, according to Torres, and the last record of them was in a 1788 deed from Mary Elks, "Indian of Hatteras Banks," to Nathan Midgett, transferring a tract of land in the old Indian town.[14] The Elks-Midgett transfer probably represented the final sale of the old Hatteras reservation tracts. As mentioned, the Hatteras had only acquired their reservation in 1759, but it was completely gone by 1788. The gradual disappearance of the Hatteras and other remaining eastern North Carolina tribes coincided with their selling off of tracts of reservation land, which had at least temporarily preserved tribal identities. The Poteskeet, Yeopin, Chowan, Meherrin, and Mattamuskeet had completely sold off the last tracts of their reservations by 1792.[15]

By the mid–18th century the remnants of the Hatteras Indians seem to have been located on the Outer Banks and at Lake Mattamuskeet, most likely limiting possible Lost Colony descendants to those locations. The historical record makes it clear that there were only a few Hatteras Indians on the Outer Banks, and that they were dwelling among the English who lived there. There is a possibility, then—but only a very slight one—that admixed Lost Colony descendants may have lived at Hatteras during this time, preserving the claim by some of today's local residents that that was indeed the case. Of course, as the reservations were being sold off, the former Indian residents did not simply disappear. Many of them "mixed with the white inhabitants," as Stewart noted in his 1761 letter. Others moved off to locations beyond the edges of white settlements and formed groups and small communities of their own.

Some of the Hatteras from Mattamuskeet may have been among these displaced people. As La Vere put it,

> In other instances, survivors from shattered villages and towns took refuge in the swamps and forests of eastern North Carolina, on marginal lands that were then of little interest to white settlers. There these Indian people joined with other refugees and created thriving Indian communities, but out of sight of the North Carolina government and most settlers.... Time and time again over the next two centuries, North Carolinians would be surprised to discover communities of Indians across the eastern part of the state.... Increasingly, even among those lying low in the swamps, Indians began wearing cloth shirts, pants, and skirts; living in log cabins; plowing their fields; converting to Christianity; and speaking English.[16]

These were the people white settlers encountered as they pushed the borders of the frontier farther inland. It was a group such as this that Hamilton McMillan claimed was a tribe of Lost Colony descendants, found by the advancing white settlers "on the waters of Lumber River ... speaking English, tilling the soil, owning slaves, and practicing many of the arts of civilized life."[17] Swanton wrote that at least part of the Indians who inhabited the Lumber River area were surviving remnants of the Siouan tribes that once dwelt along the lower Pee Dee and Waccamaw Rivers. According to Swanton, these Indians included some Cape Fears, Cheraws, Sissipahaws, Waccamaws, and Waxhaws,[18] who moved farther inland particularly along the Pee Dee and Drowning Creek, which was what the Lumber River was called prior to 1809. Neither Mooney, writing in 1894, nor Swanton, writing in 1946, mentioned the Lumbee or Coharie as an identifiable "tribe." In the North Carolina colonial records there was a description of the people at Drowning Creek, reported by the Bladen County militia in 1754: "Drowning Creek on the head of Little Pedee, 50 families a mixt Crew, a lawless People, possess the Lands without patent or paying quit rents; shot a Surveyor for coming to view vacant lands being inclosed in great swamps."[19]

McMillan supported his Lumbee-Lost Colony theory by citing the occurrence of Lost Colonist surnames found among the Lumbee people in Robeson and in other counties in the latter part of the 19th century. There are several problems with this argument. Of the 117 Lost Colony surnames (a few were repeated) listed by Hakluyt, McMillan wrote, "The names in the foregoing list in italics [fifty-six of them], are those which are found at this time [1885] among the Indians residing in Robeson county and in other counties of North Carolina."[20] This is a meaningless statistic since McMillan's fifty-six matches were not limited to Robeson County, but extended to "other counties" as well. Most of the Lost Colonists' English surnames were fairly common and could be found in large numbers in *all* of North Carolina's counties.

McMillan also declared that Henry Berry, who had received a land grant near the Lumber River in 1732, "was a lineal descendant of the English colonist, Henry Berry, who was left on Roanoke Island in 1587."[21] The fact that a land grant was issued to someone who had the same surname as a Lost Colonist is hardly evidence of a "lineal descendant." Settlers from Virginia were already moving into the area north of Albemarle Sound during the second half of the 17th century. After 1704, when Parliament offered land bounties to encourage the naval stores trade—tar, pitch, and turpentine— immigrants started arriving in large numbers, particularly from Pennsylvania and Delaware, to what would become Duplin and Bladen Counties (Robeson County was carved out of Bladen in 1787). In the meantime, Scots-Irish immigrants began arriving in the Cape Fear area in the 1730s. Thousands of land grants were issued. It is far more reasonable to conclude from the historical record that the recipients of these grants came either from the northern colonies (where the Berry surname is known to have existed) or from Ulster than it is to assume that any of the recipients could be direct descendants of Lost Colonists.

The more significant problem with McMillan's theory was his assumption that a large group of Lost Colony descendants—with their English surnames, language, and culture no less—survived for nearly two centuries and were discovered living at the Lumber River. As discussed in previous chapters, only a very small number of the original colonists could have lived past the events of 1588–89. Any possible survivors would have quickly integrated with one or more of the native tribes, most likely the Croatoans. If there were a few survivors, neither they nor their descendants could have had contact with whites in the Pamlico Sound area for another century. Their "Englishness" would have begun to disappear rather quickly, and after two or more generations their descendants would have been indistinguishable from the natives, except perhaps for the occasional manifestation of a recessive gene, such as the gray eyes Lawson noticed among the Hatteras in 1701. The English language and surnames of the original colonists had been shed long before then, or Lawson would certainly have mentioned it.

The single plausible argument in favor of a Lost Colony–Indian descendancy resides in the oral tradition of the tribes. As seen previously, the information related by the Powhatans to Smith and Strachey was quite accurate, but misinterpreted. If we accept the premise that Indian oral tradition contains an essential truth, then we must concede the possibility that *some* ancestors of *some* Indians were Lost Colonists. McMillan wrote that he first heard of the Lost Colony tradition during an inquest in 1864, when "an old Indian named George Lowrie" addressed the group and told of his tribe's blood connection with the English at Roanoke. There can be no doubt that the tradition has existed for several generations among the Lumbee and Coharie people, and there are a number of sources who have confirmed that long-standing tradition. Cherokee Indian and anthropologist, Robert K. Thomas, was skeptical about McMillan's Lost Colony hypothesis and suggested that his Lost Colony theory may have been adopted by some Lumbees in the 19th century to explain their origins, but that does not alter the fact that the same tradition existed on Hatteras as early as 1701, according to Lawson's account.

Coharie tribal member C.D. Brewington acknowledged the long-standing Lost Colony tradition among his tribe in Sampson County, but was less certain of its source. He wrote that the ancient Iroquoian ancestors of the Cherokee and the Tuscarora were people he called "Ri-Choherrians" who later divided into various clans and tribal groups in what is now North Carolina. According to Brewington, two of these groups became the Cherokee and Cheraws, also called Saura. In a similar vein as Swanton regarding the assessment of the Lumber River inhabitants, Brewington wrote, "These Indians settled on the Cape Fear and on the Saxapahaw and its tributaries. They became the ancestors of the Indians who now live in the Cape Fear Region and on the Lumbee [Lumber] in Robeson County."[22] Brewington expressed his belief in a Lost Colony–Indian tradition, but wrote, "It is impossible to point out one particular tribe of Indians as their sole ancestors." He went on to say, "These amalgamated Indians were first found on the banks of the Cape Fear and its tributaries, including Coharie, both big and little Coharie, South River, Mingo and the Neuse and Lumbee [Lumber] Rivers."[23]

What can be said with confidence is that the existence of an oral tradition among elements of the Coharie and Lumbee tribes connecting Lost Colonist and native Indian bloodlines is undeniable. We can probably conclude, then, that the first generation of admixed descendants most likely originated from contact with the Croatoans after 1587. However, Brewington was also probably correct in saying that it is impossible to know where those bloodlines might be found after several centuries. It has been suggested above that almost certainly the Hatteras, but also the Pamlicos, Corees, and Cape Fears, may have had contact with the Lost Colonists. There could have been others. There is also the possibility that subsequent admixed descendants interacted with other unidentified tribes at a later time and at unknown locations.

Of course all of this is based on the assumption that at least a few admixed descendants survived beyond the first or second generation. Given the near-certain sharp reduction of Lost Colonist numbers in 1588 and 1589, coupled with the drastic decline of the Indian population in the 17th and 18th centuries, it is very possible that no direct Lost Colonist-Indian descendants survived. The absence of surviving descendants by the late 18th or 19th century, however, does not refute the oral tradition of a tribal Lost Colonist–Indian ancestry. Such a tradition only means, as the Hatteras Indians told Lawson, that several of their ancestors were white people. It does not mean that the tribe in general was descended from those white people or that any of their admixed descendants survived to the present.

A considerable effort has been undertaken in recent years in an attempt to identify Lost Colonist descendants through DNA analysis. Roberta Estes, co-founder of the Lost Colony Research Group and administrator of the Lost Colony Y DNA and Lost Colony Family Projects, is a leading figure in this endeavor. Progress has been slow, Estes reports, due in large part to the difficulty of locating verifiable relations of the 1587 colonists in England, without whom a comparative DNA baseline cannot be established. The primary sources for 16th century genealogical records are English parish registers, but many of these records no longer exist. In 1597 Queen Elizabeth decreed that church records, originally written in Latin on individual sheets of paper, be kept in more durable vellum or parchment registers, and the earlier records transcribed, but by that time many of the original paper records had either been lost or destroyed. Records of the Lost Colonists' births, most of whom would have been born before 1567, probably disappeared during this time. In addition, many records were neglected or destroyed during the English Civil Wars in the mid–17th century.[24]

Another factor impeding the search for the 1587 colonists' family relations in England is the fact that the colonists left little or nothing of value behind when they sailed for America in 1587. They expected to be the founders and landholders of the "Cittie of Ralegh" in the new land of Virginia, and they would have sold or disbursed whatever assets they had in England to take part in the venture. Consequently there were no estates to administer when, after seven years according to English law, the 1587 colonists were considered officially deceased. The single known exception was Ananias Dare, one of John White's Assistants and son-in-law, who left a young son (illegitimate, according to Quinn[25]) named John and apparently some property in London. There is a court record indicating that John Dare, a minor and son of Ananias Dare of St. Bride's in London, was placed under the guardianship of John Nokes of London in 1594, seven years after Ananias and the rest of the colony sailed for America. John Dare obviously carried the Y DNA of Ananias Dare, but there seems to be no confirmed documentary record of John Dare or his possible descendants after 1594.[26] Efforts continue in both the U.S. and the U.K. to identify and test individuals who may have a claim to Lost Colony descendancy through old records or family histories, and the Lost Colony DNA Project maintains a database of Lost Colony surnames and DNA signatures.

The search for present-day descendants of Lost Colonists, though, brings us back once again to the question of survival probabilities. From a DNA perspective the odds are not very promising. As Estes wrote,

In order for a Y DNA match to occur, a male colonist would have to have survived and had male children who had male children down to the present generation—an unbroken line with no females. In order for a mitochondrial DNA match to occur, a female colonist would have to have survived and had female children who had female children down to the present generation—an unbroken line with no males.[27]

The search for even one Lost Colony descendant is akin to looking for the proverbial needle in a haystack. If no unbroken male or female Lost Colonist line survived to the present, however, ... there is no needle to look for.

# Summation

In the final analysis, the history of the Lost Colony was remarkably short. It began on May 8, 1587, when the colonists sailed from England with the high hopes of establishing the "Cittie of Ralegh" in America, and it essentially ended just two years and four months later. In summary:

The colonists had their first disappointing setback before they even arrived at the Outer Banks. As soon as they reached the Caribbean, master pilot Simon Fernandez learned that the Spanish knew about Raleigh's plan to establish a settlement at the Chesapeake Bay, and that they were in the process of searching for the English there. Consequently, their original Chesapeake destination had to be altered. After the flagship *Lyon* rendezvoused at Dominica with the flyboat, commanded by Edward Spicer, it was agreed that the *Lyon* and the pinnace would proceed to Roanoke Island, where Ralph Lane and Raleigh's first colony had spent the year in 1585–86. Meanwhile, Spicer and the flyboat would acquire the usual supplies and requisite cargo in the Caribbean. The *Lyon* and pinnace arrived at Roanoke with most of the colonists on July 22, and the flyboat arrived three days later on July 25 with the cargo and the rest of the colonists.

The stay at Roanoke was intended to be temporary, while a permanent settlement location could be found and prepared on the mainland. The colonists rebuilt Lane's old settlement at Roanoke, fortified and enclosed it with a strong palisade, and spent the winter there. At the same time the principal Assistants and other colonists, no doubt with the help of Manteo, explored the mainland for a good settlement site, which had to be readily accessible by way of a navigable inlet for White's return as well as for future resupply and commerce with England. With the Chesapeake eliminated, the deepest and most stable inlet on the Outer Banks was Wokokon, and consequently the new mainland settlement would likely have been somewhere west of that inlet at present-day Carteret, Pamlico, or southern Beaufort County. That area had already been explored by Grenville in 1585, probably for a future settlement site, and it had the added requirements of being beyond

the territory of the hostile Secotan tribes and also beyond the
restriction from Roanoke noted by White. The move from Roan
new mainland settlement was accomplished by mid–March of 15&
for the first spring planting in early April. Prior to their depar.u.c from
Roanoke, the colonists left carved messages directing White to Croatoan,
where a few colonists would be waiting to escort the governor, the supplies,
and the new colonists across Pamlico Sound to the settlement.

Everything changed when White failed to return by late summer or early
fall of 1588. All the colonists' hopes and expectations quickly evaporated with
the realization that their continued existence as a viable English colony was
now in serious jeopardy. Although the colony was intended to be agricultur-
ally self-sufficient, it could not survive for long without regular contact with
and resupply from England. The abandoned colonists were left with few
options available to them in 1588. Their best chance for survival was to re-
establish contact using their 30–35 tun pinnace, certainly capable of ocean
travel, and their best route was northward to Newfoundland, an English possession frequented annually by English fishing fleets between May and October. The number of colonists who embarked on this voyage could have ranged
from at least forty to perhaps eighty or ninety—nearly the entire colony—if
a second vessel was built during the six or seven month wait for a preferred
spring departure. In this likely scenario, all those who sailed for Newfoundland perished at sea in the attempt.

The colonists who remained soon faced another unforeseen calamity.
In September 1589, a powerful hurricane moved through the Caribbean and
then turned northward just off the coast of Florida, following the typical Gulf
Stream track toward the Carolina coast. Even a minor Category 2 hurricane,
like Floyd when it made landfall at Cape Fear in 1999, could be accompanied
by a nine to ten foot storm surge. Such an event would have inundated the
Outer Banks and the coastal mainland, completely eradicating the new mainland settlement and inflicting any number of fatalities there and at Croatoan
as well. Any surviving colonists, along with the Croatoans, would have been
forced to vacate the Outer Banks and the coastal mainland where the soil
was contaminated by saline residue from the surge.

The history of the Lost Colony effectively ended in September 1589,
after which the colony and the mainland settlement, by all evidence, no longer
existed. If any colonists survived, they quickly integrated with the native
tribes, most likely the Croatoans, and were somewhere on the mainland
across Pamlico Sound after September of 1589. Croatoan was still abandoned
when White finally returned in 1590, but it would be eventually reinhabited.
From this point onwards the only questions that remain unanswered are the
locations of any possible survivors and the likelihood of admixed descendants. As for the few original colonists who may have lived beyond 1589,

their subsequent total immersion in the native Algonquian culture would have eroded their English identities rather quickly. Yes, there very likely could have been first, second, and perhaps third generation admixed descendants, but their language and names would almost certainly have been Algonquian, not English, by the second generation. Other than the periodic occurrence of an unusual eye or hair color, descendants of the 1587 Lost Colonists would soon have been virtually indistinguishable from native peoples.

Given the extremely high mortality rate of the eastern Carolina tribes, the possibility of Lost Colony descendants surviving beyond the 17th and early 18th centuries would have been seriously diminished. Add to this the genetic requirements noted by Estes—an unbroken line of Y or mitochondrial DNA—and the chances of an existing 21st century direct male or female line of Lost Colonist descendants are extremely remote. Also implausible is the 19th century claim that a large group of direct descendants of the Lost Colonists with their original 16th century surnames was discovered in North Carolina tilling the soil and owning slaves and still speaking Elizabethian English. Although direct Lost Colony descendancy may not have existed beyond the mid–17th century, that does not invalidate the oral tradition of tribes asserting that some of "their ancestors were the Lost Colony of Roanoke Island," as C.D. Brewington had noted. All that unquestionably remains of the Lost Colony today are those oral traditions and legends that persist in southeast North Carolina.

Equally important as the careful *reconstruction* of the foregoing Lost Colony narrative is the *deconstruction* of the more than four centuries of myths and misinformed accounts about the supposed fate of the Lost Colonists and the rumored locations of survivors. Both elements are crucial halves of a comprehensive, whole Lost Colony analysis. With the possible exception of Wowinchopunck's report of the "cloathed men" at Pananiock, all of the stories about the Lost Colony reported from Jamestown between 1607 and 1611 were erroneous assumptions made by John Smith and William Strachey, who misunderstood the essentially accurate information provided by the Powhatans. The myths of Lost Colonists at faraway places called Pakrakanick and Ocanahonan, where they taught the Indians to build English-style houses, were hasty misinterpretations made by Smith and repeated by Strachey, and in reality were Algonquian memories of Spanish expeditions into the Piedmont of the present day Carolinas many decades earlier. They had nothing whatsoever to do with the Lost Colony.

Likewise, the 1587 colony was never slaughtered by Powhatan, or anyone else for that matter. There *was* a slaughter of sorts at Roanoke, but that occurred in 1586 and involved the assault and rout of Grenville's contingent of Englishmen and was conducted by a combined force of warriors from Aquascogoc, Secota, and Dasamonguepeuk. The Lost Colony was not involved in any way with that event or with Powhatan's massacre of the Chesapeake tribe in 1607. Nevertheless the erroneous reports about Powhatan's slaughter of the 1587 colony and Lost Colony survivors at places called Pakrakanick and Ocanahonan were officially accepted in London by 1609. Variations of that false narrative have been with us ever since.

# Chapter Notes

## Preface

1. Carl Sagan, *The Demon-Haunted World* (London: Headline Book Publishing, 1997) p. 31.
2. *Ibid.* Chapter 10, "The Dragon in My Garage," p. 160.

## Chapter 1

1. Jenny Higgins, "Uncovering Cabot: The Ruddock Riddle," Newfoundland and Labrador Heritage Web Site, 2013. http://www.heritage.nf.ca/articles/exploration/cabot-ruddock.php.
2. "A discourse of a discouerie for a new passage to Cataia." Written by Sir Humfrey Gilbert, Knight. Richard Hakluyt, *The Voyages of the English Nation to America.* Vol I, Edited by Edmund Goldsmid (Edinburgh: E & G Goldsmith, 1889). p. 34.
3. Hakluyt, *The Principal Navigations, Voyages, Traffiques, and Discoveries of the English Nation* edited by Edmund Goldsmid, XIII "America Part II. #23: "The Letters Patents, granted by the Queenes Maiestie to M. Walter Ralegh now Knight, for the discovering and planting of new lands and Countries, to continue the space of 6. yeeres and no more." This edition published by The University of Adelaide Library and available online http://ebooks.adelaide.edu.au/h/hakluyt/voyages/v13/contents.html. Hereafter referred to as Richard Hakluyt, *The Principal Navigations...*
4. Richard Hakluyt, *The Principal Navigations...* #24: "The first voyage made to the coasts of America, with two barks, wherein were Captaines M. Philip Amadas, and M. Arthur Barlowe, who discouered part of the Countrey now called Virginia Anno 1584. Written by one of the said Captaines, and sent to sir Walter Ralegh knight, at whose charge and direction, the said voyage was set forth."
5. Seth Mallios, *The Deadly Politics of Giving* (Tuscaloosa: University of Alabama Press, 2006) p. 60.
6. David Beers Quinn, *Set Fair for Roanoke: Voyages and Colonies, 1584–1606* (Chapel Hill: University of North Carolina Press, 1985) p. 35.
7. *Ibid.*
8. Richard Hakluyt, *The Principal Navigations...* #24
9. *Ibid.*
10. Richard Hakluyt, *The Principal Navigations...* #22 "A Discourse of Western Planting, written by M. Richard Hakluyt, 1584."
11. William S. Powell, *North Carolina, A Bicentennial History* (New York: W.W. Norton, 1977) p. 15.
12. Richard Hakluyt, *The Principal Navigations...* #25: "The voiage made by Sir Richard Greenuile, for Sir Walter Ralegh, to Virginia, in the yeere 1585."
13. *Ibid.*, July 15.
14. Richard Hakluyt, *The Principal Navigations...* #27: "An account of the particularities of the imployments of the English men left in Virginia by Richard Greenuill vnder the charge of Master Ralph Lane Generall of the same, from the 17. Of August 1585. Vntil the 18. Of Iune 1586 at which time they departed the Countrey; sent and directed to Sir Walter Ralegh."
15. Hakluyt, #22, Chapter IX.
16. Hakluyt, *The Principal Navigations...* #27.

17. *Ibid.*

18. *Ibid.*

19. Richard Hakluyt, *The Principal Navigations*... #29: "A briefe and true report of the new found land of Virginia: of the commodities there found, and to be raised, aswell merchantable as others: Written by Thomas Heriot, seruant to Sir Walter Ralegh, a member of the Colony, and there imployed in discouering a full tweluemonth."

20. Hakluyt, *The Principal Navigations*... #27.

21. Karen Ordahl Kupperman, *Indians and English* (Ithaca, NY: Cornell University Press, 2000) p. 186.

22. Hakluyt, *The Principal Navigations*... #27.

23. Richard Hakluyt, *The Principal Navigations*... #26: "An extract of Master Ralph Lanes letter to M. Richard Hakluyt Esquire, and another Gentleman of the middle Temple, from Virginia."

24. Hakluyt, *The Principal Navigations*... #27

25. Julian S. Corbett, editor, *Publications of the Navy Records Society of Great Britain*, Vol. II, "The Spanish War 1585–87," Printed for the Navy Records Society, 1898. p. 26. http://books.google.com/books?ei=agsJU92OEcG 0sASMvYCoBA&id=sP1aAAAAIAAJ&dq= weapons+falcons+and+fowlers&q=pinnace# v=snippet&q=pinnace&f=false

26. Richard Hakluyt, *The Principal Navigations*... #28: "The third voyage made by a ship sent in the yeere 1586, to the reliefe of the Colony planted in Virginia at the sole charges of Sir Walter Ralegh."

27. *Ibid.*

28. *The Deposition of Pedro Diaz*... "in Havana on the twenty-first day of March in the year one thousand five hundred and eighty-nine." This transcription from Andrew T. Powell, *Grenville and the Lost Colony of Roanoke* (Leicester, UK: Matador/Troubador Publishing, 2011) pp. 149–156.

29. Hakluyt, *The Principal Navigations*... #27.

30. Quinn, *Set Fair*, p. 106.

## Chapter 2

1. Richard Hakluyt, *The Principal Navigations*... #29: "A briefe and true report..."

2. *Ibid.*

3. *Ibid.*

4. *Ibid.*

5. *Ibid.*

6. Quinn, *Set Fair*, pp. 256–8.

7. *Ibid.*, p. 270

8. Richard Hakluyt, *The Principal Navigations*... #30: "The Fourth Voyage Made to Virginia with Three Ships, in Yere 1587. Wherein was transported the second Colonie."

9. Julian S. Corbett, editor, *Publications of the Navy Records Society of Great Britain*, Vol II, "The Spanish War 1585–87," p. 135.

10. The precise number of 1587 colonists is disputed. Furthermore, there a difference between the number of those who sailed from England and the number of colonists who remained at Roanoke and were "lost." Most authors have settled on 115 "lost" colonists. Author Andrew Powell has done a credible examination of this topic and arrived at 119 "lost" colonists, including Virginia Dare and a "Harvie" child, both of whom were born after the arrival at Roanoke. The number of colonists who sailed from England used here—118—is Powell's total minus the two born later, plus George Howe, who was killed by Indians upon arrival. See Andrew T. Powell, *Grenville and the Lost Colony of Roanoke* (Leicester, UK: Matador/Troubador Publishing, 2011) pp. 209–218.

11. Richard Hakluyt, *The Principal Navigations*... #30.

## Chapter 3

1. His name has been variously spelled Simão Fernandes Fernandes in his original Portuguese, Simon Fernandez in Spanish, Simon Fernando or Ferdinando in English; here and afterwards the more common "Fernandez" is used.

2. Lee Miller, *Roanoke: Solving the Mystery of the Lost Colony* (New York: Arcade Publishing, 2001) Part Three, "A Case of Conspiracy," pp. 127–261.

3. Richard Hakluyt, *The Principal Navigations*... #30: "The Fourth Voyage Made to Virginia with Three Ships, in Yere 1587. Wherein was transported the second Colonie." Entry for July 1.

4. William S. Powell, ed., *Dictionary of North Carolina Biography* D–G, Vol. 2 (Chapel

Hill: University of North Carolina Press, 1986) pp. 190–1.

5. *Ibid.*

6. Paul E. Hoffman, *A New Andalucia and a Way to the Orient* (Baton Rouge: Louisiana State University Press, 1990, 2004) p. 244.

7. Helen Wallis, *Material on Nautical Cartography in the British Library, 1550–1650* (Lisbon, Portugal: the Instituto de Investigação Científica Tropical, 1984) p. 195.

8. Powell, pp. 190–1.

9. Richard Hakluyt, *The Principal Navigations...* #30, entry for July 22.

10. Miller, pp. 181–184, 160–1, et al.

11. Richard Hakluyt, *The Principal Navigations...* #2: "A letter of Sir Francis Walsingham to M. Richard Hakluyt then of Christchurch in Oxford, incouraging him in the study of Cosmographie, and of furthering new discoueries, &c."

12. Richard Hakluyt, *The Principal Navigations...* #3: "A letter of Sir Francis Walsingham to Master Thomas Aldworth merchant, and at that time Maior of the Cittie of Bristoll, concerning their aduenture in the Westerne discouerie."

13. Giles Milton, *Big Chief Elizabeth* (New York: Farrar, Straus and Giroux, 2000) pp. 76, 131.

14. David Beers Quinn, *Set Fair for Roanoke: Voyages and Colonies 1584–1606* (Chapel Hill: University of North Carolina Press, 1985) p. 149.

15. *Ibid.*, p. 259.

16. Hakluyt. #30, entry for July 22.

17. *Ibid.*

18. *Ibid.*

19. Richard Hakluyt, *Principal Navigations...* #29 "A briefe and true report of the new found land of Virginia—The conclusion."

20. Hakluyt, #30, entry for July 22.

21. *Ibid.* entry for July 25.

22. Paul E. Hoffman, *Spain and the Roanoke Voyages* (Raleigh: North Carolina Dept. of Cultural Resources, 1987) pp. 27, 30, 32.

23. *Ibid.*, p. 32; also Irene Wright, *The Early History of Cuba 1492–1586* (New York: Macmillan, 1916) p. 349.

24. Hoffman, *Spain...*, p. 42.

25. *Ibid.*, p. 45.

26. *Ibid.*, pp. 46–7.

27. Hakluyt #30, entries for July 2, 3, 4.

28. Hoffman, *A New Andalucia and a Way to the Orient*, p. 233.

29. Hakluyt, entry for July 22.

30. Hakluyt, entry for July 23.

31. Hakluyt, entry for July 28.

32. Powell's total of "lost" colonists. See Andrew T. Powell, *Grenville and the Lost Colony of Roanoke* (Leicester, UK: Matador/Troubador Publishing, 2011) pp. 209–218.

## Chapter 4

1. Richard Hakluyt, *The Principal Navigations...* #30, "The Fourth Voyage Made to Virginia with Three Ships, in Yere 1587. Wherein was transported the second Colonie." Entry for July 30.

2. North Carolina Archaeological Council Publication Number 30, 2011, "The Archaeology of North Carolina: Three Archaeological Symposia" Ewen, Whyte, and Davis, Jr., editors.

3. David Beers Quinn, *Set Fair for Roanoke: Voyages and Colonies 1584–1606* (Chapel Hill: University of North Carolina Press, 1985) p. 347.

4. Thomas C. Parramore, "The 'Lost Colony' Found: A Documentary Perspective." *The North Carolina Historical Review*, Vol. 78, No. 1 (January 2001), pp. 70–71.

5. *Ibid.*

6. James Horn, *A Kingdom Strange* (New York: Basic Books, 2010) p. 164.

7. Horn, pp. 224, et al.; also Horn, *A Land As God Made It* (New York: Basic Books, 2005) pp. 145–6, et al.; also Lee Miller, *Roanoke: Solving the Mystery of the Lost Colony* (New York: Arcade Publishing, 2000) pp. 227–235; also Parramore "The 'Lost Colony' Found: A Documentary Perspective," p. 71; also Quinn. *Set Fair*, p. 347.

8. Hakluyt #30, entry for Aug 22.

9. *Ibid.* Single entry for May 16.

10. *Ibid.* Entry for July 25.

11. *Ibid.* Entry for June 19–21.

12. Quinn, *Set Fair*, p. 273.

13. David Stick, *Roanoke Island: The Beginnings of English America* (Chapel Hill: University of North Carolina Press, 1983) p. 199.

14. Hakluyt, #30, entry for Aug 18.

15. Richard Hakluyt, *The Principal Navigations...* #24, "The first voyage made to the coasts of America, with two barks, wherein

were Captaines M. Philip Amadas, and M. Arthur Barlowe, who discouered part of the Countrey now called Virginia Anno 1584. Written by one of the said Captaines, and sent to sir Walter Ralegh knight, at whose charge and direction, the said voyage was set forth." Description of Roanoke.

16. Hakluyt, *The Principal Navigations*... #30, Entry for July 23.

17. *Ibid.* Entry for July 28.

18. *Ibid.* Entry for August 9.

19. *Ibid.* Entry for July 23.

20. Richard Hakluyt, *The Principal Navigations*... #33, "The fift voyage of M. Iohn White into the West Indies and parts of America called Virginia, in the yeere 1590." Entry for August 18.

21. Karen Ordahl Kupperman, *Roanoke, the Abandoned Colony* (Totowa, NJ: Rowman & Allanheld, 1984) p. 108.

22. Richard Hakluyt, *The Principal Navigations*... #27, "An account of the particularities of the imployments of the English men left in Virginia by Richard Greeneuill vnder the charge of Master Ralph Lane Generall of the same, from the 17. of August 1585. vntil the 18. of Iune 1586. at which time they departed the Countrey; sent and directed to Sir Walter Ralegh."

23. "Ancient map gives clue to fate of 'Lost' Colony," published May 4, 2012, by *The Telegraph.* http://www.telegraph.co.uk/science/science-news/9244947/Ancient-map-gives-clue-to-fate-of-Lost-Colony.html; Also Joint Announcement, First Colony Foundation and British Museum, May 7, 2012 http://www.foxnews.com/scitech/2012/05/07/new-clue-to-mystery-lost-roanoke-colony/

24. A number of news outlets reported on the fort symbol discovery and cited similar quotes. See above "Ancient map gives clue..." Also "New clue to mystery of lost Roanoke colony" Published May 7, 2012 by FoxNews.com. http://www.foxnews.com/scitech/2012/05/07/new-clue-to-mystery-lost-roanoke-colony/ See also "Scientists report new clue to fate of Roanoke's Lost Colony" by Martha Waggoner of the Associated Press, published by NBC News.com 5/3/2012, http://www.nbcnews.com/id/47288500/ns/technology_and_science-science/t/scientists-report-new-clue-fate-roanoke-lost-colony/#.VwKeHPnF96U

25. Hakyluyt, *The Principal Navigations*... #27.

26. *Ibid.*

27. *Ibid.*

28. Hakluyt, *Principal Navigations*... #33.

29. *Ibid.*

30. Lee Miller, *Roanoke: Solving the Mystery of the Lost Colony* (New York: Arcade Publishing, 2001) pp. 228–9.

31. *Ibid.*

32. Francis Newton Thorpe, *The Federal and State Constitutions, Colonial Charters, and Other Organic Laws of the State, Territories, and Colonies Now or Heretofore Forming the United States of America* Vol. VII (Washington: Government Printing Office, 1909) p. 3783. "The First Charter of Virginia; April 10, 1606."

33. *Ibid.*

34. Thorpe, Vol. I, p. 53. "Charter to Sir Walter Raleigh: 1584."

35. P. Evans, M. Laird, and N. Luccketti, *2012 Archaeological Investigation of Site 31BR46 On Salmon Creek, Bertie County, North Carolina.* First Colony Foundation, March 2014, p. 65.

## Chapter 5

1. David Beers Quinn, *Set Fair for Roanoke: Voyages and Colonies 1584–1606* (Chapel Hill: University of North Carolina Press, 1985) p. 74.

2. Richard Hakluyt, *The Principal Navigations*... #25: "The voiage made by Sir Richard Greenuile, for Sir Walter Ralegh, to Virginia, in the yeere 1585."

3. *Ibid.* (An English tun referred to an old wine cask measurement of volume equivalent to 954 litres of wine which weighed roughly a ton. See Wikipedia: English tun.)

4. Quinn, *Set Fair*, p. 53, 85.

5. "Past, Present and Future Inlets of the Outer Banks Barrier Islands, North Carolina," a White Paper by Mallinson, Culver, Riggs, Walsh, Ames, Smith, Members of the North Carolina College of Arts and Sciences and Institute for Coastal Science and Policy, East Carolina University, Greenville, North Carolina. December 2008.

6. *Ibid.*, pp. 9–14.

7. *Ibid.* GPR data, pp. 5–7.

8. Quinn, *Set Fair*, p. 102.

9. "White–de Bry Map of 1590," Fort Raleigh National Historic Site website, National Park Service. U.S. Department of the Interior.

10. David Stick, *Roanoke Island, the Beginnings of English America* (Chapel Hill: University of North Carolina Press, 1983) p. 81.

11. "Past, Present and Future Inlets..." p. 10.

12. *Ibid.*

13. John Lawson, *A New Voyage to Carolina* (London, 1709) pp. 61, 64.

14. John Smith, "A True Relation," edited by Lyon G. Tyler, *Narratives of Early Virginia, 1606–1625* (New York: Scribner's, 1907) p. 53.

## Chapter 6

1. Robert Kerr, *A General History and Collection of Voyages and Travels*, volume VII, chapter VIII "Voyage of Sir Francis Drake, in 1585, to the West Indies" (Edinburgh: George Ramsay, 1812) p. 356

2. *Ibid.*

3. *Ibid.*, pp. 362–3

4. David Beers Quinn, *Set Fair for Roanoke: Voyages and Colonies, 1584–1606* (Chapel Hill: University of North Carolina Press, 1985) p. 300

5. Hakluyt's *Principal Navigations*, 1589, "John White's Account of the Abortive Voyage of the Brave and the Roe," pp. 771–773. This transcription is from Andrew T. Powell, *Grenville and the Lost Colony of Roanoke*, "The Voyages of 1588," pp. 139–147.

6. Mark Nicholls, and Penry Williams, *Sir Walter Raleigh in Life and Legend* (London and New York: Continuum International Publishing Group, 2011) p. 36.

7. Lyon Gardiner Tyler, *Encyclopedia of Virginia Biography* (New York: Lewis Historical Publishing Co., 1915) Vol. I, pp. 19–20.

8. Quinn, *Set Fair*, p. 300.

9. Email from Andy Powell to the author, May 19, 2015.

10. "John White's Account..." from Powell, p. 140.

11. *Ibid.*

12. *The Deposition of Pedro Diaz...* "in Havana on the twenty-first day of March in the year one thousand five hundred and eighty-nine." This transcription from Andrew T. Powell, *Grenville and the Lost Colony of Roa-*

noke (Leicester, UK: Matador/Troubador Publishing, 2011) pp. 155.

13. James Horn, *A Kingdom Strange* (New York: Basic Books, 2010) p. 171.

14. Quinn, *Set Fair*, p. 305.

15. *Ibid.*, p. 144.

16. *Ibid.*, p. 146.

17. *Ibid.*, p. 147.

18. Helen Rountree, *The Powhatan Indians of Virginia* (Norman: University of Oklahoma Press, 1989) p. 47.

19. Upon his return to Roanoke in 1590, White observed that the houses and been disassembled and that light cannonry and other weaponry had been removed from the settlement. See Richard Hakluyt, *The Principal Navigations...* #33, "The fift voyage of M. Iohn White into the West Indies and parts of America called Virginia, in the yeere 1590."

20. Hakluyt #33.

21. Paul Hoffman, "New Light on Vicente Gonzalez's 1588 Voyage in Search of Raleigh's English Colonies," *The North Carolina Historical Review* vol. 63, no. 2 (April 1986), p. 218.

22. Paul E. Hoffman, *Spain and the Roanoke Voyages* (Raleigh: North Carolina Dept. of Cultural Resources, 1987) p. 48.

23. Hoffman, "New Light on Vicente Gonzalez's 1588 Voyage in Search of Raleigh's English Colonies," pp. 200–201.

24. *Ibid.*, p. 50. See also Quinn, *Set Fair*, p. 308.

25. Hoffman, *Spain and the Roanoke Voyages*, p. 49. See also Fr. Luis Geronimo de Ore, *The Martyrs of Florida* (1513–1616) translated, with biographical Preface and notes, by Maynard Geiger, Franciscan Studies no. 18 (New York: J.F. Wagner, 1937).

## Chapter 7

1. Paul E. Hoffman, *Spain and the Roanoke Voyages* (Raleigh: North Carolina Dept. of Cultural Resources, 1987) p. 48.

2. Scott Dawson, "New Theory?" *The Outer Banks Sentinel*, September 13, 2006.

3. Charles Harry Whedbee, *Blackbeard's Cup and Stories of the Outer Banks* (Winston-Salem, NC: John F. Blair, 1989).

4. Richard Hakluyt, *The Principal Navigations...* #33, "The fift voyage of M. Iohn White into the West Indies and parts of America called Virginia, in the yeere 1590."

5. *Ibid.*

6. V.J. Bellis, "Ecology of maritime forests of the southern Atlantic coast: a community profile." Biological report 30, May 1995. National Biological Service, U.S. Department of the Interior. Washington, D.C. See also K. Hill, "Maritime Hammock Habitats" at the Smithsonian Marine Station website: http://www.sms.si.edu/irlspec/Hammock_Habitat.htm#top.

7. "Buxton Woods," www.hatteras-nc.com/buxton-woods.html.

8. See "Quercus Virginiana" Wikipedia. http://en.wikipedia.org/wiki/Quercus_virginiana.

9. National Wildlife Federation. "Southern Live Oak." https://www.nwf.org/Wildlife/Wildlife-Library/Plants/Southern-Live-Oak.aspx

10. *Ibid.*

11. "Seven Sisters Oak," Wikipedia. https://en.wikipedia.org/wiki/Seven_Sisters_Oak.

12. "*THE* Tree ... Angel Oak," http://www.angeloaktree.org/history.htm.

13. "The Big Tree, Rockport," Wikipedia. https://en.wikipedia.org/wiki/The_Big_Tree,_Rockport.

14. "Live Oak: Southern Ecological Heritage," by Dr. Kim Coder, Professor of Tree Biology & Health Care. Dendrology Series (Warnell School of Forestry & Natural Resources: University of Georgia, March 2015) p. 4.

15. *Ibid.*

16. William G. Haag, *The Archaeology of Coastal North Carolina*, Coastal Studies Series 2 (Baton Rouge: Louisiana State University Press, 1958). Also "The Archaeology of North Carolina: Three Archaeological Symposia," Charles R. Ewen, Thomas R. Whyte, and R.P. Stephen Davis, Jr., editors. North Carolina Archaeological Council Publication Number 30, 2011. Chapter 7, pp. 2–3.

17. Haag, *The Archaeology,* "H7 Frisco Dune Site."

18. J.C. Harrington, "Evidence of Manual Reckoning in the Cittie of Ralegh," *The North Carolina Historical Review* 33, no. 1 (1956): 1–11.

19. *Ibid.*

20. Hakluyt, *The Principal Navigations...* #33.

21. Measurements taken by LCRG members Dawn Taylor and Jennifer Creech, 2014.

22. Blair A. Rudes, "The First Description of an Iroquoian People: Spaniards among the Tuscaroras before 1522," n.d., p. 14.

23. *Ibid.*, p. 33.

24. See Al Pate, "Who Are the Coree?" and "The Coree Are Not Extinct," http://www.dickshovel.com/coreewho.html.

25. John Lawson, *A New Voyage to Carolina* (London: N.p., 1709) p. 59.

26. *Ibid.*

27. James Sprunt, *Tales and Traditions of the Lower Cape Fear, 1661–1896* (Wilmington, NC: LeGwin Brothers, 1896) p. 55.

28. *Narrative and Critical History of America*, Volume 5, Edited by Justin Winsor (New York: Houghton Mifflin and Company, 1887) p. 289.

29. "Coree" (2. Language), Wikipedia: http://en.wikipedia.org/wiki/Coree

30. Rudes, "The First Description..." p. 14. Also see Stan Allen's commentary in "Memorial: Remembering Our Friend, Blair A. Rudes, Linguistics Advisor to the CCIC" www.coastalcarolinaindians.com/memorial-remembering-our-friend-blair-a-rudes-linguistics-advisor-to-ccic/.

31. See "The Town of Swansboro," Swansboro Chamber of Commerce. http://www.swansborochamber.org/Swansboro.html.

32. Lawson, pp. 58, 171, 299.

33. "Ethnohistorical Description of the Eight Villages adjoining Cape Hatteras National Seashore and Interpretive Themes of History and Heritage." National Park Service, U.S. Department of the Interior, November 2005. Prepared for the Cape Hatteras National Seashore by Impact Assessment, Inc.

34. Charles Paul, "Colonial Beaufort: The History of a North Carolina Town," 1965 Thesis (rev. 2011), p. 11.

35. Vincent H. Todd and Julius Goebel, eds., "Christoph von Graffenried's Account of the Founding of New Bern" (Raleigh, NC: Edwards & Broughton Printing, 1920).

# Chapter 8

1. Richard Hakluyt, *Principal Navigations...* #33 "The fift voyage of M. Iohn White into the West Indies and parts of America called Virginia, in the yeere 1590." Entry for August 17.

2. See "Ships of the Roanoke Voyages,"

The National Parks Service, Fort Raleigh, North Carolina.

3. *Ibid.*

4. *Publications of the Navy Records Society of Great Britain,* Julian S. Corbett, editor, Vol. II, "The Spanish War 1585–1587," p. 1. Printed for the Navy Records Society, 1898.

5. Charles W. Livermore, *Ye Antient Wrecke—1626, Loss of the Sparrow-Hawk in 1626* (Boston: Alfred Mudge & Sons, 1865) pp. 43–4.

6. Richard Hakluyt, *The Principal Navigations...* #30: "The Fourth Voyage Made to Virginia with Three Ships, in Yere 1587. Wherein was transported the second Colonie."

7. *Ibid.*

8. *Ibid.*

9. Andrew T. Powell, *Grenville and the Lost Colony of Roanoke* (Leicester, UK: Matador/Troubador Publishing, 2011) p. 218.

10. Richard Hakluyt, *Principal Navigations...* #25 "The voiage made by Sir Richard Greenuile, for Sir Walter Ralegh, to Virginia, in the yeere 1585," entry for May 13.

11. Sherwood Harris, "The Tragic Dream of Jean Ribault," *American Heritage Society Magazine,* Volume 14, Issue 6, 1963.

12. Hobson Woodward, *A Brave Vessel: A True Tale of the Castaways Who Rescued Jamestown* (New York: Penguin Books, 2009) p. 78.

13. *Ibid.,* pp. 93–4.

14. Email communications between the author and Andrew Powell, author and former mayor of Bideford, April 30 and May 1, 2015.

15. David Beers Quinn, *Set Fair for Roanoke: Voyages and Colonies 1584–1606* (Chapel Hill: University of North Carolina Press, 1985) pp. 64, 138, 145–6.

16. Library of Congress, John Smith, *The Generall Historie of Virginia, New England & The Summer Isles* (New York: Macmillan, 1907) Third Booke: 1608, "The punishment for loyterers," p. 179.

17. William Strachey, *A True Reportory...* Part III "Their departure from Bermuda and arrival in Virginia Miseries there Departure and return upon the Lord La Warre's arriving-James Town described." From Purchas, Samuel. *Hakluytus posthumus; or, Purchas his pilgrimes* (London: William Stansby, 1625) in four volumes, beginning page 1734 in vol. IV.

18. The Library of Congress: Global Gateway, "New Maritime Routes in the 16th Century" http://international.loc.gov/intldl/fia html/fiathemela.html.

19. *Fishery Bulletin of the Fish and Wildlife Service,* No. 74, Henry Bigelow and William Schroeder, "Fishes of the Gulf of Maine" (Washington, DC: GPO, 1953) p. 182.

## Chapter 9

1. Richard Hakluyt, *The Principal Navigations...* #27 "An account of the particularities of the imployments of the English men left in Virginia by Richard Greeneuill vnder the charge of Master Ralph Lane Generall of the same, from the 17. of August 1585. vntil the 18. of Iune 1586. at which time they departed the Countrey; sent and directed to Sir Walter Ralegh."

2. Hakluyt, *The Principal Navigations...* #30 "The Fourth Voyage Made to Virginia with Three Ships, in Yere 1587. Wherein was transported the second Colonie."

3. Hakluyt, *The Principal Navigations...* #33 "The fift voyage of M. Iohn White into the West Indies and parts of America called Virginia, in the yeere 1590."

4. National Oceanic and Atmosphere Administration, National Hurricane Center, U.S. Department of Commerce, "Glossary of NHC Terms: Saffir-Simpson Hurricane Wind Scale."

5. NOAA, National Ocean Service, U.S. Department of Commerce, "Ocean Facts: What is a Hurricane?"

6. Kevin France, "Top Five U.S. Cities Most Vulnerable to Hurricanes," AccuWeaterc.com, June 25, 2015.

7. NOAA Hurricane Research Division, "Chronological List of All Hurricanes which Affected the Continental United States 1851–2014." Contributed by Chris Landsea of the National Hurricane Center.

8. R. García-Herrera, L. Gimeno, P. Ribera, and E. Hernández, "New records of Atlantic hurricanes from Spanish documentary sources," *Journal of Geophysical Research,* Volume 110, Issue D3, Feb 4, 2005.

9. In addition to the 2005 García-Herrera, et al. work, previous research included José Carlos Millás and Leonard Pardue, eds., "Hurricanes of the Caribbean and Adjacent Regions,

1492–1800," Miami: Academy of the Arts and Sciences of the Americas (1968); Huguette Chaunu and Pierre Chaunu (1955–1960), *Séville et l'Atlantique (1504–1650)* (in French) 12, Paris: Librairie Armand Colin; and David M. Ludlum (1963), *Early American Hurricanes, 1492–1870* (Boston: American Meteorological Society, OCLC 511649). All of this is summarized in "List of Atlantic hurricanes before 1600" at Wikipedia.

10. García-Herrera, et al. Unattributed notation.

11. *Scientific American,* "Why do hurricanes hit the East Coast of the U.S...." October 21, 1999. Reply by Chris W. Landsea, researcher at the Atlantic Oceanographic and Meteorological Laboratory/Hurricane Research Division of the NOAA, located in Miami, Fla.

12. See "Historical Hurricane Tracks" and "Hurricane Floyd Storm Review" at http://www.weather.gov/mhx/Sep161999EventRev iew and https://coast.noaa.gov/hurricanes/index.html.

13. "Atlantic hurricane best track (HURDAT version 2)." National Hurricane Center, Hurricane Research Division (May 7, 2015). National Oceanic and Atmospheric Administration, U.S. Department of Commerce. Retrieved July 2, 2015.

14. "Hurricane Storm Surge," *Ocean Today.* National Oceanic and Atmospheric Administration, U.S. Department of Commerce, 2015.

15. Edward N. Rappaport, National Weather Service, National Centers for Environmental Prediction, National Hurricane Center, Miami, Florida, "Fatalities in the United States from Atlantic Tropical Cyclones: New Data and Interpretation," *Bulletin of the American Meteorological Society,* Vol. 95, Issue 3, 2014.

16. "What is the difference between storm surge and storm tide?" NOAA, National Ocean Service, U.S. Department of Commerce, Ocean Facts, 2014.

17. "Event History: Hurricane Floyd 1999." Storm Surge and Coastal Inundation. NOAA, U.S. Department of Commerce.

18. Event Summaries, Hurricane Hazel October 15, 1954, "Event Overview" National Oceanic and Atmospheric Administration, U.S. Department of Commerce.

19. See the NOAA Storm Surge and Water Depth Maps for Central North Carolina at https://www.wunderground.com/hurricane/GASCNCSurge.asp.

20. Hakluyt, #33 "The fift voyage of M. Iohn White into the West Indies and parts of America called Virginia, in the yeere 1590."

21. *Ibid.*

22. Dennis J. Parker, editor, *Floods,* Vol. 1, "Health Effects of Floods" p. 181.

23. When John White finally returned to Roanoke in 1590, he noted that the colonists had left behind "heauie thinges" like "barres of iron, two pigges of lead, foure yron fowlers, Iron sacker-shotte" as well as other items presumably deemed either too cumbersome or unnecessary for the new mainland settlement. White "could perceiue no signe of" the lighter defensive armament like falconets and other small weaponry which were in the colonists' possession. See Hakluyt, "The fift voyage of M. Iohn White into the West Indies and parts of America called Virginia, in the yeere 1590."

# Chapter 10

1. "The Legend of the Coharie," by Ernest M. Bullard, reprinted in *Huckleberry Historian,* a quarterly publication of the Sampson County Historical Society, Volume XXXVI, Number 1, Jan 2014.

2. "Salt Water Inundation from Hurricane Sandy," University of Delaware College of Agricultural and Natural Resources, 2012.

3. *Ibid.*

4. J. Curtis Weaver, and Thomas J. Zembrzuski, Jr., "August 31, 1993, Storm Surge and Flood of Hurricane Emily on Hatteras Island, North Carolina." Water Supply Paper 2499, U.S. Department of the Interior, U.S. Geological Survey.

5. See "List of North Carolina hurricanes" and also "Saffir–Simpson hurricane wind scale" at Wikipedia.

6. Hamilton McMillan, *Sir Walter Raleigh's Lost Colony. An Historical Sketch of the Attempts of Sir Walter Raleigh to Establish a Colony in Virginia, With the Traditions of an Indian Tribe in North Carolina* (Wilson, NC: Advance Press, 1888) pp. 18, 20.

7. James Mooney, *The Siouan Tribes of the East* (Washington, DC: U.S. Government Printing Office, 1894) p. 7.

8. See the Coharie tribal website http://www.coharietribe.org/

9. Email from W. Stephen Lee to the author, Dec. 21, 2014.
10. *Ibid.*
11. "Brief Sketch of a Few Prominent Indian Families of Sampson County," by Enoch Emanuel and C.D. Brewington. From George Edwin Butler, *The Croatan Indians of Sampson County, North Carolina. Their Origin and Racial Status. A Plea for Separate Schools...* (Durham, NC: The Seeman Printery, 1916). p. 47.
12. Email from Don A. Grady to the author, June 7, 2016.
13. O.M. McPherson, *Report On Condition and Tribal Rights of the Indians of Robeson and Adjoining Counties of North Carolina* (Washington, DC: U.S. Government Printing Office, Sept. 19, 1914).
14. George Edwin Butler, *The Croatan Indians of Sampson County*, p. 9.
15. Adolph L. Dial, and David K. Elaides, *The Only Land I Know* (New York: Syracuse University Press, 1996) pp. 23–4.
16. Helen C. Rountree, *The Powhatan Indians of Virginia* (Norman: University of Oklahoma Press, 1989) p. 85.

## Chapter 11

1. Hakluyt, *The Principal Navigations...* #32 "A letter from John White to M. Richard Hakluyt."
2. *Ibid.*
3. *Ibid.*
4. *Ibid.*
5. David Beers Quinn, *Set Fair for Roanoke: Voyages and Colonies, 1584–1606* (Chapel Hill: University of North Carolina Press, 1985) p. 316.
6. "The Defeat of the English Armada and the 16th-Century Spanish Naval Resurgence," by Wes Ulm, Harvard University personal website. http://wesulm.bravehost.com/history/eng_armada.htm © 2004.
7. *Ibid.*
8. Richard Hakluyt, *Principal Navigations...* #33 "The fift voyage of M. Iohn White into the West Indies and parts of America called Virginia, in the yeere 1590." Entry for August 17.
9. *Ibid.*
10. *Ibid.*, August 18.
11. *Ibid.*, August 17.

12. *Ibid.*, August 12.
13. *Ibid.*, August 12–13.
14. *Ibid.*
15. *Ibid.*, August 16.
16. *Ibid.*
17. *Ibid.*, August 18.
18. Hakluyt, *The Principal Navigations...* #23: "The Letters Patents, granted by the Queenes Maiestie to M. Walter Ralegh now Knight, for the discovering and planting of new lands and Countries, to continue the space of 6. yeeres and no more."
19. *Ibid.*
20. Hakluyt, *The Principal Navigations...* #30: "The fourth voyage made to Virginia with three ships, in yere 1587. Wherein was transported the second Colonie." Entry for August 13.
21. Hakluyt, *Principal Navigations...* #33. August 15.
22. *Ibid.* August 19.
23. *Ibid.*
24. *Ibid.* August 28.
25. *Ibid.* September 27–October 24.
26. Hakluyt, *The Principal Navigations...* #32.

## Chapter 12

1. *The Discovery of Guiana* by Sir Walter Raleigh, a publication of Cassell's National Library (London: Cassell & Co. Ltd., 1887) p. 16.
2. Alexander Brown, *The First Republic in America* (Boston and New York: Houghton Mifflin, 1898) p. 121.
3. "A brief note of the sending another Bark this present year, 1602, by the Honorable Knight, Sir Walter Raleigh, for the searching out of his Colony in Virginia" in "Tracts appended to Brereton," *Collections of the Massachusetts Historical Society*, Vol. 28 (Boston: Little, Brown, 1843) pp. 94–5.
4. David Beers Quinn, *Set Fair for Roanoke: Voyages and Colonies 1584–1606* (Chapel Hill: University of North Carolina Press, 1985) pp. 356–8.
5. *Ibid.*
6. David Beers Quinn, *Explorers and Colonies: America 1500–1625* (London: Hambledon Press, 1990) p. 329.
7. *Ibid.*, pp. 350–353.

## Chapter 13

1. John Smith, "A True Relation," edited by Lyon G. Tyler. *Narratives of Early Virginia, 1606–1625* (New York: Scribner's, 1907) p. 45.
2. *Ibid.*, p. 49.
3. *Ibid.*, p. 53.
4. Alexander Brown, *The First Republic in America* (Boston and New York: Houghton Mifflin, 1898) p. 47.
5. *Ibid.*, p. 62.
6. John Smith, "A Map of Virginia: With a Description of the Countrey, the Commodities, People, Government and Religion," edited by Lyon G. Tyler. *Narratives of Early Virginia, 1606–1625* (New York: Scribner's, 1907) p. 152.
7. *Ibid.*, p. 136.
8. *Ibid.*, p. 154.
9. Brown, pp. 48–51.
10. John Smith, "A True Relation," p. 53.

## Chapter 14

1. Alexander Brown, *The Genesis of the United States* (New York: Houghton Mifflin, 1890) p. 190. (It should be noted that Brown was influenced by Hamilton McMillan, the previously mentioned advocate for Lumbee tribal recognition who claimed a Lumbee-Lost Colonist connection in Robeson, Sampson, and surrounding counties.)
2. Stephen B. Weeks, "The Lost Colony of Roanoke: Its Fate and Survival," in *Papers of the American Historical Assoc.* Vol. V (New York: G.P. Putnam's Sons, 1891) p. 470.
3. Samuel A'Court Ashe, *History of North Carolina*, Volume I (Greensboro, NC: Charles L. Van Noppen, 1908) p. 18.
4. Philip Barbour, editor, *The Complete Works of Captain John Smith in Three Volumes* (Chapel Hill: University of North Carolina Press, 1986), vol. I, footnote 111.
5. Virginia Council's "Instruccions Orders And Constitucions To Sr Thomas Gates Knight Governor of Virginia, May 1609" #15; *The Three Charters of the Virginia Company of London*, ed. Samuel M. Bemiss (Williamsburg, VA: Virginia 350th Anniversary Celebration Corporation, 1957) p. 55.
6. See *Eno People*, "Historic Eno Variations" https://en.wikipedia.org/wiki/Eno_people
7. John Smith, "A True Relation," edited by Lyon G. Tyler, *Narratives of Early Virginia, 1606–1625* (New York: Charles Scribner's Sons, 1907) Smith, "A True Relation" p. 49.
8. William Strachey, *The Historie of Travaile Into Virginia Britannia* (London: Printed for the Hakluyt Society, 1849) pp. 48–9.
9. *Ibid.*, p. 26.
10. *The Discoveries of John Lederer, Together with a General MAP of the whole Territory which he Traversed*. Collected by Sir William Talbot, Baronet (London: printed at Grays-Inne-gate in Holborn, 1672) p. iv.
11. See "Occaneechi Path," https://familysearch.org/learn/wiki/en/Occaneechi_Path
12. *The Discoveries of John Lederer*, p. 15.
13. Virginia Council's "Instruccions ... to Gates."
14. Hakluyt, *The Principal Navigations...* #27: "An account of the particularities of the imployments of the English men left in Virginia by Richard Greeneuill vnder the charge of Master Ralph Lane Generall of the same, from the 17. of August 1585. vntil the 18. of Iune 1586. at which time they departed the Countrey; sent and directed to Sir Walter Ralegh."
15. Charles Hudson, *The Juan Pardo Expeditions* (Tuscaloosa: University of Alabama Press, 2005) p. 146.
16. Charles M. Hudson (editor) and Herbert E. Ketcham (translator), *The Juan Pardo Expeditions: Spanish Explorers and the Indians of the Carolinas and Tennessee, 1566–1568. With Documents Relating to the Pardo Expeditions* (Washington, DC: Smithsonian Institution Press, 1990) pp. 254–296.
17. Hudson and Ketcham, pp. 262, 165, 187, 188.
18. Library of Congress, and Ralph Hamor, *A True discourse of the present estate of Virginia* (London: John Beale for William Welby, 1615) p. 33.
19. "Francis Yeardley's Narrative of Excursions into Carolina, 1654," from Alexander S. Salley, Jr., editor, *Narratives of Early Carolina, 1650–1708* (New York: Scribner's, 1911).
20. *The Discoveries of John Lederer*, p. 4.
21. *Ibid.*, p. 15.
22. Fred A. Olds, "Our North Carolina Indians," *The North Carolina Booklet* Vol. XVI, No. 1. The North Carolina Society of the Daughters of the Revolution (Raleigh: Commercial Printing Co., 1916) p. 39.
23. *Ibid.*, p. 16.

# Chapter 15

1. John Smith, "A True Relation," edited by Lyon G. Tyler, *Narratives of Early Virginia, 1606–1625* (New York: Scribner's, 1907) p. 53.

2. Stephen B. Weeks, "The Lost Colony of Roanoke: Its Fate and Survival," in *Papers of the American Historical Assoc.*, Vol. V (New York: G.P. Putnam's Sons, 1891) p. 469.

3. Samuel A'Court Ashe, *History of North Carolina*, Volume I (Greensboro, NC: Charles L. Van Noppen, 1908) p. 19.

4. Lee Miller, *Roanoke: Solving the Mystery of the Lost Colony* (New York: Arcade Publishing, 2001) p. 259.

5. *Ibid.*

6. Smith, "A True Relation," edited by Lyon G. Tyler, p. 53.

7. *The Complete Works of Captain John Smith (1580–1631)*, edited by Philip L. Barbour. Volume I (Chapel Hill: University of North Carolina Press, 1986) p. 105.

8. Richard Hakluyt, *The Principal Navigations*... #24, "The first voyage made to the coasts of America, with two barks, wherein were Captaines M. Philip Amadas, and M. Arthur Barlowe, who discouered part of the Countrey now called Virginia Anno 1584."

9. Hamilton McMillan, *Sir Walter Raleigh's Lost Colony. An Historical Sketch of the Attempts of Sir Walter Raleigh to Establish a Colony in Virginia, With the Traditions of an Indian Tribe in North Carolina* (Wilson, NC: Advance Press, 1888) p. 14.

10. Jonathan Culpeper, *History of English* (New York: Routledge, 2015) p. 35. Also see "double-u" digraph https://en.wikipedia.org/wiki/W and https://en.wikipedia.org/wiki/Digraph_(orthography)

11. Hakluyt, *The Principal Navigations*... #25, "The voiage made by Sir Richard Greenuile, for Sir Walter Ralegh, to Virginia, in the yeere 1585."

12. Hakluyt. *The Principal Navigations*... #27, "An account of the particularities of the imployments of the English men left in Virginia by Richard Greeneuill vnder the charge of Master Ralph Lane Generall of the same, from the 17. of August 1585. vntil the 18. of Iune 1586. at which time they departed the Countrey; sent and directed to Sir Walter Ralegh."

13. Peter C. Mancall, editor, *The Atlantic World and Virginia, 1550–1624* (Chapel Hill: University of North Carolina Press, 2007) pp. 36–7.

14. Carl Bridenbaugh, *Jamestown 1544–1699* (New York: Oxford University Press, 1980) pp. 10–17.

15. Smith, "A True Relation," p. 44.

# Chapter 16

1. David Beers Quinn, *Set Fair for Roanoke: Voyages and Colonies 1584–1606* (Chapel Hill: University of North Carolina Press, 1985) pp. 365–6.

2. James Horn, *A Kingdom Strange: The Brief and Tragic History of the Lost Colony of Roanoke* (New York: Basic Books, 2010), p. 216–17.

3. Hobson Woodward, *A Brave Vessel* (New York: Penguin, 2009) pp. 7–11.

4. *Ibid.*

5. Library of Congress. "Instructions Orders and Constitutions to Sir Thomas Gates knight Governor of Virginia May 1609" from *Records of the Virginia Company of London*. Thomas Jefferson Papers: Series 8: Virginia Records Manuscripts, 1606 to 1737 (Washington, DC: U.S. Government Printing Office, 1906–1935).

6. *Ibid.*

7. Samuel Purchas, *Hakluytus posthumus; or, Purchas his pilgrimes* (New York: Macmillan, 1906) vol. 18, p. 527.

8. *Ibid.* See also Quinn, *Set Fair*, p. 365–6. Also Quinn, *The Lost Colonists: Their Fortune and Probable Fate* (Raleigh: North Carolina Department of Cultural Resources, 1984). Eighth printing, 1999, p. 40.

9. See *The Complete Works of Captain John Smith (1580–1631)* edited by Philip L. Barbour. Volume I (Chapel Hill: University of North Carolina Press, 1986).

10. Seth Mallios, *The Deadly Politics of Giving* (Tuscaloosa: University of Alabama Press, 2006) p. 87–8.

11. Dr. Daniel Paul, Mi'Kmaq elder. "We Were Not the Savages: First Nation History" (Mi'Kmaq, Maliseet, etc., & European relations with them.) http://www.danielnpaul.com/Mi'kmaqCulture.html

12. Thomas P. Slaughter, *Exploring Lewis and Clark* (New York: Alfred A. Knopf, 2003) pp. 6–15.

# Chapter 17

1. Alexander Brown, *The First Republic in America: An Account of the Origin of the Nation* (Boston and New York: Houghton Mifflin, 1898) pp. 13, 15.

2. *Ibid.*, p. 63.

3. *Ibid.*, p. 64.

4. *American Historical Review, Vol XXV.* "Spanish Policy Toward Virginia, 1606–1612; Jamestown, Écija, and John Clark of the Mayflower" (London: Macmillan, 1920) pp. 448–479.

5. Brown, pp. 88–90.

6. "Spanish Policy Toward Virginia, 1606–1612..." pp. 448–479.

7. John H. Hann, "Translation of the Écija Voyages of 1605 and 1609 and the Gonzalez Derrotero of 1609" *Florida Archaeology No. 2* (Florida Bureau of Archaeological Research, Nov. 2, 1986) pp. 33–4.

8. *Ibid.*

9. "Spanish Policy..." pp. 448–479.

10. See "*Legua de por grado,*" League (Unit), Wikipedia https://en.wikipedia.org/wiki/League_(unit)#Spain

11. July 17–20 locations are taken from Hann, p. 76.

12. Edward-Maria Wingfield, *A Discourse of Virginia.* Edited by Charles Deane (Boston: Privately Printed, 1860). Entry for July 3, 1607.

13. George Percy, "Observations by Master George Percy 1607," edited by Lyon G. Tyler. *Narratives of Early Virginia, 1606–1625* (New York: Scribner's, 1907) p. 9.

14. John Lawson, *A New Voyage to Carolina* (London: 1709) p. 62.

15. Hakluyt. *The Principal Navigations...* #33, "The fift voyage of M. Iohn White into the West Indies and parts of America called Virginia, in the yeere 1590." Entry for August 17.

16. Lawson, p. 62.

17. Hakluyt #33, Entry for August 13.

# Chapter 18

1. William Strachey, *A True Reportory...* Part III "Their departure from Bermuda and arrival in Virginia—Miseries there—Departure and return upon the Lord La Warre's arriving—James Town described." From Samuel Purchas, *Hakluytus posthumus; or, Purchas his pilgrimes* (London: William Stansby, 1625) in four volumes, beginning page 1734 in vol. IV.

2. William Strachey, *The Historie of Travaile Into Virginia Britannia* (London: Printed for the Hakluyt Society, 1849), editor's preface.

3. Strachey, *A True Reportory...* Part III.

4. Strachey, *The Historie of Travaile* pp. 85–6.

5. *Ibid.*, p. 103.

6. *Ibid.*, p. 101.

7. *Ibid.*, p. 26.

8. *Ibid.*, p. 48.

9. *Ibid.*, p. 50.

10. *Ibid.*, pp. 19–20.

11. David Beers Quinn, *The Lost Colonists: Their Fortune and Probable Fate* (Raleigh: North Carolina Department of Cultural Resources, 1984). Published for America's Four Hundredth Anniversary Committee, Eighth printing, 1999, p. 51.

12. *Ibid.*, p.51.

13. Helen C. Rountree, *The Powhatan Indians of Virginia* (Norman: University of Oklahoma Press, 1989) pp. 9, 120; see also Strachey's *Historie*, p. 28.

14. David Beers Quinn, *Set Fair for Roanoke: Voyages and Colonies 1584–1606* (Chapel Hill: University of North Carolina Press, 1985) p. 367.

15. Thomas C. Parramore, with Peter C. Stewart, and Tommy L. Bogger, *Norfolk: The First Four Centuries* (Charlottesville: University Press of Virginia, 1994) p. 24.

16. *Ibid.*, p. 30.

17. *Ibid.*, pp. 24–5.

18. *Ibid.*, p. 18.

19. Thomas C. Parramore. "The Lost Colony and the Tuscaroras," in Roy F. Johnson, and Thomas C Parramore, *The Lost Colony in Fact and Legend* (Murfreesboro, NC: Johnson Publishing, 1983) p. 52.

20. Quinn, *Set Fair...* p. 42.

21. Parramore, et al., *Norfolk: The First Four Centuries*, p. 25.

22. Alice Granbery Walter, editor, *Lower Norfolk County, Virginia Court Records. Book "A" 1637–1646 & Book "B" 1646–1651/2* (transcribed by Walter from the 1950 microfilm of the original Journal in 1978), p. 294 in the original journal, but page 201 in Walter's transcription.

23. Roy F. Johnson, and Thomas C. Par-

ramore, *The Lost Colony in Fact and Legend* (Murfreesboro, NC: Johnson Publishing Company, 1983) p. 39.

24. Thomas C. Parramore, "The 'Lost Colony' Found: A Documentary Perspective." *The North Carolina Historical Review*, Vol. 78, No. 1 (January 2001), pp. 67–83.

25. Wilson Armistead, *The Journal of George Fox: Being an Historical Account of the Life, Travels, Sufferings, Christian Experiences, and Labours of Love* (London: W. and F.G. Cash, 1812) vol. II, p. 120.

26. *The Colonial Records Project*, Jan-Michael Poff, Editor, North Carolina Office of Archives & History, Dept. of Cultural Resources. *North Carolina Historical Review*, Vol. 51, 1974, pp. 1–21. William S. Powell, "Carolina and the Incomparable Roanoke: Explorations and Attempted Settlements, 1620–1663."

27. Library of Congress. *Records of the Virginia Company of London*, "The Court Book." Edited by Susan Myrna Kingsbury (Washington, DC: U.S. Government Printing Office, 1906).

28. Edward D. Neill, *Memoir of Rev. Patrick Copland* (New York: Scribner's, 1871) pp. 62–3.

29. William Strachey, *The Historie of Travaile...* p. 28.

30. William Bullock, "Virginia Impartially Examined" (London: Henry Whaley, 1649).

31. *Ibid.*

32. *Ibid.*

33. Hamilton McMillan, *Sir Walter Raleigh's Lost Colony. An Historical Sketch of the Attempts of Sir Walter Raleigh to Establish a Colony in Virginia, With the Traditions of an Indian Tribe in North Carolina* (Wilson, NC: Advance Press, 1888) p. 26.

34. *Ibid.*, pp. 8–9, 20.

35. *Ibid.*, p. 17.

36. Johnson and Parramore. *The Lost Colony in Fact and Legend*. p. 84: "The Lost Colony and the Tuscaroras," by Thomas Parramore.

37. "Algonquian Indians of North Carolina, Inc." Heritage: Roanoke-Hatteras Tribal History, at the Roanoke-Hatteras Indian Tribe website http://www.ncalgonquians.com/

38. *Ibid.*

39. Elizabeth Bailey, "Roanoke River," NCpedia, 2006 (http://ncpedia.org/rivers/roanoke).

40. "History of Roanoke" Virginia's Blue Ridge Roanoke Valley website at http://www.visitroanokeva.com/visitors/history/roanoke-history/, also "Roanoke River" at http://en.wikipedia.org/wiki/Roanoke_River.

41. Library of Congress. *The Thomas Jefferson Papers Series 8. Virginia Records Manuscripts. 1606-1737.* Susan Myra Kingsbury, editor, "Records of the Virginia Company, 1606–26, Volume III: Miscellaneous Records."

42. Richard Hakluyt, *The Principal Navigations...* #24: (1584 Amadas and Barlowe expedition), 2 "Roanoak" Island references. #25: (1585 Grenville voyage), 1 "Roanook" Island reference. #27: (1585–6 Grenville-Lane account), 13 "Roanoak" Island references. #28: (1586 Raleigh, Grenville relief ships), 1 "Roanoak" Island reference. #30: (1587 White colony), 11 "Roanoak" Island references. #33: (1590 White return voyage), 3 "Roanoak" Island references.

43. Library of Congress. John Smith, *The Generall Historie of Virginia, New England & The Summer Isles* (New York: Macmillan, 1907), 21 references to "Roanoak" Island (various spellings: "Roanok," Roanoack," Roanoacke," etc.; some are repetitions of accounts contained in Hakluyt).

44. Richard Hakluyt, *The Principal Navigations...*#29: "A briefe and true report of the new found land of Virginia: of the commodities there found, and to be raised, aswell merchantable as others: Written by Thomas Heriot, seruant to Sir Walter Ralegh, a member of the Colony, and there imployed in discouering a full tweluemonth." Ten references to "Roanoac" Island.

45. Robert Beverley, *The History of Virginia In Four Parts* (Richmond, VA: J.W. Randolph: 1855). Nine references to "Roenoke" Island, four to "Roenoke" shell ornaments.

46. Strachey. *The Historie...* In addition to the several references in the Index there are 27 "Roanoak" Island references in the text.

## Chapter 19

1. Natalie Zacek, "William Strachey," *Encyclopedia Virginia*, a Publication of the Virginia Foundation for the Humanities, updated April 4, 2012. See also Helen C. Rountree, *The Powhatan Indians of Virginia* (Norman: University of Oklahoma Press, 1989) p. 4.

2. See "Preposition 'at' (Place)" Cambridge Dictionary online. (http://dictionary.cambridge.org/dictionary/british/at_1).

3. William Strachey, *The Historie of Travaile Into Virginia Britannia* (London: Printed for the Hakluyt Society, 1849) p. 50.

4. *Ibid.*, p. 26.

5. *Ibid.*, p. 28.

6. George Percy, *Observations by Master George Percy 1607*, edited by Lyon G. Tyler. *Narratives of Early Virginia, 1606–1625* (New York: Scribner's, 1907) p. 17.

7. Library of Congress. John Smith, *The Generall Historie of Virginia, New England & The Summer Isles* (New York: Macmillan, 1907) pp. 26–7.

8. Robert Beverley, *The History of Virginia In Four Parts* (Richmond, VA: J. W. Randolph, 1855) p. 13.

9. Hakluyt. *The Principal Navigations* #30: "The fourth voyage made to Virginia with three ships, in yere 1587. Wherein was transported the second Colonie."

10. Giles Milton, *Big Chief Elizabeth* (New York: Farrar, Straus and Giroux, 2000) p. 193.

11. *Ibid.*

12. Johnson and Parramore, p. 16.

13. *Ibid.*, p. 150

14. Rountree, p. 85.

15. *Ibid.*

16. Hakluyt, #27: "An account of the particularities of the imployments of the English men left in Virginia by Richard Greeneuill vnder the charge of Master Ralph Lane Generall of the same, from the 17. of August 1585. vntil the 18. of Iune 1586. at which time they departed the Countrey; sent and directed to Sir Walter Ralegh."

17. David Stick, *Roanoke Island, the Beginnings of English America* (Chapel Hill: University of North Carolina Press, 1983), p. 147.

## Chapter 20

1. Maurice A. Mook, "Algonquian Ethnohistory of the Carolina Sound," *Journal of the Washington Academy of Sciences* 34 (1944), pp. 6–7. See also Christian F. Feest, "North Carolina Algonquians," *Handbook of North American Indians*, Vol. 15, Bruce Trigger, editor (Washington, DC: Smithsonian, 1978) pp. 271–281.

2. "The Ethnic Position of the Southeast-

ern Algonquian," by Frank G. Speck. *American Anthropologist* 26 (1924): pp. 184–200.

3. Karen Ordahl Kupperman, *Indians & English, Facing Off in Early America* (Ithaca, NY: Cornell University Press, 2000) pp. 88–91.

4. Thomas C. Parramore, "The Lost Colony and the Tuscaroras," in Johnson and Parramore, *The Lost Colony in Fact and Legend* (Murfreesboro, NC: Johnson Publishing Company, 1983).

5. Elias Johnson, a Native Tuscacora Chief. *Legends, Traditions and Laws, of the Iroquois, or Six nations, and History of the Tuscarora Indians* (Lockport, NY: Union Printing and Publishing Co., 1881) p. 61–2.

6. *Ibid.*

7. William G. Haag, *The Archaeology of Coastal North Carolina*, Coastal Studies Series 2 (Baton Rouge: Louisiana State University Press, 1958), "Physiography of the Coastal Region, Pamlico Sound," p. 47.

## Chapter 21

1. Lynda Payne, "Health in England (16th–18th c.)" in *Children and Youth in History*, Item #166. http://chnm.gmu.edu/cyh/primary-sources/166 (Accessed July–August 2016).

2. James Mooney, *The Siouan Tribes of the East* (Washington, DC: U.S. Government Printing Office, 1894) p. 6.

3. *Ibid.*, p. 66.

4. John Lawson, *A New Voyage to Carolina* (London: 1709) p. 54.

5. William Bright, *Native American Placenames of the United States* (Norman: University of Oklahoma Press, 2004) pp. 165, 425. See also http://en.wikipedia.org/wiki/Haw_River

6. John Reed Swanton, *The Indian Tribes of North America* (Washington, DC: U.S. Government Printing Office, 1952) p. 84.

7. David La Vere, *The Tuscarora War* (Chapel Hill: University of North Carolina Press, 2013) p. 105.

8. Swanton, p. 186.

9. "Francis Yeardley's Narrative of Excursions into Carolina, 1654," from Alexander S. Salley, Jr., editor, *Narratives of Early Carolina, 1650–1708* (New York: Scribner's, 1911) pp. 25–6.

10. David Beers Quinn, *Set Fair for Roanoke: Voyages and Colonies 1584–1606* (Chapel Hill: University of North Carolina Press, 1985) p. 381.

11. "Francis Yeardley's Narrative..." pp. 25–6.

12. *Ibid.*, p. 26.

13. *Ibid.*, p. 27.

14. Swanton, p. 206.

15. *Ibid.*; also Lawson p. 234.

16. David LaVere, *The Tuscarora War* (Chapel Hill: University of North Carolina Press, 2013) p. 15.

17. "Ethnohistorical Description of the Eight Villages Adjoining Cape Hatteras National Seashore and Interpretive Themes of History and Heritage," U.S. Department of the Interior, Cape Hatteras National Seashore, Manteo, North Carolina, November 2005. Vol 1, p. 10.

18. Lawson, p. 200.

19. Richard Hakluyt, *The Principal Navigations...*#24, "The first voyage made to the coasts of America, with two barks, wherein were Captaines M. Philip Amadas, and M. Arthur Barlowe, who discouered part of the Countrey now called Virginia Anno 1584. Written by one of the said Captaines, and sent to sir Walter Ralegh knight, at whose charge and direction, the said voyage was set forth."

20. Lawson, p. 62.

21. Karen Ordahl Kupperman, *Indians and English* (Ithaca, NY: Cornell University Press, 2000) p. 34.

22. Richard Hakluyt, *The Principal Navigations...*#29: "A briefe and true report of the new found land of Virginia: of the commodities there found, and to be raised, aswell merchantable as others: Written by Thomas Heriot, seruant to Sir Walter Ralegh, a member of the Colony, and there imployed in discouering a full tweluemonth."

23. "Archdale's Description of Carolina, 1707," from Alexander S. Salley, Jr., editor, *Narratives of Early Carolina, 1650–1708* (New York: Scribner's, 1911) p. 286.

24. Lawson, p. 10.

25. *Ibid.*, p. 224.

26. La Vere, p. 98.

27. *Ibid.* See pp. 97–99.

28. E. Lawrence Lee, *Indian Wars in North Carolina 1663–1763* (Raleigh: Office of Ar-chives and History/North Carolina Department of Cultural Resources, 2011), p. 3.

29. Lawson, p. 234.

## Chapter 22

1. David La Vere,. *The Tuscarora War* (Chapel Hill: University of North Carolina Press, 2013), p. 185.

2. *Ibid.*, pp. 197–200.

3. Swanton, John Reed. *The Indian Tribes of North America* (Washington, D.C.: U.S. Government Printing Office, 1952), p. 170. Also La Vere, pp. 147–8.

4. La Vere, p. 198.

5. C. D. Brewington, *The Five Civilized Indian Tribes of Eastern North Carolina*. Edited by Oscar M. Bizzell (Newton Grove, NC: Sampson County Historical Society, 1994) pp. 15–24.

6. Swanton, pp. 15–24.

7. Richard Hakluyt, *The Principal Navigations...*#29: "A briefe and true report of the new found land of Virginia: of the commodities there found, and to be raised, aswell merchantable as others: Written by Thomas Heriot, seruant to Sir Walter Ralegh, a member of the Colony, and there imployed in discouering a full tweluemonth."

8. *The Colonial Records of North Carolina*. Edited by William S. Saunders, Secretary of State. Vol II, 1713–1728 (Raleigh: P. M. Hale, Printer to the State, 1886), p. 129.

9. La Vere, p. 176.

10. *Colonial Records...* Vol. II, p. 172.

11. Louis Torres, *Historic Resource Study of Cape Hatteras National Seashore* (U.S. Department of the Interior: National Park Service, Denver Service Center, 1985) pp. 17–18.

12. *Colonial Records...* Vol. VI (Raleigh, NC: Joseph Daniels, Printer to the State, 1888), p. 563.

13. *Ibid.*, p. 995.

14. Torres, pp. 27–8.

15. La Vere, pp. 203–4.

16. *Ibid.*, pp. 205–6.

17. Hamilton McMillan, *Sir Walter Raleigh's Lost Colony. An Historical Sketch of the Attempts of Sir Walter Raleigh to Establish a Colony in Virginia, With the Traditions of an Indian Tribe in North Carolina* (Wilson, NC: Advance Press, 1888), p. 11.

18. Swanton, pp. 103, 110, 186, 203, 206.

19. *Colonial Records...* Vol V. "Report concerning the militia in each county of North Carolina" p. 162.

20. McMillan, pp. 23–4.

21. *Ibid.*, p. 4.

22. Brewington, pp. 15–24.

23. *Ibid.*

24. Roberta Estes, email to the LCRG on the status of the Lost Colony DNA Project. August 5, 2016.

25. David Beers Quinn, *Set Fair for Roanoke: Voyages and Colonies 1584–1606* (Chapel Hill: University of North Carolina Press, 1985) p. 255.

26. Estes email August 5, 2016; also see "Ananias Dare," Wikipedia.

27. Estes email August 5, 2016.

# Bibliography

Armistead, Wilson. *The Journal of George Fox: Being an Historical Account of the Life, Travels, Sufferings, Christian Experiences, and Labours of Love*. London: W. and F.G. Cash, 1812.

Ashe, Samuel A'Court. *History of North Carolina*. Greensboro, NC: Charles L. Van Noppen, 1908.

Barbour, Philip L., editor. *The Complete Works of Captain John Smith (1580–1631)*. Chapel Hill: University of North Carolina Press, 1986.

Bellis, V.J. "Ecology of maritime forests of the southern Atlantic coast: a community profile." Biological report 30. National Biological Service, U.S. Department of the Interior. Washington, D.C. May 1995.

Bemiss, Samuel M., editor. *The Three Charters of the Virginia Company of London*. Williamsburg, VA: Virginia 350th Anniversary Celebration Corporation, 1957.

Beverley, Robert. *The History of Virginia in Four Parts*. Richmond, VA: J.W. Randolph, 1855.

Bigelow, Henry and Schroeder, William. "Fishes of the Gulf of Maine." *Fishery Bulletin of the Fish and Wildlife Service*. No. 74. Washington, DC: Government Printing Office, 1953.

Brewington, C.D. *The Five Civilized Indian Tribes of Eastern North Carolina*. Edited by Oscar M. Bizzell. Newton Grove, NC: Sampson County Historical Society, 1994.

Bridenbaugh, Carl. *Jamestown 1544–1699*. New York and Oxford: Oxford University Press, 1980.

"A brief note of the sending another Bark this present year, 1602, by the Honorable Knight, Sir Walter Raleigh, for the searching out of his Colony in Virginia." *Collections of the Massachusetts Historical Society*. Vol 28. Boston: Charles C. Little and James Brown, 1843.

Bright, William. *Native American Placenames of the United States*. Norman: University of Oklahoma Press, 2004.

Brown, Alexander. *The First Republic in America*. New York: Houghton Mifflin, 1898.

———. *The Genesis of the United States*. New York: Houghton Mifflin, 1890.

Bullock, William. *Virginia Impartially Examined*. London: Henry Whaley, 1649.

Butler, George Edwin. *The Croatan Indians of Sampson County, North Carolina. Their Origin and Racial Status. A Plea for Separate Schools*. Durham, NC: The Seeman Printery, 1916.

Coder, Kim. "Live Oak: Southern Ecological Heritage." Dendrology Series. Warnell School of Forestry & Natural Resources: University of Georgia, March 2015.

Corbett, Julian S., editor. *Publications of the Navy Records Society of Great Britain*, Vol. II, "The Spanish War 1585–1587." Printed for the Navy Records Society, 1898.

Culpeper, Jonathan. *History of English*. London: Routledge, 2015.

Dial, Adolph L., and David K. Elaides. *The Only Land I Know*. New York: Syracuse University Press, 1996.

*The Discoveries of John Lederer. Together with a General MAP of the whole Territory which he Traversed*. Collected by Sir William Talbot, Baronet. London: Printed at Grays-Inne-gate in Holborn, 1672.

"Ethnohistorical Description of the Eight Villages adjoining Cape Hatteras National Seashore and Interpretive Themes of History and Heritage." Prepared for the Cape Hatteras National Seashore by Impact Assessment, Inc. National Park Service, U.S. Department of the Interior, November 2005.

Evans, P., M. Laird, and N. Luccketti. "2012 Archaeological Investigation Of Site 31BR46 on Salmon Creek, Bertie County, North Carolina." First Colony Foundation, March 2014.

"Event Overview, Hurricane Hazel October 15, 1954." National Oceanic and Atmospheric Administration, U.S. Department of Commerce. www.weather.gov.

Feest, Christian F. "North Carolina Algonquians." *Handbook of North American Indians* Vol. 15. Bruce Trigger, Editor. Washington, DC: Smithsonian Institution Press, 1978.

France, Kevin. "Top Five U.S. Cities Most Vulnerable to Hurricanes." AccuWeatherc.com, June 25, 2015.

García-Herrera, R., L. Gimeno, P. Ribera, and E. Hernández. "New records of Atlantic hurricanes from Spanish documentary sources." *Journal of Geophysical Research*, Volume 110, Issue D3, Feb. 4, 2005.

Golay, Michael, and John S. Bowman. *North American Exploration*. Hoboken, NJ: John Wiley, 2003.

Haag, William G. *The Archaeology of Coastal North Carolina*. Coastal Studies Series 2. Baton Rouge: Louisiana State University Press, 1958.

Hakluyt, Richard. *The Principal Navigations, Voyages, Traffiques, and Discoveries of the English Nation*. XVI Volumes, edited by Edmund Goldsmid, 1885–1890. Vol. XIII "America Part II." Edinburgh: E. & G. Goldsmid, 1889.

_____. *The Voyages of the English Nation to America Before the Year 1600*, Vol I. Edited by Edmund Goldsmid. Edinburgh: E. & G. Goldsmid, 1889.

Hamor, Ralph. *A True discourse of the present estate of Virginia*. London: John Beale for William Welby, 1615. Library of Congress.

Hann, John H. "Translation of the Écija Voyages of 1605 and 1609 and the Gonzalez Derrotero of 1609." *Florida Archaeology No. 2*. Florida Bureau of Archaeological Research, Nov. 2, 1986.

Harrington, J.C. "Evidence of Manual Reckoning in the Cittie of Ralegh." *The North Carolina Historical Review* 33, no. 1, 1956.

Harris, Sherwood. "The Tragic Dream of Jean Ribault." *American Heritage Society Magazine*. Volume 14, Issue 6, 1963.

Hawks, Francis. *History of North Carolina*. Fayetteville, NC: E.J. Hale and Son, 1858.

Hoffman, Paul E. *A New Andalucia and a Way to the Orient*. Baton Rouge: Louisiana State University Press, 2004.

_____. *Spain and the Roanoke Voyages*. Raleigh: N.C. Dept. of Cultural Resources, 1987.

_____. "New Light on Vicente Gonzalez's 1588 Voyage in Search of Raleigh's English Colonies." *The North Carolina Historical Review*. Vol. 63, No. 2, April 1986.

Horn, James. *A Kingdom Strange*. New York: Basic Books, 2010.

_____. *A Land As God Made It*. New York: Basic Books, 2005.

Hudson, Charles M., editor, and Herbert E. Ketcham, translator. *The Juan Pardo Expeditions: Spanish Explorers and the Indians of the Carolinas and Tennessee, 1566–1568*. Washington, DC: Smithsonian Institution Press, 1990.

Hudson, Charles. *The Juan Pardo Expeditions*. Tuscaloosa: University of Alabama Press, 2005.

"Hurricane Storm Surge." *Ocean Today*. National Oceanic and Atmospheric Administration, U.S. Department of Commerce, 2015.

Johnson, Elias, a Native Tuscacora Chief. *Legends, Traditions and Laws, of the Iroquois, or Six nations, and History of the Tuscarora Indians*. Lockport, NY: Union Printing and Publishing Co., 1881.

Johnson, Roy F., with Thomas C. Parramore. *The Lost Colony in Fact and Legend*. Murfreesboro, NC: Johnson Publishing Company, 1983.

Julian S. Corbett, editor. *Publications of the Navy Records Society of Great Britain*. Vol II, "The Spanish War 1585–87." Printed for the Navy Records Society, 1898.

Kerr, Robert. *A General History and Collection of Voyages and Travels*. Edinburgh: George Ramsay and Co., 1812.

Kingsbury, Susan Myra, editor. *Records of the Virginia Company, 1606–26*. Library of Congress. Washington, DC: U.S. Government Printing Office, 1906.

Kupperman, Karen Ordahl. *Indians and English, Facing Off in Early America*. Ithaca, NY: Cornell University Press, 2000.

_____. *Roanoke: The Abandoned Colony*. Totowa, NJ: Rowman & Allanheld, 1984.

_____. The Jamestown Project. Cambridge, MA: The Belknap Press of Harvard Univ. Press, 2007.La Vere, David. *The Tuscarora War*. Chapel Hill, NC: University of North Carolina Press, 2013.

La Vere, David. *The Tuscarora War*. Chapel Hill, N.C.: Univ. of N.C. Press, 2013.

Landsea, Chris, contributor. "Chronological List of All Hurricanes which Affected the Continental United States 1851–2014." NOAA Hurricane Research Division, National Hurricane Center, n.d.

Lawson, John. *A New Voyage to Carolina*. London: N.p., 1709.

Lee, E. Lawrence. *Indian Wars in North Carolina 1663–1763*. Raleigh: Office of Archives and History/North Carolina Department of Cultural Resources, 2011.

Livermore, Charles W. *Ye Antient Wrecke–1626, Loss of the Sparrow-Hawk in 1626*. Boston: Alfred Mudge and Sons, 1865.

Mallinson, Culver, Walsh Riggs, Ames Smith and Members of the North Carolina College of Arts and Sciences and Institute for Coastal Science and Policy. "Past, Present and Future Inlets of the Outer Banks Barrier Islands, North Carolina." White Paper. Greenville, NC: East Carolina University, December 2008.

Mallios, Seth. *The Deadly Politics of Giving*. Tuscaloosa: University of Alabama Press, 2006.

Mancall, Peter C., editor. *The Atlantic World and Virginia, 1550–1624*. Chapel Hill: University of North Carolina Press, 2007.

McMillan, Hamilton. *Sir Walter Raleigh's Lost Colony. An Historical Sketch of the Attempts of Sir Walter Raleigh to Establish a Colony in Virginia, With the Traditions of an Indian Tribe in North Carolina*. Wilson, NC: Advance Press, 1888.

McPherson, O.M. *Report on Condition and Tribal Rights of the Indians of Robeson and Adjoining Counties of North Carolina*. Washington, DC: U.S. Government Printing Office, Sept. 19, 1914.

Miller, Lee. *Roanoke: Solving the Mystery of the Lost Colony*. New York: Arcade Publishing, 2001.

Milton, Giles. *Big Chief Elizabeth*. New York: Farrar, Straus and Giroux, 2000.

Mook, Maurice A. "Algonquian Ethnohistory of the Carolina Sound." *Journal of the Washington Academy of Sciences* 34, 1944.

Mooney, James. *The Siouan Tribes of the East*. Washington, DC: U.S. Government Printing Office, 1894.

Neill, Edward. D. *Memoir of Rev. Patrick Copland*. New York: Charles Scribner and Company, 1871.

Nicholls, Mark, and Penry Williams. *Sir Walter Raleigh in Life and Legend.* New York: Continuum International Publishing Group, 2011.

Oberg, Michael Leroy. *The Head in Edward Nugent's Hand.* Philadelphia: University of Pennsylvania Press, 2008.

Olds, Fred A. "Our North Carolina Indians." *The North Carolina Booklet.* Vol. XVI, No. 1. The N.C. Society of the Daughters of the Revolution, Raleigh: Commercial Printing Co., 1916.

de Ore, Fr. Luis Geronimo. *The Martyrs of Florida (1513–1616)* translated, with biographical preface and notes, by Maynard Geiger. Franciscan Studies no. 18. New York: J.F. Wagner, 1937.

Parker, Dennis J., editor. *Floods.* New York: Routledge, 2000.

Parramore, Thomas C. "The 'Lost Colony' Found: A Documentary Perspective." *The North Carolina Historical Review.* Vol. 78, No. 1, January 2001.

_____, with Peter C. Stewart, and Tommy L. Bogger. *Norfolk: The First Four Centuries.* Virginia: University Press of Virginia, 1994.

Paul, Charles. "Colonial Beaufort: The History of a North Carolina Town." 1965 Thesis, republished 2011. www.beaufortnc.org.

Percy, George. "Observations by Master George Percy 1607," edited by Lyon G. Tyler. *Narratives of Early Virginia, 1606–1625.* New York: Charles Scribner's Sons, 1907.

Poff, Jan-Michael, editor. *The Colonial Records Project. North Carolina Historical Review,* Vol. 51, 1974. North Carolina Office of Archives and History, Dept. of Cultural Resources.

Powell, Andrew T. *Grenville and the Lost Colony of Roanoke.* Leicester, UK: Matador/Troubador Publishing, 2011.

Powell, William S. *North Carolina, A Bicentennial History.* New York: W.W. Norton, 1977.

_____, editor. *Dictionary of North Carolina Biography.* Chapel Hill: University of North Carolina Press, 1986.

Purchas, Samuel. *Hakluytus Posthumus; or, Purchas his pilgrimes.* New York: Macmillan, 1906.

Quinn, David Beers. *Set Fair for Roanoke: Voyages and Colonies, 1584–1606.* Chapel Hill: University of North Carolina Press, 1985.

_____. *Explorers and Colonies: America 1500–1625.* London: Hambledon Press, 1990.

_____. *The Lost Colonists: Their Fortune and Probable Fate.* Raleigh, NC: North Carolina Department of Cultural Resources, 1984.

Raleigh, Sir Walter. *The Discovery of Guiana.* A publication of Cassell's National Library. London: Cassell, 1887.

Rappaport, Edward N. "Fatalities in the United States from Atlantic Tropical Cyclones: New Data and Interpretation." *Bulletin of the American Meteorological Society* Vol. 95, Issue 3, 2014.

Rountree, Helen. *The Powhatan Indians of Virginia.* Norman: University of Oklahoma Press, 1989.

Rudes, Blair A. "The First Description of an Iroquoian People: Spaniards among the Tuscaroras before 1522." Paper, Testimony of Chicora Conference on Iroquis Research, Rensselaerville, New York, Oct. 2002.

Sagan, Carl. *The Demon-Haunted World.* London: Headline Book Publishing, 1997.

Salley, Alexander S., Jr. editor. "Francis Yeardley's Narrative of Excursions into Carolina, 1654." *Narratives of Early Carolina, 1650–1708.* New York: Charles Scribner's Sons, 1911.

"Salt Water Inundation from Hurricane Sandy." University of Delaware College of Agricultural and Natural Resources, 2012.

Saunders, William S., Secretary of State. *The Colonial Records of North Carolina.* Vol. II, 1713–1728. Raleigh: P.M. Hale, Printer to the State, 1886.

Smith, John. "A True Relation." Edited by Lyon G. Tyler. *Narratives of Early Virginia, 1606–1625*. New York: Charles Scribner's Sons, 1907.

_____. *The Generall Historie of Virginia, New England & The Summer Isles*. New York: Macmillan, 1907.

Southern, Ed, editor. *The Jamestown Adventure*. Winston Salem, NC: John F. Blair, 2004.

"Spanish Policy Toward Virginia, 1606–1612: Jamestown, Écija, and John Clark of the Mayflower." *American Historical Review*, Vol XXV. London: Macmillan, 1920.

Speck, Frank G. "The Ethnic Position of the Southeastern Algonquian." *American Anthropologist* 26, 1924.

Spelman, Henry. *Relation of Virginia*. London: J. F. Hunnewell at the Chiswick Press, 1872.

Sprunt, James. *Tales and Traditions of the Lower Cape Fear, 1661–1896*. Wilmington, NC: LeGwin Brothers, 1896.

Stick, David. *Roanoke Island; The Beginnings of English America*. Chapel Hill: University of North Carolina Press, 1983.

Strachey, William. *A True Reportory... From Samuel Purchas, Hakluytus posthumus; or, Purchas his pilgrims*. London: William Stansby, 1625.

_____. *The Historie of Travaile Into Virginia Britannia*. London: Printed for the Hakluyt Society, 1849.

Swanton, John Reed. *The Indian Tribes of North America*. Washington, DC: U.S. Government Printing Office, 1952.

Thorpe, Francis Newton. *The Federal and State Constitutions, Colonial Charters, and Other Organic Laws of the State, Territories, and Colonies Now or Heretofore Forming the United States of America*. Washington, DC: U.S. Government Printing Office, 1909.

Torres, Louis. *Historic Resource Study of Cape Hatteras National Seashore*. U.S. Department of the Interior, National Park Service, Denver Service Center, 1985.

Tyler, Lyon Gardiner. *Encyclopedia of Virginia Biography*. New York: Lewis Historical Publishing Co., 1915.

_____, editor. *Narratives of Early Virginia. 1606–1625*. New York: Charles Scribner's Sons, 1907.

Todd, Vincent H., and Julius Goebel, editors. *Christoph von Graffenried's Account of the Founding of New Bern*. Raleigh, NC: Edwards & Broughton Printing, 1920.

Wallis, Helen. *Material on Nautical Cartography in the British Library, 1550–1650*. Lisbon, Portugal: Instituto de Investigação Científica Tropical, 1984.

Weaver, J. Curtis, and Thomas J. Zembrzuski, Jr. "August 31, 1993, Storm Surge and Flood of Hurricane Emily on Hatteras Island, North Carolina." Water Supply Paper 2499, U.S. Department of the Interior, U.S. Geological Survey.

Weeks, Stephen B. "The Lost Colony of Roanoke: Its Fate and Survival." *Papers of the American Historical Association*, Vol V. New York: G.P. Putnam's Sons, 1891.

Whedbee, Charles Harry. *Blackbeard's Cup and Stories of the Outer Banks*. Winston-Salem, NC: John F. Blair, 1989.

"Why do Hurricanes hit the East Coast of the U.S.?" *Scientific American Magazine*. October 21, 1999.

Wingfield, Edward-Maria. *A Discourse of Virginia*. Edited by Charles Deane. Boston: Privately printed, 1860.

Winsor, Justin, editor. *Narrative and Critical History of America*. New York: Houghton Mifflin, 1887.

Woodward, Hobson, *A Brave Vessel: A True Tale of the Castaways Who Rescued Jamestown*. New York: Penguin Books, 2009.

Wright, Irene. *The Early History of Cuba, 1492–1586*. New York: Macmillan, 1916.

# Index

Menatonon 16–17, 141, 145–146, 212
Menéndez de Aviles, Pedro 27, 33–34
Menéndez Marques, Pedro 32–33, 66–67, 168
*Michaell* 9–10
Miller, Lee 25, 27, 29–30, 41, 43, 48, 146, 149
Milton, Giles 192
Mongoack/Mangoag Indians 154, 201, 138
Mooney, James 106, 207–208, 221
*Moonlight* 113–114, 116, 119
Moratico also Moratoc (Roanoke) River 16, 18, 46, 135, 138, 146, 185
Mouzon, Henry 58, 81

National Oceanic and Atmospheric Administration (NOAA) 92, 98–99, 103; *see also* hurricane of 1589; hurricane storm surge; hurricanes
Neuse Indians 59, 124, 217; *see also* Neusiok Indians
Neusiok Indians 59–60, 77, 106, 150; *see also* Neuse Indians
Newfoundland 9, 11–12, 16, 26–27, 29, 49, 54, 83, 161, 174; colonists probable attempt to reach 88–90, 100, 119, 122–123, 168, 173, 198, 203, 206–207, 227
Newport, Christopher 127, 129–130, 133, 145, 151, 155–157, 161, 170, 176, 178, 191
Norfolk County, VA 179–180
Norris, John 112
Northwest Passage 9–10, 13
Nugent, Edward 17

Ocanahonan 5–6, 129, 133; "men cloathed" at 134–144; 145, 151, 153–154, 156, 158–162, 177, 197, 201–205, 228–229
Okisco 41
Olds, Frederick 142
Olmos, Alonso de 152
Opechancanough 17, 129, 133, 143, 152, 158, 160, 197

Pakrakanick 5–6, 131, 133; "men cloathed" at 134–144; 145, 151, 153, 156, 158–162, 177, 201, 203–204, 228–229
Pamlico County, NC 49, 59, 81, 97–100, 103, 105, 124, 205, 226
Pamlico Indians 79, 106, 148, 212–213, 215–218, 223; *see also* Pomouik Indians
Pananiock: "men apparelled" at 131, 133–134, 145–146, 148–149, 151–154, 172, 203–205, 228; not to be confused with Pomeiock 148; *see also* Pananuaioc; Panauuaiock; Panawicke
Pananuaioc 148–149; *see also* Pananuaioc; Panauuaiock; Panawicke
Panauuaiock 147–150; *see also* Pananuaioc; Panauuaiock; Panawicke
Panawicke: "many men appareled" at 61, 129, 133–134, 145–149, 151, 204; *see also* Pananuaioc; Panauuaiock; Panawicke
Paquiquineo 27, 67, 152–153

Paquiwoc 53, 56
Pardo, Juan 139–141, 143, 159, 197, 203
Parramore, Thomas C. 40–41, 48, 177–181, 183–187, 190, 195
Paspahegh chief 60, 129, 132–133, 145–146, 151–152, 204; *see also* Wowinchopunck
Paspahegh Indians 151–153, 170
Pasquatank Indians 212
*Patience* 86–87, 89–90, 173–174
Paul, Charles 80
Payankatank Indians 160, 200
Pemisapan 17, 21, 23, 41, 51, 59, 190, 194, 207; *see also* Wingina
Perquiman Indians 212
Phelps, David 4, 39
Philip II, King 34, 62, 66, 112
Philip III, King 131, 164–165
*Phoenix* 129–130
pinnace *see* 1587 pinnace
"Pitch 'n' Tar" 107
Plat, James 30
Plymouth Company 127, 165
Pocahontas 161–162
Pomeiok/Pomeiock 14, 148, 192
Pomouik Indians 59–60, 106, 148, 150–151, 204, 213; *see also* Pamlico Indians
Poole Anne 4
Popham, John 127
Pory, John 182, 210
Poteskeet Indians 212
Powell, Andrew 64, 85
Powell, Nathaniel 154
Powell, William S. 181–183
Powhatan (Chief) 8, 89, 152, 172, 228–229; and the Chesapeake tribe 160, 176–177, 191–192, 195, 198, 200, 210, 229; meeting with Newport 130; and the "men cloathed" 133, 136, 197; and the "slaughter" references 5, 155, 157–163, 174–178, 187, 189, 191, 194–199, 200–201, 203–204, 210, 228–229; Smith's captivity by 129, 162; *see also* Wahunsunacock
Powhatan Indians 7, 17, 110, 128, 130, 134–135, 138, 142, 145, 153, 155, 159–161, 187, 189, 193–205, 210, 222, 228
Preston, Amias 54
Pring, Martin 84
Purchas, Samuel 157, 159–161, 163, 177–178, 199; *Hakluytus Posthumus or Purchas His Pilgrimes* 157

Quinn, David Beers 2, 12, 22–23, 29, 54–55, 63, 65, 155, 210–211, 224; and the Chesapeake theory 40–41, 68, 120, 177, 187, 191; and the Samuel Mace voyages 125–126; and the "slaughter at Roanoke" 177–180, 199

Raleigh, Walter 8–9, 25, 27–30, 33, 49–50, 52, 62–64, 88, 91, 111, 117–119, 123–124, 127, 139, 154, 158, 171, 180–183, 189–190, 195, 214–215, 226; and the Cittie of Ralegh 20–24, 30–31,